THE OLD ENGLISH IN
EARLY MODERN IRELAND

Irish Historical Monograph Series

ISSN 1740-1097

Previous titles in the series are listed at the back of the volume.

THE OLD ENGLISH IN EARLY MODERN IRELAND

The Palesmen and the Nine Years' War, 1594–1603

Ruth A. Canning

THE BOYDELL PRESS

First published 2019
The Boydell Press, Woodbridge

ISBN 978-1-78327-327-0

The Boydell Press is an imprint of Boydell & Brewer Ltd
PO Box 9, Woodbridge, Suffolk IP12 3DF, UK
and of Boydell & Brewer Inc.
668 Mt Hope Avenue, Rochester, NY 14620–2731, USA
website: www.boydellandbrewer.com

A CIP catalogue record for this title is available from the British Library

The publisher has no responsibility for the continued existence or accuracy of URLs for external or third-party internet websites referred to in this book, and does not guarantee that any content on such websites is, or will remain, accurate or appropriate

This publication is printed on acid-free paper

Printed and bound in Great Britain by
TJ International Ltd, Padstow, Cornwall

For Anne and Rody

Contents

Acknowledgements

First and foremost, I owe immeasurable thanks to Hiram Morgan. Hiram has been a constant source of guidance and support since my very first voyage into the history of the Nine Years' War. This book, like so many other endeavours, would not have been possible without his patience and sage advice. It hasn't always been the most graceful of journeys but, as a mentor and friend, Hiram has helped me over more scholarly, professional, and personal hurdles than even he can imagine. I will be forever grateful.

This project would have been considerably more difficult to complete without the generous financial support of a Marie Curie International Outgoing Research Fellowship. I also appreciate the additional funding provided by the Marie Curie Alumni Association. My thanks to the School of History at University College Cork and the School of Canadian Irish Studies at Concordia University, Montreal, for hosting me as a research fellow and providing me with fantastic professional support. The Moore Institute at NUI Galway gave me the time, space, and resources thanks to a visiting fellowship in 2017. I would like to express my deep appreciation to the archivists and librarians at UCC's Boole Library, the National Library of Ireland, the James Hardiman Library at NUIG, Trinity College Dublin, the British Library, University Library Cambridge, the Bodleian, Oxford, and the Jesuit Archives in Dublin and London. My only regret is that there was not more time to pore over the many manuscripts housed in these libraries.

I have had the good fortune of meeting many great colleagues and friends along the way. Very special thanks are due to Steven Ellis who has been a very generous reader, providing me with steady encouragement and expert knowledge over many years. I have had the great pleasure of spending many hours discussing the finer points of this period with my fellow Nine Years' War fanatic, James O'Neill. His knowledge is as boundless as his generosity, and my own work has been greatly enhanced by having recourse to him. It goes without saying (but I'll say it anyway) that the Hugh O'Neill roadshow would have been considerably less vibrant, and certainly less eventful, without James, Hiram, and Malachy O'Neill. I owe a great deal of thanks to Valerie McGowan-Doyle and Brendan Kane whose friendship, stimulating discussions, and meticulous scholarship have been motivational. There are many other early modernists who lent an ear, advice, and shared many a comforting pint, for which I am particularly grateful to Matthew Woodcock, John Appleby, Fiona

Pogson, Dave Edwards, Mark Hutchinson, Aine Sheehan, Claire Connolly, John Morrill, Bob Tittler, Vincent Carey, and Sarah Covington. To the many friends and colleagues without whom I could not have endured the long hours of toil, isolation, and repetitive relocation, very special thanks are due to John Borgonovo, Susan Cahill, Emer O'Toole, Sarah Anne Buckley, Jane McGaughey, Michael Kenneally, Matina Skalkogiannis, Linda Connolly, Sonja Tiernan, Kate Mattocks, Andy Bielenberg, Miriam Haughton, Sarah Thelan, Dave Fitzgerald, James Ryan, and Ania Geerts. There are so many others, in Ireland, Canada, and the UK to whom I am indebted, especially all the family and friends who have repeatedly supplied me with encouraging thoughts and heartening reminders of life beyond academe.

I am eternally beholden to Mark Empey; at every turn, his support has been enthusiastic, obliging, and unfaltering. And last, but never least, to my parents and siblings, Rody, Anne, Stephanie, and Gareth, for whom talk of this book must have seemed like Groundhog Day in purgatory. I will never have adequate words to express how truly grateful I am to have them in my corner. This book is for them.

Note on Conventions

The term 'Old English' is employed to identify members of a community descended from the original twelfth-century Anglo-Norman conquerors of Ireland. Frequently considered anachronistic, there is evidence to suggest that this term was coming into currency during the mid-1590s. It was first employed by Edmund Spenser in 1596 and then used by an anonymous Pale author in 1598 when he set out to write a definitive explanation of how this community differed from their Gaelic Irish compatriots.[1] The term was again employed by the Baron of Dunsany in 1600 in a context which implied readers would know exactly to whom this appellation applied.[2]

Spelling has been preserved in quoted material, with a few modernisations where original phrasing was unclear.

Currency referred to here is in sterling, unless otherwise stated.

---

[1]   E. Spenser, *A View of the State of Ireland*, ed. A. Hadfield and W. Maley (Oxford, 1997); TNA, SP 63/202(4)/75 ('A discourse to show "that planting of colonies, and that to be begun only by the Dutch, will give best entrance to the reformation of Ulster"', 1598). Another version is available in BL, Cotton Titus B XII, ff. 112–17.
[2]   TNA, SP 63/207(5)/34 (Dunsany to R. Cecil, 18 Sep. 1600).

Abbreviations

AFM	*Annála Ríoghachta Éireann: Annals of the kingdom of Ireland by the Four Masters, from the earliest period to the year 1616*, ed. and trans., J. O'Donovan, 7 vols (Dublin, 1848–51)
Anal. Hib.	*Analecta Hibernica*
APC	*Acts of Privy Council*
BL	British Library
Cal. Carew	*Calendar of the Carew manuscripts preserved in the archiepiscopal library at Lambeth, 1551–1642*, ed. J.S. Brewer and William Bullen, 6 vols (London, 1867–73)
CELT	Corpus of Electronic Texts (https://celt.ucc.ie/index.html)
CSPD	*Calendar of State Papers, Domestic*
CSPI	*Calendar of State Papers, Ireland*
CSP Sp.	*Calendar of State Papers, Spain*
CUL	University Library, Cambridge
DIB	*Dictionary of Irish Biography*, ed. James McGuire and James Quinn (Cambridge, 2009) and online edition
HJ	*Historical Journal*
HMC	Historical Manuscripts Commission
IHS	*Irish Historical Studies*
NLI	National Library of Ireland
ODNB	*Oxford Dictionary of National Biography*
PRIA	*Proceedings of the Royal Irish Academy*
Salisbury MSS	*Calendar of the manuscripts of the marquis of Salisbury: preserved at Hatfield House, Hertfordshire*, ed. R.A. Roberts, E. Salisbury, G. Montague, and O. Geraint Dyfnallt, 24 vols (London, 1883–1976)
TCD	Trinity College Dublin
TNA	The National Archives [of the UK], Kew

1

Pale Politics: An Old English Community and the Outbreak of War

In autumn 1599 Hugh O'Neill, earl of Tyrone and leader of the Irish Catholic Confederacy, aimed to penetrate the loyal English Pale through County Westmeath. This presented an immediate threat to crown defences in the area, as well as to the man in charge of them, Christopher Nugent, the baron of Delvin. As the rebels approached, Delvin hastily wrote to the Council in Dublin: 'I mistrust a great part of the country will revolt, some according their own lewd disposition… and others in respect [that] they have no defence.'[1] Delvin's fears were well founded: five years of war had taken its toll on his barony, and now that O'Neill's incursions coincided with the harvest, many of Delvin's tenants and neighbours were inclined to submit. The reality was that as the war had dragged on and O'Neill's strength continued to grow, it had become increasingly difficult for border lords like Delvin to maintain their defences.[2] And now this danger coincided with the deployment of a sophisticated nationalist rhetoric which called upon all Irish Catholics to defend their homeland from the centralising forces of the English Protestant crown. This could be strong incentive and justification for any vacillating borderer or haggard husbandman, and a number of formerly loyal Old Englishmen did switch sides. Surrounded by the forces of O'Neill, O'Rourke, and their Leinster allies, 'the whole country being on fire', Delvin assured the Dublin Council that his own doubts were never about whether he would remain loyal to the queen; rather, he doubted his ability to withstand further rebel incursions without military assistance from the crown.[3] Delvin begged administrators for reinforcements to defend this vital frontier, but his pleas were ignored; he begged for directions – should he make a stand, or run and fight another day – but little sympathy or instruction was forthcoming. Finally, the desperate Delvin, 'subject to all adventures of fortune, in a weak house, not possible long to be kept',[4] requested permission to parley with the wily O'Neill in the hope of gaining some time to regroup. The lord lieutenant, Thomas Butler, earl of Ormond, reluctantly

---

1   *CSPI, 1599–1600*, p. 267.
2   C. Lennon, 'Christopher Nugent', *ODNB*.
3   *CSPI, 1599–1600*, p. 267.
4   Ibid.

agreed, and Delvin, through his agents, entered a series of discussions with the Confederate leader and achieved a temporary truce. To assure the Council that there had been no foul play, Delvin dutifully submitted his proceedings to the state. These records, which included exchanges about the sincerity of O'Neill's crusade for an Irish Catholic nation, were scrutinised, but the temporary truce benefited all, including the crown army, whose energies were directed in other parts of the country, and Delvin, who did indeed fight many more days in the service of the English crown. However, three years later the stakes had changed. The Confederacy was on the run and crown officials were determined to root out suspected sympathisers, especially those living within the Pale. The openly recusant, bilingual, and politically active Delvin was swiftly arrested on allega-tions of treason, and while rumours were collected as evidence, he died in a Dublin Castle gaol cell. The evidence against him was weak at best, and given the situation in Ireland at this time, it is probably safe to assume that Delvin's greatest crimes were his Irish birth and his attachment to the old faith.

Recent historiography has drawn attention to ideas of identity, nationalism, and conflicting allegiances in Tudor Ireland. However, these concepts have not been adequately addressed in relation to the Old English community during the Nine Years' War. This book is an attempt to rectify that omission. By no means is it *the* definitive study of Old English identity; nor is it an exhaustive history of the Nine Years' War. What it does aim to offer is a comprehensive examination of a minority community undergoing significant socio-political development during a traumatic period. This was a multidimensional social group which had been shaped by a complex history. Given that they were variously known at the time as 'English Irish', 'Anglo Irish', 'English born in Ireland', 'English of Ireland', 'Hiberno-English', and other forms of 'the loyal English lieges of Ireland', it is understandable that historians have long quibbled over the appropriateness of different nomenclature.[5] There was no all-embracing term used by contemporaries to define this population, and while the label 'Old English' has been the subject of much debate, the term was coming into use during the Nine Years' War. In each instance of its use no definition was required because its meaning was transparent to both the authors and their readers.[6] It will, therefore, be employed in this book to identify a

---

[5] For example, A. Clarke, 'Colonial Identity in Early Seventeenth-Century Ireland', in D. Ó Corráin and T.W. Moody (eds), *Nationality and the Pursuit of National Independence*, *Historical Studies*, Vol. XI (Belfast, 1978), p. 58; N.P. Canny, 'Identity Formation in Ireland: The Emergence of the Anglo-Irish', in N.P. Canny and A. Pagden (eds), *Colonial Identity in the Atlantic World*, *1500–1800* (Princeton, NJ, 1987), p. 160; N.P. Canny, 'Spenser's Irish Crisis: Humanism and Experience in the 1590s', *Past & Present*, No. 120 (1988), p. 203; C. Brady, 'Spenser's Irish Crisis: Humanism and Experience in the 1590s', *Past & Present*, No. 111 (1986), p. 24.

[6] E. Spenser, *A View of the State of Ireland*, ed. A. Hadfield and W. Maley (Oxford, 1997); TNA, SP 63/207(5)/34 (Dunsany to R. Cecil, 18 Sep. 1600); SP 63/202(4)/75 ('A discourse to show

community which comprised the descendants of Ireland's twelfth-century Anglo-Norman invaders along with subsequent English settlers who arrived in Ireland prior to the 1541 creation of the Kingdom of Ireland. The term 'Old English' should not obscure the fact that this population descended from a heterogeneous collection of Anglo-Normans, Welshmen, Flemings, and Englishmen who, notwithstanding some intermarriage with the Gaelic natives, regarded themselves as subjects of the English crown. The manner of their occupation of Ireland, along with their experiences over successive generations, ascribed to them a certain demographic, ethnic, and historical identity. However, this was by no means a uniform society in which all members shared the same ambitions, concerns, and general life experiences. It was composed of urban merchants and patricians, clerics and lawyers, labourers and craftsmen, husbandmen and freeholders, servants and peasants, border barons and feudal-style soldiers, crown officials and outlaws. Geography and socio-economic interests dictated a range of responses to political and religious changes over the course of the sixteenth century. What members of this community did have in common was a general attachment to an ancestral Englishness, a sense of isolation living on a Tudor periphery, and for the majority anyway, a growing commitment to the now banned Catholic religion.

There were clusters of Old English settlement throughout the country, but the main concentration of this population was within the region of the Pale. This was the defensible core of Ireland's original English colony, roughly comprising the modern counties of Dublin, Kildare, Meath, Westmeath, and Louth, which, according to one contemporary, was 'not much larger in all then Yorckshire in England'.[7] Since the original Anglo-Norman conquest, the march surrounding the Pale shires had been described as a physical and psychological barrier separating a land of civility carved out from the dark savagery and tyranny of the Gaelic beyond. But this border was far more flexible and porous than these records imply. There had been a constant ebb and flow of the Pale's physical boundaries, particularly with respect to the marchlands which insulated the five shires.[8] These boundaries had receded during the fourteenth and fifteenth centuries, but there was no sixteenth-century Gaelic resurgence to shrink the Pale even further. Instead, the Tudors' reinvigorated commitment to reconquest entailed land confiscations and plantations which extended the reach of crown influence beyond the traditionally defined Pale. During the Nine

"that planting of colonies, and that to be begun only by the Dutch, will give best entrance to the reformation of Ulster'", 1598). Another version is available in BL, Cotton Titus B XII, ff. 112–17.

[7]   TNA, SP 63/202(4)/60 ('The greevances of the Englishe Pale', 1598).

[8]   P.J. Duffy, 'The Nature of the Medieval Frontier in Ireland', *Studia Hibernica*, No. 22/23 (1982/1983), pp. 21–38; C. Maginn, 'Gaelic Ireland's English Frontiers in the Late Middle Ages', *PRIA*, Vol. 110C (2010), pp. 173–90.

Years' War, the Pale marches could be seen to extend into Cavan and Longford on account of a series of royal grants to loyal servitors.[9] Other English areas in the vicinity of the Pale, such as the city of Waterford and parts of counties Kilkenny and Tipperary, could also be considered within the ambit of the Pale, since the inhabitants of these areas not only shared certain characteristics with their Pale counterparts but also found themselves treated in much the same manner by crown authorities. For instance, while the merchants and civic officials of Waterford were just as vociferous in their professions of loyalty as the citizens of Dublin, they were equally inclined to profit from the illegal weapons trade with the Confederate enemy.[10] Like the more rural inhabitants of Westmeath and Louth, the inhabitants of Ormond-controlled Kilkenny and Tipperary endured the same trespasses of rebels and crown soldiers while they were simultaneously called upon to serve the crown with military services and supplies.[11] By the 1590s the Pale was as much a concept as it was a reality, and this study will therefore refrain from giving exact geographical coordinates – which were never really lasting – and focus instead on a region and population which possessed distinct cultural, social, and political traits.

Within this region geography did play an important role in determining patterns of cultural and political diversity. In spite of the 'us versus them' situation described by many sources, including those written by proud Palesmen like Richard Stanihurst, survival in Ireland had necessitated varying degrees of acculturation, accommodation, and interaction between the Old English population and their Gaelic Irish neighbours. This was especially true along the Pale's frontiers and other more isolated pockets of Old English habitation. While the inhabitants of Dublin could brag about the purity of English culture and society within their city's walls, the lords living beyond this cocoon accepted Gaelic tenants, learned the Irish language, utilised Gaelic law when convenient, and even married their children to their Gaelic Irish equiva-lents. What is more, there are plenty of examples of prominent Pale families sponsoring and engaging in Gaelic literary culture, amongst whom the Nugents of Delvin are a prime example. They not only patronised Multyfarnham Abbey, a Franciscan centre of Gaelic learning, but Christopher Nugent and his father Richard were competent linguists while his brother William Nugent was an accomplished Gaelic poet.[12] Acculturation had indeed occurred, but

9 TNA, SP 63/198/129 (grant to baron of Delvin, Apr. 1597); TNA, SP 63/199/17 (grant to baron of Delvin, 7 May 1597).
10 R.A. Canning, 'Profits and Patriotism: Nicholas Weston, Old English Merchants, and Ireland's Nine Years' War, 1594–1603', *Irish Economic and Social History*, Vol. 43, No. 1 (2016), pp. 14–16.
11 TNA, SP 63/206/43 (baron of Upper Ossory to Cecil, 27 Nov. 1599); TNA, SP 63/183/96 (Wallop, Gardiner, Napper, Sentleger and Wilbraham to Burghley, 20 Oct. 1595).
12 V.P. Carey, '"Neither Good English Nor Good Irish": Bi-lingualism and Identity Formation in Sixteenth-Century Ireland', in H. Morgan (ed.), *Political Ideology in Ireland, 1541–1641* (Dublin,

some individuals and groups had gone too far, especially the disenfranchised who lived on the geographic, social, and legal margins of Old English society. Degenerate families, like the infamous 'Bastard Geraldines', the Harolds, and the Archbolds, not only acquired a new language, but they also adopted a Gaelic lineage culture and its attendant socio-political structures.[13] Having become 'more Irish than the Irish themselves', by the sixteenth century these groups had become appropriate focal points for New English attacks on the quality and character of Old English loyalties. As Lord Deputy Mountjoy's secretary, Fynes Moryson, pontificated:

> I will say for the English Irish … But as horses Cowes and sheepe transported out of England into Ireland, doe each race and breeding declyne worse and worse, till in a fewe yeares they nothing differ from the races and breeds of the Irish horses and Cattle. So the posterities of the English planted in Ireland, doe each discent, growe more and more Irish, in nature manners and customes, so as wee founde in the last Rebellion diuers of the most ancient English Familyes planted of old in Ireland, to be turned as rude and barbarous as any of the meere Irish lords.[14]

This alleged degeneration prompted sporadic efforts to implement cultural legislation, but far more detrimental to this community's interests was that it had also become one of many convenient excuses for removing the Old English from positions of authority.

English monarchs had long ruled Ireland through aristocratic delegation, and this had permitted the greatest Old English magnates control over the staffing and running of the crown's Irish administration. The situation was to change following the suppression of the Kildare Rebellion in 1534, when the office of viceroy became the preserve of men sent directly from England. Their mission was to reform Ireland and mould it into a little England beyond the sea. This transformation was anything but smooth, implemented as it was by a revolving door of Tudor deputies armed with inconsistent reform policies which oscillated between conciliation and subjugation by violent conquest. Centralising reform

1999), p. 53; D. Casey, *The Nugents of Westmeath and Queen Elizabeth's Irish Primer* (Dublin, 2016); C. Nugent, 'Queen Elizabeth's Primer of the Irish Language', in J.T. Gilbert (ed.), *Facsimiles of National Manuscripts of Ireland*, IV(i) (London, 1882), no. 22; G. Murphy, 'Poems of Exile by Uillim Nuinseann Mac Barúin Dealbhna', *Éigse*, Vol. 6 (1948–52), pp. 9–15; O. Bergin (ed.), 'Unpublished Irish Poems. II: In Memoriam Ricardi Nugent', *Studies: An Irish Quarterly Review*, Vol. 7, No. 26 (1918), pp. 279–82; É. Ó Tuathail, 'Nugentiana', *Éigse*, Vol. 2 (1940), pp. 4–14; B. Iske, *The Green Cockatrice* (Dublin, 1978); NLI, MS G 992.

[13] See C. Maginn, 'English Marcher Lineages in South Dublin in the Late Middle Ages', *IHS*, Vol. 34, No. 134 (2004), pp. 113–36; C. Parker, 'Paterfamilias and Parentela: The Le Poer Lineage in Fourteenth-Century Waterford', *PRIA*, Vol. 95C, No. 2 (1995), pp. 93–117; W. FitzGerald, 'Walter Reagh Fitz Gerald, a Noted Outlaw of the Sixteenth Century', *Journal of the Royal Society of Antiquaries of Ireland*, ser. 5, Vol. 8, No. 4 (1898), pp. 299–305.

[14] F. Moryson, *Shakespeare's Europe*, ed. C. Hughes (London, 1903), p. 481.

efforts were ushered in through legislation like the 1541 creation of the Kingdom of Ireland, the enactment of the Protestant Reformation, and the redistribution of dissolved monastic properties. Implementation was to be effected through the dismantling of feudal networks and the establishment of provincial presidencies supported by permanent garrisons funded by new taxation methods. Accompanying these changes was a renewed commitment to 'civilising' Ireland through new plantations in Ulster, Laois, Offaly, and Munster, all of which were entrusted to a second wave of colonial élite comprising English-born Protestants. The crown's Irish bureaucracy expanded correspondingly, and its offices were filled by men sent from England who espoused the new state religion. Thus, Ireland was effectively transformed during the Tudor period from a nominally Catholic peripheral lordship governed by over-mighty subjects into a kingdom ruled by English viceroys buoyed up by a new breed of Protestant administrator, colonist, and soldier: the New English. In this new Ireland the Old English soon found themselves relegated to subordinate status.

There is a growing body of literature which focuses on issues of Old English alienation, degeneration, and loyalties in early modern Ireland. Nicholas Canny's work on the Old English élite set the agenda for the study of Old English identities.[15] He expanded this through his work on colonial mentalities and the Anglicisation of Ireland, noting that different periods of conquest gave rise to two competing English colonial communities.[16] Steven Ellis has focused on crown and community under the early Tudors, with particular attention to how Tudor ambitions to control, or at least contain, Ireland caused relations between Irish subjects and English monarchs to erode.[17] Ellis has also detected certain characteristics which connected Ireland's Old English nobility with their equivalents in northern England as a frontier élite who were forced to define themselves in relation to a growing discourse on ideas of 'English civility'.[18] Kenneth Nicholls approached the Old English from the opposite angle by examining the sources of their alleged 'incivility', or 'Gaelicisation',

[15] N.P. Canny, 'The Formation of the Old English Elite in Ireland', O'Donnell Lecture (Dublin, 1975); Canny, 'The Formation of the Irish Mind: Religion, Politics and Gaelic Irish Literature 1580–1750', *Past & Present*, No. 95 (1982), pp. 91–116.

[16] N.P. Canny, *Making Ireland British, 1580–1650* (Oxford, 2001); Canny, *Kingdom and Colony: Ireland in the Atlantic World, 1560–1800* (London, 1988); Canny, 'Edmund Spenser and the Development of an Anglo-Irish Identity', *The Yearbook of English Studies*, Vol. 13 (1983), pp. 1–19; Canny and Pagden (eds), *Colonial Identity in the Atlantic World*.

[17] S.G. Ellis, *Ireland in the Age of the Tudors 1447–1603: English Expansion and the End of Gaelic Rule* (Harlow, 1998); Ellis, *Tudor Ireland: Crown, Community and the Conflict of Cultures, 1470–1603* (Harlow, 1985); Ellis, *Defending English Ground: War and Peace in Meath and Northumberland, 1460–1542* (Oxford, 2015); Ellis and C. Maginn, *The Making of the British Isles: The State of Britain and Ireland, 1450–1660* (London, 2007).

[18] S.G. Ellis, *Tudor Frontiers and Noble Power: The Making of the British State* (Oxford, 1995); Ellis, 'A Border Baron and the Tudor State: The Rise and Fall of Lord Dacre of the North', *HJ*, Vol. 35,

and detailing certain acculturation trends amongst segments of the population, particularly those living on the margins of society.[19] It is generally understood that fears of a Gaelic resurgence spurred Old Englishmen to urge the crown and Privy Council to carry out a major social and political reform of Ireland, but they quickly lost control of the movement they had founded. Nicholas Canny and Brendan Bradshaw have both argued that the Old English fell out of tune with changing intellectual currents in England over the course of the mid-century and this served to accelerate their displacement from positions of authority.[20] Other historians have focused on the link between Old English alienation and rising recusancy. Investigating the Palesmen's mysterious move 'from passive church-papistry to active and decisive recusancy', Ciaran Brady has offered a convincing argument that economic grievances, particularly in relation to 1570s and 1580s cess controversy, prompted political protest in the form of religious non-conformity.[21] Colm Lennon's research on recusancy, Mass in the manor house, and the patronage of Catholic institutions and clerics has provided equally intriguing insight into the particular brand of Catholicism practised by members of the Pale community.[22] More broadly, his prosopographical study of the Dublin patricians, along with his biographical works on Richard Stanihurst and Archbishop Richard Creagh, have been instrumental in identifying the key socio-political concerns and ambitions of the Old English community. A number of other historians have followed suit with biographical studies which survey the careers of the baron of Howth and the earls of Ormond, Kildare, and Desmond, exposing their responses to specific social and political changes over the course of the sixteenth century and the implications for the wider community.[23] And finally, addressing the first half of the seventeenth

No. 2 (1992), pp. 253–77; Ellis, 'The Pale and the Far North: Government and Society in Two Early Tudor Borderlands', O'Donnell Lecture (Galway, 1986).

[19] K.W. Nicholls, *Gaelic and Gaelicised Ireland in the Middle Ages* (Dublin, 2003).

[20] Canny, 'The Formation of the Old English Elite'; B. Bradshaw, *The Irish Constitutional Revolution of the Sixteenth Century* (Cambridge, 1979).

[21] C. Brady, 'Conservative Subversives: The Community of the Pale and the Dublin Administration, 1556–86', in P. Corish (ed.), *Radicals, Rebels and Establishments* (Belfast, 1985), p. 13; Brady, *The Chief Governors: The Rise and Fall of Reform Government in Tudor Ireland, 1536–1588* (Cambridge, 1994).

[22] C. Lennon, *Archbishop Richard Creagh of Armagh, 1523–1586: An Irish Prisoner of Conscience of the Tudor Era* (Dublin, 2000); Lennon, *The Lords of Dublin in the Age of Reformation* (Blackrock, 1989); Lennon, *Richard Stanihurst the Dubliner, 1547–1618* (Blackrock, 1981); Lennon, 'Richard Stanihurst (1547–1618) and Old English Identity', *IHS*, Vol. 21, No. 82 (1978), pp. 121–43; Lennon, 'The Nugent Family and the Diocese of Kilmore in the Sixteenth and Early Seventeenth Centuries', *Breifne*, Vol. 10 (2001), pp. 360–74; Lennon, 'Mass in the Manor House: the Counter-Reformation in Dublin, 1560–1630', in J. Kelly and D. Keogh (eds), *History of the Diocese of Dublin* (Dublin, 2000), pp. 112–26.

[23] V. McGowan-Doyle, *The Book of Howth: The Elizabethan Re-conquest of Ireland and the Old English* (Cork, 2011); D. Edwards, *The Ormond Lordship in County Kilkenny, 1515–1642: The Rise*

century, Aidan Clarke has concluded that sixteenth-century developments helped forge a unique Old English identity which would, under a combination of socio-political pressures, lead to a rupture in crown–community relations and ultimately push the Old English to join their Gaelic Irish co-religionists in rebellion in 1641.[24]

There has, therefore, been substantial and significant research produced on Ireland's Old English community over the past forty years. Historians of the sixteenth and seventeenth centuries generally agree that the Old English regarded themselves as English (but a little different from those born in England); that they were mostly Catholic (but their increasing attachment to that faith was not an inevitable historical fact); and that their Irish birth endowed them with a unique cultural and political perspective (but one that was a lot different from their Gaelic Irish compatriots). Yet there remains a gap in the narrative because these concepts and issues have not been adequately addressed in relation to the Old English community during the Nine Years' War. It is as if the cess controversy of the 1570s–80s marked the end of a period of evolution, while the quest to wrest Catholic concessions from the new Scottish king of England, James I, marked the commencement of another. But what about that last Tudor decade, 1593–1603? Surely, the socio-political development of this community did not simply halt as if the Nine Years' War was a chrysalis from which a yet-to-be defined population emerged as a fully-formed Catholic community professing allegiance to a Protestant English king. No; an awful lot happened during this war. The Nine Years' War was as brutal and as sanguinary as the Tudor reconquest of Ireland could get, and the Palesmen's responses to that war, the actions they undertook, and the allegiances they professed were conditioned by prior events and experiences.

Thus far, research on the Nine Years' War has focused on political, military, and ideological developments. There has been no systematic analysis of the war's human, economic, agricultural, and cultural impact on the inhabitants of Ireland, and this is especially true of the Pale region. With the exception of a handful of short studies, which address an individual or episode during this conflict, the position of the Old English Pale community during this war has been left virtually untouched.[25] This is largely owing to the fact that the war overshadowed the production of any readily identifiable evidence pertaining to

---

and Fall of Butler Feudal Power (Dublin, 2003); V.P. Carey, Surviving The Tudors: The 'Wizard' Earl of Kildare and English Rule in Ireland, 1537–1586 (Dublin, 2002); A.M. McCormack, The Earldom of Desmond, 1463–1583 (Dublin, 2005).

[24] A. Clarke, The Old English in Ireland, 1625–42 (Dublin, 2000).

[25] For example, V. McGowan-Doyle, '"Spent Blood": Christopher St Lawrence and Pale Loyalism', in H. Morgan (ed.), The Battle of Kinsale (Bray, 2004), pp. 179–92, and K. Nicholls, 'Richard Tyrrell, Soldier Extraordinary', in Morgan (ed.), Battle of Kinsale, pp. 161–78.

the shifting social and political mentalities of the Old English community. Until recently, the work of Richard Bagwell, Cyril Falls, and Gerard Hayes-McCoy were the indispensable texts on which to rely for details of military engagements, the operation of military apparatuses, and the careers of military men.[26] While these still warrant consideration, the political and military historiography of the war has progressed. John Silke's examination of Iberian–Irish relations and Spanish intervention at Kinsale remains an invaluable assessment of the role of Catholicism and international politicking in foreign conspiracies.[27] Exploring some of the social and economic consequences of the conflict, John McGurk has appraised the war's drain on England's manpower and resources while detailing the abysmal living conditions and experiences of Elizabethan soldiers operating in Ireland.[28] More recently, Hayes-McCoy's pioneering research on major engagements and tactics has been expanded and enhanced by James O'Neill.[29] Remarkably, O'Neill's monograph is the first comprehensive history of the entire Nine Years' War, and it offers a much more sophisticated interpretation of Irish military history than previous studies. Indeed, O'Neill convincingly argues that the Irish were far from the primitive tribesmen popularly described by preju- diced English contemporaries and that there was, in fact, a process of military revolution occurring in Ireland during this war period.[30] Darren McGettigan has examined the life of Hugh O'Neill's chief ally, Red Hugh O'Donnell, and his leadership during this war.[31] Hiram Morgan's work remains essential reading for any investigation of this war period. He has produced thorough assessments of the genesis, escalation, and main protagonists of the Nine Years' War.[32] In doing so, his work has provided great insight into the character, ambitions, and life of Hugh O'Neill, the enigmatic earl of Tyrone. Morgan's other great contribution to the study of this war is his analysis of the evolution and deployment of an

---

[26] R. Bagwell, *Ireland Under the Tudors* (London, 1963); C. Falls, *Elizabeth's Irish Wars* (London, 1996); G.A. Hayes-McCoy, *Irish Battles: A Military History of Ireland* (Belfast, 1990).

[27] J.J. Silke, *Kinsale: The Spanish Intervention in Ireland at the End of the Elizabethan Wars* (New York, 1970).

[28] J. McGurk, *The Elizabethan Conquest of Ireland: the 1590s Crisis* (Manchester, 1997). More recently, Rhys Morgan has commented on the recruitment of Welsh soldiers and servitors during this war. R. Morgan, *The Welsh and the Shaping of Early Modern Ireland, 1558–1641* (Woodbridge, 2014).

[29] J. O'Neill, *The Nine Years War, 1593–1603: O'Neill, Mountjoy and the Military Revolution* (Dublin, 2017).

[30] O'Neill, *The Nine Years War*. This opinion was also aired by Eoin Ó Néill in 2009: E. Ó Néill, 'Towards A New Interpretation of the Nine Years' War', *Irish Sword*, Vol. 26, No. 105 (2009), pp. 241–62.

[31] D. McGettigan, *Red Hugh O'Donnell and the Nine Years' War* (Dublin, 2005).

[32] H. Morgan, *Tyrone's Rebellion: The Outbreak of the Nine Years War in Tudor Ireland* (Woodbridge, 1993); Morgan, 'Hugh O'Neill and the Nine Years War in Tudor Ireland', *HJ*, Vol. 36. No. 1 (1993), pp. 21–37.

Irish Catholic faith and fatherland ideology, along with its purposefully tailored rhetoric for a target audience: the Old English of Ireland.[33]

The Old English felt both the physical and ideological pressures of the Nine Years' War, and it was not unnatural to suspect that some would be tempted to join a 1590s national crusade to defend Catholicism and their positions in a rapidly changing Ireland. In fact, with the exception of Shane O'Neill, it was from amongst the supposedly loyalist Old English populations of Ireland that the most serious resistance to Tudor ambitions had sprung, starting with the 1534 Kildare Rebellion and then, in quick succession from the late 1560s onwards, two Desmond Rebellions, and the risings of Baltinglass and William Nugent. The true motivations behind these rebellions were consistent: a deep and justified fear of displacement by English Protestant newcomers. Anticipating stricter enforcement of religious conformity in Ireland, the leaders of these rebellions also took up the Catholic banner. This helped galvanise more militantly minded clerics and continentally educated laymen and it afforded their movements a certain legitimacy to international observers. More crucially, by adopting these justifications, these Old English revolts effectively entwined socio-political grievances with religious discontent and thus sparked the beginnings of an Irish faith and fatherland ideology. It was therefore entirely reasonable for Hugh O'Neill and crown administrators to expect that Old English Palesmen would be attracted to the 1590s Confederate cause.

Contrary to the Confederates' hopes and officials' fears, existing evidence strongly infers that the majority of the Old English Pale population remained steadfast to the queen's cause throughout the Nine Years' War. Notwithstanding this fact, the Old English did not act in unison because the immediate concerns, ambitions, and daily realities of members of this community varied widely depending on place of residence, social status, and degrees of political and religious conformity. For instance, the Catholic Christopher Nugent, baron of Delvin, was one of the wealthiest and most powerful nobles in Ireland. Delvin lived on the embattled frontier of Westmeath, where he served the crown valiantly by providing military leadership, defending the borders, offering advice, and, by his own personal account, executing or apprehending at least 246 rebels.[34] Yet, in 1602 Delvin had died in prison while awaiting trial on

---

[33] H. Morgan, 'Policy and Propaganda in Hugh O'Neill's Connection with Europe', in M.A. Lyons and T. O'Connor (eds), *The Ulster Earls and Baroque Europe: Refashioning Irish Identities, 1600–1800* (Dublin, 2010), pp. 18–52; Morgan, 'The 1597 Ceasefire Documents', *Dúiche Néill*, Vol. 11 (1997), pp. 1–21; Morgan, 'Faith and Fatherland in Sixteenth-Century Ireland', *History Ireland*, Vol. 3, No. 2 (1995), pp. 13–20; Morgan, 'Faith and Fatherland or Queen and Country? An Unpublished Exchange Between O'Neill and the State at the Height of the Nine Years War', *Dúiche Néill*, Vol. 9 (1994), pp. 1–49.

[34] TNA, SP 63/207/88(I) (services done by Delvin from 1596 to 1 Feb. 1600). Although there is

trumped-up charges of treason. The experiences of other Old Englishmen were considerably different. Patrick Plunkett, baron of Dunsany, was also a Catholic border lord, but he never suffered imprisonment or interrogation even though his own foot company deserted their garrison post and joined the rebellion, his son had been suspected of fraternising with the enemy, and one of his servants had been apprehended on suspicion of financing seminarians.[35] The sheriff of Kildare, James Fitzpiers Fitzgerald, who was probably a Protestant, did commit treason by joining forces with the Leinster rebels. He was not only forgiven for his misdemeanours, but he was actually rewarded with a knighthood soon after.[36] And then there was the infamous Captain Richard Tyrrell, O'Neill's leading Old English officer who was followed by many other lesser Palesmen.[37] These were all prominent military men who came from the countryside, yet their actions and interactions with the crown and Confederates were diverse. More different still were the wartime experiences and behaviours of those inhabiting urban centres. The residents of cities and large towns were relatively immune to the depredations of the rebels; it was only if border defences, in the charge of men like Delvin and Dunsany, collapsed, that there was any real threat of rebel attack. Nevertheless, the war took a massive toll on urban areas. While the crops of husbandmen were requisitioned or destroyed by plundering crown troops or marauding Confederates, the inhabitants of towns and cities suffered the burdens of billeting large numbers of soldiers, constant material and monetary levies, famine, disease, and fatal accidents like the 1597 gunpowder explosion.[38] Like their rural compatriots, the townsmen's responses to the war were not uniform, nor was their treatment. Sir Patrick Barnewall passed valuable intelligences to the Dublin administration; but being a notorious recusant meant that the loyalist gentleman was overlooked

---

no way of verifying this number through other accounts, Lord Deputy Russell's campaign journal includes several entries noting Delvin's delivery of rebel heads and prisoners as well as reporting a number of his successful victories against the insurgents; there can, therefore, be little doubt that Delvin performed many services for the crown. Lambeth, Carew MS, 612, No. 270 (Russell's journal); TNA, SP 63/202(2)/13 (note of principal traitors slain or executed since 3 March, 19 Apr. 1598).

[35] TNA, SP 63/206/31(I) (R. Heath to Lords Justices Loftus, Carey and Council, 17 Nov. 1599); TNA, SP 63/206/33 (R. Napper, Chief Baron of the Exchequer, to Cecil, 18 Nov. 1599); TNA, SP 63/188/8 (J. Blakney to Dunsany, 3 Apr. 1596); TNA, SP 63/189/54 (Dunsany to Cecil, 29 May 1596); HMC *Salisbury MSS*, vii, 58 (Dunsany to Cecil, 8 Feb. 1597).

[36] R.A. Canning, 'James Fitzpiers Fitzgerald, Captain Thomas Lee, and the Problem of "Secret Traitors": Conflicted Loyalties During the Nine Years' War, 1594–1603', *IHS*, Vol. 39, No. 156 (2015), pp. 93–4.

[37] Nicholls, 'Richard Tyrrell, Soldier Extraordinary', pp. 161–78.

[38] C. Lennon, 'The Great Explosion in Dublin, 1597', *Dublin Historical Record*, Vol. 42, No. 1 (1988), pp. 7–20; Lennon, 'Dublin's Great Explosion of 1597', *History Ireland*, Vol. 3, No. 3 (1995), pp. 29–34.

for promotion to office and his house was searched for priests.[39] Nicholas Weston, a Protestant merchant and Dublin alderman, provisioned the crown army with finance, food, and apparel, for which he received great favour.[40] But, at the same time as Nicholas Weston was doing his bit for the crown, his brother Richard was acting as personal secretary to Hugh O'Neill.[41] Another Old English merchant named John Bathe was illegally importing arms from Scotland for the Confederates.[42] Meanwhile, James Fleming, a merchant from Drogheda, was transporting Counter-Reformation agents to and from the continent.[43] The Palesmen therefore experienced the war in different ways in different places, but they were all nonetheless affected by its consequences.

This book will explore the many ways in which the Nine Years' War impacted and affected Old English individuals and groups within the Pale region. Chapters 2 and 3 will investigate the deployment of patriotic ideology during Hugh O'Neill's rebellion, along with certain conspiracies which infiltrated the Pale, in order to assess the dissemination of propaganda and its reception amongst the Old English Pale community. The first of these examines the religious dimension of the war through a discussion of the activities of O'Neill's clerical allies and the responses afforded them by the Palesmen. The second builds upon the work of previous historians, particularly that of Hiram Morgan, by addressing the evolution of O'Neill's 'faith and fatherland' ideology as a national platform and the impact these notions may have had on certain members of the Pale community. In doing so, these two chapters aim to examine if and how patriotic ideas may have affected the allegiances of certain Palesmen

---

39 TNA, SP 63/182/12(I) (docquet of 1,350li. borrowed, Aug. 1595); TNA, SP 63/178/4 (P. Barnewall to Burghley, 9 Jan. 1595); C. McNeill (ed.), 'Harris: Collectanea De Rebus Hibernicis', *Anal. Hib.*, No. 6 (1934), p. 377; *CSPI, 1600–1601*, p. 117.

40 Canning, 'Profits and Patriotism', pp. 1–28.

41 Although Richard operated as one of O'Neill's confidantes, from an early date he had also been providing the English administration with valuable intelligence directly from O'Neill's camp. TNA, SP 63/180/48 (Fenton to Burghley, 24 June 1595); TNA, SP 63/186/13 (Fenton to Burghley, 12 Jan. 1596); TNA, SP 63/198/35 (Fenton to R. Cecil, 24 Mar. 1597); TNA, SP 63/198/87 (Fenton to R. Cecil, 15 Apr. 1597); HMC *Salisbury MSS*, xiii, 529–30 (R. Eastfeild to Burghley or R. Cecil, 20 Dec. 1596); TNA, SP 63/207(5)/6 (N. Dawtrey to J. Fortescue, Chancellor of the Exchequer, 7 Sep. 1600). Ó Báille has drawn attention to Richard Weston's role as 'chief auditor for Tyrone' and in charge of paying O'Neill's troops. See M. Ó Báille, 'The Buannadha: Irish Professional Soldiery of the Sixteenth Century', *Journal of the Galway Archaeological and Historical Society*, Vol. 22, Nos 1/2 (1946), p. 74.

42 TNA, SP 63/178/53(V) (advertisements sent to H. Duke by several espials, 20 Feb. 1595); TNA, SP 63/203/19(I) (extracts of a letter, 15 Jan. 1599); Morgan, *Tyrone's Rebellion*, p. 182, 194n; Moryson, *An Itinerary containing his ten yeeres travell through the twelve dominions of Germany, Bohmerland, Scotland and Ireland* (4 vols, Glasgow, 1907), ii, p. 237.

43 TNA, SP 63/174/45(II) (declaration of Taylor, 10 May 1594); TNA, SP 63/179/85 (Fenton to Burghley, 19 May 1595); M. Kerney Walsh, 'Archbishop Magauran and His Return to Ireland, October 1592', *Seanchas Ardmhacha*, Vol. 14, No. 1 (1990), p. 74.

while identifying other more mundane and practical concerns which may have exerted an equal or greater influence upon the otherwise loyal Palesmen. The fourth and fifth chapters explore the Pale community's service to the crown. The former assesses the military participation of Old English Palesmen in order to determine if, or to what extent, the Palesmen were willing to support the crown during this conflict. The latter surveys the material burden of war on the loyalist Pale population by outlining the normal and extraordinary demands placed upon the Palesmen's resources, the massive debts owed to them, and the economic decline precipitated by this conflict. Finally, through an analysis of the Palesmen's petitions and treatises, the sixth chapter explores how the Old English expressed political loyalty, grievances, and their rights as crown subjects. Particular attention will be given to the efforts of the Old English élite to preserve their status and authority from the encroachment of New English Protestant *arrivistes* and protect their positions in an emerging English Ireland. Ultimately, the Nine Years' War would teach the Old English some harsh lessons, and these would be instrumental in shaping their future relations with the English crown and their Irish homeland.

2

Instruments of Sedition: Priests and the Pale

> It is Popery that hath alienated the heartes of that people from the faith, fidelity, obedience, loue and loyaltie, that is required in Subiects towardes theyr Souereignes. It is Popery that hath set afoot so many rebellions in Ireland, that hath cost the liues of multitudes, that hath ruined that whole Realme, and made it subiect to the oppression of Theeus, Robbers, Spoilers, Murtherers, Rebels and Traitors.
>
> Barnaby Riche, 1610[1]

By the 1590s, both Hugh O'Neill and English crown administrators had every right to think that a war fought in the name of the Catholic Church would rouse the Old English population of the Pale from passive recusancy to armed revolt. A 'faith and fatherland' ideology had struck roots in Ireland long before the outbreak of the Nine Years' War. It had found early expression in the revolts of James Fitzmaurice (1579), Viscount Baltinglass (1580), and William Nugent (1581). Not only had the Old English leaders of these uprisings espoused a Catholic cause, but their actions and assertions had been bolstered by the ministries of Counter-Reformation clerics who openly denounced English heresy and solicited foreign intervention for Ireland. These clerics were some of the earliest proponents of an Irish 'faith and fatherland' philosophy and they would come to be regarded as the chief propagandists of the nationwide revolt led by Hugh O'Neill. How this came to be and how the work of the clergy became coterminous with the ideological wing of O'Neill's rebellion is crucial to understanding the Nine Years' War and the predicament of Ireland's Catholic inhabitants. The involvement of Catholic clerics gave many administrators cause to fear the kind of religious fervour they might inspire, and this anxiety was clearly articulated in official records. This chapter will therefore examine the activities of some of O'Neill's chief clerical conspirators to illustrate that O'Neill's hopes and administrators' concerns were not groundless. However, it will also challenge the assumption that an appeal for a Catholic crusade would find wide and enthusiastic support in Ireland, and especially amongst the population of the Pale. Although religious concerns are clearly apparent in the State Papers, evidence suggesting that religion and the Catholic clergy played a decisive role in this conflict is inconclusive. There were indeed a number of Catholic clerics who championed O'Neill's rebellion through subversion at

---

1   B. Riche, *A New Description of Ireland* (London, 1610), pp. 90–1.

home and solicitation of foreign intervention abroad; but these were the efforts of a select number of individuals and the beliefs and actions of these men were not representative of the entire Irish population. While the intentions of this minority were sincere, the reception afforded them was not necessarily what they had hoped for or expected. Surviving evidence suggests that the religious dimension of this conflict has been mistakenly exaggerated, as has the activity and success of religious radicals. Thus, after exploring the real and perceived dangers of clerical activities in Ireland, this chapter will consider the reception afforded Catholic clerics and crusading rhetoric within the Pale. Religion could indeed bridge many gaps, but centuries of animosities between the Old English and Gaelic Irish were far more difficult to overcome than either Hugh O'Neill or crown administrators imagined. Nevertheless, clerics and religious fervour did play a role in a number of serious plots against the crown and therefore the exertions and attitudes of Catholic clerics, militant and otherwise, require attention in order to assess the impact of religion and the religious on the progress of this war.

Early Clerical Instigators

Before Hugh O'Neill became the administration's primary concern, crown administrators were already anxious about Jesuits and seminarians operating in Ireland. After the formation of the established Church of Ireland, countless Irish students, along with members of the Catholic clergy, left home for the Catholic colleges of the continent where they were imbued with the spirit of a militant Counter-Reformation movement.[2] A significant number of these returned home through the 1580s and 1590s to preach the merits of Catholicism, denounce English heresy, and encourage Irishmen in their resolve to reject Protestantism.[3] It was a dangerous time to do so, and even Edmund Spenser, the English poet and planter, expressed wonder at the perils Catholic priests were willing to face in their determination to further the Catholic cause in Ireland. He wrote: 'they spare not to come out of Spaine, from Rome, and from Remes, by long toyle and daungerous travayling hither, where they know perill of death awayteth them, and no reward or richesse is to be found, onely to draw the people unto the Church of Rome'.[4] Once back in Ireland, these

---

[2] For a discussion on patterns of Old English education, see H. Hammerstein, 'Aspects of the Continental Education of Irish Students in the Reign of Queen Elizabeth', in T.D. Williams (ed.), *Historical Studies*, Vol. 8 (Dublin, 1971), pp. 137–53.

[3] R.D. Edwards, *Church and State in Tudor Ireland: A History of Penal Laws Against Irish Catholics, 1534–1603* (Dublin, 1935), p. 164.

[4] Spenser, *A View*, pp. 153–4.

Catholic 'Bishops, doctors and preests' found shelter and sustenance 'in sertayne lawyers howses and aldermens howses and men of great substance'.[5] Although many of them confined themselves to simple missionary work, a number entered conspiratorial plots at home and abroad in the hope of overthrowing English heresy and domination.[6] Crown officials were convinced that these ecclesiastics were exerting undue influence over rebelliously inclined Irish lords. They were equally worried that priests were sowing seeds of sedition amongst the otherwise loyal Catholic community of the Pale.[7] Since these Catholic clerics presented a destabilising threat, sincere efforts were made to keep abreast of their movements and activities, yet administrators were unable to stem the flow of Catholic clergy into Ireland.

As early as November 1594 Lord Deputy Sir William Russell complained that O'Neill was 'a man now altogether gouerned by Jesuitts and seminarye pristes the fore runners of rebellions'.[8] Six years later, Lord Chancellor Adam Loftus and Bishop Thomas Jones of Meath likewise asserted that the rebels had been 'perverted and seduced by traitorous priests'.[9] There has been some debate about whether O'Neill manipulated the Counter-Reformation clergy in order to legitimise his rebellion or whether the clergy, who 'saw in Hugh O'Neill their deliverer from an imposed alien religion', used O'Neill as a pawn to serve their own ends.[10] It was clear by this time that secular and spiritual affairs had become inseparable in Ireland and it is far more likely that a mutually dependent, or symbiotic, relationship existed between the two. For the Catholic episcopacy, O'Neill's rebellion offered the means to achieving a Catholic Ireland; for O'Neill, Catholic ideology and the ministries of its clerical leaders provided his war with a righteous cause. Amongst the clergy, Peter Lombard saw the benefit of supporting O'Neill's rebellion, regardless of whether O'Neill's motivation was real or contrived, because 'if this Prince comes out conqueror in this war, the cause of the orthodox religion will also triumph throughout all Ireland'.[11] The role of the Catholic clergy in fomenting unrest and allying various interests in the north was important, but they were not the orchestrators of this rebellion.

5   TNA, SP 63/202(1)/70 (P. Hackett to Burghley, 1 Mar. 1598); TNA, SP 63/202(1)/69 (D. Rowghane to Burghley, 1 Mar. 1598).
6   Edwards, *Church and State*, p. 230; C. Maginn, 'Whose Island?: Sovereignty in Late Medieval and Early Modern Ireland', Éire-Ireland, Vol. 44, Nos 3/4 (2009), p. 241.
7   TNA, SP 63/177/9 (lord deputy to Burghley, 15 Nov. 1594); HMC *Salisbury MSS*, iv, 564–5; V.P. Carey, 'John Derricke's "Image of Irelande", Sir Henry Sidney, and the Massacre at Mullaghmast, 1578', IHS, Vol. 31, No. 123 (1999), pp. 314–15.
8   TNA, SP 63/177/9 (lord deputy to Burghley, 15 Nov. 1594).
9   CSPI, 1600, pp. 79–80.
10 McGurk, *Elizabethan Conquest*, p. 21.
11 M.J. Byrne (ed.), *The Irish War of Defence, 1598–1600: Extracts from the De Hibernia Insula Commentarius of Peter Lombard* (Cork, 1930), p. 41.

Seeing O'Neill as the means to achieving a Catholic Ireland, these clerics put themselves at O'Neill's disposal, acting as his 'instruments' to be directed as he willed.[12] In fact, as the war progressed, crown administrators often referred to them by this term, indicating an appreciation of their function in the wider scheme of the rebellion.[13] Nevertheless, there were a number of Irish clerics who played a leading role in nourishing unrest during the various stages of the rebellion, and their activities as well as their powers of persuasion warrant consideration in order to better understand official concerns.

In 1592, in spite of warnings of inevitable doom should he venture to Ireland, Edmund Magauran, Catholic archbishop of Armagh, returned from Spanish exile in order to rally his Irish flock to a higher cause. Magauran arrived bearing promises of Spanish assistance provided the northern lords united in a war against the English crown. This proved propitious, as an emerging Ulster confederacy, which included MacMahon, O'Rourke, Maguire, and O'Donnell, was on the point of revolt against English centralising policies and the officials and soldiers implementing them.[14] Magauran's involvement was short-lived, but before his untimely death on the battlefield in 1593, the newly confederated northern lords dispatched James O'Hely, Archbishop of Tuam, to Spain to continue Magauran's lobby for military assistance.[15] O'Hely was successful – or would have been had his mission been completed. On the return journey to Ireland, O'Hely, along with John Lacie and the earl of Desmond's son, were lost at sea, as was the Spanish king's response and a significant stock of supplies for the war effort.[16] In spite of his brief involvement, O'Hely played a decisive role in fuelling the fires of what would come to be the greatest native challenge to English suzerainty in Ireland. Like Magauran, O'Hely actively encouraged Irishmen to rebel but, more importantly, he was quick to recognise a certain weakness in the initial confederacy. While he may have secretly endorsed the

---

[12] TNA, SP 63/202(3)/135 (Irish Council to Privy Council, 31 Oct. 1598).

[13] Ibid.; TNA, SP 63/207(4)/94 (Fenton to Cecil, 28 Aug. 1600).

[14] The earliest Confederates were composed of MacMahon, O'Rourke, Maguire, O'Donnell, and Cormac O'Neill, brother of Hugh O'Neill. Byrne (ed.), *Irish War of Defence*, pp. 23–7; Morgan, *Tyrone's Rebellion*, pp. 140–3; M. O'Reilly, *Memorials of Those Who Suffered for the Catholic Faith in Ireland* (London, 1868), pp. 131–3; Kerney Walsh, 'Archbishop Magauran', pp. 68–79; Silke, *Kinsale*, p. 25; Bagwell, *Ireland under the Tudors*, pp. 233–4. See also T. Gainsford, *The true exemplary, and remarkable history of the Earle of Tirone* (London, 1619), pp. 17–18.

[15] TNA, SP 63/177/9(I) (Advertisements, 11 Nov. 1594); *CSP Sp.*, *1587–1603*, p. 599 (H. O'Donnell to viscount Baltinglass and T. Geraldine, 8 Apr. 1593); *CSP Sp.*, *1587–1603*, pp. 609–611 (statement of Archbishop of Tuam to Philip II, Sep. 1593); *CSP Sp.*, *1587–1603*, pp. 611–612 (statement handed to the King by Archbishop of Tuam, Sep. 1593).

[16] TNA, SP 63/183/71(VIII) (examination of P. O'Cullan, 29 Sep. 1595); TNA, SP 63/186/22(II) (Examination of T. O'Hogan, 18 Jan. 1596); TNA, SP 63/178/24 (Dr. R. Brown to lord deputy, 28 Jan. 1595); TNA, SP 63/196/31(III) (examination of R. Folan, priest, 16 Dec. 1596). M. Walsh, 'The Military Order of Saint Patrick, 1593', *Seanchas Ardmhacha*, Vol. 9, No. 2 (1979), pp. 274–85.

actions of his neighbours, Hugh O'Neill, soon to be the leader of the rebellion, was still conducting himself as a loyal subject of the English crown.[17] O'Hely knew that this chief's support would be crucial for the success of an Irish rebellion, and he therefore asked King Philip II of Spain to write to O'Neill and personally entreat the most powerful northern lord to join the revolt.[18]

The loss of both Magauran and O'Hely at the very outset of this war could have been a serious setback for the future of the rebellion, but there were to be many more Catholic clerics who would take their place in furthering a militant Catholic tendency in Ireland.[19] Records detailing the careers of some of O'Neill's religious partners appear almost heroic. Dr Dermot McCreagh's role in committing a large part of Munster to the Catholic faith was renowned amongst contemporaries and later writers.[20] Amongst the Jesuits, the labours of James Archer have resonated through Irish history.[21] The career of Peter Lombard has likewise received much acclaim.[22] More recently, the politico-religious dealing and foreign intrigues of Franciscan Florence Conry have been detailed.[23] Following the defeat of O'Neill and his Confederates, clerics like Franciscan Mícheál Ó Cléirigh would immortalise O'Neill and his allies as the freedom fighters of a Catholic Ireland.[24] Generations of such men would continue to produce propaganda depicting this period as the naissance of a universal Catholic nation moulded from the once feuding Gaelic Irish and Old English populations. However, these are only a few representative members of the nationalised religious community and the work of many other Catholic clerics who advocated Irish unrest, or disavowed it, has not received the same

[17] O'Neill's proxy war has been comprehensively detailed by Hiram Morgan and James O'Neill: Morgan, *Tyrone's Rebellion*; O'Neill, *The Nine Years War*. See also J. Perrot, *The Chronicle of Ireland, 1584–1608*, ed. H. Wood (Dublin, 1933), pp. 73–89.

[18] *CSP Sp.*, *1587–1603*, pp. 611–12 (statement handed to the King by Archbishop of Tuam, Sep. 1593); TNA, SP 63/174/18(VI) (declaration of R. Nugent, 19 Apr. 1594); TNA, SP 63/174/45(II) (declaration of H. Taylor, 10 May 1594); TNA, SP 63/177/9(I) (advertisements, 11 Nov. 1594).

[19] For example, TNA, SP 63/196/31(III) (examination of Folan, 16 Dec. 1596).

[20] TNA, SP 63/203/25 ('Proclamation for Ireland', 25 Jan. 1599); H.A. Jefferies, *The Irish Church and the Tudor Reformations* (Dublin, 2010), pp. 260–2; H. Morgan, 'Hugh O'Neill and the Nine Years War in Tudor Ireland', *HJ*, Vol. 36, No. 1 (1993), p. 26. His relative Miler Magrath was particularly outspoken against him.

[21] E. Hogan, *Distinguished Irishmen of the Sixteenth Century* (London, 1894), ch. 11; T.J. Morrissey, *James Archer of Kilkenny, an Elizabethan Jesuit* (Dublin, 1979); J. Corboy, 'Father James Archer, S.J., 1550–1625(?)', *Studies*, Vol. 33 (1944), pp. 99–107; Corboy, 'Father Henry Fitzsimon, S.J., 1566–1643', *Studies*, Vol. 32 (1943), pp. 260–6; H. Fitzsimon, *Words of Comfort to Persecuted Catholics*, ed. E. Hogan (Dublin, 1881); J. Corboy, 'Father Christopher Holywood, S.J., 1559–1626', *Studies*, Vol. 33 (1944), pp. 543–9; Jesuit Archives, London, 46/17/8/4 ('Letters between Holywood and Acquaviva').

[22] Byrne (ed.), *Irish War of Defence*; J.J. Silke, 'The Irish Peter Lombard', *Studies*, Vol. 64, No. 254 (1975), pp. 143–55.

[23] B. Hazard, *Faith and Patronage: The Political Career of Flaithrí Ó Maolchonaire* (Dublin, 2010).

[24] J. O'Donovan (ed.), *Annals of the Kingdom of Ireland, by the Four Masters* (Dublin, 1854).

attention. It is therefore necessary to examine the efforts of those clerics who actively promoted rebellion in Ireland as well as those who maintained their distance. It is also essential to consider the ways in which these clerics and their ministries were received by the lay community and how crown administrators responded. By doing so, it is possible to begin assessing the degree to which religion impacted affairs in the Pale and Ireland as a whole, both in terms of its threat to the state as well as its actual influence on the consciences and actions of the people.

Francis Mountford and His Associates

By 1594 an English seminary priest named Francis Mountford had been identified as one of O'Neill's leading clerical agents.[25] It was believed that Mountford had initially come from England into the Pale from whence the Palesmen had sent him north in order to encourage Hugh O'Neill 'to proceed in this action'.[26] As is the case with many of O'Neill's English Catholic collaborators, it is unclear how and when Mountford became acquainted with Ireland's simmering troubles, nor is there any distinct evidence to explain why he decided to join O'Neill and participate in the Irish rebellion. The fact that an English cleric had involved himself in Irish affairs during this period was not particularly unusual; Dr Nicholas Sanders had been an important agitator during the ill-fated Fitzmaurice revolt just over a decade earlier. Like Sanders, Mountford proved to be a very tricky customer and Dublin administrators, though lacking concrete evidence against him, portrayed Mountford as one of the principal threats to crown government in Ireland.[27]

Mountford was a busy man and government intelligence implicated him in many treasonous activities at home and abroad. Domestically, it was supposed that Mountford sent seditiously minded clerics into the Pale to rally support for the rebellion and that he was sometimes present there himself.[28] His name also appears in connection with communications sent from the north into Scotland,

[25] The Irish State Papers label Mountford as an English Jesuit; however, Robert Dudley Edwards contends that Mountford was actually a secular priest, and that English officials habitually ascribed Catholic clerics to the Order of Jesus. Edwards, *Church and State*, p. 284.

[26] TNA, SP 63/178/58 (Russell to Burghley, Feb. 1595). Although there is no evidence to confirm this allegation, in 1599 it was contended that while Mountford was in the Pale he had been a guest in the house of Captain William Warren, a crown servitor and friend of O'Neill's. It was argued that it was here that O'Neill first met Mountford before he travelled north to become one of O'Neill's chief councillors. TNA, SP 63/203/58 (articles against W. Warren, Feb. 1599).

[27] TNA, SP 63/179/85 (Fenton to Burghley, 19 May 1595); TNA, SP 63/180/32(I) (Bishop of Meath to lord deputy, 12 June 1595); TNA, SP 63/202(4)/61 ('A sumerie discourse of this Realme of Ireland', 1598).

[28] TNA, SP 63/178/58 (Russell to Burghley, Feb. 1595).

England, and Spain, and on two occasions it was reported, but never verified, that Mountford had personally ventured to Spain as O'Neill's emissary.[29] It was widely believed that O'Neill held Mountford in very high regard, so much so that the baron of Slane was under the mistaken impression that it was solely on Mountford's advice that O'Neill refused to deliver his son as a crown hostage.[30] Mountford was also credited with converting O'Neill's New English Protestant wife, Mabel Bagenal, to Catholicism.[31] These unproven allegations served to confirm official fears about the influence of seminarians on Irish rebels.

What is particularly noteworthy about Mountford's rumoured intrigues is the depth and scale of the conspiracies surrounding him. Documentary evidence concerning Mountford's activities demonstrates that clerical involvement in O'Neill's rebellion was an international and ethnically diverse affair. Contrary to the common assumption that ethnic boundaries not only determined preference for religious orders, but seriously impeded collaboration between the various religious and cultural groups of Ireland, affiliations between Mountford and other Catholic clerics indicate that at least some individuals could ignore traditional divisions. His connections with other clerical conspirators, amongst whom the names of Gravenor, Hales, and O'Cullan are prominent, is proof that the religious dimension of O'Neill's rebellion transcended ethnic boundaries and that there were English, Old English, and Gaelic Irish clerics working together to achieve the same end. All showed impressive dedication to the cause and all went to great lengths to conceal their activities from the government. The secrecy of Mountford and his colleagues meant that in mid-1595 Fenton, who was usually remarkably well-informed about these things, was unable to describe 'the complection hayre, or other owtwarde token wherby Monfort might be knowen'.[32] In spite of their efforts, all those whose names are recorded, with the exception of Mountford, were captured and it is largely as a result of their apprehension that any information concerning their activities has survived.

It was well known that O'Neill had been soliciting military support from Spain through his Jesuit and seminary associates and, in October 1594, Lord Deputy Fitzwilliam received intelligences from three Palesmen about several priests and laymen associated with O'Neill. Thomas Fleming, baron of Slane, reluctantly, but in accordance with his duty as a loyal subject, reported that there were four Englishmen 'named Bennett, Gravener, Dickinson, and Mountffortie'

---

29 TNA, SP 63/178/13 (R. Beacon to Lord Keeper, 21 Jan. 1595); TNA, SP 63/179/85 (Fenton to Burghley, 19 May 1595); TNA, SP 63/197/6 (H. Knowlis to Cecil, 10 Jan. 1597).
30 TNA, SP 63/176/60(XI) (baron of Slane to lord deputy, 12 Oct. 1594).
31 Morgan, 'Policy and Propaganda in Hugh O'Neill's Connection with Europe', p. 21; T. Lee, 'A brief declaration of the government of Ireland' (1594), in J. Lodge (ed.), *Desiderata Curiosa Hibernica* (Dublin, 1772), p. 111.
32 TNA, SP 63/179/85 (Fenton to Burghley, 19 May 1595).

greatly favoured by O'Neill at that time.[33] Of these, Mountford, the priest, was with O'Neill 'and of greate councell with him', Bennett was schoolmaster to O'Neill's children, and Gravenor and Dickinson had departed Ireland for an unknown destination.[34] Slane was ignorant as to the whereabouts of Gravenor and Dickinson, but Sir Patrick Barnewall was able to inform Fitzwilliam that O'Neill had sent Gravenor to Spain.[35] Barnewall's testimony was corroborated by an examination of Mr Udall, a servant to the earl of Kildare.[36]

The Dublin administration took immediate action to prevent Gravenor's mission and, in January 1595, Thomas Gravenor, along with two companions, later identified as brothers John and Edward Hales, were captured 'coming out of Ireland and going into Scotland upon some message from the Earl of Tyrone'.[37] This was a 'very happie' event for Lord Deputy Russell who believed that examinations of Gravenor and Hales would 'reveal great matters concerning the Earl of Tirone's practising with Spain'.[38] Russell's happiness was to be short-lived, as Gravenor, who was supposed to be transported from York to London for interrogation, had mysteriously fallen ill and was unable to endure travel.[39] Several days later his guardian and interrogator, Richard Topcliffe, reported Gravenor dead, having 'died like a dumb dog'.[40] The death of this Catholic conspirator was unwelcome news for English officialdom; the bishop of Limerick fretted that if only Gravenor had lived, he 'could have spoken mutch for he knewe all'.[41] Russell was particularly upset because he believed an examination of Gravenor would have revealed 'the Earles practises with those of the Pale, amonge which I assure myself there are many hollow harted, and were meete to be discovered'.[42] Although the death of Gravenor impeded government intelligence gathering, Topcliffe expressed hope that one of Gravenor's companions would 'utter all the secrets that Gravener or the Earl of Tyrone did impart to him'.[43]

Gravenor's companions, John and Edward Hales, had been imprisoned in Newgate, and examined, and were to be indicted for recusancy, 'whereby [they] may be lawfully detained'.[44] Before their indictment the brothers were

[33] TNA, SP 63/176/60(XI) (Slane to lord deputy, 12 Oct. 1594).
[34] Ibid.
[35] TNA, SP 63/176/50 (W. Fitzwilliam to Burghley, 2 Oct. 1594).
[36] TNA, SP 63/184/41 (Bishop John Thornburgh of Limerick to Cecil, Nov. 1595).
[37] CUL, Ms. Ee III 56, No. 38 (14 Jan. 1594); TNA, SP 63/178/58 (Russell to Burghley, Feb. 1595); TNA, SP 63/185/7 (Cecil to Kildare, 10 Dec. 1595); TNA, SP 63/184/41 (Thornburgh to Cecil, Nov. 1595); HMC *Salisbury MSS*, vi, 427–8.
[38] *CSPI, 1592–96*, p. 292; TNA, SP 63/178/58 (Russell to Burghley, Feb. 1595).
[39] HMC *Salisbury MSS*, v, 81, 83; CUL, Ms. Ee III 56, No. 38 (14 Jan. 1594).
[40] HMC *Salisbury MSS*, v, 91.
[41] TNA, SP 63/184/41 (Thornburgh to Cecil, Nov. 1595).
[42] TNA, SP 63/178/58 (Russell to Burghley, Feb. 1595).
[43] HMC *Salisbury MSS*, v, 91.
[44] HMC *Salisbury MSS*, vi, 427–8.

questioned about letters found in their possession from prisoners in Bridewell prison and a priest named Pearcie. According to the examiners, Pearcie claimed that his letters were in response to a request, delivered by John Hales, for advice on affairs concerning O'Neill. The examiners noted that the content of communications meant for Pearcie was 'very suspicious in divers points, but both of them do interpret the same only to concern prayer and meditation'. Equally troubling was that 'there is mention made of a priest called Father Frauncys, whom... is well known unto Hale'.[45] John Hales, the elder of the two, refused to confirm any of this, thus leading his examiners to conclude that he was a particularly 'obstinate and dangerous person'. The brothers were also asked about Gravenor's dealings with O'Neill, to which they admitted that the two men had held secret conferences but that they themselves were unaware of what had been discussed. Asked where they had intended to go after Scotland if they had not been apprehended, the brothers responded that they were destined for France, where they planned 'to learn the language'; the examiners argued that 'it was more evident it should be for Spain or Rome'.[46]

Not to be confused with the Hales brothers, another priest named Hall was captured around the same time in Waterford on his return from Spain.[47] Hall is depicted as another clerical conspirator associated with O'Neill and Mountford and he was suspected of carrying out a mission similar to that of Gravenor and the Hales brothers. While it was unclear where the Hales brothers typically operated, Hall was considered particularly active within the Pale where he 'not only said masse in manie places abroad in the contrey, but even here in this cittie of Dublin'.[48] There is, however, no mention of where Hall actually lodged, where he preached, or who supported him, financially or otherwise. Like every other clerical detainee, Hall was examined about other suspected ecclesiastical agents operating abroad on behalf on O'Neill, but he too pleaded ignorance.[49]

Government officials failed to ascertain anything substantial about Mountford or O'Neill from these captives, but they were soon to learn by other means more about Mountford's activities. In January 1595, Richard Beacon, an English administrator and author, drew attention to a rumour that O'Neill had sent

---

45   This 'Father Frauncys' is almost certainly Francis Mountford.

46   HMC *Salisbury* MSS, vi, 427–8.

47   Russell's letter suggests that Hall was captured sometime around the end of February 1595. TNA, SP 63/179/90 (lord deputy to Cecil, 23 May 1595); TNA, SP 63/179/93 (lord deputy to Cecil, 24 May 1595); Lambeth, Carew MS, 612, No. 270 (Russell's journal).

48   TNA, SP 63/179/90 (lord deputy to Cecil, 23 May 1595).

49   Hall was examined about another priest named Donnell as well as 'that counsellor contayned in your nott'. It is possible that this councillor was Mountford; however, over the course of the war the State had identified a number of other individuals acting as O'Neill's councillors (i.e. James Nott), and it is unclear exactly to whom Russell was referring in this instance. TNA, SP 63/179/93 (lord deputy to Cecil, 24 May 1595).

Mountford, 'the cheife' of his clerical allies, to the Spanish court to further his suit for assistance.[50] The following May, Fenton reported that Mountford and 'one Fleminge an Irishman… are now upon their dispatch to go from therle for Spaine'.[51] According to Fenton's intelligence, the conspirators were to travel to Spain via Scotland, and Fenton hoped to make arrangements with the English ambassador to capture Mountford and Fleming, 'together with their letters and instructions', while they awaited transportation to Spain.[52] Mountford successfully evaded efforts to apprehend him, but it is possible that the administration's intelligence was incorrect because there are no records to indicate that Mountford did, in fact, arrive in Spain, nor are there any records of his return journey to Ireland.

Mountford's supposed companion, the unidentified Fleming, may have been the same James Fleming, a Drogheda merchant, who was responsible for transporting Magauran from Spain to Ireland in 1592 and O'Hely from Ireland to Spain in 1593.[53] Unlike his dealings with Magauran and O'Hely, it appears that on this occasion Fleming was unable to arrange direct shipping from the north of Ireland. Instead, Fleming allegedly accompanied Mountford on a Scottish ship destined for Scotland, from whence they meant to sail for Spain.[54] Merchants like Fleming, whether they intended it or not, were indispensable to O'Neill's rebellion and the Counter-Reformation in Ireland. They supplied the rebels with weapons and intelligence, provided the means for correspondence with foreign powers, transported Irish students to continental Catholic colleges, and shipped zealous clerics back to Ireland to bolster the Counter-Reformation and rebellion back home.[55] All this they did at considerable personal risk as the crown had ordered the execution of any such aiders and abetters of rebellious Catholic conspirators. Religious fervour may not have been the motivating factor for many of these merchants since the Protestant Nicholas Weston was also accused of assisting the Confederates with shipments of gunpowder.[56] It was generally accepted that the Confederates were willing to pay higher prices

---

[50] TNA, SP 63/178/13 (Beacon to Lord Keeper, 21 Jan. 1595).
[51] TNA, SP 63/179/85 (Fenton to Burghley, 19 May 1595).
[52] Ibid.
[53] TNA, SP 63/174/45(II) (declaration of Taylor, 10 May, 1594). See also Kerney Walsh, 'Archbishop Magauran', p. 74.
[54] TNA, SP 63/179/85 (Fenton to Burghley, 19 May 1595). This was corroborated by Captain Charles Egerton a few months later, who reported that Mountford was in Scotland awaiting transport to Spain. TNA, SP 63/183/78 (C. Egerton to Burghley, 7 Oct. 1595); TNA, SP 63/183/84(IV) (Egerton to Russell, 5 Oct. 1595).
[55] For example, see TNA, SP 63/178/53(V) (advertisements sent to H. Duke, 20 Feb. 1595); TNA, SP 63/179/90 (lord deputy to Cecil, 23 May 2595); TNA, SP 63/177/5 (lord deputy to Burghley, 8 Nov. 1594); TNA, SP 63/187/19 (Dowdall to Burghley, 9 Mar. 1596); TNA, SP 63/202(2)/100 (Privy Council to Irish Council, 13 July 1598).
[56] HMC *Salisbury MSS*, vi, 529–30; Canning, 'Profits and Patriotism', pp. 1–28.

than the crown for supplies and other services, and this would have been strong incentive for many merchants like Fleming.[57]

Mountford had escaped the crown's grasp on this occasion, but another one of his envoys was not so fortunate. At the beginning of October 1595, Russell announced the capture of a priest carrying letters containing 'the traytorly Erles intentions to bring in Spanish forces'.[58] This priest was Piers O'Cullan of Clogher, and his interrogation was to provide the administration with much wanted intelligence regarding the foreign intrigues of O'Neill and his clerical colluders.[59] O'Cullan had been captured at Drogheda, en route to Spain, in possession of letters from O'Neill and O'Donnell which 'plainly discovered their intent both to bring in Spanish forces, and to make religion the ground of this their Rebellion'.[60] Being examined by Robert Bowen, Provost Marshal of Leinster, and Richard Cooke, the viceroy's secretary, O'Cullan confessed that he had spent three years in Spain, France, and Italy where he had become acquainted with O'Neill's foreign conspiracies.[61] O'Cullan insisted, however, that his sole purpose in returning to Ireland was to take up a parsonage in his native Clogher, for which he had been granted a papal bull. He claimed he had arrived in Dublin about twenty days earlier and had immediately travelled northwards to take up his post. When O'Cullan arrived in the north, O'Neill summoned him to Dungannon for a night meeting with Mountford and O'Neill's wife. He complied, and the following morning he accompanied Mountford away from Dungannon in order to join O'Neill. According to O'Cullan, O'Neill then 'gave Momford direction… to write letters to the king of Spaine, Don Carolo, and Don John Daguila'. Of the three letters he carried, O'Cullan acknowledged that two were written by Mountford, 'and the third by a tall black man whom he knoweth not, attending vpon the Countesse'.[62] Although he insisted that he was not privy to the content of these letters, O'Cullan had considerably detailed knowledge of the message. He confessed O'Neill was seeking the assistance of three to four thousand soldiers with money and munitions by the following May, vowing that if the Spanish king agreed, 'they would mainteyne the warres, toguether with the Catholick relligion, and submit them selves to be governed by him as anie naturall Spaniard'.[63] The

---

57 Moryson, *Itinerary*, ii, p. 240; *CSPI, 1599–1600*, pp. 181, 285–6.
58 TNA, SP 63/183/71 (Russell to Burghley, 4 Oct. 1595).
59 TNA, SP 63/183/71(VIII) (examination of O'Cullan, 29 Sep. 1595).
60 TNA, SP 63/183/73 (Russell to Cecil, 4 Oct. 1595); TNA, SP 63/183/71(VIII) (examination of O'Cullan, 29 Sep. 1595); Perrot, *Chronicle*, p. 112.
61 TNA, SP 63/183/71(VIII) (examination of O'Cullan, 29 Sep. 1595).
62 Ibid. Hiram Morgan has suggested that this unnamed cleric was probably Robert MacArthur, alias Chamberlain, originally from County Louth. See Morgan, 'Policy and Propaganda', pp. 24, 30.
63 However, the letters also noted that if this aid was not forthcoming O'Neill and his allies

government acquired a great deal of incriminating evidence in these intercepted letters, and O'Cullan's interrogation only confirmed what the examiners had discovered in the communications.[64] What O'Cullan's testimony did reveal was that by permitting the poor priest only one night's rest before departing on his mission, O'Neill was desperately eager for a speedy resolution on this point.

Interestingly, O'Cullan avoided implicating himself in any conspiracy. He claimed that when in Spain he had refused Don Carlos's request to carry letters to O'Neill.[65] He explained that he had only met with O'Neill because he had left the bull for his parsonage in St Malo and, because his benefice was located within O'Neill's territory, he was obliged to inform the rebel earl. O'Neill subsequently refused to allow O'Cullan, a man of little importance, to take up his post without papal documentation and ordered him to return to St Malo and fetch his proof. While doing so, O'Neill stipulated that O'Cullan was to deliver certain letters and await answer.[66] O'Cullan's testimony portrays him as an unassuming, apolitical, cleric whose involvement was accidental and unintended. This does not mean it was entirely true. It is impossible to determine whether O'Cullan was forced to carry out this mission or whether he had a hand in it, but he knew the purpose of his journey and he must have been well aware of the risks involved. It is unlikely that O'Cullan would have run such a dangerous errand unless he was willing to advance these rebellious intrigues; it is therefore quite plausible that he himself espoused the cause. Notwithstanding his tacit complicity, O'Cullan was simply the messenger, obliged to carry out this task in return for O'Neill's permission to take up his clerical post.[67]

The men discussed thus far were only a few of O'Neill's clerical co-conspirators. They were not alone, and the government received numerous other advertisements concerning O'Neill's relations with Spain and the activities of Irish clergy abroad in procuring foreign assistance. It is evident from the intercepted letters and examinations of men like O'Cullan, Hall, and the Hales brothers, that O'Neill was mindful of the possibility of interception and that he was careful to dispatch several copies of his communications by different messengers and different routes.[68] It is even possible that O'Neill

'might make their peace with the English'. TNA, SP 63/183/71(VIII) (examination of O'Cullan, 29 Sep. 1595)

[64] All three were written in Latin and were dated 27 September 1596. The three letters are can be found in both the Irish State Papers and the Carew Manuscripts. *Cal. Carew*, iii, 122–3; *CSPI, 1592–96*, p. 409.

[65] TNA, SP 63/183/71(VIII) (examination of O'Cullan, 29 Sep. 1595).

[66] Ibid.

[67] It is also possible that O'Neill orchestrated the whole affair in order to instill the fear of foreign conspiracy amongst government officials.

[68] For example, TNA, SP 63/202(4)/13 (statement by B. O'Donnell to Bishop of Limerick, 8 Dec. 1598).

wanted these communications to be intercepted in order to further unsettle nervous administrators. The letters found on the Hales brothers indicate that they, or some other individuals, had succeeded in carrying out at least part of their mission. And, although the government had prevented the delivery of the letters carried by O'Cullan, correspondence to the same effect had made its way into Spain and received answer around the same time.[69] This was a tactic employed throughout the war, and no matter how many letters crown officials seized, O'Neill and his agents continued to communicate with allies abroad.

While O'Neill and his agents' efforts to secure Spanish assistance had the appearance of becoming more assured, they were also aware of the need for support at home. The Confederates faced a dilemma, a double-edged sword so to speak. They could not be confident of Spanish intervention without widespread support at home; however, they could not rally support within Ireland without some assurance that the promise of foreign aid would actually materialise. It was therefore sometimes suggested that the Spanish should land near the Pale as it would be the best means to encourage the country to rise.[70] Before that could happen, it was necessary to establish some local alliances. Under O'Donnell's influence, Connacht stood relatively firm with the Confederates.[71] In Munster, agents, supported by a series of circular letters exhorting the leading inhabitants to rise, were favourably received and the province would eventually be the centre of rebellion for a period.[72] But the same could not be said for Leinster, and it was towards the Pale that O'Neill now directed his attentions. By the summer of 1596, O'Neill's efforts to seduce leading Irish lords in Leinster were well known and it was reported that his 'Messengers are with Feagh mac Hugh and divers others in the pale, drawing them to combine with him in this conspiracie'.[73] While O'Neill's messengers found a strong ally in Feagh

---

[69] TNA, SP 63/193/20(I) (O'Neill and O'Donnell to King of Spain, 23 Aug.–2 Sep. 1596); *CSP Sp., 1587–1603*, Nos. 634; 635; 636; 637; 638; 639; 641; 643; 644; 645; 654.

[70] TNA, SP 63/190/44(XIII) (J. Morgan to Russell, 23 June 1596); TNA, SP 63/193/35 (Russell to Burghley, 26 Sep. 1596).

[71] See Bingham's reports on the state of Connacht. See also TNA, SP 63/196/31(VII) (H. Bagenal to Russell, 23 Dec. 1596).

[72] The Munster plantation was overthrown in 1598 and the province suffered great instability for a period. W. Maley (ed.), 'The Supplication of the Blood of the English Most Lamentably Murdered in Ireland, Cryeng Out of the Yearth for Revenge (1598)', *Anal. Hib.*, No. 36 (1995), pp. 3–77; Bagwell, *Ireland under the Tudors*, pp. 271–2. For earlier disturbances, see *Cal. Carew*, iii, 179; TNA, SP 63/192/20 (lord deputy to Burghley, 21 Aug. 1596); TNA, SP 63/193/20 (Irish Council to Privy Council, 17 Sep. 1596); TNA, SP 63/194/15 (Russell to Privy Council, 14 Oct. 1596); TNA, SP 63/194/19 (Irish Council to Privy Council, 15 Oct. 1596); TNA, SP 63/195/15 (T. Norreys to Cecil, 15 Nov. 1596).

[73] TNA, SP 63/191/26 (lord deputy to Burghley, 16 July 1596); TNA, SP 63/191/23 (Irish Council to Privy Council, 16 July 1596); TNA, SP 63/193/45(V) (O'Neill to F. McHugh, 12 Sep. 1596); Perrot, *Chronicle*, 124–5.

McHugh, a man already inclined towards rebellion, they could make little headway with the vast majority of loyal subjects residing in the heart of English Ireland. Many of these distrusted O'Neill and suspected that his leadership of the rebellion was motivated by self-interest and ambition rather than any altruistic notion of national liberation.[74] For them, O'Neill was just another Gaelic tyrant and they would need more convincing reasons to join his revolt. And so, where O'Neill's political emissaries failed, he employed clerical agents to move the peoples' consciences.

Notwithstanding a truce made that summer, by mid-1596 it was accepted that O'Neill had little intention of pursuing peace and that demonstrations of any such desire were merely a means to buy him time while he consolidated his position and awaited the arrival of Spanish aid.[75] A number of clerics were already at work in the Pale at this time, but in July 1596 O'Neill dispatched Francis Mountford towards the Pale where he began 'secretly seeking whome he may seduce'.[76] Administrators' worst fears had come true and the situation described by Russell betokens a genuine anxiety for the potential success of O'Neill's agents in rousing support within the Pale:

> They... send their messingers aswell into the pale as into other partes, to sound howe every man stood affected towardes them, and such as by that meanes they could not worke, they haue most cunningly found another way to entyse, which is by the perswasion of Mumford the priest, a verie pestilent and craftie seducer, who for certeine is at this present in the pale, and hath been since the sealing of therles pardon; so as whensoever therle shall againe declare him self to bee in Action... [he] will pretend the ground thereof to be for freedom of Relligion & conscience, a matter which he hath heretofore stood vpon. Yt may well bee doubted his partie wilbe so great as will giue a strong push to endaunger the whole Realm, in as much as it is certenly thought, the greatest part of the pale are combined with him, and are deeply interessted in this conspiracie.[77]

Little is known about Mountford's activities in the Pale; yet, four months after he allegedly entered the area, Elizabeth was 'offended that one Montford, should walke as he doth, without being apprehended'.[78] Russell and the rest of the Council attempted to excuse their inactivity by arguing that they were restrained from taking decisive action against O'Neill's agents, and specifically Mountford, because 'wee had no certeine knowledge of his being in the Pale, so

---

[74] Morgan, 'Faith and Fatherland in Sixteenth-Century Ireland', p. 17.
[75] TNA, SP 63/191/27 (Russell to Cecil, 16 July 1596); TNA, SP 63/191/37(VI) (E. Moore to Russell, 22 July 1596); Perrot, *Chronicle*, p. 115.
[76] TNA, SP 63/191/23 (Irish Council to Privy Council, 16 July 1596); TNA, SP 63/191/26 (lord deputy to Burghley, 16 July 1596).
[77] TNA, SP 63/191/27 (Russell to Cecil, 16 July 1596).
[78] TNA, SP 63/194/19 (Irish Council to Privy Council, 15 Oct. 1596).

men of his qualletie many and doe raunge vpp and downe in the contrey and Townes, and shall haue all meanes and favor to cover them and keepe them from our knowledge'. Equally problematic was that an agreement made with O'Neill that summer extended a pardon to many of his adherents; and, having been 'pardoned by speciall name', administrators were prevented from pursuing Mountford despite having 'good will therevnto'.[79] Following this missed opportunity, Mountford appears to have left Ireland. The last mention of him in the Irish State Papers was made by Henry Knowlis who, in January 1597, reported that Mountford was acting as O'Neill's representative in Spain.[80] There is no record of him returning to Ireland, though he continued to be active in England where he was arrested in 1602 before being exiled to Paris.[81]

Mountford and his affairs are shrouded in secrecy. Examinations of Gravenor, the Hales brothers, Hall, and O'Cullan revealed embarrassingly little about O'Neill or his chief clerical conspirator, Mountford. They did, however, expose the impressive determination of these agents and indicate that O'Neill was especially careful in his selection of clerical co-conspirators. All of these men were considered exceptionally devout and dangerous Catholics, and many of them had a strong English extremist connection. Although deeply involved in traitorous conspiracies, these messengers refused to disclose any details regarding their missions, nor would they divulge anything about any other suspected persons. Hall refused to confess anything under examination, except that 'hee hath benn a prist but toe years'.[82] Neither would the Hales brothers corroborate any evidence presented against them. More interesting was Gravenor's method of keeping silent. Topcliffe believed that Gravenor had poisoned himself before he could be interrogated, 'a resolution taught in the Church to such as to whom they commit these desperate acts and practices'.[83] His suspicion was confirmed nearly two years later by Gravenor's colleague, John Hales.[84] Although the examination of O'Cullan uncovered much, he disclosed little more than officials could ascertain for themselves from the letters

---

[79] TNA, SP 63/191/27 (Russell to Cecil, 16 July 1596); TNA, SP 63/194/19 (Irish Council to Privy Council, 15 Oct. 1596). That Mountford was included in a 1596 pardon of O'Neill allies is corroborated by Robert Dudley Edwards's analysis of the Fiants. Edwards, *Church and State*, p. 285. Edwards cites *Fiants, Elizabeth*, No. 5996.

[80] TNA, SP 63/197/6 (Knowlis to Cecil, 10 Jan. 1597).

[81] G. Anstruther, *The Seminary Priests: A Dictionary of the Secular Clergy of England and Wales 1558–1850, I Elizabethan 1558–1603* (Durham, 1968), p. 232.

[82] TNA, SP 63/179/93 (lord deputy to Cecil, 24 May 1595).

[83] HMC *Salisbury MSS*, v, 91.

[84] HMC *Salisbury MSS*, vi, 427–8. Hales's admission of the suicide might have been just an expression of the pride he felt in his companion's dedication to the cause. Much like Gravenor, Topcliffe described John Hales as 'a man less savouring of loyalty, obedience, honest religion and humanity than ever I did see, even very red fire itself', a thing also asserted by his examiners in London. HMC *Salisbury MSS*, v, 91.

he carried. A few months later O'Cullan was reported dead, having broken his neck in an attempted escape from Dublin Castle. Russell dismissed this as an act of desperation arising from O'Cullan's fear of further torture; but it is unclear whether any believed he was innocent or whether he may have had more to tell.[85] The secrecy of these individuals and the self-destructive acts of Gravenor and O'Cullan are testaments to their sincere dedication to preserve Catholicism in English dominions; few other men would be so willing to sacrifice themselves for such an idea. The reality was that Catholicism did not automatically lend itself to radical ideas and the promotion of violence; many Catholic clerics, especially those sheltered within the Pale, were content to confine themselves to performing the mass while avoiding entanglements in weighty political matters like these.

Henry Fitzsimon, SJ: Reluctant Radical

Following the lead of Mountford and his colleagues, other clerics would do much to further the Confederate cause and the Counter-Reformation in Ireland. Amongst them was Kilkenny native James Archer, who took to the woods and bogs with the rebels, participated in parlays, and was accused of orchestrating the capture of the earl of Ormond in April 1600.[86] O'Neill found equally militant allies in number of other Irish-born clerics, including Friar Peter Nangle, Bishop Dermot McCreagh, and Owen McEgan.[87] McCreagh and McEgan were powerful allies in Munster, but Palesmen like Nangle were particularly useful for penetrating Old English society. By virtue of their birth, along with ties of blood, marriage, and friendship to members of that community, they could potentially 'persuade many of the best sort of the English Pale and thereabouts to enter bad actions'.[88] For this reason, O'Neill endeavoured to link himself to other Pale ecclesiastics, including a few less radical clerics, namely the Jesuit Fathers Henry Fitzsimon and Christopher Holywood, whose piety and records of imprisonment made them appropriate religious figures to rally around.

In the minds of Irish Catholics and crown officials, James Archer represented the Society of Jesus in its most radical and militant form.[89] Of all the

---

[85] Although there is no mention of torture during his examination, Russell's explanation for O'Cullan's desperate act indicates that he was, in fact, questioned under duress and that he expected further cruelty if he remained in captivity. TNA, SP 63/185/30 (Russell to Burghley, 26 Dec. 1595).

[86] Morrissey, *James Archer*; Hogan, *Distinguished Irishmen*; Corboy, 'James Archer', pp. 99–107.

[87] TNA, SP 63/207/108 (Bishop Lyon to Cecil, 15 Feb. 1600).

[88] HMC *Salisbury MSS*, vii, 218. See also Morgan, 'Hugh O'Neill', p. 26.

[89] TNA, SP 63/202(III)/152(I) (N. Walsh to Loftus and Gardener, 30 Oct. 1598); Morrissey, *James Archer*; Hogan, *Distinguished Irishmen*; Corboy, 'James Archer', pp. 99–107.

orders operating in Ireland at this time, the Jesuits were regarded as the most dangerous, being 'the forerunners [of] attemptes by preparing the peoples mindes… and most devillishly bent to doe mischief'.[90] But not all newly arriving clerics, Jesuit or otherwise, were so overtly militant. Though equally committed to confirming Ireland for the Catholic Church, there is no evidence to indicate that Henry Fitzsimon endorsed the Confederate cause or personally adhered to O'Neill. Instead of joining Confederate ranks or preaching sedition and violence, Fitzsimon confined himself to the Pale where he preferred to busy himself with academic debate, delivering regular masses, and hearing confessions. The ideological differences between Archer and Fitzsimon highlighted internal divisions within the Catholic clergy whereby some were branded exceptionally subversive while others were accused of practically condoning heresy. As Christopher Holywood, the imprisoned Superior of the Irish Jesuit Mission, reported to Claudio Acquaviva, the Superior General of the Order, in 1599: 'Bertram's first-born (Father Archer), who lives in one part of the island, is called a favourer of sedition, and Bertram's younger son (Fitzsimon), who dwells in another part, is looked on as a propagator of heresy.'[91] In no way did the Dublin-born, continentally educated Fitzsimon approve of Protestantism, but he was certainly a different kind of missionary to James Archer. This was because Fitzsimon 'keeps within bounds', even though Holywood fretted that he was still 'not cautious enough'.[92] These two Jesuits, sent to Ireland at the same time to reopen the Mission, exemplified different strands of political thought amongst Irish Catholic clerics. Archer had much in common with Mountford and his associates, and he proved to be even more dangerous to crown interests. Once in Ireland, Archer worked tirelessly as one of O'Neill's instruments, rousing support in Munster and Leinster and penning propagandist letters to leading Irish lords.[93] He was also an agent of communication with continental powers, both by letter and in person, and he was notorious for his propagation of the supposed papal excommunication of Elizabeth and all those who supported her. Adding to his reputation and fame, Archer played a key role in the capture of Ormond, advocated the earl's elevation to king of Ireland, and was even credited with converting Ormond to Catholicism.[94] Unsurprisingly, busy clerics like Archer tend to dominate narratives of Catholic clerical activities during this war, but there were countless others whose tales

[90] TNA, SP 63/194/1 (Russell to Privy Council, 2 Oct. 1596); HMC *Salisbury MSS*, vi, 539.
[91] Hogan, *Distinguished Irishmen*, p. 211.
[92] Ibid.
[93] TNA, SP 63/206/136 (Elizabeth to ——, 1599); TNA, SP 63/206/142 ('A brief declaration of the state wherein Ireland now standeth', 1599).
[94] TNA, SP 63/207(I)/130(I) (copy of papers by O'Neill and Archer, 27 Feb. 1600); TNA, SP 63/207(4)/5 (Mountjoy to Cecil, 4 July 1600). For a detailed assessment of Archer's career, see, Morrissey, *James Archer*.

have escaped attention, and especially those who did not fit the militant radical mould. Though long celebrated as a leading Catholic controversialist who defied the greatest Protestant minds and suffered harsh imprisonment for his faith, Henry Fitzsimon was more representative of these. More importantly, his behaviour and attitude towards Hugh O'Neill, the Confederates, and the war itself was more characteristic of Catholic clerics operating within the Pale. For this reason, his activities and wartime experiences deserve some exploration.

Returning to Ireland around the end of 1597, Fitzsimon believed Ireland was ripe for a mission, and he assured the General of his Order that 'the whole face and condition of the country will soon be changed'.[95] In September 1598 he informed Acquaviva that he had spent 'the whole summer' travelling through 'various parts of the kingdom, [and] not without very good results. I converted six heretics and very many schismatics, and heard an immense number of confessions. I preached every Sunday and holiday, and not a few came even twenty miles to hear me.'[96] The following year he reported, '[t]here are so many joining the Church, that in one day I received four Englishmen, three of whom were men of distinction and great note'.[97] Having found shelter amongst the many recusants of Dublin and its environs, Fitzsimon owed his success at least partly to the fact that he was a native of the Pale and connected with many of its leading members. According to Loftus and Jones, because of Fitzsimon's 'alliance to many, both in city and country, and of this course of his proceeding in the erection of Popery, he was generally received as an angel amongst this ignorant and idolatrous people'.[98] Fitzsimon had earned a reputation for evangelising and debate, but there is little evidence that he endorsed war or openly supported the Confederates. In fact, in a letter to Acquaviva in November 1598, Fitzsimon critiqued the activities and sincerity of O'Neill and his allies:

> They boast of being Catholics, but they are only so in name, and they do not allow any one to correct their ignorance, or to curb their wickedness. They are so bent on plunder, that I fear it was that which gave occasion to the insurrection... Though the whole of my country is not subject to the insurgent lords, yet it is all open to their incursions. They roam about everywhere, and carry off the property of the good as well as of the bad... They venerate externally all venerable things, but their works are far from God.[99]

This was a rather damning assessment of Confederate morality, and, for a Palesman who was raised with contempt for Gaelic society, it was an opinion

95 Fitzsimon to Acquaviva, 25 Nov. 1598 (*Words of Comfort*, p. 47).
96 Ibid., pp. 46–7.
97 Fitzsimon to Acquaviva, 1 Sep. 1599 (*Words of Comfort*, p. 49).
98 *CSPI*, 1600, p. 76.
99 Fitzsimon to Acquaviva, 25 Nov. 1598 (*Words of Comfort*, p. 47).

that was unlikely to change. Nevertheless, Fitzsimon's dedication to advancing the Catholic faith in Ireland, and especially within the Pale, troubled authorities, who branded him 'a busy traveller and practiser in the Pale'.[100] Administrators feared that the spread of Counter-Reformation Catholicism and a corresponding decline in outward conformity could lead to unrest. Although crown officials had been loath to act against many clerics and their patrons for fear of alienating the Catholic Palesmen, Fitzsimon's success amongst them, as well as his affiliation with the Society of Jesus, prompted administrators to call for his arrest. A reward of 20*l.* was offered and, after nearly three years of evading capture, Fitzsimon was apprehended on 2 December 1599 by a Mr Serjeant Hoye.[101]

Fitzsimon was brought before the Irish Council and charged with violating the queen's laws 'by his open saying of mass, and preaching'. As a member of the Society of Jesus, Fitzsimon was also deemed 'a person justly to be suspected by the State (both in regard he was sent from the Pope, Her Majesty's mortal enemy… and in regard the practices of the Jesuits in these perilous times did… work bad offices between our prince and her subjects)'.[102] Interestingly, and probably on account of his conscience as an Old English man born and raised in the Pale, Fitzsimon initially made 'a kind of protestation of his loyalty to Her Majesty'. Under interrogation, however, Fitzsimon soon conceded that he believed Pius V's bull against Elizabeth was lawful, and specifically in relation to the pope's right to depose the queen and absolve her subjects of their obedience.[103] This was a common opinion amongst Catholic clerics operating in Ireland, and it was rightly believed that a number of Irish clerics were lobbying the pope for a renewal of that general excommunication. Fitzsimon does not appear to have been one of them and, fortunately for the crown, the pope did not acquiesce to those requests.[104] Such an event would have had the potential to seal the fate of English rule in Ireland by forcing all nominally loyal Catholics to choose between their faith and their queen.

By accepting the lawfulness of the original bull, Fitzsimon could be condemned as a traitor. But the Irish administration was not in a position to convict Fitzsimon of any religious crime for fear of creating a martyr or politico-religious figure for aggrieved Catholics to rally around. Consequently,

---

[100] *CSPI, 1599–1600*, p. 324.
[101] TNA, SP 63/206/65 (G. Carey to Cecil, 3 Dec. 1599); TNA, SP 63/206/84 (Irish Council to Privy Council, 15 Dec. 1599); TNA, SP 63/207(1)/134 ('A brief of concordatums', Feb. 1600).
[102] *CSPI, 1600*, p. 76.
[103] Ibid., p. 77.
[104] For Fitzsimon's position, see TNA, SP 63/207(3)/114 (G. Carew to Cecil, 17 June 1600); TNA, SP 63/208(2)/20(I) (intelligences delivered to Jones and R. Gardener, 23 Apr. 1601). Pope Clement VIII did issue a Bull of Indulgence to O'Neill, but he stopped short of granting excommunications against O'Neill's Catholic opponents.

as was the norm with other high-profile clerical prisoners, it was determined that Fitzsimon would be examined in Dublin and then transferred to England, where he could be found guilty of various political and religious crimes.[105] In the meantime, the administration endeavoured to build a case against him by accumulating all evidence which might link Fitzsimon to O'Neill and the Confederate cause. This evidence was more convenient than convincing, but it served its purpose. Statements taken from Henry Duckworth, William Tipper, and George Taylor about a dinner-party conversation at George Blackney's house in Swords, County Dublin, implied that Fitzsimon did indeed endorse the Confederate cause.[106] According to Duckworth, Fitzsimon was one of three priests present and he 'began to speak of the success of the Irishry, saying, "You see what fortune O'Neill and his kern and followers have against the Queen's forces; but where God blesseth, all things prosper; a land that is won by the sword, and kept by the sword, without authority from the Pope, is not lawful by the word of God"'.[107] Taylor supposedly countered Fitzsimon by arguing that Henry II had won Ireland by the sword and that the pope had confirmed his right to rule the island. Adding to the legitimacy of English princes, argued Taylor, was that the Irish lords had surrendered their titles to King Henry and received them back upon promises of obedience.[108] Fitzsimon retorted that these agreements were now null and void because the queen had broken with the Roman church and thereby rendered the contract with God and his representative, the pope, invalid.[109] At the core of his argument was the opinion that not 'every conquest is lawful' because not every conquest was papally approved.[110]

The deponents' testimonies indicated that Fitzsimon challenged Elizabeth's right to rule Ireland, yet they did not offer absolute proof that Fitzsimon supported Confederate violence or ideology. His comment on the rebels' progress was more one of wonder and restricted to the fact that God would have the final say in who ruled Ireland. Rather conveniently, another event would provide administrators with the tenuous evidence they needed to link Fitzsimon to O'Neill. In November 1599, a Palesman named Thomas Barnewall accompanied Sir William Warren to a meeting with Hugh O'Neill. While at Dungannon,

---

[105] TNA, SP 63/206/65 (Carey to Cecil, 3 Dec. 1599); TNA, SP 63/207(2)/92 (Loftus and Jones to Whitgift, 7 Apr. 1600). As things transpired, Fitzsimon spent the following five years in Dublin Castle before being released and exiled to the continent.

[106] TNA, SP 63/206/85 (accusation taken before Gardener, 15 Dec. 1599); TNA, SP 63/206/101 (declaration of W. Tipper, 24 Dec. 1599); TNA, SP 63/206/102 (declaration of G. Taylor, 24 Dec. 1599); TNA, SP 63/207(2)/92 (Loftus and Jones to Whitgift, 7 Apr. 1600).

[107] CSPI, 1599–1600, p. 326.

[108] Ibid.; TNA, SP 63/206/101 (declaration of Tipper, 24 Dec. 1599); TNA, SP 63/206/102 (declaration of Taylor, 24 Dec. 1599).

[109] Ibid.

[110] TNA, SP 63/206/10 (declaration of Taylor, 24 Dec. 1599).

Richard Owen, one of O'Neill's chief men, showed Barnewall 'several writings, to the number of 6 or 7... all of them being by Tyrone's own hand subscribed'. Having heard one read aloud, Owen informed Barnewall that O'Neill 'purposed to have them cast abroad in the streets of Dublin and Drogheda'.[111] Barnewall convinced Owen to give him a copy to deliver to whomever O'Neill 'might best trust' in the Pale. But instead of carrying through with that promise, Barnewall dutifully delivered the writing to the Irish Council.[112] This was O'Neill's famous nationalist proclamation, more commonly known in official circles as the 'libel' in which O'Neill 'took in hand the Catholic cause, [and] called the Governors tyrants and enemies to God and man'.[113] According to crown administrators, it was 'full of horrible treasons against Her Majesty and her kingdom', and it revealed 'the malicious pride of the Archtraitor, and the venom of his stomach against Her sacred Majesty'.[114] While the content of the libel deeply troubled administrators, what also kindled their interest was to whom the first letter was to be delivered: Henry Fitzsimon. Specifically named by O'Neill, administrators could now implicate Fitzsimon in Confederate plotting and this, combined with Fitzsimon's 'disloyal speeches lately uttered' at Blackney's house, was enough to prove that he was indeed 'a very dangerous person'.[115] More interesting, and more damning, was that because Fitzsimon was supposed to be the first to receive a copy, Loftus and Jones were 'partly drawn into a kind of suspicion that that pernisious writing and instrument was first penned by Fitzsimmons, seeing it is thought Tyrone hath about him no person of learning to devise such a writing'.[116] This he most certainly did not, though there is a strong possibility that Fitzsimon's Jesuit colleague James Archer had a hand in its composition.[117] And finally, far from helping Fitzsimon's cause, within two weeks of his imprisonment, O'Neill demanded that the Jesuit 'be presently enlarged'. According to O'Neill, 'I am noe more beholding [to Fitzsimon] then to an Irish Katholick that is restrained in Turkie for his religion, but... I must vndertake... for all Irish catholicks... that one should [not] be for his religion restrained in tyme of cessation'.[118] This personal entreaty gave administrators further reason to

---

111 *CSPI, 1599–1600*, p. 253.
112 TNA, SP 63/206/16 (book of concordatums, 10 Nov. 1599); TNA, SP 63/206/20 (Carey to Cecil, 13 Nov. 1599); TNA, SP 63/206/25(III) (declaration of Barnewall, 15 Nov. 1599).
113 *CSPI, 1599–1600*, pp. 258, 246.
114 Ibid.
115 *CSPI, 1599–1600*, p. 324.
116 *CSPI, 1600*, p. 77. See also TNA, SP 63/206/20 (Carey to Cecil, 13 Nov. 1599); TNA, SP 63/206/25(III) (declaration of Barnewall, 15 Nov. 1599); TNA, SP 63/206/84 (Irish Council to Privy Council, 15 Dec. 1599).
117 TNA, SP 63/207(I)/136 (E. FitzHarries to N. Walsh, Feb. 1600); Morgan, 'Policy and Propaganda', pp. 18–52.
118 TNA, SP 63/206/86 (O'Neill to Warren, 15 Dec. 1599); TNA, SP 63/206/100 (Warren to Cecil, 24 Dec. 1599).

suspect Fitzsimon since one 'may plainly discern how acceptable a person this Jesuit is unto Tyrone and his confederates'.[119]

In the absence of any other evidence signalling an association between O'Neill and Fitzsimon, it must be wondered whether O'Neill had directed the proclamation to Fitzsimon in the hope of convincing the Jesuit of the sincerity of his cause. O'Neill was clearly determined to acquaint Fitzsimon with his ideology because Fitzsimon admitted that he had previously encountered an unidentified man on the road who had also tried to give him a copy of O'Neill's proclamation with instructions to publish it in the Pale. According to Fitzsimon, he refused and 'put spurs to my horse, and there left the man'.[120] It is impossible to know whether Fitzsimon was telling the truth but, already imprisoned and facing an uncertain future, he had little to lose by being honest. What evidence exists for Fitzsimon's activities in Ireland prior to his imprisonment does not suggest he was a man of intrigue. And, had he been of the same radical tendency as Gravenor and O'Cullan, he probably would have chosen death before revealing O'Neill's repeated overtures towards him. The reality was that O'Neill had his own agenda for trying to acquaint Fitzsimon with his propaganda and for demanding his release. First, Fitzsimon was a revered clerical figure, especially within the Pale where he was connected to many leading inhabitants through blood and marriage. Fitzsimon would therefore have been a most useful instrument for O'Neill since many Palesmen were inclined to follow his persuasions. O'Neill's demand for Fitzsimon's release was likewise calculated. Having presented himself as a champion of Catholicism, it was imperative that O'Neill provide the appearance of protecting all Catholics, and especially clergymen. What is more, O'Neill probably recognised an opportunity to draw public and international attention to Fitzsimon as a persecuted clerical figure to unite around.

The evidence collected by the administration did not confirm any definite alliance between Fitzsimon and O'Neill, nor did it prove that Fitzsimon openly endorsed the Confederate cause. Nevertheless, Fitzsimon spent the following five years in Dublin Castle where he continued to be accused of traitorous dealings; these included meetings with priests and sending secret communications to the continent.[121] Crown officials may have desired his capture, but it has been suggested by a number of historians that Fitzsimon actually wanted to be imprisoned so that he could engage Protestant ministers in academic debate.

---

[119] *CSPI, 1600*, p. 78.
[120] Ibid.
[121] TNA, SP 63/207(6)/124 (W. Udall's memorials concerning Delvin, Dec. 1600); TNA, SP 63/208(2)/20(I) (intelligences delivered to Jones and Gardener, 23 Apr. 1601); Neville to Cecil, 28 Dec. 1599, in E. Sawyer (ed.), *Memorials of Affairs of State in the Reigns of Queen Elizabeth and King James I*, Vol. 1 (London, 1725), p. 122.

As a matter of fact, Fitzsimon was, and is, better known as a competent controversialist than as a supporter of violent revolution. Once in prison Fitzsimon challenged leading Protestant academics to debate the finer points of religion, including Meredith Hamner, Dean John Rider, and Fitzsimon's younger cousin, James Ussher, the future primate of Ireland.[122] As the example of Fitzsimon demonstrates, just as the methods of Catholic clerics operating in Ireland differed, so too did their support of armed action. As a group, they all strove to confirm Ireland and its inhabitants for the Roman Catholic Church, and in this they succeeded. But, in doing so, they were not all radicals, nor were they all militants. Very few marched onto the battlefield or openly preached sedition; instead, they found succour in the houses of noblemen and gentry where they tended to the souls of their patrons and their associates.

Priest Hunting

Crown officials believed the evangelising efforts of Catholic clerics were a ubiquitous problem in Ireland, yet the State Papers offer surprisingly little evidence to substantiate this in terms of intelligence reports or records on the apprehension and prosecution of suspects. Administrators often claimed their task was made virtually impossible because Catholic clerics operated under the protection of the local population, particularly the leading nobles and gentry whose political and military support of the crown was indispensable for the time being.[123] For this reason, Russell lamented that the capture of the Irish priest Hall was 'a thing not vsiall hyer'.[124] He complained in a similar manner when he elaborated on his difficulties apprehending Piers O'Cullan. According to Russell, the inhabitants of Drogheda were stubbornly opposed to arresting the priest and it was only by the fortuitous accident of his own presence in the vicinity that he was able to employ one of his own men to that end.[125]

Assisting authorities in the capture of priests was uncommon in Ireland and it seems the vast majority of inhabitants refused to participate in the prosecution

---

[122] A. Ford, *James Ussher, Theology, History and Politics in Early-Modern Ireland and England* (Oxford, 2007), ch. 1; A. Ford, 'Goliath and the boy David: Henry Fitzsimon, James Ussher and the Birth of Irish Religious Debate', in S. Ryan and C. Tait (eds), *Religion and Politics in Urban Ireland, c. 1500–c. 1750* (Dublin, 2016), pp. 108–33; B. Jackson, 'The Construction of Argument: Henry Fitzsimon, John Rider and Religious Controversy in Dublin, 1599–1614', in C. Brady and J. Ohlmeyer (eds), *British Interventions in Early Modern Ireland* (Cambridge, 2005), pp. 97–115. Following his release from prison, Fitzsimon penned a number of important treatises on matters of faith.

[123] TNA, SP 63/177/31(II) (Irish Council to Elizabeth, 5 Dec. 1594).

[124] TNA, SP 63/179/90 (lord deputy to Cecil, 23 May 1595); TNA, SP 63/179/93 (lord deputy to Cecil, 24 May 1595).

[125] *CSPI, 1592–96*, p. 472.

of their Catholic clerics. This, however, is not conclusive proof that the entire lay and clerical population championed rebellion. For much of the population, the protection of the Roman Church and its agents had more to do with the preservation of souls than it did with politics; many people were unwilling to risk their place in the hereafter for the sake of the crown's politico-religious agenda. There were nevertheless a number of individuals whose attempts at self-preservation occasionally advanced government interests. In December 1595, Sir Robert Cecil informed the earl of Kildare that his servant, Udall, had been imprisoned for recusancy. Cecil explained that Udall was 'suspected to be conversant with Priestes' and had been registered as 'an ill affected personne in Religion' for three or four years.[126] This may have been so, but Udall was not keen to pay recusancy fines or spend any time in prison. A month earlier, the bishop of Limerick reported that the same Udall had not only offered his services as a spy, but had voluntarily divulged all his knowledge of O'Neill's activities, including details of Gravenor's Spanish mission.[127] Udall's assistance in this instance had been conditional because, in exchange for his services in espionage, he would receive his freedom.[128] More revealing was the exoneration and state pension given to an informant named John Leynan who revealed the 1598 plot to seize Dublin Castle.[129] He had been amongst the original conspirators and many of his accomplices were put to death immediately after the discovery of the plan. The informant was spared this fate as 'recompence for this good seruice done therein'.[130] Anticipating similar acquittals, many other offers of assistance came directly from gaol cells.[131]

The Irish administration was forced to rely heavily on such means for intelligence gathering; but to supplement this dysfunctional system, the administration enlisted the help of what, for lack of a better term, can only be called priest-hunters. In late 1597 and early 1598 the government employed the services of John Burnell, a Dublin merchant, and William Paule, a former muster officer.[132] Like the majority of government informants, both of these men were of questionable character. Burnell had been confined to the Marshalsea and Paule had been imprisoned in Dublin Castle for his bad conduct as a muster officer.[133]

---

[126] TNA, SP 63/185/7 (Cecil to Kildare, 10 Dec. 1595).

[127] TNA, SP 63/184/41 (Thornburgh to Cecil, Nov. 1595).

[128] TNA, SP 63/194/32 (draft by Burghley or Cecil to Kildare, Oct. 1596).

[129] See Chapter 3.

[130] TNA, SP 63/202(3)/135 (Irish Council to Privy Council, 31 Oct. 1598).

[131] TNA, SP 63/202(1)/70 (P. Hackett to Burghley, 1 Mar. 1598); TNA, SP 63/202(1)/69 (D. Rowghane to Burghley, 1 Mar. 1598).

[132] TNA, SP 63/199/118 (Burgh and Wallop to Cecil, 24 June 1597); TNA, SP 63/202(1)/17 (Loftus, Gardener, and Wallop to Cecil, 17 Jan. 1598).

[133] TNA, SP 63/200/56 (J. Burnell to Cecil, 28 July 1597); TNA, SP 63/202(1)/17(I) (W. Paule to Loftus, 15 Jan. 1598); TNA, SP 63/202(1)/45 (Paule to Cecil, 2 Feb. 1598).

In mid-January 1598, Paule informed Loftus that prior to his imprisonment Lord Deputy Thomas Burgh had authorised him to use all lawful means to discover and apprehend priests in Ireland.[134] This was a service he wished to continue, and it seems that time spent in prison was extremely conducive to this sort of task. While in gaol, Paule collected information on suspicious persons and drew up a lengthy report on the activities of many suspects.[135] Between these two men, the administration acquired intelligence on four 'principall men', identified as 'Stanley, Archer, Walshe & Mercer', all of whom were considered especially dangerous.[136] In November 1597, based on the information provided by Burnell and Paule, Wallop was able to announce the successful arrest and detention of a priest named Hugh Walshe.[137] This was no mean feat and the two priest-hunters emphasised their hardships in this service.

Early efforts to capture Walshe failed. At one point Walshe had been residing in Dublin 'bouldly vnderneathe the nose of the State 10 or twelue dayes togeather', but no man would dare apprehend him.[138] Having discovered the exact Dublin address where Walshe could be found, Paule and Burnell hatched a plot for the priest's apprehension. According to Burnell, Walsh had spent Easter in his own Dublin home, but had slipped off to London before Burnell could lay hands on him. Shortly after this failed attempt, Walshe was reportedly back in Ireland and within the environs of Dublin at the house of a Mr Luttrell. Burnell immediately made his way to Luttrell's home only to discover that Walshe had again departed for England.[139] Paule and Burnell finally caught up with Walshe in Munster and delivered him to the authorities at Dublin Castle where he was examined.[140]

Walshe was apprehended while carrying two gold rings which 'one Chapman deceased' had instructed Walshe to deliver to 'Whittinghams wief an Alderman in Oxford the other to a gentleman that she knewe of'.[141] The details of Walshe's purpose in this exchange are unclear, but Wallop nonetheless recommended the priest be sent to England for detention, 'for heer he remaineth to noe other end then as other of his sorte do, to be relieved and meinteined by such as are

---

134 TNA, SP 63/202(1)/17(I) (Paule to Loftus, 15 Jan. 1598); TNA, SP 63/202(1)/45 (Paule to Cecil, 2 Feb. 1598).

135 Ibid.

136 TNA, SP 63/199/118 (Burgh and Wallop to Cecil, 24 June 1597); TNA, SP 63/202(1)/17(I) (Paule to Loftus, 15 Jan. 1598).

137 TNA, SP 63/199/118 (Burgh and Wallop to Cecil, 24 June 1597).

138 Ibid.; TNA, SP 63/202(1)/17(I) (Paule to Loftus, 15 Jan. 1598); TNA, SP 63/202(1)/45 (Paule to Cecil, 2 Feb. 1598).

139 TNA, SP 63/199/118 (Burgh and Wallop to Cecil, 24 June 1597).

140 TNA, SP 63/202(I)/17(I) (Paule to Loftus, 15 Jan. 1598); TNA, SP 63/202(1)/45 (Paule to Cecil, 2 Feb. 1598).

141 TNA, SP 63/201/56 (Wallop to Cecil, 5 Nov. 1597).

addycted to the fauoring of him and all of his profession'.[142] This was a common request because government officials knew they would have great difficulty proceeding against religious delinquents in Ireland.[143] Just as the capture of such men proved exasperating, it was practically impossible to indict Irish clerics for any offence because juries composed of locals were disinclined to convict other Catholics, especially men of the cloth.[144] Equally significant though, was that many English officials thought it unwise to proceed publicly against clerics in Ireland since it would send an undesirable message to the lay community. It would only serve to confirm that religious persecution was in effect and that the time had come to take a determined stand against the Protestant establishment.

Even before O'Neill entered rebellion, the queen and her administration had reached the logical conclusion that the 1590s were really not the time to pick the religious bone too seriously. In her 1592 instructions for the discovery of priests and their patrons, Elizabeth dictated that 'the lord deputy shall seriously consider how in *secrett* manner the s[ai]d persons and their Menteynors and the like... may be apprehended and comitted to Prison'.[145] This remained the policy throughout the war.[146] Although the Dublin administration had not entirely desisted in the search for clerical conspirators, or in their efforts to reform, both the Protestant administration and the proponents of the Counter-Reformation understood the reactionary power of religious persecution.[147] Thus, with the exception of certain clergymen who were considered particularly active in fomenting rebellion, the crown opted to overlook the vast majority of religious transgressions within the Pale and English enclaves so as to avoid making 'the people more obdurate'.[148] When any ostentatiously Catholic individual was targeted, officials were adamant that their prosecution had absolutely nothing to do with religion and that conviction rested solely on political considerations.[149] The official line was that these were traitors, not martyrs. For example, the charges against Henry Fitzsimon were given a secular slant; rather than an indictment for recusancy, he was charged with breaching the laws by saying

---

[142] Ibid.

[143] Edwards, *Church and State*, p. 275; TNA, SP 63/158/38 (Irish Council to Privy Council, 14 June 1591).

[144] For example, TNA, SP 63/206/119(I) ('Caveat delivered to Her Majesty in November, 1591', Dec. 1599); TNA, SP 63/202(4)/9 (Saxey to Cecil, 5 Dec. 1598).

[145] BL, Add. MS 4819, f. 120v. Emphasis added.

[146] BL, Add MS 4757, Milles Collection, Vol. III, f. 8v (instructions for Mountjoy, 1599); TNA, SP 63/207(2)/124 (memoranda on affairs in Ireland, 19 Apr. 1600); TNA, SP 63/207(3)/139 ('Certain instructions conceived' by the queen, June 1600).

[147] For a discussion of early modern Irish martyrdom, see C. Tait, 'Adored for Saints: Catholic Martyrdom in Ireland, c. 1560–1655', *Journal of Early Modern History*, Vol. 5, No. 2 (2001), pp. 128–59; P.J. Corish and B. Millett (eds), *The Irish Martyrs* (Dublin, 2005).

[148] McGurk, *Elizabethan Conquest*, p. 23.

[149] Edwards, *Church and State*, pp. 225, 296. For example, see *Cal. Carew*, iii, 457–9; 469–70.

Mass. He was also placed under the charge of being a suspected person because, as a Jesuit, he had been sent to Ireland by the queen's enemy, the pope.[150] Also significant is that while some priests and laymen had been apprehended and detained, the administration claimed, with a large degree of truth, that the majority obtained their release within a very short period. This was not necessarily a demonstration of goodwill; it may have had more to do with potential financial gains as it seems that their freedom had been secured by bribes.[151] As Fitzsimon noted, '[d]uring the time of my incarceration, one bishop, three Franciscans, and six secular priests recovered their liberty by solicitation, money, or exchange of prisoners'.[152] Consequently, many suspected persons escaped court verdicts and the hardships of long imprisonment.[153]

It was in the crown's best interests to deny charges of religious persecution. In his effort to rally domestic support, O'Neill had railed against religious oppression.[154] Yet, contrary to O'Neill's pronouncements, the administration had refrained from excessive modes of religious enforcement during this interval; instead, existing evidence suggests that the crown unofficially tolerated a larger degree of religious freedom than previously supposed. The queen and her administration refuted accusations of religious persecution in Ireland by comparing the Irish situation with that of England. It was admitted that the prosecution of Catholics for their faith did occur in England, but that the same laws were not in force in Ireland.[155] As Cecil scoffed in late 1599, O'Neill 'pretends matter of religion, that he will have it free for all men, and… that none in that kingdom should suffer for their conscience. Whereas in that kingdom it is well known the laws are not for religion, as they are in England; to receive a priest or hear a mass in Ireland is no felony.'[156] Granted, these proclamations were issued by officials who hoped to discredit O'Neill and the Confederate cause. But further evidence of toleration may be drawn from David Edwards's study of English Catholic migration to Ireland at the turn of the century.[157] In order to avoid the vigour of religious laws in England, Edwards has demonstrated that

---

[150] TNA, SP 63/207(2)/92 (Loftus and Jones to Whitgift, 7 Apr. 1600).

[151] Unsurprisingly, the release of suspects raised strenuous objections amongst the more reform minded Protestants who used it as proof of government corruption. BL, Harl. MS 292, ff. 168–174 ('A Direction to the Queenes Majestie how to conquer Ireland. A.D. 1599'); Lee, 'The Discovery and Recovery of Ireland with the Author's Apology', ed. J. McGurk (CELT, 2009), ff. 62–3.

[152] Fitzsimon, *Words of Comfort*, p. 53.

[153] TNA, SP 63/207(6)/126 (paper on the causes of the rebellion in Ireland, Dec. 1600); TNA, SP 63/212/135 (Irish Council to Privy Council, 24 Feb. 1603); TNA, SP 63/207(2)/92 (Loftus and Jones to Whitgift, 7 Apr. 1600).

[154] For example: TNA, SP 63/206/136 (Elizabeth to ——, 1599); TNA, SP 63/206/142 ('brief declaration', 1599).

[155] CUL, Ms. Kk. I. 15, ff. 151v; 154r–154v; 178v. See also Edwards, *Church and State*, pp. 273–7.

[156] *CSPI, 1599–1600*, pp. 223–4.

[157] D. Edwards, 'A Haven of Popery: English Catholic Migration to Ireland in the Age of

many English Catholics attempted to emigrate to Ireland during this period, some with greater success than others. These English migrants had been given reason to hope for greater religious freedom in Ireland and evidence of English Catholic settlement indicates that they did find a religious toleration which was non-existent in England at this time.[158] In fact, during the Nine Years' War the crown's claim of religious leniency extended so far as to assert that not a single Irish Catholic martyr had been made.[159]

Not all English administrators were pleased with the situation. In 1600, Loftus and Jones complained to John Whitgift, archbishop of Canterbury, that 'it is now generally conceived amongst them [the Palesmen], that Her Highness either will not, nor dare not call them into question for the daily and most contemptuous breach of her sacred laws'.[160] Whether people actually doubted the queen's resolve in religious matters is debateable, but the testimonies of several Old Englishmen who rejected O'Neill's call to arms are telling. Many of those who offered written excuses for their non-defection averred that they did not believe their spiritual interests were under attack since they had not felt the sharp hand of correction in religious matters.[161] It may be fairly assumed that these men were equally unwilling to force the queen's hand by partaking in any outwardly defiant religious displays. Nevertheless, O'Neill's allegations of religious persecution failed to persuade a population which, according to both the government and a few of his Old English co-religionists, had not experienced the severity of the anti-recusancy laws which were in full effect in England.

Proof of the government's leniency in matters of religion can be seen in the continued existence and functioning of Catholic organisations right in the heart of English Ireland. Colm Lennon has investigated the survival of Catholic religious houses and guilds under the protection of leading citizens and local magnates during this period.[162] The government was well aware of the activities

Plantations', in A. Ford and J. McCafferty (eds), *The Origins of Sectarianism in Early Modern Ireland* (Cambridge, 2005), pp. 95–126.

[158] Ibid. See also TNA, SP 63/191/8 (Bishop Lyon to Lord Hudson, 6 July 1596); TNA, SP 63/207(2)/92 (Loftus and Jones to Whitgift, 7 Apr. 1600); HMC *Salisbury MSS*, xiv, 239; Moryson, *Shakespeare's Europe*, p. 209; Edwards, *Church and State*, p. 296.

[159] CUL, Ms. Kk. I. 15, ff. 151v; 154r–154v; 178v. Interestingly, that Elizabeth was not in the business of creating Irish martyrs was corroborated by the exiled Irish Catholic John Copinger, who bemoaned Ireland's recent shortage of holy martyrs. J. Copinger, *Mnemosynim or Memoriall to the afflicted Catholickes in Irelande* (Bordeaux, 1606).

[160] *CSPI*, 1600, p. 79.

[161] T. Stafford, *Pacata Hibernia* (Dublin, 1810), pp. 37–8. TNA, SP 63/207(1)/44 (T. Dillon to O'Neill, 25 Jan. 1600); TNA, SP 63/206/63(I) (Delvin's instructions to Leicester and Archbold, 25 Nov. 1599). See also Hazard, *Faith and Patronage*, p. 39 (notes 197 and 198); Morgan, 'Faith and Fatherland or Queen and Country?', pp. 14–15.

[162] Lennon, *Lords of Dublin*, pp. 144–50; 'The Dissolution to the Foundation of St Anthony's

of these organisations but chose not to interfere, as much for lack of power as to avoid the further alienation of loyalist participants. The case of Multyfarnham and its patron Christopher Nugent, the baron of Delvin, is indicative of the crown's unofficial, albeit uneasy, toleration of unsanctioned religious practices. Delvin had long been considered a Pale malcontent due to his suspected involvement in his brother's rebellion and his open hostility towards certain political issues.[163] Like so many other Old English nobles at the close of the century, Delvin was also an open supporter of the Catholic Church and Counter-Reformation. The Nugent family had acquired control over numerous parish lands following the Henrician dissolutions and they, like other Old English magnates, directed at least a portion of the proceeds towards maintaining 'an unofficial Catholic ministry'.[164] Much like his ancestors had done before and after the Reformation, Delvin continued to patronise Catholic institutions, like Multyfarnham, and provide shelter for priests, like Richard Brady, Franciscan bishop of Kilmore.[165] Government officials expressed reservations about Delvin's blatant disregard for the established church and intelligences on the activities of Catholic clerics under his care did bring the baron under some scrutiny. In April 1590, Miler Magrath, archbishop of Cashel, captured Walter Faranan, 'pretended Bisshop of Kildare and Prior of Connell and St Patrikes purgatorie of the Bisshop of Romes institution', who had recently returned to Ireland in order to 'animat the people against the State, and to prepare them for the Spanishe attempts'.[166] Considered a devout martyr by some, the imprisoned Faranan quickly suffered a change of

College, Louvain, 1534–1607', in E. Bhreathnach, J. MacMahon, and McCafferty (eds), *The Irish Franciscans, 1534–1990* (Dublin, 2009), pp. 3–26; 'The Parish Fraternities of County Meath', *Riocht na Midhe*, No. 19 (2008), pp. 85–101; 'Fraternity and Community in Early Modern Dublin', in R. Armstrong and T. Ó hAnnracháin (eds), *Community in Early Modern Ireland* (Dublin, 2006), pp. 167–78; 'The Nugent Family and the Diocese of Kilmore', *Breifne*, Vol. 10 (2001), pp. 360–74; 'Mass in the Manor House: the Counter-Reformation in Dublin, 1560–1630', in J. Kelly and D. Keogh (eds), *History of the Diocese of Dublin* (Dublin, 2000), pp. 112–26; 'The Chantries in the Irish Reformation: the Case of St Anne's Guild, Dublin, 1550–1630', in R.V. Comerford, M. Cullen, J.R. Hill, and C. Lennon (eds), *Religion, Conflict and Coexistence in Ireland* (Dublin, 1990), pp. 6–25.

163 TNA, SP 63/147/25 (note of suspected men, 18 Oct. 1589); TNA, SP 63/149/32 (the doubtful men, 1589).

164 Lennon, 'Nugent Family and the Diocese of Kilmore', pp. 368–9.

165 See TNA, SP 63/154/8 (lord deputy and others to lords chancellor and treasurer, 20 Aug. 1590); TNA, SP 63/154/35 (lord deputy, Archbishop of Dublin and Bishop of Meath to lords chancellor and treasurer, 21 Sep. 1590); TNA, SP 63/154/35(I) (examination of W. Faranan, no date); TNA, SP 63/156/12 (note by Magrath, 17 Dec. 1590); I. Fennessy, 'Richard Brady OFM, Bishop of Kilmore, 1580–1607', *Breifne*, Vol. 9 (2000), pp. 225–42; Lennon, 'Nugent Family and the Diocese of Kilmore', pp. 360–74. James Blake told Thomas Jones, bishop of Meath, that Bishop Brady was in communication with a friar who had returned to Ireland from Spain. TNA, SP 63/194/1(I) (Jones to Loftus, 28 Sep. 1596); B. Bradshaw, *Dissolution of the Religious Orders* (Cambridge, 1974), p. 141.

166 TNA, SP 63/154/8 (lord deputy and others to lords chancellor and treasurer, 20 Aug. 1590).

heart and felt the need to clear his conscience by relating any knowledge he had which might endanger crown government.[167] In doing so, Faranan provided the names of certain individuals whom administrators had 'cawse heretofore to be more then suspected' as well as some possible Irish conspiracies then in progress.[168] Amongst these suspected persons, Delvin and the Nugents were singled out as especially dubious, 'who sending so latelie to the Prince of Parma[169] seeme to be ready for an oportunitie'.[170] It was further assumed that Bishop Richard Brady, a man known to be under Nugent protection and a frequent resident of Multyfarnham, 'was the medium of communications between the disaffected and the Prince of Parma'.[171]

These seemingly credible allegations of treachery worried crown administrators; but Delvin's illicit religious activities, and those of the clergy under his care, had to be considered alongside political expediency.[172] Regardless of administrators' confidence that the Nugents and Bishop Brady were involved in treasonous dealings, it was felt that 'it might be bad policy to arrest him as the others might be frightened into flight or otherwise'.[173] Notwithstanding his commitment to the Catholic Church or his former clashes with crown government, Delvin was a loyal military servitor and the religious activities of both himself and Multyfarnham did not present an immediate political threat – unless administrators made it one. As political and religious discontent escalated, the crown was unwilling to force the hands of powerful Catholic loyalists in case they might choose their spiritual ruler over their temporal. Thus, the government was reluctant to act against Delvin, Brady, or Multyfarnham for fear of alienating one of the Pale's most powerful and influential border lords. Officials were aware that such an act would provoke Delvin and the result could only give rise to a formidable enemy who would, in the minds of the Catholic majority at any rate, have the 'true' God on his side.[174] As much as administrators may have wished to rid the country of Catholic clergy, they were reluctant to disturb the native political heavyweights by tearing their houses apart in the search for clerical operatives. Not only would that perturb the local elites, but the related fines and imprisonments of patrons would surely provoke an undesirable backlash.

This was definitely the case throughout the 1590s; however, by June 1600 official attitudes may have been shifting and Delvin was to find his religious

167 O'Reilly, *Memorials*, pp. 129–30.
168 TNA, SP 63/154/8 (lord deputy and others to lords chancellor and treasurer, 20 Aug. 1590).
169 Alessandro Farnese, duke of Parma, governor of the Spanish Netherlands.
170 TNA, SP 63/154/8 (lord deputy and others to lords chancellor and treasurer, 20 Aug. 1590).
171 *CSPI, 1588–1592*, p. 361; TNA, SP 63/154/35(I) (examination of Faranan, n.d.).
172 TNA, SP 63/154/8 (lord deputy and others to lords chancellor and treasurer, 20 Aug. 1590).
173 *CSPI, 1588–92*, p. 361.
174 TNA, SP 63/207(2)/96 (F. Shane to Cecil, 8 Apr. 1600); TNA, SP 63/208(1)/53 (Shane to Cecil, 22 Feb. 1601).

activities under severe pressure. Bishop Brady and Multyfarnham had been implicated in the 1593 bishops' plot to solicit Spanish assistance.[175] Seven years later, Elizabeth reproved her Irish Council that in 'the hart of thenglish pale, there is suffred to stand vntouched, a howse of fryars, called Multifernan, the onely place of assembly and conventicle of all the trayterus Iesuits of the Realme, and where was the first conspiracy and plottinge of this great Rebellion'.[176] She especially reprimanded Bishop Jones of Meath because 'the fryars, and all other popish aduersaries to her Ma:ties gouernement, haue their recourse and passage to and frow thether, in as open and publick manner, as yf their Idolatrous profession where Iuestified by the authoritie of the clargy'.[177] Elizabeth ordered Jones and Lord Deputy Mountjoy to investigate 'how this howse may be demol-ished, or at least the fryars expelled, and the howse conuerted to a place of garrison, or some other good vse'.[178] A year later Multyfarnham was attacked and its inhabitants captured by Sir Francis Shane, sheriff of Westmeath. Shane, however, failed in his purpose and the Nugents rose to the challenge. While leading his clerical hostages to Dublin for reward, Shane was intercepted by Sir Walter Nugent's men who safely returned the friars to their establishment. Notwithstanding the queen's earlier reprimand, this action was conducted for Shane's own personal reasons and was not, in fact, sanctioned by the admin-istration.[179] With the exception of Elizabeth's complaint and allegations made by Shane, there is no other evidence amongst the Irish State Papers to suggest that Multyfarnham was in fact a location of Confederate plotting. And after this event, it seems that the existence and operation of Multyfarnham was tolerated again.[180]

Not all loyal Catholic subjects were as fortunate as Delvin in the 1590s, and there are several examples of individuals suffering certain discomforts for their Catholicism and their supposed protection of its agents. The case of Sir Patrick Barnewall demonstrates the complexities of balancing a devotion to Catholicism with obedience to the crown while revealing some of the subtleties

---

[175] Brady's name was among the signatures of five northern lords and six bishops contained in a 1593 letter to Phillip II. Fennessy, 'Richard Brady OFM', p. 233; Kerney Walsh, 'Archbishop Magauran', pp. 68–79; J.J. Silke, 'The Irish Appeal of 1593 to Spain', *The Irish Ecclesiastical Record*, ser. 5, Vol. 92 (1959), pp. 279–90, 361–71.

[176] TNA, SP 63/207(3)/139 (Elizabeth to Irish Council, June 1600). Also see, BL, Add MS 11,402, f. 76r (Privy Council to Irish Council, 17 July 1600).

[177] TNA, SP 63/207(3)/139 (Elizabeth to Irish Council, June 1600).

[178] Ibid.

[179] TNA, SP 63/207(2)/96 (Shane to Cecil, 8 Apr. 1600); J. Mannion, '"As trew Englishe as any man borne in Myddlesex": Sir Francis Shane, 1540–1614', in C. Maginn and G. Power (eds), *Frontiers, States and Identity in Early Modern Ireland and Beyond* (Dublin, 2016), pp. 164–87.

[180] TNA, SP 63/207(2)/96 (Shane to Cecil, 8 Apr. 1600); TNA, SP 63/208(1)/53 (Shane to Cecil, 22 Feb. 1601). For a discussion of the event, see Lennon, 'Nugent Family and the Diocese of Kilmore', pp. 360–74; Fennessy, 'Richard Brady OFM'.

of Irish politics at this time. Before the war, Barnewall had been considered a doubtful man and a known supporter of Catholic institutions and personnel, yet he had served the crown faithfully with rebel intelligences.[181] Shortly after informing the government of Gravenor's mission to the continent, Barnewall's Dublin residence was searched for a priest.[182] It was not unknown for men of his sort to harbour clergymen in their homes where they frequently held private masses, but their private religious affairs were usually left alone so long as they publicly performed the duties of loyal subjects. This seems to hold true in Barnewall's case. The investigation into his affairs stemmed not from any reports that Barnewall's private life posed a threat to the crown, but from Loftus's personal animosity towards him. Indeed, Barnewall argued that accusations of suspicious behaviour had arisen solely from 'a dislike betwixt my Lord Chaunceler and me'.[183] He appealed to Burghley about this invasion of his private affairs, arguing that the grounds for the search of his residence were entirely unfounded. He also claimed to have investigated the matter personally, insisting that there was no priest and that he was entirely innocent of the charges. It is hard to believe that Barnewall did not shelter Catholic priests or hold services in his home, but had it not been for Loftus's personal interest it is quite possible that Barnewall's private religious affairs would have been tolerated or, at least, overlooked for the time being.

Clerical Participation

There has been much recent speculation about whether the majority of Counter-Reformation clergy were genuinely convinced by O'Neill's religious objective. Certainly, the vast majority of government officials were confident that Catholic clerics were unanimously in favour of rebellion and, if Peter Lombard's description of O'Neill as a charismatic man who 'captivates the feelings of men' was accurate, then there must have been other religious men who felt the same way.[184] Yet, there have been frequent assertions by a number of historians that the majority of clerics did not support armed revolt and their

---

[181] TNA, SP 63/149/32 (Doubtful men, 1589). He and his family patronised the convent of Gracedieu and his son was known to be attending the Catholic college of Douai. H. Jefferies, 'The Early Tudor Reformations in the Irish Pale', *Journal of Ecclesiastical History*, Vol. 52, No. 1 (2001), p. 49; McGowan-Doyle, '"Spent Blood": Christopher St Lawrence and Pale Loyalism', in H. Morgan (ed.), *Battle of Kinsale*, p. 181.

[182] TNA, SP 63/178/4 (Barnewall to Burghley, 9 Jan. 1595).

[183] Ibid.

[184] Byrne (ed.), *Irish War of Defence*, p. 29. This sentiment had been expressed earlier by Patrick Sedgrave: Archivo General de Simancas, Estado, 612–106, 'Breuis rerum declaration', by Patrick Sedgrave, Brussels, c. 1595.

scepticism is warranted.[185] In addition to the example of Henry Fitzsimon, Jesuit Fathers Richard de la Field and Christopher Holywood were noticeably aloof.[186] Other testimony comes from the baron of Dunsany, who, in 1600, explained that '[o]ur massinge preests heere be at variance, for Tyrones preestes affyrme his proceedinge by burninge and cruellness to be lawefull, the English Pale preests denye yt'.[187] Following the 1607 Flight of the Earls, an English observer likewise averred that some members of the Catholic clergy 'are very virtuous and conteine themselues within their boundes of their Allegiance and duty to his Maiestie and doe oppose themselues all they can to the proceedings of thother'.[188] Although he offered a number of plausible and more secular reasons for the inactivity of Old English laymen during this rebellion, Philip O'Sullivan Beare contended that some priests had actively dissuaded Old English Catholics from taking arms.[189] It is doubtful that a devout and militant Catholic of O'Sullivan Beare's vintage would have laid even the faintest hint of blame on the Catholic clergy unless he had reason to believe it. What is more, the State Papers reveal that a number of Catholic priests actually assisted the crown against O'Neill and his Confederates.[190] In fact, one priest, William Atkinson, even offered to assassinate O'Neill though a poisoned host.[191] Based on such evidence, it is likely that the majority of Irish clerics, especially those of the Pale, strove to maintain the status quo by denouncing upheaval, even if it was for the sake of the Catholic religion. Considering how little evidence there is in contemporary records concerning those who did promote rebellion, clerical neutrality is plausible. Excepting men like Archer, Nangle, and Mountford, many clerics did not wish to endanger the souls of their congregations by forcing them to choose between earthly survival and eternal salvation. Rather than concerning themselves with what were weighty political matters, many clerics simply busied themselves with performing the sacraments and confirming the Catholicity of their Irish flocks.

---

185 Edwards, *Church and State*, pp. 288–9; Silke, *Kinsale*, pp. 29–30, 117–19; J. Murray, *Enforcing the English Reformation in Ireland: Clerical Resistance and Political Conflict in the Diocese of Dublin, 1534–1590* (Cambridge, 2009).

186 Hogan, *Distinguished Irishmen*, pp. 170–1.

187 TNA, SP 63/207(I)/2 (Dunsany to Cecil, 2 Jan. 1600).

188 Exeter College, Oxford, MS 154, f. 68r (discourse on the mere Irish).

189 P. O'Sullivan Beare, *Chapters Towards A History of Ireland in the Reign of Elizabeth*, ed. M.J. Byrne (CELT), pp. 54–5.

190 For example: TNA, SP 63/182/10(II) (Mr. Whitchurch to Bagenal, 1 Aug. 1595); TNA, SP 63/181/47 (intelligence out of Tirconnell by a priest, 21 July 1595); TNA, SP 63/182/10(III) (D. Quiran's declaration relative to the Scots, 1 Aug. 1595); TNA, SP 63/203/48(I) (extracts of intelligence sent to Fenton by an Irish priest, 6 Feb. 1599); TNA, SP 63/206/81 (Fenton to Cecil, 12 Dec. 1599); SP 63/207/84(II) (O'Donnell to Waad, Jan. 1600); TNA, SP 63/207(3)/27(I) (advertisements received by Fenton, 10 May 1600).

191 TNA, SP 12/251/49 (W. Atkinson to Cecil, Feb. 1595).

Henry Jefferies has argued that Catholicism and the Catholic clergy played a 'central role in forging support for the war against England' during the 1590s.[192] This conclusion cannot be easily dismissed, as there is limited evidence to suggest that Catholic clergymen did not support the rebellion. However, just as evidence of clerical non-complicity is scanty, evidence concerning those who sanctioned rebellion is incomplete and, in many cases, inconsistent. Existing documentation is overwhelmingly represented by English sources, and one must presume that like all one-sided records the natural inclination of English officialdom was to paint all members of the Catholic clergy with the same brush. Considering how prolific Dublin administrators claimed these seditious priests to be, one must wonder why there are so few records documenting the activities, apprehension, and interrogation of Catholic clergymen. In their determination to extirpate the Catholic episcopacy it is unlikely English officials would have missed opportunities to relate potentially condemning evidence against Catholic clerics. Indeed, one can be sure they were disinclined to record any evidence which contradicted their negative opinion of these ecclesiastics. The lack of concrete evidence indicating widespread collaboration amongst the religious rank and file is surprising. The absence of such information may be explained by a few possible scenarios. First, and most obviously, Catholic clerics of both political persuasions operated under great secrecy. This fact was made clear by the queen when she complained that 'Iesuits and Seminarie Priests are in many places openly mainteyned and followed… [but] in some places Namely the English Pale secretly mentained in the houses of some Noble persons and in many gentlemens houses partly disguised in apparell of servingmen'.[193] This made it considerably more difficult for administrators to ascertain much about their locations and activities.[194] Second, and significantly, not all Catholic clerics supported rebellion, in which case it would have been difficult to pass censure. There is convincing evidence to support this since several clerics willingly supplied the state with evidence against O'Neill and his allies, while Captain Thomas Lee proposed employing Catholic priests to help recruit and confirm former rebels to the crown's cause.[195] And third, many of the clerics operating within the Pale were not only patronised by leading members of the lay community, but were also related to them. Since the majority of Old English gentry and merchants were reluctant to rise against their monarch, their clerical employees and cousins would have been disinclined to disagree and risk the loss of both their protective sponsors and the income they provided. It is, therefore,

---

[192] Jefferies, *The Irish Church*, pp. 262, 259–75.
[193] BL, Add. MS 4819, f. 120v.
[194] TNA, SP 63/177/31(II) (Irish Council to Elizabeth, 5 Dec. 1594).
[195] TNA, SP 63/176/50 (Fitzwilliam to Burghley, 2 Oct. 1594); TNA, SP 63/202(3)/171(V) (report of certain speeches between Lee and the Bishop of Meath, 18 Nov. 1598).

conceivable that many Catholic clergymen chose to 'toe the line'. As Father James Archer explained to Acquaviva: 'The chiefs in the south wish also to have our Fathers, but they do not dare to patronise and protect them openly. They will protect them, however, and take every care of them.'[196]

While religion must be an ever-present theme in any study of early modern Ireland, there is a remarkable absence of detailed commentaries concerning religion in the State Papers during these war years. With surprisingly few extant examples, it seems as if there was a concerted effort on the part of administrators to ignore one of the most important controversies of the time. This was because administrators were well aware of the dangers in forcing religious conformity on an Irish public which already had enough grievances to make their loyalties worrisome. By drawing attention to the issue, they would have been inadvertently advertising O'Neill's cause. One must accept that existing information focused on those who did support rebellion rather that those who adopted a more idle political stance; it is the absence of detailed evidence against those who advocated insurrection which must be taken as proof that O'Neill's rebellion did not receive universal support from the Irish clerical community.

As for the contention that Catholic clerics were spreading sedition far and wide, one should not assume that their influence was absolute. Although it is true that the church played a more prominent role in sixteenth-century society than it does at present, it would be a mistake to accept that our ancestors possessed higher moral principles than we do now. They may have been more attentive to the orations of their priests, but that does not mean they acted upon the decrees of their spiritual shepherds. Religion certainly complicated things in Ireland, but it was not the single deciding factor in Ireland's struggle against English suzerainty. Sincerity to the actual cause amongst those who sided with O'Neill in the 1590s may be discredited to some extent since even O'Neill's most trusted Old English commander, Captain Richard Tyrrell, had ensured there was something material in it for him before he wholeheartedly committed to the revolt.[197] Besides, the Irish Catholic Church had long been divided into two, often competing, institutions: one, 'English', and the other, 'Gaelic Irish'.[198]

---

196 From Archer's letter to Acquaviva, 10 Aug. 1598, in Hogan, *Distinguished Irishmen*, p. 325.

197 Kenneth Nicholls has reproduced an agreement made between Tyrrell, O'Neill, and the Spanish king, by which Tyrrell guaranteed himself large land grants in return for his military support. Nicholls, 'Richard Tyrrell, Soldier Extraordinary', pp. 161–78.

198 Hazard, *Faith and Patronage*; H.A. Jefferies, *Priests and Prelates of Armagh in the Age of Reformations, 1518–1558* (Dublin, 1997); Jefferies, 'Why the Reformation Failed in Ireland', *IHS*, Vol. 40, No. 158 (2016), pp. 151–70; Jefferies, 'The Early Tudor Reformations in the Irish Pale', pp. 34–62; Jefferies, 'The Church Among Two Nations: Armagh on the Eve of the Tudor Reformations', *History Ireland*, Vol. 6, No. 1 (1998), pp. 17–21; Jefferies, 'The Role of the Laity in the Parishes of Armagh *Inter Anglicos*, 1518–1553', *Archivium Hibernicum*, Vol. 52 (1998), pp. 73–84; Jefferies, 'The Irish Parliament of 1560: The Anglican Reforms Authorised', *IHS*, Vol. 26,

Even if the ethnic gulf in Irish Catholicism was not enough to hinder unity, the fact that the Old English distrusted the Gaelic Irish generally, and in particular doubted the true intentions of O'Neill, makes it unlikely that religion would have been enough to ally these two communities at this time. For instance, when O'Hely arrived in Madrid seeking Spanish aid, Dublin-born Richard Stanihurst cautioned against placing any trust in Irish promises.[199] Thus, the contention that the Old English and Gaelic Irish were unified by Catholicism and the work of Catholic missionaries is impractical. Although those who revolted were prepared to endorse the religious cause, the vast majority were far more incensed over what they perceived to be English oppressions and infringements on their traditional privileges rather than the imposition of an alien religion.

No, 102 (1988), pp. 128–41; P. Corish, 'The Origins of Catholic Nationalism', in P. Corish (ed.), A History of Irish Catholicism (Dublin, 1968), p. 8.
[199] Morgan, Tyrone's Rebellion, p. 142.

3

Secret Traitors and Crown Colluders: The Palesmen's Response to Patriotic Pressures

By the 1590s the majority of Old English Palesmen were conscious of an ever-widening gulf between them and their English-born brethren, yet they were still a long way from conceding to any theory which suggested that they now had more in common with their Gaelic Irish compatriots.[1] Ironically, this was one area in which the English crown and Hugh O'Neill could agree. For these two enemies, the Old English shared two crucial national characteristics with the Gaelic Irish: their faith and their fatherland. O'Neill seized on these two features as the foundations for a revitalised nationalist philosophy during the Nine Years' War.[2] He did so because he recognised that he would need the support of the Old English population if he was to ever achieve the overthrow of English authority in Ireland. Without even minimal assistance from the Pale and southern towns, the Confederates would lack the military and victual supply system necessary for waging a full-out war. More importantly, lacking the artillery necessary for taking fortified towns, O'Neill would need at least tacit support from within the Pale if he hoped to oust the English government from its Dublin stronghold. O'Neill therefore targeted the Palesmen with passionate words and fair promises. Meanwhile, crown officials, conscious of growing discontent with English policies and administrators, worried that the Palesmen might be convinced and so they gravely entertained accusations of treason against many leading Old English figures. Some, of course, did join the rebellion but, contrary to O'Neill's hopes and administrators' fears, convincing the Old English to join him was not such an easy task.

Prior to the outbreak of hostilities, Hugh O'Neill had shown little interest in spiritual matters and it is probably fair to assume that his ambitions were far

---

[1] TNA, SP 63/202(4)/60 ('greevances', 1598). Two other versions of this text are available: Lambeth, Carew MS, 632, No. 271, ff. 163–70; BL, Cotton Titus B XII, ff. 97–105b. See also TNA, SP 63/202(4)/75 ('A discourse to show "that planting of colonies, and that to be begun only by the Dutch, will give best entrance to the reformation of Ulster"', 1598).

[2] Morgan, 'Policy and Propaganda', pp. 18–52; Morgan, 'The 1597 Ceasefire Documents', pp. 1–21; Morgan, 'Faith and Fatherland in Sixteenth-Century Ireland', pp. 13–20; Morgan, 'Faith and Fatherland or Queen and Country?', pp. 1–49; Morgan, 'Hugh O'Neill and the Nine Years War', pp. 21–37.

greater than a religious settlement for Ireland.[3] On earlier visits to Dublin he had regularly accompanied lords deputy to Protestant services without expressing any struggle of conscience. The more likely impetus for O'Neill's rebellion lay in his political grievances and his personal aspirations. More than anything else, he wanted to attain unqualified authority over the north. Achieving this would require an all-Ireland agenda and he would need to provide legitimate and just reasons for intransigence. To this end, O'Neill was quick to use the religious crisis as a means to rally support. In January 1596 he presented the crown with his demand for liberty of conscience and this would remain a sticking point throughout subsequent negotiations. Although his early demand was not publicised, it probably reached the ears of some well-placed Old Englishmen.[4] Then, in the summer of 1597, O'Neill claimed to be acting on behalf of 'all the Catholics of the land'.[5] Without a doubt, defending the faith tugged at the consciences of a number of conflicted Catholic subjects or, at least, forced loyal Irish Catholics to reconsider where their allegiances ought to lie. A religious crusade tempted some contemporaries, but most Old Englishmen, especially those within the Pale, would offer little more than inert neutrality.[6] In order to extend agitation beyond Ulster, O'Neill had to expand the grounds of his appeal. As the war dragged on, his claim to a Catholic crusade began to evolve into a more clearly defined national ideology steeped in the concepts of faith and fatherland. This two-pronged approach of defending the national religion and the ancestral homeland provided O'Neill with a wider and more inclusive base on which to appeal to Ireland's inhabitants. Fatherland ideology, which naturally appealed to the Gaelic Irish, was employed to establish that the Old English had a vested interest in the socio-political and geographical landscape of Ireland. Place of birth was emphasized above bloodline origin in a plea to convince the Old English that they too had a responsibility to protect Ireland. As such, the island of Ireland was portrayed as the birthright of all the nation's inhabitants.

O'Neill was not the first Irishman to conceive the idea of an Irish nationality, nor was his vision of a nationwide alliance between the Gaelic Irish and Old English without precedent. Far from inventing the Irish nation, O'Neill adopted and expanded ideas propagated during Fitzmaurice's rebellion more than a decade earlier. He also borrowed and built upon a developing commonwealth

---

[3] Although Catholic, O'Neill was not a devout one. Morgan has argued that it was in O'Neill's political interests to oppose Protestantism, especially in Ulster, because the appointment of alien Protestant ministers would frustrate his authority by obstructing his control over church patronage and appointments. Morgan, 'Policy and Propaganda', p. 21.

[4] CUL, MS Kk. I. 15, f. 134.

[5] Morgan, 'Faith and Fatherland or Queen and Country?', p. 8.

[6] A. Clarke, 'Alternative Allegiances in Early Modern Ireland', *Journal of Historical Sociology*, Vol. 5, No. 3 (1992), p. 258.

rhetoric which had emerged from within the politicised Old English community over preceding decades. O'Neill's application of the individual's patriotic duty to the nation was reminiscent of Edward Walshe's earlier treatise, *Office and Duety in Fighting for our Country*.[7] However, O'Neill's national concept differed dramatically from that of the loyalist from Waterford. Walshe regarded the English monarch as a central and defining feature in the national spirit. For O'Neill, queen and country were no longer synonymous and the patriotic defence of one's country now called for the expulsion of that same monarch who was once so vital to the nation's existence. Religion and place of birth replaced monarchical rule as the fundamental core of the nation and the identity of its denizens. In O'Neill's estimation, or those who advised him, these two features had transformed two formerly divergent communities into one single and common entity – Irish Catholic – and this was now endangered by the despotic forces of English heresy.

O'Neill was keen to exploit every possible opportunity which might convince the Old English that it was in their best interests to align themselves with their Gaelic Irish Catholic neighbours. He was acutely conscious of this audience and he tailored his nationalistic rhetoric to appeal to them in terms which played upon their insecurities: religion; political exclusion; and social displacement by English newcomers. These issues would become central in O'Neill's formation of a patriotic platform which was designed to include all Irish 'natives', be they Gaelic Irish or Old English. He portrayed the rebellion as a national one which transcended traditional ethnic boundaries and advertised himself as the only solution for the rehabilitation of a blended Irish Catholic nation.[8] To sway them, O'Neill had to make the case that Ireland would be better off once liberated from English overlordship. His propaganda and communications strove to discredit the current regime while intimating that he had taken it upon himself to protect and defend the land and people of Ireland. He repeatedly denounced the treachery and broken promises of English administrators and the betrayal of powerful, but loyal, Gaelic Irish and Old English lords.[9] During negotiations in 1597, O'Neill specifically complained that 'divers good gent of thenglishe Pale, in the Lo: Grayes gouer[n]m[en]t, [were]

---

7   E. Walshe, *The office and duety in fighting for our countrey* (London, 1545); Morgan, 'Faith and Fatherland', p. 13.

8   TNA, SP 63/201/80(III) (O'Neill to T. Norreys and Council, 27 Nov. 1597).

9   TNA, SP 63/207(2)/79 ('Certain conferences' between F. McCarthy and D. McCarthy, 2 Apr. 1600). Red Hugh O'Donnell, Hugh Roe MacMahon, Maguire, and the O'Reillys of East Breifne were model examples, as was the Monaghan settlement. B. Cunningham, 'The Anglicisation of East Breifne: The O'Reillys and the Emergence of County Cavan', in R. Gillespie (ed.), *Cavan: Essays on the History of an Irish County* (Dublin, 1995), pp. 51–72; P. Moore, 'The Mac Mahons of Monaghan (1500–1593)', *Clogher Record*, Vol. 1, No. 3 (1955), pp. 22–38; Moore, 'The Mac Mahons of Monaghan (1593–1603)', *Clogher Record*, Vol. 1, No. 4 (1956), pp. 85–107. See also

attainted and executed, for supposed treason, vpon the witnes of a raskall horseboy and protected Traytor, their landes and goods taken for forefeicture'.[10] According to O'Neill, English policies had led to the estrangement of Ireland's traditional political élite and this, by implication, amounted to an infringement on Ireland's national autonomy. He likewise concentrated on Old English fears regarding their declining position of authority by declaring that it was the crown's intention to suppress the Irish nobility and replace them with newly installed Englishmen.[11] O'Neill had definitely hit a chord since experience had already convinced many Palesmen of the veracity of this charge.[12] As much as the crown may have wanted to contest it, numerous contemporary treatises penned by Englishmen had explicitly recommended the destruction of Ireland's native élite as the only means of achieving a reconstructed English society in Ireland.[13] O'Neill further argued that the government's underhand dealings, especially in terms of fuelling factional rivalries within families and between neighbours, had misled the Irish into participating in their own demise. This had forced him to rebel because he refused to take part in the disgrace of his countrymen.[14] O'Neill was thus provided with a political platform which he could use, in combination with religious grievances, as the honourable rationale for his revolt.

O'Neill's demands were designed to appeal to the general public's sense of tradition and entitlement and, in his effort to seduce members of the Old English community, he was willing to promise anything they wanted to hear.[15] He fulminated against recent land confiscations and newly erected English plantations. He demanded the full restoration of ancestral lands and possessions and pressed for the re-establishment of all hereditary privileges once enjoyed by Ireland's social élite.[16] But while O'Neill's message may have appealed to a wide audience, even he knew that some groups would be harder to persuade than others. For this reason, O'Neill purposefully directed his propaganda and agents at the most vulnerable elements of society, particularly the lower ranking

BL, Cotton Titus C VII, ff. 156–61 (Sir Henry Wallops Relation of the Progresse of Tiroens rebellion, 1600); Exeter College, Oxford, MS 154, f. 55r (discourse on the mere Irish).

[10] Bodleian Library, MS Laud 612, f. 59.

[11] TNA, SP 63/192/7(XI) (advertisements by J. Fitzgarrett, 12 Aug. 1596); TNA, SP 63/206/142 ('A brief declaration of the state wherein Ireland now standeth', 1599).

[12] For example, TNA, SP 63/195/15 (Norreys to Cecil, 15 Nov. 1596); TNA, SP 63/206/14 ('A brief declaration', 1599). See also A. Hadfield, 'English Colonialism and National Identity in Early Modern Ireland', Éire-Ireland, Vol. 28, No. 1 (1993), pp. 69–86.

[13] Spenser, A View; Maley (ed.), 'The Supplication', p. 38; TNA, SP 63/196/2 ('Observations', 3 Dec. 1596).

[14] TNA, SP 63/192/7(XI) (advertisements by Fitzgarrett, 12 Aug. 1596).

[15] TNA, SP 63/194/41 (Fenton to Burghley, 22 Oct. 1596.); TNA, SP 63/202(2)/26 (Irish Council to Privy Council, 4 May, 1598); TNA, SP 63/206/81 (Fenton to Cecil, 12 Dec. 1599).

[16] TNA, SP 63/206/55 (articles intended to be stood upon by Tyrone, Nov. 1599).

or disenfranchised members of important families. He also employed Palesmen like Richard Nugent, one Shelton, 'a young man of Dublin', and priests like Peter Nangle as instruments to propagate his message amongst their kinsmen and followers.[17] He was clever and endowed with the kind of cunning needed to direct man's natural greed to his own advantage. To those Old Englishmen who would join him, O'Neill pledged to restore their alienated possessions or establish them as great lords as he had done for his Gaelic Irish allies.[18] This was happily greeted by the most disaffected elements who, 'pretendinge a generall Irish quarrell, for old titles, and recouerye of lands, long since lawfully evicted from them', flocked to O'Neill's camp expecting large rewards.[19] English observers retorted that, like religion, this was a ruse to beguile the Old English into his confidence and that in the event of a Confederate victory they would soon find themselves expelled from the country, like their New English counterparts.[20] As Fenton complained: 'the Irish can make a grounde of any matter, how vnt[rue] or weake soeuer, to serue their torne'.[21] It is possible, however, that both O'Neill and the crown had overlooked one significant detail; it was unlikely that O'Neill's support of certain troublesome Gaelic Irish borderers, like Owny O'Moore, would serve as bait for most Old English lords. These men had no desire to see the installation of violent and uncivil Gaelic Irish lords in their vicinity, nor would they seriously consider allying themselves with such men.[22]

For much of the war it seemed the Confederates were gaining the upper hand, which caused O'Neill to become ever more confident and uncompromising in his stance.[23] His demands took on the appearance of a political manifesto articulating the concerns of his target audience, the Old English Palesmen.[24] Because these demands reflected both universal and specific Irish

---

17 HMC *Salisbury MSS*, vii, 218; TNA, SP 63/206/20 (G. Cary to Cecil, 13 Nov 1599); TNA, SP 63/206/44(VIII) (Irish Council to Ormond, 27 Nov. 1599); TNA, SP 63/207(2)/63(I) (intelligences out of the north, 21 Mar. 1600).

18 TNA, SP 63/186/22 (Russell to Privy Council, 26 Jan. 1596); TNA, SP 63/192/7(IX) (R. Greame to Russell, 8 Aug. 1596); TNA, SP 63/193/32 (Russell to Burghley, 25 Sep. 1596); TNA, SP 63/194/15 (Russell to Privy Council, 14 Oct. 1596); TNA, SP 63/195/9 (Russell to Cecil, 9 Nov. 1596); TNA, SP 63/202(1)/87 (Fenton to Burghley, 21 Mar. 1598); TNA, SP 63/202(2)/57 (N. Dawtrey to Cecil, 6 June 1598); TNA, SP 63/205/197 (memoranda by Essex, 5 Oct. 1599).

19 TNA, SP 63/202(3)/142 (Irish Council to Privy Council, 3 Nov. 1598).

20 Exeter College, Oxford, MS 154, ff. 55–74 (discourse on the mere Irish).

21 TNA, SP 63/194/41 (Fenton to Burghley, 22 Oct. 1596).

22 Morgan, 'Hugh O'Neill and the Nine Years War', pp. 35–6. For an example of an incident which reinforced their distrust, see TNA, SP 63/205/218 (Loftus and Carey to Privy Council, 23 Oct. 1500).

23 Morgan, 'Faith and Fatherland or Queen and Country?', p. 17; Edwards, *Church and State*, p. 287.

24 TNA, SP 63/186/32(I) (Wallop and Gardiner to lord deputy and Council, 25 Jan. 1595); TNA, SP 63/188/27 ('The effect of Her Majesty's pleasure', 12 Apr. 1596); TNA, SP 63/189/46(I) (report

grievances, many crown officials had difficulty believing he had drawn them up on his own. Following a parley late in 1597, Ormond was convinced that O'Neill's demands had been 'deuised by persons of the Pale'.[25] For similar reasons, O'Neill's 1599 proclamation was erroneously attributed to Henry Fitzsimon.[26] True, some of his articles for redress are reminiscent of those submitted by the baron of Delvin in 1584, and it is almost certain that O'Neill received substantial assistance from another Jesuit father, James Archer, in the formation of his faith and fatherland logic.[27] As Hiram Morgan has argued, O'Neill was no philosopher; but the Palesmen and clerics educated abroad were well versed in the new political and national ideas taking hold on the continent. These concepts, useful in the Irish context of the 1590s, are apparent in much of O'Neill's propaganda, especially following Archer's return to Ireland and his endorsement of the rebellion then raging throughout the country.[28] Nevertheless, it is conceivable that O'Neill devised the main points of contention himself and that certain advisors, like Archer, merely elaborated on his meaning. Although of Gaelic Irish stock, Hugh O'Neill's upbringing and humanistic education in the Pale had endowed him with a unique ability to understand the inner workings of Old English Pale society.[29] While resident in the Pale, he had received the same education and social experiences as many privileged Palesmen and, in doing so, he had become familiar with Ireland's political and social élite. By this lucky event, O'Neill was well acquainted with prevailing socio-political anxieties in the Pale, and was also well aware that not all members of this community shared identical social and political values or ambitions. No other Gaelic lord had comparable experience and O'Neill was intelligent enough to employ it to his advantage.

by G. O'Flanigane, 12 May 1596); TNA, SP 63/201/112 (O'Neill's answers to the articles, 22 Dec. 1597); TNA, SP 63/201/114 (O'Neill's petition to Ormond, 23 Dec. 1597); TNA, SP 63/201/117 (Fenton to Cecil, 26 Dec. 1597); TNA, SP 63/201/117(II) (articles prescribed to O'Neill, 22 Dec. 1597); TNA, SP 63/201/122 (T. Jones to Burghley, 28 Dec. 1597); TNA, SP 63/202(1)/1 (Irish Council to Privy Council, 3 Jan. 1598); TNA, SP 63/202(2)/9 (Jones to Burghley, 18 Apr. 1598); TNA, SP 63/106/55 (articles stood upon by O'Neill, Nov. 1599); CUL, MS Kk. I. 15, ff. 130–73. For a full assessment of O'Neill's nationalistic platform, see Morgan, 'The 1597 Ceasefire Documents', pp. 1–21; 'Faith and Fatherland or Queen and Country?', pp. 1–49.

[25] TNA, SP 63/202(1)/5 (Ormond to Burghley, 4 Jan. 1598).

[26] TNA, SP 63/207(2)/92 (Loftus and Jones to J. Whitgift, 7 Apr. 1600).

[27] TNA, SP 63/108/58 (Delvin's plot for the reformation of Ireland, 26 Mar. 1584); TNA, SP 63/207(1)/136 (E. Fitzharries to N. Walsh, Feb. 1600).

[28] Morgan, 'Policy and Propaganda', pp. 18–52. See also Morrissey, *James Archer of Kilkenny*; Corboy, 'James Archer', pp. 99–107. There were other Palesmen who did their bit to further the cause. For instance, it was believed that a Palesman was responsible for inventing and spreading a rumour that the queen was dead, a rumour which would have been welcomed by the disaffected. TNA, SP 63/205/226 (notes from a letter out of the Brenny to Fenton, 28 Oct. 1599).

[29] Morgan, *Tyrone's Rebellion*, pp. 92–4; 97; Canny, 'Hugh O'Neill, Earl of Tyrone, and the Changing Face of Gaelic Ulster', *Studia Hibernica*, No. 10 (1970), pp. 7–35.

An Adaptable, Evolving, and Opportunistic Ideology

As the war progressed, O'Neill's propaganda machine grew in scope and sophistication, especially after he enlisted the help of men like James Archer.[30] From an early date the Dublin administration expressed concerns about the probable success of O'Neill's propaganda and proselytisers, but the danger of his attempts at persuasion amongst the otherwise loyal population of the Pale became fully apparent when O'Neill's intrigues with James Fitzpiers Fitzgerald, sheriff of Kildare, were revealed in November 1598.[31] Months earlier, in March, O'Neill had written to Fitzpiers in an effort to seduce the sheriff into rebellion. This letter is one of the best surviving examples of O'Neill's employment of a sophisticated faith and fatherland rhetoric in his campaign to entice loyalist Old English servitors into the Confederate fold.[32] In addition to illustrating O'Neill's persuasive tactics, the letter also demonstrates just how adaptable O'Neill and his propaganda machine could be. The 'faith' aspect in this communication was carefully worded. Although O'Neill invoked the name of God, His 'Commaundements', referred to Heaven and Hell, and even employed the term 'converte' twice, he made no specific reference to the Roman Catholic Church, the pope, or 'Christ's true religion'. The demand to 'converte' was probably religiously motivated, yet in the context of this letter it seemed to be Fitzpiers's general behaviour, in both political and religious matters, which needed reform. This was a new and significant departure which becomes more apparent when compared to similarly intended letters directed to other individuals. In a circular letter to the lords of Munster in 1596, O'Neill portrayed his war solely in terms of a religious struggle for the preservation of the Catholic Church, for which he specifically employed the terms 'Christ's Catholic religion' and 'God's just cause'.[33] The letter to Fitzpiers does not explicitly present itself as plea for a Catholic crusade; instead, O'Neill placed greater emphasis on Fitzpiers's patriotic duty to defend his native soil: the fatherland. Since the letter to the Munster nobility made no obvious mention of duty to one's native land, this may have been a more recent development, thus signalling the evolution of a more broadly nationalistic ideology.

Over the course of the war O'Neill stressed the common bonds of religion and native land in order to motivate the Old English to join the Gaelic Irish in a fight against foreign heresy. The fact that this letter makes no specific

---

30 Morgan, 'Policy and Propaganda', pp. 18–52.

31 For a full account of Fitzpiers's revolt, see Canning, 'James Fitzpiers Fitzgerald', pp. 573–94.

32 TNA, SP 63/202(3)/168(II) (O'Neill to J. Fitzpiers, 11 Mar. 1598). Hiram Morgan has also identified the significance of this letter in O'Neill's conception of fatherland ideology. See Morgan, 'Hugh O'Neill and the Nine Years War', p. 24.

33 *Cal. Carew*, iii, 179.

reference to the Catholic church indicates that O'Neill was conscious of the existence of heterogeneous religious interests in Ireland, even amongst those whom he wished to attract to his Confederacy. Although the letter to Fitzpiers contains definite Christian overtones, the absence of what might be considered distinctly 'Catholic' rhetoric would suggest that religion was not an issue for which Fitzpiers had any concern. Fitzpiers's father, Piers Fitzjames, was Protestant, and while O'Neill declared he was rotting in hell, he did not specifically attribute this damnation to heresy, but rather to his father's 'cruell and bloody' treatment of the Gaelic Irish. Following the example set by his father, Fitzpiers may have been amenable to the established church, and so O'Neill would have been foolish to insult him by accusing him of heresy at a time when Fitzpiers's military support was far more valuable than his eternal soul. This seems even more likely when the Fitzpiers letter is compared with another composed in early 1600. In his letter to Lord Barry, O'Neill's call to arms did evoke a sense of patriotism, but far more strenuous was his reprimand to Barry for his 'impietie to God, crueltie to your soule and body, tyrannie & ingratitude both to your followers and country are inexcusable & intolerable. You separated your selfe from the unitie of Christs mysticall Bodie, the *Catholike Church*.'[34] O'Neill frequently railed against Catholics who refused to fight for the church, repeatedly threatening them with the power of excommunication he so desired from the papacy. In his communication with Fitzpiers however, O'Neill stopped short of calling the sheriff a traitor to Christ's true church; instead, Fitzpiers would be a traitor to his country if he failed to defend it.

As an Old Englishman born and bred in Ireland, Fitzpiers may have felt a need to defend his *patria*, and his position within it, from ambitious newcomers. Thus, O'Neill focused on the fatherland and the righteousness in defending one's country against foreign oppressions. This duty, O'Neill asserted, was part and parcel of one's obligation to the one true but, in this case, seemingly non-denominational God. The emphasis here was on God as a moral adjudicator rather than as the head of a single religious institution. O'Neill seemed to grasp that one's personal responsibility to serve God and, through him, one's country was a notion which could be shared by both Irish Catholics and Protestants and, for the moment anyway, the nation could belong to them both, so long as they were 'Irish'. While his toleration of Fitzpiers's Protestantism may appear to be an aberration, the reality was that O'Neill's crusade had initially called only for freedom of conscience; it is possible that returning Ireland firmly to the Roman Catholic fold and redeeming men like Fitzpiers was to be the end result of this revolution. Many of O'Neill's declarations, proclamations, and

---

[34] Emphasis added. Stafford, *Pacata Hibernia*, p. 20; TNA, SP 63/207(1)/130 (O'Neill to Lord Barry, 25 Feb. 1600).

letters appealed to people's sense of identity in a similar manner by encouraging them to engage in the honourable pursuit of defending the two critical items which had combined to create a national identity: religion and birth. When he was appealing to Fitzpiers, the national tradition transcended that of religion. While O'Neill avoided naming the Catholic Church as a unifier in this case, he still ensured his message conveyed that God and country were mutually inseparable. O'Neill has often been cast as a militant nationalist, but the fact that he included or excluded certain ideological elements in his appeals to certain individuals indicates that he was acutely aware of what he was up against.[35]

One wonders then if Fitzpiers, who was probably a Protestant, received such an emotionally charged appeal, whether O'Neill wrote similar letters to all the magnates and lesser gentry of Ireland? If he did, surely one would expect to find many more examples amongst the Irish State Papers, especially of those directed to loyal, but devoutly Catholic, individuals like the barons of Dunsany or Delvin. Although it was suggested that the steadfast Dunsany had received similar correspondence in 1601, no letter was turned over to the administration.[36] Presumably, had individuals of Dunsany's ilk received dispatches of this nature, at least some would have elected to deliver the messages to the government as proof of their loyalty. Owing to the absence of similar letters, it is possible that these loyal Catholics felt exactly the opposite, fearing administrators would assume that they had given O'Neill cause to make such overtures. This is borne out by O'Neill's communications with the baron of Delvin. There is no evidence to suggest that the ever-doubted but loyal Delvin had been approached by O'Neill until that crucial juncture in the autumn of 1599. It was only when Delvin found himself between a rock and a hard place – that is, surrounded by O'Neill and his allies with no hope of reinforcement from the crown army – that O'Neill attempted to win him over by preying upon his vulnerability.[37] It would therefore seem that there was calculated method behind O'Neill's dissemination of propaganda and it might be reasonable to assume that O'Neill targeted Fitzpiers in the spring of 1598 because he had reason to believe that the sheriff was open to switching sides. In all likelihood, O'Neill was aware of Fitzpiers's personal grudge against the queen's lieutenant-general, 'Black' Tom, the great earl of Ormond. The role played by factional rivalries cannot be dismissed, considering that men like James Butler, son of Viscount Mountgarrett, admitted that their 'brethren were in rebellion, not

---

35 For example, Seán Ó Faoláin's fictionalised account of Hugh O'Neill portrays the Confederate leader as an Irish nationalist. S. Ó Faoláin, *The Great O'Neill: A Biography of Hugh O'Neill, Earl of Tyrone, 1550–1616* (New York, 1942).

36 TNA, SP 63/209(2)/201 (Jones to Cecil, 25 Nov. 1601).

37 TNA, SP 63/206/63(II) (proceedings of Delvin's agents, 26 Nov. 1599).

with malicious hearts against the Queen, but to be revenged upon the Earl of Ormonde'.[38]

As it transpired, Fitzpiers did rebel. After thorough investigation it was discovered that his revolt had nothing to do with faith and fatherland, but stemmed from his desire to undermine Ormond's paramountcy. The timing of O'Neill's communication was propitious because Fitzpiers had only just joined his friend Captain Thomas Lee in a secret plot to this end. Although their plot required that Fitzpiers join the rebels in order to infiltrate them, it had all the appearances of genuine treason.[39] Consequently, crown administrators, only too willing to brand Old Englishmen as traitors, readily accepted that the sheriff had been seduced from his loyalty. There were, however, a few crown officials who offered cautionary notes that rancour towards Ormond was at least partially responsible for pushing Fitzpiers into the arms of the enemy.[40] Like these administrators, O'Neill probably knew about Fitzpiers's strained relations with the queen's cousin. He had an ear to the ground and was informed of all political matters prevailing in, and pertaining to, Ireland.[41] He was also acutely conscious of destabilising flaws in the existing political system, namely the factional rivalries obtaining within each of Ireland's prominent families as well as those which split the administration.

Throughout the preceding centuries crown administrators had exploited the chronic and combative factionalism existing within the Irish political system.[42] They continued doing so throughout this war by pitting claimants for traditional territorial titles against one other, as was the case with the Maguires in Fermanagh, the MacMahons in Monaghan, the Fitzgeralds of Desmond, and the lesser Butlers.[43] O'Neill recognised the same opportunity and, once firmly established in Ulster, began manipulating the endemic power struggles

---

[38] *CSPI, 1600*, p. 109; TNA, SP 63/207(2)/126 (Carew to Mountjoy, 19 Apr. 1600).

[39] Canning, 'James Fitzpiers Fitzgerald', pp. 573–94. For more on the Irish career of Thomas Lee, see J.P. Myers, '"Murdering Heart… Murdering Hand": Captain Thomas Lee of Ireland, Elizabethan Assassin', *The Sixteenth Century Journal*, Vol. 22, No. 1 (1991), pp. 47–60; McGurk, 'A Soldier's Prescription for the Governance of Ireland, 1599–1601: Captain Thomas Lee and his Tracts', in B. MacCuarta (ed.), *Reshaping Ireland 1550–1700: Colonization and its Consequences* (Dublin, 2011), pp. 43–60.

[40] TNA, SP 63/202(3)/167 (T. Reade to Cecil, 20 Nov. 1598); TNA, SP 63/202(4)/46(I) (R. Lane's project for service, 23 Dec. 1598).

[41] For example, see TNA, SP 63/191/18 (J. Morgan to Russell, 10 July 1596); TNA, SP 63/202(2)/54 (memorandum by Stafford, May 1598); Lee, 'Apologie', f. 34.

[42] It was also recommended that she continue doing so. TNA, SP 63/206/120 (notes on a plan to recover Connacht, Dec. 1599). See also TNA, SP 63/207(2)/111 (Stafford to Cecil, 16 Apr. 1600); TNA, SP 63/207(4)/116 (H. Cuff to Carew, Aug. 1600); TNA, SP 63/207(5)/110(I) (letters sent by O'Neill to Lords in Munster, 20–21 Sep. 1600).

[43] TNA, SP 63/207(2)/63(I) (intelligences out of the north, 21 Mar. 1600); TNA, SP 63/207(4)/105 (Carew to Privy Council, 30 Aug. 1600); TNA, SP 63/208(1)/38 (Irish Council to Privy Council, 7 Feb. 1601).

and personal rivalries of his neighbours.[44] With the outbreak of war, he cast his eye further abroad and exploited existing feuds while attempting to create new ones by resorting to allegations of treachery to draw already insecure Old English lords to his side. For instance, in 1594 O'Neill made overtures to the earl of Kildare.[45] He attempted to twist the details of recent events by claiming that certain attacks committed against Kildare's lands, supposedly perpetrated by some of O'Neill's kinsmen and allies, had in fact been executed under the authority of Marshal Henry Bagenal.[46] O'Neill further insisted that if Kildare could procure the lord deputy's warrant to proceed against these villains, he would find O'Neill 'redie to performe anie thing I maie that shall work your contentment'.[47] Fortunately for Kildare, following the discovery of O'Neill's letter Lord Deputy Fitzwilliam assured Burghley that there was no reason to doubt the earl.[48]

O'Neill was a tricky customer and knew exactly how to play on the vulnerabilities of individuals; he knew Kildare was irate at the recent spoliation of his lands and he also knew that there was no love lost between Bagenal and any of the Irish nobility. In his communication with Kildare, circumstances allowed O'Neill to attempt to shift the blame from his own adherents to his personal nemesis, Bagenal. The situation with Fitzpiers was far more delicate because Fitzpiers's father and family had been murdered by men who had since become O'Neill's allies. O'Neill glossed over this fact by saying it was at the behest of these allies that he now kindly entreated Fitzpiers to reform his ways and join the Confederacy. However, it was as much a warning as it was an invitation, and O'Neill counselled Fitzpiers that failure to perform his natural duty to his country would not go unpunished. This same threat propped up all of his communications; no matter how opportunistic or passionate O'Neill's patriotic appeals were, they were always backed up with warnings of physical violence.[49]

---

[44] For a discussion of O'Neill's manipulation of Ulster politics, especially his elimination of competitors, see H. Morgan, '"Slán Dé fút go hoíche": Hugh O'Neill's Murders', in D. Edwards, P. Lenihan, and C. Tait (eds), *Age of Atrocity: Violence and Political Conflict in Early Modern Ireland* (Dublin, 2007), pp. 95–118; Morgan, 'Hugh O'Neill and the Nine Years War', pp. 34–5; G.A. Hayes-McCoy, 'Strategy and Tactics in Irish Warfare, 1593–1601', *IHS*, Vol. 2, No. 7 (1941), p. 257.

[45] TNA, SP 63/174/37(XIII) (O'Neill to Kildare, 8 Apr. 1594).

[46] Ibid. For an official report on these attacks on Kildare, see TNA, SP 63/178/53(V) (advertisements sent to Sir Henry Duke, 20 Feb. 1595).

[47] TNA, SP 63/174/37(XIII) (O'Neill to Kildare, 8 Apr. 1594). See also TNA, SP 63/192/7(XI) (advertisements by Fitzgarrett, 12 Aug. 1596).

[48] TNA, SP 63/174/38 (Fitzwilliam to Burghley, 5 May 1594).

[49] As Sir Henry Power noted: 'By letters and menaces, he sought all the means he could to draw the gentlemen, who are subjects, into his faction', *CSPI, 1600*, p. 15, TNA, SP 63/207(2)/9 (H. Power to Privy Council, 4 Mar. 1600). TNA, SP 63/207(I)/65 (Fenton to Cecil, 31 Jan. 1600);

As the war dragged on, O'Neill went on progresses, seducing and overawing the inhabitants of Ireland with impressive shows of strength while taking pledges to guarantee adherence.[50] It was widely accepted that the more successful O'Neill's military enterprise was and the more publicity his patriotic rhetoric received, the more likely wavering Old English borderers and Palesmen were to join him.[51] Assuredly, some submitted because they sympathised with the cause, but many others feared the violent retribution meted out upon those who dared resist. Just as O'Neill had warned Fitzpiers of the carnage awaiting him if he did not join the rebellion, O'Neill's messages to other Palesmen were equally menacing. In fact, O'Neill's communications with Old English lords always coincided with the presence of his forces in their vicinity. O'Neill's alleged letter to Dunsany was only sent when his forces were at the baron's doorstep and, no doubt, Dunsany was reminded of the damage they could do.[52] Having surrounded Delvin with the combined forces of the Leinster and Ulster Confederates in the autumn of 1599, it was harassment and physical intimidation which compelled the baron to negotiate and engage with O'Neill's ideology.[53] Although it could not be proven, it was suspected that Delvin had capitulated since he had so much to lose due to his frontier situation.[54] Many other Old Englishmen were just as vulnerable, and administrators openly fretted

TNA, SP 63/207/85 (A. Savage to Cecil, 3 Feb. 1600); TNA, SP 63/207/86 (Irish Council to Privy Council, 4 Feb. 1600); TNA, SP 63/207(4)/1 (T. Dillon to Cecil, 1 July 1600).

[50] TNA, SP 63/205/42 (Essex to Privy Council, 29 Apr. 1599); TNA, SP 63/207(2)/1 (Irish Council to Privy Council, 1 Mar. 1600); TNA, SP 63/207(2)/9 (Power to Privy Council, 4 Mar. 1600); TNA, SP 63/207(2)/41 (Mountjoy to Cecil, 18 Mar. 1600).

[51] TNA, SP 63/202(3)/117 (Ormond to Privy Council, 21 Oct. 1598); TNA, SP 63/202(3)/125 (Norreys to Cecil, 23 Oct. 1598); TNA, SP 63/202(3)/132 (C. Clifford to Cecil, 30 Oct. 1598); TNA, SP 63/202(3)/135 (Irish Council to Privy Council, 31 Oct. 1598); TNA, SP 63/202(3)/142(I) (—— to Lords Justices Loftus and Gardener, 1 Nov. 1598); TNA, SP 63/202(3)/152(I) (N. Walsh to Loftus and Gardener, 30 Oct. 1598); TNA, SP 63/202(3)/153 (Fenton to Cecil, 7 Nov. 1598); TNA, SP 63/206/81 (Fenton to Cecil, 12 Dec. 1599); TNA, SP 63/206/120 (notes to recover Connacht, Dec. 1599); Perrot, *Chronicle*, pp. 156–7. This was also the case when O'Neill went on progress in 1600: TNA, SP 63/207(I)/11(1) (intelligences from several letters to Fenton, 7 Jan. 1600); TNA, SP 63/207(I)/86 (Irish Council to Privy Council, 4 Feb. 1600); TNA, SP 63/207(I)/89 (Fenton to Cecil, 4 Feb. 1600); TNA, SP 63/207(2)/3 (Mountjoy to Cecil, 3 Mar. 1600).

[52] TNA, SP 63/208(1)/44 (Dunsany to Cecil, 10 Feb. 1601); TNA, SP 63/209(2)/201 (Jones to Cecil, 25 Nov. 1601).

[53] TNA, SP 63/206/44(I) (Delvin to Irish Council, 22 Nov. 1599); TNA, SP 63/206/44(III) (motions made on behalf of Delvin, 24 Nov. 1599); TNA, SP 63/206/68(V) (Delvin to Ormond, 25 Nov. 1599); TNA, SP 63/206/63(I) (Delvin's instructions to T. Leicester and M. Archbold, 25 Nov. 1599); TNA, SP 63/206/63(II) (proceedings of Delvin's agents, 26 Nov. 1599).

[54] AFM, Vol. 6, p. 2147; TNA, SP 63/206/68(I) (W. Warren to Loftus and Carey, 23 Nov. 1599); TNA, SP 63/206/65 (Carey to Cecil, 3 Dec. 1599); TNA, SP 63/206/74 (Warren to Cecil, 5 Dec. 1599); TNA, SP 63/206/81 (Fenton to Cecil, 12 Dec. 1599); TNA, SP 63/207(6)/124 (W. Udall's memorials concerning Delvin, Dec. 1600); TNA, SP 63/208(2)/49 (Fenton to Cecil, 8 May 1601); Iske, *The Green Cockatrice*, p. 127.

that 'the longer he [O'Neill] is suffred to range… as a sponge he [sucketh to] him all the Irish, and shaketh the loyalty of many good subiects that haue stand [stood] firme hethervnto'.[55]

The autumn of 1599 marked a crisis point when O'Neill's ideology and the threat of Confederate forces became a very pressing reality. The Confederates were multiplying throughout the country, notching up victories against a disorganised crown army and its weakened fortifications, while, at the same time, letters were being circulated amongst prospective allies. Negotiators, led by Sir William Warren, were dispatched to the north to discuss a ceasefire, and they found O'Neill so confident in his position that '[h]e hath both his wife and his daughters in the camp with him, and the most part of all their wives with them, which maketh me think that they regard our army but a little'.[56] Officials were concerned that O'Neill had designs on the Pale, but their fears were fully realised when O'Neill's proclamation was brought to the administration's attention following its discovery by a Palesmen named Thomas Barnewall.[57] His participation in the crown's 1599 negotiating team was providential since it is unlikely that any New English official could have gained the confidence of O'Neill's man, Richard Owen, and even less likely that Owen would have entrusted a copy to a New English agent. Barnewall was exactly the kind of person this propaganda targeted and so Owen 'shewed unto me several writings, to the number of 6 or 7, whereof having read one unto me, he told me that he purposed to have them cast abroad in the streets of Dublin and Drogheda'. Owen had clearly misjudged Barnewall's interest in the thesis because:

> I, the said Thomas, fearing some inconvenience might grow by that course of casting them abroad, moved him to another course, which was, that he would send one of them by me to whom he thought he might best trust, to the end that party might acquaint many others in more secret manner with the same; whereof he liked well, and thereupon delivered one of them unto me, which I, according my duty, delivered to your Lordships and Council.[58]

This was O'Neill's proclamation, known to English contemporaries as his 'infamous' and 'villainous libel'.[59] It was the fruit of a constantly evolving ideology, founded on his 1596 religious demands and moulded over the following years into the sense of patriotic love for one's country seen in the letter to Fitzpiers. He combined his own knowledge, ambitions, and wiles with

---

55 TNA, SP 63/207(I)/120 (Irish Council to Privy Council, 18 Feb. 1600).
56 *CSPI, 1599–1600*, p. 300.
57 *CSPI, 1599–1600*, pp. 252–3.
58 Ibid.
59 TNA, SP 63/206/20 (Cary to Cecil, 13 Nov. 1599); TNA, SP 63/206/25(III) (declaration of Thomas Barnewall, 15 Nov. 1599).

the commonwealth rhetoric of Palesmen and the advice and wisdom of educated counsellors – especially, it seems, the Jesuit James Archer.[60] The culmination was a diatribe against any who dared to go against the laws of reason and nature by betraying their fatherland. To those who would join him, O'Neill pledged:

> I will imploye myselfe to the utmost of my power in their defence and for the extirpation of heresie, the planting of the Catholike Religion, the deliverie of our country of infinite murders, wicked and detestable policies by which this kingdome was hetherto governed, norished in obscuritie and ignorance, mayntained in barbarity and incivility and consequently of infinite evills which weare to lamentable to be rehearsed.[61]

This proclamation was backed up with a series of twenty-two articles.[62] With respect to religion, the articles stipulated that laws against practising the Catholic faith be abolished and that the Church of Ireland was to be restored to the pope's jurisdiction. All church lands which had been confiscated as part of the dissolutions were to be restored. All Irish Catholic clerics who had been imprisoned on account of their faith in both Ireland and England were to be released and henceforth no Englishman was to be allowed any church office in Ireland. O'Neill also demanded the establishment of an Irish university in which instruction would follow the manner of the Catholic church, not the Protestant aims of the recently founded Trinity College, Dublin. He insisted that no Irishman should be denied access to education or membership to any profession. Politically, all administrative offices in Ireland were to be held by men born in Ireland and Irishmen were to have the same commercial rights and trading liberties as any man born in England. And finally, he stipulated that the queen and her successors could not make any Irishman serve in any military capacity against his will. Marked as utopian, these articles constituted O'Neill's manifesto and, as Morgan has noted, '[t]he enactment of these proposals would have made Ireland a kingdom in fact, not just in name'.[63]

Combined, the proclamation and articles amounted to 'an ideological bombshell' which specifically targeted the Palesmen who 'would have been the main beneficiaries of its proposals'.[64] They were 'meant to be sent and divulged in cities and towns by the Jesuits and priests' in order to stir them into action.[65] While the articles were designed to entice the Palesmen with 'Ewtopian' promises, the proclamation also intimated that O'Neill had preserved them

---

60 Morgan, 'Policy and Propaganda', pp. 28–35.
61 TCD MS 578/12, f. 31.
62 TNA, SP 63/206/55 (articles intended to be stood upon by Tyrone, Nov. 1599).
63 Morgan, 'Hugh O'Neill and the Nine Years War', p. 26.
64 Ibid.; Morgan, 'Faith and Fatherland', p. 19.
65 CSPI, 1599–1600, p. 258.

from serious harm thus far, having patiently waited for them to realise that they should join the crusade 'against the Enemies of god and our poore country'. They had not. Thus, much like in the letter to Fitzpiers, O'Neill warned the Palesmen that if they did not heed these written declarations, the Confederate army was ready to punish them.[66] This was not a hollow threat as administrators had already 'received intelligence out of the county of Tyrone, that that Archtraitor was drawing to the borders, and, before the ending of the letter, we understood that he is entered the pale'.[67] At the very same time, administrators expressed their deepest reservations about the fidelity and reliability of the Palesmen:

> we have not that confidence in the Pale-men, which we have had, for that we have daily information of some gentlemen, being younger brothers, that run to the rebels, which is not without suspicion that they make way for their friends and parents; and, in the time of the cessation, some gentlemen of living went into Ulster to the Archtraitor for divers ends, to serve their own turn; who, we have reason to think, will break out manifestly upon any advantage of the time.[68]

Delvin's 1599 exchange with O'Neill remains the best documented because the baron turned his records over to the administration. It is unlikely that he was the only Pale borderer forced to negotiate with O'Neill at this time and it is equally unlikely that all other borderers were as unyielding as Delvin. There is ample evidence that a number of Palesmen did join the Confederacy during the autumn of 1599. Maybe they agreed with the ideas and arguments put forth by O'Neill and his proselytisers; Sir Robert Napper certainly thought so when he insisted that 'we must think, now this matter breaketh out to open flame, that all is drawn from the fountain of this pestilent libel, long past from time to time persuaded by their priests'.[69] However, the proclamation and articles were never actually published, so it is impossible to determine how many people may have seen them or been influenced by their contents.[70] It is more likely that self-preservation was the key consideration for many and, unlike his New English colleagues, Ormond stressed that fear of violence was the chief reason for defections.[71] Intimidation was effective, and throughout November,

---

66 Lord Barry in Munster suffered great destruction because he refused to join with O'Neill. TNA, SP 63/207(2)/19 (Barry to Cecil, 7 Mar. 1600); TNA, SP 63/207(2)/43 (H. Pyne to Cecil, 18 Mar. 1600); TNA, SP 63/207(2)/43(I) (Barry to Pyne, 17 Mar. 1600); TNA, SP 63/207(2)/8 (Commissioners of Munster to Privy Council, 4 Mar. 1600); TNA, SP 63/207(2)/9 (Power to Privy Council, 4 Mar. 1600).
67 CSPI, 1599–1600, p. 247; TNA, SP 63/206/33 (Napper to Cecil, 18 Nov. 1599).
68 CSPI, 1599–1600, pp. 247–8.
69 CSPI, 1599–1600, pp. 258–9.
70 Morgan, 'Faith and Fatherland of Queen and Country?', p. 13.
71 TNA, SP 63/207(1)/61 (Ormond to Privy Council, 30 Jan. 1600). Fenton also believed that

December, and January came reports of newly confederated Palesmen. Those named were mostly members of the Gaelicised Geraldines, such as Garrald Oge Fitzgerald and Murrough Nycogg Fitzgerald, and it was specifically noted that they had done so in exchange for O'Neill ordering his Leinster allies to 'suffer him to carry away his corn, without troubling him'.[72] The news was disconcerting because 'Garrold Oge is a Geraldine, a gentleman of good sort, and well reckoned of with the State. A dangerous example that such a one should run to the Archtraitor, to seek a safeguard for his corn.'[73] In County Kildare, O'Neill won more allies by creating McOrish as the head of the 'Bremicham' sept. This was a blow to the administration because McOrish 'is now followed by the most of all the rest of that sept, who have so infected that barony, called Bremicham's country, which hath always been one of the most civil and quiet places in the county of Kildare, as there are very few in it to be trusted'.[74] Less than a month later came news that 'eight or ten gentlemen of the Darcys, and as many of the Daltons of Westmeath, all gentlemen of English nation, are gone into rebellion, and we cannot but think that sundry others within the Pale and borders thereof will run the same course'.[75] At the very same time came news that while the steadfast Dunsany was away in England, his foot company, stationed in Kells, had run to the enemy and handed over their garrison place.[76] Recounting these events, Fynes Moryson wrote that 'at this time… the rebellion was at the greatest strength', and '[t]he meere Irish puffed up with good successe, and blouded with happy incounters, did boldly keepe the field, and proudly disdaine the English forces'. Moryson specifically noted that Confederate forces in Leinster increased by 1,280 men, most of whom were Palesmen and many of whom had been considered reliable servitors.[77] These were only the numbers which Moryson could say with certainty, and he remarked that 'most part of the rest temporised with the State, openly professing obedience, that they might live under the protection thereof, but secretly relieving the rebels, and practising with them for their present and future safeties'.[78] Fenton strongly believed Delvin was one of these temporisers, noting that 'I cannot thinke he will starte in his owne person, for that he will not loose the stake he hath at home, But yt may be, he will suffer his contrey and tennaunts to make their way with the rebells, wherein his owne saffety, howses, and goodes wilbe Included'.[79] Delvin denied

---

this was a key consideration: TNA, SP 63/206/81 (Fenton to Cecil, 12 Dec. 1599).
[72] *CSPI, 1599–1600*, p. 204.
[73] Ibid.
[74] *CSPI, 1599–1600*, p. 194.
[75] *CSPI, 1599–1600*, p. 252.
[76] TNA, SP 63/206/33 (Napper to Cecil, 18 Nov. 1599).
[77] Moryson, *Itinerary*, ii, pp. 272–3.
[78] Ibid., p. 273.
[79] TNA, SP 63/206/81 (Fenton to Cecil, 12 Dec. 1599).

it till his death, but in the minds of most administrators, it was very plausible that the baron would unite with the rebels; after all, he was an ardent Catholic who had contested government policies in the past, had healthy relations with many of his Gaelic neighbours, had relatives in rebellion, and had a great deal of land and wealth to protect on that frontier.

Irish councillors were shaken and they explored various avenues to respond to O'Neill's propaganda and growing support. Thomas Jones, bishop of Meath, decided to compose a reply aimed at the Palesmen, but Fenton recommended that it not be published because it might 'raise conceits and apprehensions in the minds of the unsettled multitude, when they should see an answer proclaimed to a matter that was not as yet published'.[80] While the publication of Jones's response was being considered in London, a second answer was prepared. This much longer invective was supposedly written by the lords of the Pale but, as Morgan has discussed in detail, it was more likely drawn up by a government official.[81] Neither of these responses were published for fear of inadvertently advertising O'Neill's cause, but the fact that crown administrators were in such a hurry to counter O'Neill's proclamation, and that the second response was ten times longer than the initial libel, is indicative of how dangerous they considered O'Neill's propaganda.[82]

O'Neill, however, was aware that his claim to a religious crusade still lacked teeth and, through his agents, he continued his appeals to Rome for an endorsement of his cause. Peter Lombard, an esteemed theologian and future primate of Armagh, laboured in Rome to secure an excommunication from the pope which would require all Irish Catholics to fight English heresy or risk eternal damnation. His treatise, *De Hibernia Insula Commentarius*, presented a robust case for intervention in Ireland by harking back to the island's past as a land of saints and scholars while presenting O'Neill as a pious crusader.[83] At the same time, O'Neill and his allies back home tried to wrest similar concessions from the Irish clergy. At the end of January 1600, Thady Doyne notified Lords Justice Loftus and Carey that O'Neill, accompanied by 2,800 foot and 300 horse, was on his way to meet Desmond at the Abby of Holy Cross to see 'if he can procur the byshopes and other pastors of the romyshe profession to geue out an excomunycation to all such as do Imbras that religion, if the[y] do not take part with hym making that now his quarrell of revolt'.[84] This was beyond their power but, in April 1600, Pope Clement VIII

---

[80] *CSPI, 1599–1600*, p. 308.

[81] Morgan, 'Faith and Fatherland or Queen and Country?', pp. 10–13.

[82] For a detailed discussion of O'Neill's proclamation and articles, as well as the government's written responses, see Morgan, 'Faith and Fatherland or Queen and Country?', pp. 1–49.

[83] Byrne (ed.), *Irish War of Defence*.

[84] TNA, SP 63/207(I)/63 (T. Doyne to Loftus and Carey, 30 Jan. 1600).

partially yielded to the requests of Lombard and other Confederate supporters by issuing a plenary indulgence to those who would support 'our beloved son, Hugh O'Neale, styled Earl of Tyrone, Baron Dungannon', who was now elevated to the title 'captain general of the Catholic army in Ireland'.[85] The indulgence legitimised the Confederate cause and certainly empowered O'Neill with its leadership; but it was not the same as an excommunication. Because it did not spiritually condemn them for eternity, the papal indulgence could not compel Catholics loyal to the crown of England to abandon their worldly allegiances. This was undoubtedly a comfort to many Catholic Palesmen because, as far as many of them were concerned, the overlordship of a heretical English queen was still better than that of a tyrannical Gaelic lord.[86] And, even if this indulgence could have moved their consciences, the papal proviso came too late. The arrival of Charles Blount, Lord Mountjoy, as lord deputy in February 1600 marked a turning point in the war as English forces under Docwra, Chichester, and Mountjoy strategically closed in on O'Neill's northern stronghold. With O'Neill distracted in the north, the Palesmen did not suffer the same degree of harassment, with the result that many of those recently formed affiliations with O'Neill were fraying. In the meantime, Carew crushed the remaining embers of rebellion in Munster so that the arrival of the Spanish nineteen months later did not have the desired effect of inspiring the country to rise. The tide had begun to turn against O'Neill, and the Confederate defeat at Kinsale in December 1601 effectively broke the back of the rebellion for good.[87] In its aftermath, ideology was of little use to a weakened O'Neill whose subsequent inability to instil fear in adherents and would-be allies during the closing years of the war meant his propaganda lacked credibility and potency. This does not mean administrators had been wrong to worry.

The Problem with Secret Traitors

Old English loyalty was not beyond reproach and administrators' anxieties about the effectiveness of O'Neill's propaganda were justified. The failure of Old English constitutional appeals to the crown in previous decades had left some favouring more drastic measures. Although they had repeatedly declared anathema the very notion of a partnership with the Gaelic Irish, the reality was that similar alliances had taken place in the recent past. In fact, during

[85] Cal. Carew, iii, 523.
[86] TNA, SP 63/202(4)/75 ('A discourse', 1598); BL, Cotton Titus B XII, ff. 112–17.
[87] For a detailed assessment of military affairs during the Nine Years' War, see O'Neill, The Nine Years War; chapter 6 provides an excellent account of the war's closing years.

the risings of Viscount Baltinglass and William Nugent it was the Old English who had drawn the Gaelic Irish into their fight.[88] These revolts, along with the rebellions of Kildare and Desmond earlier that century, had served to highlight a growing rift in crown–community relations as well as a capacity to collaborate with their Gaelic Irish neighbours. The severity of government reaction to these disturbances inadvertently legitimised their purpose and, rather than extinguishing political and economic resentment, the government's response hardened opinions and attitudes among the Palesmen, especially amongst those affected by the harsh penalties of confiscation and execution following their suppression.[89] In the aftermath, the Old English had grown more indignant, yet they had also become more closeted in their criticisms. As Secretary Fenton opined in February 1596, the nobility of the Pale 'seame to be discontented, but touching the causes, they are closs and pryvat to themselves, which makes me dowtfull of further hydden matter then I dare ayme at'.[90] Clearly, Fenton believed that their undisclosed but obvious dissatisfaction could have potentially catastrophic consequences. If common ground could be found in the early 1580s, it was conceivable that a similar coalition could be achieved a decade later.

As the Old English were predominantly residents of the Pale, the seat and heart of English authority, the unreliability of their allegiances had serious strategic implications. This was because O'Neill not only recognised their importance for toppling the English government, but he actively sought their assistance by playing upon their strained relations with the administration. In light of communications like that to Fitzpiers, and the defection of a number of formerly loyal crown servitors, administrators feared he would prevail. And, owing to the importance of the Pale region for the survival of English rule, many officials had come to deem the Old English more of a menace to the realm's security than any provincial Gaelic Irish rebel or malcontent.[91] Interestingly, a number of English observers were convinced that there was a hierarchy of treason. Captain Thomas Lee, amongst others, delineated various gradations of Irish traitors under the headings 'open traitors' and 'secret traitors'.[92]

---

[88] C. Maginn, 'The Baltinglass Rebellion, 1580: English Dissent or a Gaelic Uprising?', *HJ*, Vol. 47, (2004), pp. 205–32.

[89] Brady, 'Conservative Subversives', pp. 26–8. Lennon has posited that government reaction 'provoked a variety of responses under the general aegis of the movement for the defence of the Catholic heritage'. C. Lennon, 'The Counter-Reformation in Ireland, 1542–1641', in C. Brady and R. Gillespie (eds), *Natives and Newcomers* (Blackrock, Co. Dublin, 1986), p. 86.

[90] TNA, SP 63/186/90 (Fenton to Burghley, 29 Feb. 1596).

[91] See T. Lee, 'Brief declaration of the government', p. 111; Spenser, *A View*, p. 175.

[92] The most detailed analysis of these groupings was provided by Lee. See Lee, 'The Discovery and Recovery of Ireland with the Author's Apology', ed. J. McGurk (CELT, 2009). Similar views were expressed by other authors. See BL, Harl. MS 292, f. 173 ('A Direction to the Queenes Majestie

Open traitors applied to the Gaelic Irish and those defiant and perverted Old English borderers who were perpetually occupied in some armed action. People like Feagh McHugh O'Byrne, Brian Reagh Fitzgerald, and Captain Richard Tyrrell qualified under this category. Lee's more interesting designation was that grouping he termed 'secret traitors'. These, Lee argued, were far more dangerous than open traitors. Open traitors could be identified and neutralised with relative ease, but secret traitors were extremely difficult to detect as they 'seeme to bee subjectes yet doe covertly succore mayntayne and relieve the open Traytours'.[93] It was felt that the population of the Pale was predisposed towards becoming secret traitors because they were naturally attracted to the nationalist and religious cause but, reminded of the harsh punishments suffered by some of their colleagues in the early 1580s, were terrified by the idea of openly partici-pating in armed insurrection against their monarch. The supposed existence of these secret traitors seriously undermined the administration's sense of security because they were situated in places of utmost importance: the Pale and the port towns. These traitors were therefore well positioned to fuel the fires of rebellion through the illegal munitions trade, the supply vital information, subterfuge, and covert acts of sabotage where it most hurt: Dublin and the Pale.[94] O'Neill was eager to capitalise on this fact and some of his allies actually bragged that 'our frends amongst youe doe us more good than all those that are forth in action with us'.[95]

Amongst the most worrisome secret traitors were the merchants. In addition to what he had stockpiled and had received from Spain, a significant proportion of O'Neill's munitions were transported out of Scotland, England, and other places by Irish merchants, the vast majority of whom appear to have been Old English townsmen.[96] The scale of the problem is highlighted by numerous calls for legislation against trade between the rebels and 'the

how to conquer Ireland' (1599)); Exeter College, Oxford, MS 154, f. 66v (discourse on the mere Irish); TNA, SP 63/209(1)/28 (articles to be preferred by Desmond, c. 13 Aug. 1601); Maley (ed.), 'The Supplication', p. 71.

[93] Lee, 'The Discovery', f. 5.

[94] For example, TNA, SP 63/205/201 (W. Saxey to Essex, 9 Oct. 1599); TNA, SP 63/207(3)/114 (Carew to Cecil, 17 June 1600).

[95] Lee, 'Apologie', f. 17.

[96] A significant proportion of the Scottish trade was conducted by John Bath, a Palesman and 'close associate of the earl. He had established himself as "a great merchant of Strabane" and owned a ship to expedite his business.' Morgan, *Tyrone's Rebellion*, p. 182; Moryson, *Itinerary*, ii, p. 237. An advertisement to Sir Henry Duke provides some names of O'Neill's allies, including a John Bath who appears to have been a close associate of O'Neill's, close enough that he came with O'Neill and Henry Hovenden to a conference with O'Neill's brother, Art McBaron. TNA, SP 63/178/53(V) (advertisements sent to Henry Duke, 20 Feb. 1595). John Bath was later rumoured to have received a trade monopoly from the rebels. See TNA, SP 63/203/19(I) (extracts of a letter from Richard Weston, 15 Jan. 1599).

merchants in the borough townes & Citties', yet these efforts did little to halt illegal arms trading.[97] As John Dowdall exclaimed, 'The Erle of Tyrone hath fraighted Shippes to Danske for powder, and to England for Leadd, out of her Maiesties civill Townes.'[98] A year later Sir Edward Fitton, an undertaker in the plantation of Munster, lamented O'Neill's acquisition of 'lead for Bullett muskettes murryones Hed peeces sordes and dagers', all of which was transported out of England by Irish merchants, who 'as I learne are most obstynate papistes and recusants'.[99] They may have been recusants, and they may have been 'the transportors of Jesueytes, Semenaryes, and such licke papisticall traytors', but there can be little doubt that the promise of profit provided at least as strong incentive as religion when supplying the enemy.[100] As Thomas Stafford complained, the Irish townsmen were the 'principall ayders, abettors, and upholders of this unnatural Rebellion, which proceeded partly out of malice to the State for matters of Religion, but principally for their owne benefit'.[101] At the local level, Stafford explained that these merchants first bought up 'the Countrey Commodities at their owne prizes', that is, cheaper than the same could be purchased by crown commissioners. They then sold these commodities to the royal army rank and file whenever the soldiers managed to obtain disposable cash. The unreliable dispensation of army pay meant that crown soldiers were not a consistent source of income. This loss could be remedied through alternative business practices, and merchants were well known to 'issue their Marchandise to the Rebells (underhand) at very excessiue rates'.[102] Indeed, Fynes Moryson complained that 'the Rebels will give such extreme and excessive prices, that they will never be kept from them'.[103] The same situation applied to the merchants' international trading interests. While war presented certain hazards to overseas trade due to embargos, piracy, and detainment by foreign enemies,[104] it was also a particularly profitable time for business due to an elevated demand for military supplies and corresponding price inflation. Thus, taking advantage of present economic circumstances,

97 For example, Lambeth, Carew MS, 612, No. 270 (Russell's journal); TNA, SP 63/178/57(I) (motions made by the master for the supply of munition, 27 Feb. 1595); TNA, SP 63/187/19 (Dowdall to Burghley, 9 Mar. 1596); TNA, SP 63/200/67 (memorandum by James Nott for R. Cecil, July 1597); TNA, SP 63/202(2)/28 (Fenton to Cecil, 7 May 1598).
98 TNA, SP 63/187/19 (Dowdall to Burghley, 9 Mar. 1596).
99 TNA, SP 63/199/116 (E. Phyton (Fitton) to Burghley, 22 June 1597).
100 TNA, SP 63/190/10 (Dowdall to Burghley, 7 June 1596); Moryson, *Itinerary*, ii, p. 298.
101 Stafford, *Pacata Hibernia*, p. 109. See also, CUL, MS Kk. I. 15, ff. 387–89v ('Some errors to be reformed in the goverment of Ireland', Aug. 1598).
102 Stafford, *Pacata Hibernia*, p. 109.
103 Moryson, *Itinerary*, ii, p. 240.
104 TNA, SP 63/202(I)/29 (H. Brouncker to Cecil, 22 Jan. 1598). For Weston's problems, see TNA, SP 63/198/49(I) (N. Weston to Cecil, 27 Mar. 1597); TNA, SP 2/24/178 (Privy Council meeting, 7 Nov. 1598).

many Pale merchants, intent on profit, played a crucial role in maintaining O'Neill's rebellion.[105]

In addition to the treasonous activities of merchants, English officials were agreed that the Pale and administration had been compromised by clandestine agents. As early as 1594 Lord Deputy Russell was 'greatly suspecting that the earle hath som great practis with many in the english pall and som others of great account or ells hee wold never carye him self so vndutyfully as he doth'.[106] O'Neill even boasted of being informed of Council resolutions almost immediately after they had been passed, while William Warren gave out that 'almost nothinge can be keapt from him', including the 'closset of matters concerninge her Ma:ties service' discussed in private meetings.[107] During the early stages of rebellion, O'Neill still enjoyed the friendship, albeit a wary one, of many Palesmen and members of the Irish Council; some of these may have passed him information in the naïve hope that mutual understanding might lead to a peaceful solution. Most New English administrators were reluctant to blame one of their own of such duplicity, preferring to cast their eyes upon the usual suspects: Irish-born councillors. As Fynes Moryson argued, 'our secrett Counsells' must have been betrayed by Old English insiders because 'who could more iustly be suspected of this falsehood, then the Counsellors of State, borne in that kingdome'.[108] Moryson was of the firm opinion 'that the English Irish made Counsellors of State, and Judges of Courts did euidently hurt the publike good, and that their falseharted helpe, did more hinder refor-mation, then the open Acts of the Rebells'.[109] Whether this was true cannot be proven, but there can be little doubt that someone or some people were relaying a great deal of information to the Confederates. The continual leak of information greatly perturbed the queen and even as late as 1599 she felt the need to reprimand her Irish Council because 'either some of you cannot forget

---

[105] TNA, SP 63/187/19 (Dowdall to Burghley, 9 Mar. 1596); TNA, SP 52/56/586 (G. Nicolson to R. Bowes, 8 July 1595); TNA, SP 52/61/98 (Bowes to Burghley, 6 Nov. 1597); TNA, SP 52/56/620 (J. Auchinross to Nicolson, 1 Aug. 1595); TNA, SP 52/61/98(I) (Bowes to Burghley, 6 Nov. 1597); TNA, SP 52/64/329 (Nicolson to Cecil, 27 Feb. 1599); TNA, SP 59/38/1149 (Scrope to Cecil, 21 Feb. 1600); TNA, SP 63/178/53(V) (advertisements sent to Henry Duke, 20 Feb. 1595); TNA, SP 63/203/19(I) (extracts of a letter from Richard Weston, 15 Jan. 1599); TNA, SP 63/207(4)/105 (Carew to Privy Council, 30 Aug. 1600); TNA, SP 63/207(6)/78 (Chichester to Cecil, Dec. 16, 1600). For a more detailed discussion about Old English merchants and this illegal trade, see Canning, 'Profits and Patriotism', pp. 11–16.

[106] TNA, SP 63/176/33 (lord deputy to Cecil, 22 Sep. 1594).

[107] For example, TNA, SP 63/191/18 (J. Morgan to Russell, 10 July 1596); TNA, SP 63/196/31(VII) (H. Bagenall to Russell, 23 Dec. 1596); TNA, SP 63/202(2)/54 (memorandum by Stafford, May 1598); TNA, SP 63/207(4)/21 (articles of detections by Owen McHugh McNeil More O'Neill, 17 July 1600); Lee, 'Apologie', f. 34; TNA, SP 63/206/100 (Warren to Cecil, 24 Dec. 1599).

[108] Moryson, *Shakespeare's Europe*, p. 204.

[109] Ibid.

your old good wills to that Traitor, or else are insensible of all things, save your own particulars'.[110]

The very notion of 'secret traitors' meant that no Irishman was immune to charges of treason. Besides sharing intelligence, the inhabitants in all parts of Ireland were accused of supplying the rebels with food, shelter and money.[111] Although this was interpreted as proof of their disloyalty, it is equally possible that in many cases it was something akin to blackrent[112] and that the inhabitants were merely complying with the Confederates' demands in order to preserve themselves, their families, and their livings.[113] Conspiracy theories were rampant and rumours involving some of the leading Old English inhabitants of Leinster and Munster had been widely circulated since the war's inception. As the rebellion gained momentum the most prominent and trusted Old English servitors were subjected to close scrutiny and allegations of treachery. It was believed that the retinues of the most commendably loyal Old Englishmen had been infiltrated and questions were raised about the earl of Kildare and his associates on multiple occasions.[114] In 1595, the baron of Howth, a beacon of Old English loyalism, was allegedly implicated in a treasonous plot involving some exiled Irish nobility in Spain.[115] The baron of Louth was occasionally linked to O'Neill through his supposed involvement in a Pale conspiracy.[116] Theobald Dillon, whose lands were destroyed and who had ventured his life to warn the garrison at Athlone of an impending attack, was accused of being a 'very bad, [and] a greater abettor and temporiser with the rebels'.[117] More seriously, the baron of Delvin, who had served the crown valiantly, died in a Dublin Castle gaol cell after being indicted for treason even though no concrete evidence could be brought against him. Even the most esteemed earl of Ormond raised eyebrows. His personal secretary was suspected of colluding with the

---

110 *CSPI, 1599–1600*, p. 115.
111 TNA, SP 63/206/68 (Ormond to Privy Council, 4 Dec. 1599); TNA, SP 63/207(2)/42 (Saxey to Cecil, 18 Mar. 1600).
112 Illegal 'protection' money commonly extorted by Gaelic lords from the vulnerable residents of English marches.
113 For example, see TNA, SP 63/207(4)/4 (William Bourke and Morrogh Ny Moe O'Flaherty to Carew, 3 July 1600).
114 For example, TNA, SP 63/196/39 ('Memorandum on the state of Ireland', Dec. 1596).
115 TNA, SP 63/178/24 (R. Brown to lord deputy, 28 Jan. 1595). By contrast, for official recommendation of Howth, see TNA, SP 63/179/82 (Irish Council to Privy Council, 18 May 1595). For an account of the St Lawrences's crown loyalty, see McGowan-Doyle, '"Spent Blood"', pp. 179–91. See also V. McGowan-Doyle, 'The Book of Howth: The Old English and the Elizabethan Conquest of Ireland' (unpublished PhD thesis, University College Cork, 2005).
116 SP 12/275/5 (J. Chamberlain to D. Carleton, 13 June 1600).
117 *CSPI, 1600*, p. 293. For Dillon's services, see TNA, SP 63/207/85 (Savage to Cecil, 3 Feb. 1600); TNA, SP 63/207(1)/65 (Fenton to Cecil, 31 Jan. 1600); TNA, SP 63/207/86 (Irish Council to Privy Council, 4 Feb. 1600); TNA, SP 63/207(3)/25 (Dillon to Cecil, 8 May 1600); TNA, SP 63/207(4)/1 (Dillon to Cecil, 1 July 1600); TNA, SP 63/207(1)/65 (Fenton to Cecil, 31 Jan. 1600).

rebels and 'doth play some bad parts in discovering the enemy'.[118] Ormond was quick to respond that 'I haue knowen manye other abused by such as they haue trosted, and do think I may be so, thogh I hardlye beleue hit.'[119] Far more irritating for Ormond though was when Captain Lee announced that Ormond was the chief of Ireland's secret traitors, some administrators were willing to humour him.[120]

Most of the evidence acquired by the administration was based on hearsay and hypotheses; indisputable proof was hard to find.[121] However, by 1596 crown officials believed that 'many of the better sort' within the Pale 'haue bin practised withall, of whose sowndnes wee are rather dowtfull then otherwaies, specially yf the forreine ennemy come'.[122] In fact, it was assumed that many Palesmen, even within the gates of Dublin city itself, were 'alreadie generally in rebellion or conspiracie'.[123] As the war progressed and the prospect of a Spanish invasion became more likely, under the guise of a religious and national liberation, the rebellion's religious objective became increasingly assertive and threatening. It was widely believed that Counter-Reformation clergy, particularly the Jesuits under which label many clerics were erroneously labelled, were exerting a dangerous influence over the northern rebels. Equally concerning were reports that Jesuits and seminary priests had infiltrated all parts of Ireland, including the Pale and towns, where they laboured to persuade otherwise loyal communities to renounce their crown allegiance for that of Rome. The Irish Council was aware of the presence of such men in the households of Old English nobles and it was greatly feared what troubles might ensue from their activities.[124]

The constancy of the Palesmen had always been questionable, but their uncertainty became even more alarming when O'Neill's military progress critically endangered the Pale in late 1598. That summer, O'Neill's formidable associate Captain Richard Tyrrell was successfully campaigning and raising support in parts of Leinster and Munster.[125] In August, the crown army, under

[118] CSPI, 1598–99, pp. 222–3; TNA, SP 63/202(3)/35 (Ormond to Cecil, 24 Aug. 1598). Ormond's secretary is identified in the Calendar as 'Mr. Sherwood', CSPI, 1598–99, p. 238.
[119] TNA, SP 63/202(3)/35 (Ormond to Cecil, 24 Aug. 1598).
[120] For a full account of Fitzpiers's revolt, see Canning, 'James Fitzpiers Fitzgerald', pp 573–94.
[121] For example, one of the many rumours of a Spanish invasion, see TNA, SP 63/190/44(XIII) (J. Morgan to Russell, 23 June 1596).
[122] TNA, SP 63/191/23 (Irish Council to Privy Council, 16 July 1596).
[123] TNA, SP 63/192/30 (Irish Council to Privy Council, 28 Aug. 1596).
[124] For example, see TNA, SP 63/202(1)/70 (P. Hackett to Burghley, 1 Mar. 1598). Similarly, by the end of 1598 it was common knowledge that James Archer and Doctor Dermot McCreagh were entertained by the baron of Cahir whom they endeavoured to encourage to persevere in his revolt. TNA, SP 63/202(4)/34 (Ormond to Privy Council, 17 Dec. 1598); TNA, SP 63/202(4)/34(VII) (Ormond's response to Mountgarrett, 13 Dec. 1598); TNA, SP 63/202(4)/35 (Ormond to Cecil, 18 Dec. 1598); TNA, SP 63/202(4)/40 (Fenton to Cecil, 22 Dec. 1598).
[125] TNA, SP 63/202(1)/28 (Clifford to Burghley, 22 Jan. 1598); TNA, SP 63/202(2)/110(I)

the leadership of Marshal Henry Bagenal, suffered an embarrassing defeat at the Yellow Ford which left the army weakened and the country vulnerable.[126] The momentum was in O'Neill's favour and the Dublin administration, deeply conscious of the physical threat now posed by enemy forces, found itself under the most extreme pressure it had yet experienced.[127] The rebels pressed their advantage; raids and spoliation were reported everywhere, but more disconcerting was that these incursions were occurring within a few miles of the city of Dublin with no perceptible resistance made by the inhabitants.[128] It was reported that very few places, even within the most loyalist areas of Leinster, still held out for the queen. Far more worrying was that many of the fortifications lost to the enemy 'were betrayed by some of the Irish, whome the owners did specyally trust, the most of them beinge persons, as wee vnderstand, either norished vp by the owners from their cradle, or otherwaies tyed to them by many benefits'.[129] Then, in October, the same month that the Munster plantation was overthrown, the Dublin Castle plot which Sir George Carew had predicted more than four years earlier was put into practice.[130] This was confirmation that rebel conspiracies had entered the seat and heart of English jurisdiction in Ireland.

Uncovered at the end of October 1598, the plot to seize Dublin Castle had the potential to topple the English administration of Ireland. It constituted a serious Confederate conspiracy in which O'Neill employed some of his agents within the Pale 'to surprise this her maiesties castle of Dublin, and to subuert this Citty, and consequently to comitt to massacre and havocke all the English and their goods'.[131] The principal participants in the planned assault were clerics and laymen from the Pale, thus proving official doubts about the Palesmen's allegiances were not without grounds. The attack, very near fruition,

(extracts of a letter to Fenton, 20 July 1598); Perrot, *Chronicle*, p. 144; Nicholls, 'Richard Tyrrell, Soldier Extraordinary', pp. 161–78.

[126] See Falls, *Elizabeth's Irish Wars*, pp. 213–29; Hayes-McCoy, *Irish Battles*, pp. 106–31.

[127] The Irish Council complained 'that vpon these sodden perillous occasions, which wee see do apparauntly threaten to distress this citty and castle of Dublin, which is the best parte of the liffe of the kingdome, and the borders adiacent'. TNA, SP 63/202(3)/142 (Irish Council to Privy Council, 3 Nov. 1598).

[128] TNA, SP 63/202(3)/117 (Ormond to Privy Council, 21 Oct. 1598); TNA, SP 63/202(3)/119 (Ormond to Elizabeth, 21 Oct. 1598); TNA, SP 63/202(3)/124 (T. Norreys to Privy Council, 23 Oct. 1598); TNA, SP 63/202(3)/167 (T. Reade to Cecil, 20 Nov. 1598); TNA, SP 63/202(4)/3 (Reade to Cecil, 1 Dec. 1598); TNA, SP 63/202(4)/19(I) ('Garrison Plot by Reade', n.d.); TNA, SP 63/202(4)/40 (Fenton to Cecil, 22 Dec. 1598); TNA, SP 63/202(4)/46(I) (Lane's project for service, 23 Dec. 1598); HMC *Salisbury MSS*, viii, 433.

[129] TNA, SP 63/202(3)/168 (Irish Council to Privy Council, 23 Nov. 1598).

[130] TNA, SP 63/174/13(1) (treatise on Ireland by Carew, Apr. 1594). For a discussion of the Dublin Castle Plot, see Chapter 2.

[131] TNA, SP 63/202(3)/135 (Irish Council to Privy Council, 31 Oct. 1598).

was to be executed by thirty 'resolute men, sett on by 29 preests lyinge in Dublin', 1,000 men from Tyrone, and a further 1,000 of 'the mountaine rebells'.[132] Following the plot's discovery, administrators were convinced the plan had been devised and promoted by Catholic clerics, and the leading conspirators, 'all of this countrey', were identified as Lapley, Cawell, John Shelton,[133] Friar Peter Nangle, John Leynan, and Bethall.[134] Of these, John Lapley had only weeks before told Lord Justice Gardiner that he had been dispatched to Ireland by Cecil and Sir Walter Raleigh to effect some secret piece of service against O'Neill.[135] Lapley was therefore a secret traitor and yet another example of why Irish-born servitors could not be trusted. Many of the conspirators, including Lapley, Cawell, and Shelton, were tried according to the law and put to death as traitors 'within these 2 daies'.[136] Bethall was captured shortly after and shared the same fate. As for the remaining heads of this conspiracy, Leynan was granted a pardon for informing on his colleagues, and Nangle, 'beinge a chief plotter of the treason', escaped the government's search.[137] Nangle had been considered particularly active in rousing support within the Pale, but by 1 December he had successfully absconded into the north with O'Neill, 'whose lyenge in those partes will encrease much mischeife'.[138]

The Irish Council was lucky to have foiled this Confederate conspiracy which, they reported, 'was so farr advaunced, as yt was very nere the tyme of

---

[132] TNA, SP 63/202(3)/135 (Irish Council to Privy Council, 31 Oct. 1598).

[133] John Shelton was a member of a prominent Dublin merchant family and was the elder brother of Thomas Shelton, translator of *Don Quixote*. After uncovering the Dublin Castle Plot, the Dublin administration also seems to have been keen to apprehend Thomas due to his own association with known rebels, especially Peter Nangle and Richard Nugent (son of William Nugent, brother of the baron of Delvin). The Sheltons were also related to the Cusacks. See E.B. Knowles, 'Thomas Shelton, Translator of Don Quixote', *Studies in the Renaissance*, Vol. 5 (1958), pp. 160–75.

[134] TNA, SP 63/202(3)/135 (Loftus, Gardener, Bingham and Irish Council to Privy Council, 31 Oct. 1598); HMC *Salisbury MSS*, viii, 412.

[135] SP/63/202(3)/114 (Gardener to Cecil, 17 Oct. 1598). Lapley had recently arrived in Ireland from England with an unidentified friar, perhaps one of those named by the Irish Council. HMC *Salisbury MSS*, viii, 412. Ormond calls Lapley a captain and his name falls under the list of men 'all of this countrey'. TNA, SP 63/202(4)/34 (Ormond to Privy Council, 17 Dec. 1598); TNA, SP 63/202(3)/135 (Loftus, Gardener, Bingham and Irish Council to Privy Council, 31 Oct. 1598); HMC *Salisbury MSS*, viii, 412.

[136] TNA, SP 63/202(3)/135 (Loftus, Gardener, Bingham and Irish Council to Privy Council, 31 Oct. 1598); HMC *Salisbury MSS*, viii, 412.

[137] Nangle, a Franciscan friar, was a 'member of another well-known Anglo-Irish family' and 'was, by some accounts, the master mind of the Dublin Castle plot. He had been guardian of the Franciscan Convent at Armagh and long active in the Catholic cause. His sister was the wife of Henry Shelton' and mother of Nangle's co-conspirator, John Shelton. Through the Nangles, the Sheltons were 'also distantly related to the Nugents'. Knowles, 'Thomas Shelton', p. 165.

[138] Nangle would continue as a close associate of O'Neill's throughout the following war years. HMC *Salisbury MSS*, vii, 218; TNA, SP 63/202(3)/135 (Irish Council to Privy Council, 31 Oct. 1598); TNA, SP 63/202(4)/3 (Reade to Cecil, 1 Dec. 1598).

execucion'. It served to validate prior claims that 'the Citties and Porttownes of the Pale are not free from the treasonable practises of Tyrone'.[139] It also proved William Paule correct that there were 'Certaine euil disposed Seminary Priests & such lik leude persons arryved & lurcking in Corners in this land with wicked traiterus intents & purposes. Not onely to stir vp the inhabitants of the same, to vnduetifull disloyall behauiour towards their naturall & Soueraign Princesse, but also to extend the drift of their mallicious plotts and deuises.'[140] It is surprising that so little documentary evidence has survived about an event which would have been, had it succeeded, a monumental disaster for English governance in Ireland.[141] However, falling hot on the heels of the crown's humiliating defeat at Yellow Ford, an open investigation might have amounted to an admission of just how vulnerable the Dublin administration really was.

The 1598 plot was not the only conspiracy to threaten the Castle during this war. In December 1599, Loftus noted that three other plots to seize Dublin Castle had been foiled during his joint lord justiceship with Sir Robert Gardener. Like the 1598 plot, Loftus offered no details other than to announce his centrality in thwarting them.[142] It is, therefore, quite plausible that officials preferred not to draw attention to these incidents so as to avoid advertising the administration's vulnerability. Equally important though is that the government had no desire to make public its reaction for fear of what it would beget. Not only would it signal that such a coup was possible, but the manner in which the administration handled conspirators would have provoked immeasurable outrage amongst the local population. Nevertheless, what the 1598 Dublin Castle Plot did demonstrate was that treason and conspiracy had indeed infiltrated the Pale and that O'Neill's clerical 'instruments' had succeeded in seducing a number of otherwise loyal Palesmen to rise against their government.

Old English Responses to O'Neill's Overtures

Unfortunately, we cannot conveniently divide the Old English Pale population into those who supported English government and those who strove for its overthrow. This community was not a homogeneous unit in which all members

---

[139] TNA, SP 63/202(3)/135 (Loftus, Gardener, Bingham and Irish Council to Privy Council, 31 Oct. 1598).

[140] TNA, SP 63/202(1)/17(I) (Paule to Loftus, 15 Jan. 1598).

[141] The Dublin Castle Plot receives only passing mention in a handful of documents. HMC *Salisbury MSS*, viii, 412; TNA, SP 63/202(3)/135 (Irish Council to Privy Council, 31 Oct. 1598). Several contemporary treatises do comment on the Dublin Castle Plot but, again, they do not treat the incident in any great detail. For example, see C.L. Falkiner (ed.), 'William Farmer's Chronicles of Ireland from 1594–1613', *The English Historical Review*, Vol. 22, No. 85 (1907), p. 109.

[142] TNA, SP 63/206/64 (Loftus to Cecil, 3 Dec. 1599).

shared the same cultural values and political ambitions. An example of the political disparity obtaining within this community is provided by the voluntary report of one Richard Nugent to the government concerning his encounter in Spain with a Munster gentleman named Ned Lacie. Lacie assumed by Nugent's readily identifiable Old English name that they were of like minds and freely disclosed information concerning James O'Hely's efforts to solicit Spanish aid as well as his confidence of Scottish support. Unfortunately for Lacie, Nugent turned state's evidence. Lacie and Nugent represent Old English individuals on opposite sides of the war: Lacie, eager for rebel success, and Nugent, who believed that it was his duty as a crown subject to deliver this information to the Dublin administration.[143]

There was nothing straightforward about the loyalties and behaviour of the Old English population. Some, like Captain Richard Tyrrell, the earl of Ormond, and Christopher St Lawrence remained steadfast to one party or the other throughout the war. But many others, like Viscount Mountgarrett and James Fitzpiers Fitzgerald, were on one side at the beginning and later switched to the other, sometimes on multiple occasions.[144] As Lord Lieutenant Essex grumbled, 'those whom yesterday I led to the field, fight against me to-day; and those who shot at me to-day, will come in, and fight on my side to-morrow. Such is the nature of this people, and of this war'.[145] Discussing the 'Irish Catholic party's' failure to achieve a united nationalist movement, Philip O'Sullivan Beare likewise explained that the inhabitants 'did not confederate at the same time, but when some had laid down their arms, others took them up. When some were annihilated, others renewed the war.'[146] The apparent capriciousness of many Old Englishmen depended largely on whether they were under pressure from one side or the other, or whether circumstances were favourable to declare themselves according to their own political beliefs. Personal relations also helped dictate behaviour because the loyalty of a local or family leader could be enough to deter individuals from following their own inclinations towards rebellion.[147] However, external conformity did not negate the possibility of private duplicity. Although the majority of high-ranking Palesmen remained outwardly loyal, administrators were deeply sceptical about their personal dealings. It was inevitable that virtually every Palesman had kinsmen and associates in rebellion and it was greatly feared that obedient subjects were

[143] TNA, SP 63/174/18(VI) (declaration of R. Nugent, 19 Apr. 1594). This is not the same Richard Nugent, son of William Nugent, who had joined the rebels.
[144] TNA, SP 63/206/116 (opinion and advice of J. Baynard, Dec. 1599); TNA, SP 63/207(I)/104(I) (advertisements written to Fenton, 13 Feb. 1600).
[145] CSPI, 1599–1600, pp. 124–5.
[146] O'Sullivan Beare, History of Ireland, p. 53.
[147] TNA, SP 63/202(3)/171(IV) (substance of speeches between T. Lee and R. Hoper, 24 Nov. 1598).

secretly assisting and protecting their wayward kin and followers.[148] This constituted the largest group of secret traitors.[149] For those who may have been able to
overcome the pollution of family ties and their instinct for survival, there was
a genuine worry that they could be bullied into compliance by rebels, kinsmen,
neighbours, or even priests. And, while many individuals' actions and affiliations may have seemed questionable, there were others who avoided openly
declaring themselves for one party or the other. This had been expected and, as
early as 1590, Sir George Carew hypothesised that even if the Spanish arrived
in Ireland 'those of English race, and especially the gentlemen of the Pale
(although for the most part throughout the kingdom they be degenerated and
Papists)... will either fight for the Crown of England or at the least continue
neuters'.[150] Carew had clearly overestimated the quality of crown loyalty within
the Pale, but he was correct that some would prefer neutrality. Such indeci-
siveness may have been an effort at self-preservation to protect themselves and
their positions regardless of the outcome of the war because it is very likely that
most people realised that if they found themselves in the wrong camp at the
war's conclusion they stood to lose everything, including their lives.[151]

Status, religion, family ties, location of lordship, extent of interaction
with Gaelic Irish neighbours, and political faction all played a role in determining the actions and loyalties of individuals. It was also widely accepted
that political beliefs could be set aside in favour of profits and, for many Old
English merchants, economics alone drove them to tacitly support the rebellion
through the arms and munitions trade.[152] Generally speaking though, the heads
of leading Old English families backed the crown and those Old Englishmen
who were tempted to throw in their lot with the Confederates came from
lesser, often rival, family branches.[153] This may be due largely to the fact that
those lower ranking family members had less to lose and more to gain by the
overthrow of English rule. For them, should the rebels be victorious, they stood
to be installed as the new heads of their families while the existing heads would
be overthrown along with English government. This scenario was exploited by
O'Neill, who purposefully directed his propaganda at the lower social levels. As
Captain Nicholas Dawtrey explained, 'the rebellious earl, hath both Jesuits and

---

148 Moryson, *Shakespeare's Europe*, p. 206. TNA, SP 63/205/41 (Essex to Cecil, 28 Apr. 1599);
TNA, SP 63/205/201 (Saxey to Essex, 9 Oct. 1599); TNA, SP 63/206/116 (opinion and advice of
Baynard, Dec. 1599); TNA, SP 63/208(1)/53 (F. Shane to Cecil, 22 Feb. 1601).
149 For example, see TNA, SP 63/206/81 (Fenton to Cecil, 12 Dec. 1599).
150 *Cal. Carew*, iii, 18. Carew's opinion did, however, alter over time.
151 For example, see T. Gainsford, *The true exemplary*, p. 30.
152 Canning, 'Profits and Patriotism', pp. 1–28.
153 For example, see Lee, 'The Discovery', ff. 5–6; TNA, SP 63/205/201 (Saxey to Essex, 9
Oct. 1599); TNA, SP 63/205/25 (Irish Council to Privy Council, 17 Nov. 1599); TNA, SP
63/207(I)/122 (Barry to Cecil, 18 Feb. 1600); O'Sullivan Beare, *History of Ireland*, pp. 51–2.

seminaries to employ in all places to stir the base-born of every house, or other discontented men of any family that are left without living, promising them that, if they beat the English out of Ireland, that the pope and his lieutenant, the traitor Tyrone, shall make them great lords'.[154] It was an effective strategy, and many men, like William Darcy, the poorer Butlers, and the 'Bremichams' of Kildare answered the call in the hopes of gaining titles and advancement.[155] Conversely, the existing heads of great families owed their positions to the English crown, and to rise against that which had established them would ultimately lead to their ruin. In the event that they rebelled and the English won they could be attainted and executed for treason. However, should they rebel and their contribution result in a rebel victory, there was no guarantee that they would benefit from the new order since the positions they held were representative of the former regime.[156]

Individual standing at the outbreak of war did much to determine the side with which Old English individuals aligned themselves; therefore, private interest, more than familial, ethnic, or religious motivations, dictated the actions of individuals. Understandably, the leading members of Old English society were concerned about the retention of lands, titles, and goods, and, as one anonymous Palesmen averred, 'no one of 10l. freeholde is gone to the Ennemye'.[157] The administration must have taken some comfort in this fact, as seemed to be the case when the earl of Kildare's loyalties came under scrutiny in 1598. Fenton dismissed suspicions because 'I see not how by breakinge his duty he cann better his estate, but rather make it desperate for euer'.[158] This is consistent with O'Sullivan Beare's opinion that the Old English, 'influenced by the favour and gifts of the Kings of England, for the most part took sides with the heretics, although themselves Catholics, preferring the cause of kith and kin to the Catholic religion'.[159] O'Neill was conscious of this, and so he focused on reminding Old English lords of their duties to God and country while admonishing them for their worldliness. For instance, in 1599 he chided Delvin because he knew the baron 'would not hassard the losse of a foote of land, or forgo his good meate, drink, and lodging, to advaunce the Catholick Religion'.[160] O'Neill was probably right about Delvin. But, like Delvin, many

---

[154] CSPI, 1598–99, p. 172; Morgan, 'Hugh O'Neill and the Nine Years War', p. 36.
[155] TNA, SP 63/207(I)/24 (Fenton to Cecil, 11 Jan. 1600); TNA, SP 63/207(I)/24(I) (O'Neill to W. Darcy, 6 Jan. 1600); TNA, SP 63/207(2)/126 (Carew to Mountjoy, 19 Apr. 1600); TNA, SP 63/205/218 (Loftus and Carey to Privy Council, 23 Oct. 1599).
[156] TNA, SP 63/207(I)/44 (Dillon to O'Neill, 25 Jan. 1600); TNA, SP 63/207(I)/136 (E. Fitzharries to N. Walsh, Feb. 1600); TNA, SP 63/207(2)/10 (Walsh to Cecil, 4 Mar. 1600).
[157] TNA, SP 63/202(4)/75 ('A discourse', 1598).
[158] TNA, SP 63/202(3)/147 (Fenton to Cecil, 5 Nov. 1598).
[159] O'Sullivan Beare, History of Ireland, p. 51.
[160] TNA, SP 63/206/63(II) (proceedings of Delvin's agents, 26 Nov. 1599).

other Old Englishmen were unwilling to risk losing their positions to advance the cause. Many doubted they would be rewarded, or even continued, if O'Neill's rebellion succeeded. Some, like Theobald Dillon, carefully noted how and why they were better off under the English crown. He declared that 'hyr Ma:tie… hau geven me more then the Revenu of my anchitors [ancestors]… & is in possibilitie to get more'. Dillon knew O'Neill could not offer him the same and he therefore ridiculed O'Neill's overtures: 'Do you thenke that I wold for sake so Royall a M[aste]r & my naturall prince for your sodden comyng to Dillons contrie, assuring my self I shall never see you there agayne, you must not thenk them to be andgels [sic] that wyshed you to send me such a letter.'[161] No doubt, this exclamation was at least partially for the benefit of crown officials should Dillon's correspondence be intercepted. His message was nonetheless clear. As far as most of the Old English nobility and gentry were concerned, O'Neill could not guarantee them any more land or income than they already enjoyed under their queen and they therefore refused to commit treason.

Security of land tenure weighed heavily on the minds of all men of property, and this was a point which Edward Fitzharries belaboured during an exchange with O'Neill's chief clerical propagandist, James Archer, in 1600. Pontificating about the cause, Archer stated that liberty of religion was not enough to satisfy the Confederates who would not rest until 'everie one disposed of their lyving this manie yeres were restored'.[162] If all Irish land was to be repossessed and English rule overthrown, Fitzharries demanded to know who would control Ireland. Archer responded that each territory would be ruled by its traditional chief in the same manner as an English earldom and, if necessary, they would pay the queen 'a yerelie rent & themselves to enioy & govern the whole Realme'. However, Fitzharries argued that the Old English had ruled Ireland in the name of the English crown since the Anglo-Norman conquest, and 'if that [the Confederate] course weare held & the mere right examined it shold then fall out that the Irishe nacion shold enioy the whole as before the Conquest'. This would mean the displacement of the entire Old English population, leaving Ireland to 'the Irishe who had neither learning nor anie waie inclined to civilitie to rule as superiors'. Archer, who clearly envisaged a role for men like himself, countered that the Old English would be continued as the counsellors and educators of these Irish chiefs. Fitzharries doubted this, and retorted that if O'Neill were to become the chief lord of Ireland, then the suddenly defenceless Old English would 'in tyme be banished aswell for suspicion of our loialtie to the Crowne of England, as for the desire of the possessions which we enioyed'.

---

161 TNA, SP 63/207(I)/44 (Dillon to O'Neill, 25 Jan. 1600).
162 TNA, SP 63/207(I)/136 (Fitzharries to Walsh, Feb. 1600).

As Fitzharries reasoned, one of O'Neill's proposed aims was the restoration of all confiscated lands to their supposed original proprietors, and it was therefore unlikely that Old Englishmen would be rewarded or maintained since all land had, at one time, been possessed by the Gaelic Irish. In fact, they were more likely to lose land than gain it if O'Neill stuck to this utopian objective.[163] To this, Archer's response must have seemed rather flippant and naïve. He averred that 'it was a vaine ymaginacion, considering the auncient Englishe were so manie which being banished… wold weaken the whole Realme' and that it was impossible to actually determine 'who had those places vppon the conquest'.[164]

Archer may have believed his own rhetoric about the future role of the Old English in a new Ireland. Others, like Justice Nicholas Walsh, did not. Walsh had received news of the contrary; according to his intelligences, O'Neill's Leinster allies had 'brought forth their Irish books, importing what lands the several stirps [sic] of the Irishry have had before the conquest, and… they have disclosed their purposes… to exclude all the ancient English gentlemen from their possessions'.[165] Walsh was not alone in this belief.[166] During negotiations in 1599, Delvin accused O'Neill of trying to destroy the Pale and its inhabitants in order to make good on false claims to lands there.[167] This fear must have served to deter many Old Englishmen from joining the Confederacy, and it probably made them all the more determined to defeat it. This was certainly the case for Walshe, who '[p]rays God to "beat down these cursed caterpillars, to the comfort of all Her Majesty's faithful subjects, who now are called out and most hatefully prosecuted by those miscreants"'.[168]

The testimonies of those Old Englishmen who rejected O'Neill's call to arms are telling. They were not as gullible as crown officials imagined and many were fully cognisant that O'Neill was merely pandering to their grievances. As Sir Patrick Barnewall declared in 1601, O'Neill:

useth all his instruments and means possible to uphold that combination, which by his practice hath spread itself throughout most parts of the kingdom … Wherein he useth this as a most forcible and potent persuasion; that he is acquainted with the condition of our estate, our defects and want of means in what kind soever, our purposes and designments, which himself frameth for the present, as may best serve the drift of his own practice.[169]

---

[163] TNA, SP 63/202(4)/75 ('A discourse', 1598); Exeter College, Oxford, MS 154 ff. 55–74 (discourse on the mere Irish); TNA, SP 63/207(I)/136 (Fitzharries to Walsh, Feb. 1600).
[164] TNA, SP 63/207(I)/136 (Fitzharries to Walsh, Feb. 1600).
[165] CSPI, 1600, p. 17.
[166] For instance, TNA, SP 63/202(4)/75 ('A discourse', 1598).
[167] TNA, SP 63/206/63(I) (Delvin's instructions, 25 Nov. 1599).
[168] CSPI, 1600, p. 17.
[169] CSPI, 1600–1601, p. 166.

There was a deep distrust of O'Neill and many Palesmen were convinced that his rebellion was motivated by ruthless personal ambition rather than any sense of obligation to his fellow countrymen or their religion.[170] In response to O'Neill's call for a crusade, a number of Old Englishmen pointedly stated that they had not been subjected to any form of religious persecution. As Lord Barry declared in 1600, 'Hir highness hath never rest[ra]ined me for matter of religion… and… I haue setteled my selfe never to forsake her.'[171] A number of Palesmen also challenged the sincerity of O'Neill's commitment to a religious and nationalist cause. In 1599 the baron of Delvin instructed his commissioners to remind O'Neill that if he pretended his actions were for the preservation or advancement of the Catholic religion, 'all the inhabitants of the English Pale… and specially myself, are Catholics, and were so when he was not thought to be one'.[172] Delvin further argued that the Palesmen were better informed than O'Neill on church doctrine and they 'could never find in Scripture, General Council, by the Fathers, or any other authentical authority, that subjects ought to carry arms against their anointed Christian Prince, for religion or any other cause, and specially against so gracious a Prince as we have'. Delvin therefore warned O'Neill that 'the world in general must judge that he useth pretence of religion but as a cloak of tyranny, for which he may expect no other reward in this world, or in the world to come'.[173] Edward Fitzharries likewise argued with James Archer that 'accions of burning, spoiling and other misdeameanors, [are] contrarie to gods lawes [and] was not tollerable in men of their profession'.[174] Responses like these have survived because they were relayed to crown authorities as proof of the authors' continuing loyalty to the English crown. These were often accompanied by declarations of services and personal explanations emphasising the supplicants' desire to see the overthrow of the queen's enemies. As Theobald Dillon proclaimed to Cecil, '[t]hese rebels do say that the cause of their rebellion is for religion', but 'they have no more religion than dogs… [and] I protest I would sooner trust Turks than them'.[175] As contrived as these ripostes may seem, for many Old Englishmen, O'Neill was just another Gaelic tyrant and becoming his vassals would be an insult to their Old English heritage. No matter how hard they tried, they could not convince the crown of this fact.

Political allegiances were complicated and multifaceted, something which O'Neill and some crown officials seem to have grasped at the time. The

---

170 Morgan, 'Faith and Fatherland or Queen and Country?', p. 17.
171 TNA, SP 63/207(I)/123(III) (Barry's answer to O'Neill, 16 Feb. 1600). See also Stafford, *Pacata Hibernia*, pp. 37–8; Hazard, *Faith and Patronage*, p. 39, n. 197 and n. 198; Morgan, 'Faith and Fatherland or Queen and Country?', p. 14.
172 *CSPI, 1599–1600*, p. 292.
173 Ibid.
174 TNA, SP 63/207(I)/136 (Fitzharries to Walsh, Feb. 1600).
175 *CSPI, 1600*, p. 291.

experiences of Fitzpiers, Delvin, Dillon, and Fitzharries reveal the complexity of the times while highlighting some very intriguing features at play during the Nine Years' War. They demonstrate O'Neill's desire to draw the Old English Palesmen into his fight. In doing so, he was shrewd, calculating, and adaptable. He addressed their community by preying upon their grievances with progressively sophisticated logic and promising them a 'native' solution. He also appealed to them individually with terms designed to tug at spiritual and patriotic heartstrings. Should that not work, O'Neill was prepared to use force under the pretence that he could not stand by while Irish-born Catholics served a heretical foreign prince. Conscious of already strained crown–community relations and past revolts, crown administrators greatly feared O'Neill's faith and fatherland propaganda would persuade the Old English to join him. They appreciated that promises of lands, titles, and riches, combined with threats of destruction, could easily sway members of an increasingly disaffected community. Particularly worrisome was the thought that many would do so secretly. Because they had access to the most important political and economic centres, crown officials were agreed that no Palesman could be trusted. There were a number of Old Englishmen who eagerly joined the revolt, but most of these were the disenfranchised and younger sons of younger sons. In spite of all administrative fears and suspicions, O'Neill found it an uphill task to persuade leading members of this community to defend their homeland from foreign aggression. Personal ambition, internecine rivalries, and self-protection loomed large in the minds of all individuals, and these were equally, if not more, important than notions of loyalty to a distant monarch or attachment to a native soil. Many Palesmen genuinely believed that they had a more prosperous future as subjects of the English crown than as vassals of a Gaelic lord. This was not merely declared through words but, as the following chapters will elaborate, it was demonstrated through military action, support, and sacrifice. The fact was that no matter how eloquent and persuasive his rhetoric, the Old English of the Pale would never accept O'Neill – or any other man of Gaelic blood – as their ruler.

4

'Patriot Games': *Old English Participation in the Crown's Military Enterprise*

Sixteenth-century English commentators constantly denigrated the dedication, dependability, and loyalty of Ireland's Old English Pale community. Yet contemporary records pertaining to the Nine Years' War show that large numbers of Old Englishmen willingly served the crown against their Gaelic Irish Catholic countrymen. These records suggest that the military contribution of the Old English Pale community has been grossly underestimated and that the role of the Palesmen in the eventual victory of the English crown deserves more detailed examination.[1] In order to do this, disparaging comments must be weighed against surviving testimonies of military performance. The rare laudatory commendations of certain servitors demand consideration as a means for exploring the achievements and careers of those involved. Condemnation is the overriding theme, but there are a number of records which praise extraordinary feats of martial service by specific Old English individuals and these offer important insight into the military participation of the wider community. A case in point is James Sedgrave, 'a gentleman Cornett' and 'an Irish Meath-man of great size and courage', who distinguished himself on the battlefield at Clontibret on 27 May 1595.[2]

Clontibret was the first true test of arms during this conflict at which the Irish Confederacy inflicted an embarrassing 'moral' defeat on the queen's army.[3] Though badly shaken and demoralised, that the crown army managed to escape total annihilation can be almost entirely attributed to the valiant actions of one man, James Sedgrave. The details of this battle have been recounted elsewhere and need only be summarised here.[4] On 25 May 1597 Hugh O'Neill's nemesis, Marshal Henry Bagenal, marched out of Newry at the head of an impressive

---

[1] In his study of English recruitment and supply for this war, John McGurk drew attention to this problem. McGurk, *Elizabethan Conquest*, p. 43.

[2] TNA, SP 63/180/23 (Lane to Burghley, 9 June 1595); O'Sullivan Beare, *History of Ireland*, p. 87.

[3] As Hayes-McCoy has noted, this was a 'moral victory' for Hugh O'Neill and his confederates because they had now shown they were fully capable of confronting and battering the English army on its own terms. Hayes-McCoy, *Irish Battles*, p. 88.

[4] Hayes-McCoy, *Irish Battles*, pp. 87–105; Hayes-McCoy, 'The Tide of Victory and Defeat: I. The Battle of Clontibret, 1595', *Studies: An Irish Quarterly Review*, Vol. 38, No. 150 (1949), pp. 158–68; L. Ó Mearáin, 'The Battle of Clontibret', *Clogher Record*, Vol. 1, No. 4 (1956), pp. 1–28.

crown force, supposedly so large as to intimidate the enemy from showing its face. Their mission was to relieve the beleaguered Monaghan fort, which they achieved with relative ease.[5] Having successfully supplied the garrison, the army began the return journey to Newry on 27 May, but by an alternate route. This time the marching column was ambushed in a terrain unconducive to its preferred methods of combat. By midday, the crown army, already handicapped by large numbers of raw recruits and a severe shortage of experienced military commanders, was running short on powder and faltering under a constant barrage of well-aimed musket volleys and cavalry charges by the Irish enemy. In effect, the great crown army was fighting a losing battle. Amidst the ensuing melee, Hugh O'Neill had ridden to the front to encourage and lead his troops in the final push towards their imminent victory; it was at this point that James Sedgrave made a daring but decisive move.

Upon hearing that O'Neill was visible at the head of a rebel company, Sedgrave took the initiative and assembled 'a troop of picked Irish and English horse' to charge O'Neill's company.[6] According to the crown muster master, Sir Ralph Lane, Sedgrave 'chardged the greate troupe of Therle... and there incounter was soe rude, that they booth were vnhorsed'. Once on the ground, the two opponents engaged in hand-to-hand combat. Initially, Sedgrave had the upper hand, 'having Therle about the neck' but, blindly stabbing at O'Neill's body, 'could not perce him nether with his stafe nor sworde'. In the meantime, O'Neill's men had stood aghast, but recovering from their initial shock, they now came to their leader's aid. 'Occahans sonne' attacked Sedgrave with his sword, struck off the arm which strangled O'Neill and thereby enabled O'Neill to stab his assailant 'with his skeane'. '[A]nd so he [Sedgrave] died.'[7]

Contemporary accounts vary somewhat in the specific details of this encounter, but all are consistent in the outcome: Sedgrave's actions permitted the crown army to make its escape.[8] Sedgrave's bravery had temporarily paralysed O'Neill's men with fear at the possible loss of their great leader, and by the time O'Neill and his forces had recovered their composure, the crown army had regrouped and was on the run.[9] Now all O'Neill could do was pursue the fleeing column, and this would inflict only minimal damage. The crown army may have lost pride and confidence at this engagement, but many soldiers

---

[5] There were a few minor incidents along the way, but O'Neill made little attempt to seriously challenge the relief convoy's sizable military escort.

[6] O'Sullivan Beare, *History of Ireland*, p. 87.

[7] TNA, SP 63/180/23 (Lane to Burghley, 9 June 1595).

[8] O'Sullivan Beare's account, written twenty-six years later, contains some glaring errors, including naming Sir John Norreys as the English commander when, in fact, Norreys was still in Munster. O'Sullivan Beare, *History of Ireland*, p. 87. See also BL, Add. MS 4819, f. 135; Perrot, *Chronicle*, pp. 95–6.

[9] TNA, SP 63/180/23 (Lane to Burghley, 9 June 1595).

managed to escape with their lives and for this they owed immense gratitude to the dead gentleman from Meath. Had Sedgrave lived in a modern totalitarian state he would have been hailed as the heroic poster boy of state-sponsored propaganda; but in sixteenth-century Ireland the value of Sedgrave's propagandist gallantry was tarnished by his membership in the doubtful Old English community.

The dramatic retellings of the O'Neill–Sedgrave duel almost epitomise the popular romanticised idea of the struggle for Ireland. However, while O'Neill represented the forces of Catholic Ireland, Sedgrave can hardly be said to represent those of Protestant England. Like O'Neill, Sedgrave was a native, albeit of English ancestry, of the very land which the English queen now wished to subjugate. What is more, Lane's account of the event noted that Sedgrave 'knewe' O'Neill, though it is unclear whether this was by personal acquaintance or by reputation. Whatever the case, this association makes it more remarkable that Sedgrave was willing to risk his own person against his notorious countryman, and all for the sake of the English crown. If there was ever an opportunity for an Old English Palesman to reconsider his political position and defect to the enemy, surely this would have been it – he may have been damned if he did, but he was dead because he did not. Without a doubt, the Old English community had its fickle members, but Sedgrave was proof that the crown had underestimated the quality of crown loyalty amongst sections of this population. Although his actions have attracted much comment since the event, the question of Sedgrave's ethnicity has thus far failed to draw attention to the military involvement of his community during this war.[10] The fact that the most courageous actor in the English army at Clontibret was not actually English raises an important, but daunting, question: how 'English' was this English army of conquest? The answer, it would seem, was not very; the 'Irish' contribution was impressive.

Assessing the Native Contribution

The focus of this study is the role of the Old English community during the Nine Years' War, and the purpose of this particular chapter is to examine their military participation in Elizabeth's final effort at conquest. Unfortunately, contemporary records present certain ambiguities which render an accurate assessment of the Old English military contribution practically impossible. This is largely because the ethnic identity of native soldiers is rarely explicit, and thus determining the Old English contribution from that of the loyal

10 O'Sullivan Beare, *History of Ireland*, p. 87; Perrot, *Chronicle*, pp. 95–6; Hayes-McCoy, 'The Tide of Victory and Defeat', p. 166.

Gaelic Irish poses certain challenges. Nevertheless, this subject is of critical importance for a study of Old English political allegiances and it is therefore necessary to establish some criteria on which to base an evaluation. After all, actions speak louder than words and it is only by studying the actions of Old Englishmen that we can determine whether their behaviour was consistent with their declarations of allegiance.

Existing records demonstrate that English officials had a definite preference for native recruits of Old English stock.[11] As Ralph Lane stipulated in August 1595, Irish-born soldiers employed in English bands were to be 'palemen and of Leynster and Mounster'.[12] Lord Deputy Burgh expressed the same opinion, insisting that when recruiting native troops, 'Choyse shalbe made of the most civill partes of the kingdome'.[13] Sir John Norreys, always reluctant to enlist local backup, specifically instructed Captain Warren to levy men within the Pale when filling his diminished ranks.[14] Similarly, Sir Richard Bingham in Connacht preferred that the native reinforcements sent to him should have been raised amongst the inhabitants of the Pale rather than among the natives of his own locale.[15] Thus, it would seem that references to native recruits generally meant those of Old English stock, and ideally from the Pale, unless otherwise stated. This, however, is far too simplistic an interpretation.

Because there was no systemised use of statistics during this period, determining the actual contribution of any ethnic group, be it Gaelic Irish, Old English, or New English, is virtually impossible.[16] Although there were occasions when officials attempted to gather detailed lists on the number of men employed in the crown's military establishment, very few of these accounts were preserved, and even fewer can be considered accurate. An illustration of this problem is a February 1598 communication from the Irish Council on English forces recently delivered into Ireland. The councillors explained that although the troops had arrived in an acceptable condition – and this was a rare occurrence – they were unable to reappraise the strength of these soldiers now that

---

[11] TNA, SP 63/182/13 (Irish Council to Privy Council, 6 Aug. 1595); TNA, SP 63/182/77(I) (Norreys to Russell, 25 Aug. 1595); TNA, SP 63/200/120 (Burgh to Cecil, 10 Sep. 1597).

[12] TNA, SP 63/182/7 (Lane to Burghley, 3 Aug. 1595).

[13] TNA, SP 63/200/120 (Burgh to Cecil, 10 Sep. 1597).

[14] TNA, SP 63/182/77(I) (Norreys to Russell, 25 Aug. 1595).

[15] TNA, SP 63/182/13 (Irish Council to Privy Council, 6 Aug. 1595).

[16] Only one thing can be said with any certainty when dealing with military statistics for this period: companies listed as 100 men were never actually that due to the allowance of six 'dead pays', and there were usually more. However, as Gervase Phillips has shown, there were incredible irregularities in the numbers which made up what were considered companies in Tudor armies, some could be as large as 250 men and others as small as twenty. G. Phillips, '"Home! Home!": Mutiny, Morale, and Indiscipline in Tudor Armies', *Journal of Military History*, Vol. 65 (2001), 322–3. See also C.G. Cruickshank, 'Dead-Pays in the Elizabethan Army', *English Historical Review*, Vol. 53 (1938), pp. 93–7.

they were engaged in active service. This was partially due to the itinerant existence of soldiers in Ireland as they were constantly shifted from one place to another. A far more troubling trend was that 'many of them by the yll handling of their Captens haue bin changed from English to Irish, and many dischardged withowt our knowledge' with the result that 'yt is impossible for vs to giue any certaine account, either of their bodies or furnitures'.[17]

Elizabethan muster officers were instructed to conduct regular checks and provide exact numbers for 'howe manye Englishe, howe many Palemen, and howe many myer Irishe' were employed in the queen's army.[18] But theory and practice were two separate matters. The greatest impediment to a quantitative assessment of the actual military contribution of the Old English community is that most contemporary sources refer to 'native' or 'Irish' soldiers without clearly distinguishing between the Gaelic Irish and Old English populations.[19] In late March 1597, Lane complained that the muster rolls submitted by the recently appointed Maurice Kyffin were inaccurate and accused his colleague of incompetence. Lane ridiculed Kyffin's inability to tell English, Old English, and Gaelic Irish soldiers apart, 'not hauinge beene able vpon the sudden to discerne an englisheman from an Irisheman, neyther by theire speeche nor by theire apparell, neither an englishe Irishe allowed from a meere Irishe'.[20] In Kyffin's defence, segments of the Old English population had, by this time, adopted the language, dress, and customs of their Gaelic Irish neighbours so it is hardly surprising that inexperienced English muster clerks had difficulty with these classifications. And, for all his criticisms of Kyffin, even Lane had to admit that all muster officers encountered deceptions which made drawing up accurate army surveys a tedious task. For Lane, it was not just distinguishing the Old English from the Gaelic Irish which proved challenging; he found it difficult to discern any type of Irishman from Englishmen because peculating army captains dressed Irish recruits in English apparel and entered these men into their rolls under English names.[21] So, as difficult as it was to distinguish the Old English from the Gaelic Irish, it was often just as difficult to differentiate between

---

[17] TNA, SP 63/202(1)/56 (Loftus, Gardener, Ormond, and Council to Privy Council, 27 Feb. 1598).

[18] TNA, SP 63/202(1)/54 (Wackely to Lane, 19 Feb. 1598); TNA, SP 63/202(1)/66 (Lane to Burghley, 1 Mar. 1598); TNA, SP 63/202(1)/91 (Lane to Burghley, 25 Mar. 1598).

[19] The Irish State Papers offer the most detailed accounts for muster rolls and expenses; however, in addition to the many exaggerations and other inaccuracies contained within these documents, these records are not considered complete as there are many documents which are known to be missing and there is no accounting for those which were never recorded to exist. Therefore, this chapter will not offer a complete and absolutely accurate assessment of Old English military participation during the Nine Years' War, but will attempt to examine their contribution so far as the sources permit.

[20] TNA, SP 63/198/45 (Lane to Burghley, 25 Mar. 1597).

[21] TNA, SP 63/198/83 (Lane to Burghley, 11 Apr. 1597).

soldiers of Irish birth and those of English. To complicate matters further, muster checks, and the officers conducting them, were subjective. Commenting on the recently approved allowance of twenty Irish soldiers in bands of a hundred, Kyffin argued that this did not accurately reflect the actual numbers of native soldiers entertained in English ranks because some councillors did not consider Old English soldiers 'Irish', and allowed them to pass muster checks as 'English'.[22] The fraudulent treatment of muster rolls was likely designed to portray a more 'English' army to the queen and her privy councillors in England, who were greatly incensed over the ethnic impurity of English forces. This poses a significant challenge for determining the actual military contribution of the Old English community since Old English soldiers could be considered either, or both, 'Irish' and 'English' at the same time and were hardly ever identified for what they were: Old English.

The problem of ethnic distinction must be kept in mind when examining the military participation of Ireland's Old English population. It is presumed that the numerous risings out from the Pale comprised mainly Old English individuals, amongst whom there would have been a small number of anglicised Gaelic Irish Pale residents. When discussing native companies and Irish recruits enrolled in English companies it is far more ambiguous.[23] With respect to companies of horse, the native component was largely composed of Palesmen; however, the strength of the army, resting on its foot companies, was made up of the least desirable elements, be they English or Irish.[24] For the purpose of this chapter, the terms 'native' and 'Irish' are used loosely with the understanding that contemporary records employ these terms to identify a group which could comprise either or both of Ireland's two dominant ethnic populations.

Military Traditions in the Pale

From the very first effort to exert crown authority in Ireland, the Pale had been the centre and strength of the English presence and the security of its frontiers had always been an overriding concern. The strategic importance of the Pale

[22] TNA, SP 63/197/105 (Kyffin to Burghley, 18 Feb. 1597).
[23] It would seem that when employing natives to fill the ranks of garrison companies in Gaelic areas the captains drew largely from the local Gaelic Irish population since this was far more convenient. This was indeed the case in Connacht. See Canny, *Making Ireland British*, pp. 97–8. Although one might assume when the same was done along the Pale borders that native levies were largely of Old English extraction it is, in fact, far more complicated and virtually impossible to determine whether those Irishmen employed were indeed Gaelic Irish or Old English unless explicitly stated.
[24] According to Sir John Norreys, there were too many Palesmen compared to English-born horsemen. CUL, MS Kk. I. 15, f. 223 (instructions from J. Norreys, 27 July 1596).

was twofold. It was the administrative heart of Ireland where, for the moment anyway, English authority reigned supreme. It was also the hub of domestic production and supply, and thus crown government relied heavily on this area to sustain its existence. Without this foothold, English rule could not survive in Ireland. However, it was not England which provided the equipment for the region's protection; this heavy responsibility had been the hereditary obligation of the Pale's Old English community.

Since the twelfth-century introduction of English rule in Ireland, the inhabitants of the Pale and the isolated quasi-independent English lordships had led a highly militarised existence. They did not constitute a standing army *per se*, but they did provide a defensive buffer zone, or 'military frontier'.[25] Magnates maintained their own private armies to defend and expand their lordships and, although they occasionally rose up against the crown over some perceived grievance, they usually acted on its behalf by taking responsibly for raising local forces to respond to localised threats. In addition to the lords' permanent retinues, their tenants were required to perform certain military services according to tenures dictated by statute. Each year all able-bodied male tenants could be called upon by their local lords to 'rise out' and present themselves for forty days of service. These local retinues or militias often joined with other local or crown forces as part of a hosting (i.e. a military expedition). Hostings had been a frequent occurrence since the arrival of the Anglo-Normans.[26] Notwithstanding periodic attempts to expand the boundaries of the Pale or confront enemies like Shane O'Neill, the primary purpose of these martial undertakings was to defend the Pale's frontiers from marauding Gaelic neighbours and protect the lives, lands, and goods of the Pale's inhabitants. Undoubtedly, there were years during which the Palesmen were required to exceed their traditional terms of service but, for the most part, conflicts were short-lived and the mandatory forty days service sufficed.[27]

---

[25] R. Morgan and G. Power, 'Enduring Borderlands: The Marches of Ireland and Wales in the Early Modern Period', in S.G. Ellis *et al.* (eds), *Frontiers, Regions and Identities in Europe* (Pisa, 2009), p. 120.

[26] Local participation was mandatory and, as in England, military tenure in Ireland was established by regulation; all able-bodied men between the ages of sixteen and sixty were required to maintain weapons appropriate to their status and perform up to forty days of military service each year, usually in connection with State-ordered hostings. By statute, only those individuals recognised as crown subjects were required to fulfil this duty; however, those who were not considered 'full subjects' but resided within the limits of English ruled territories were encouraged, rather forcefully, to do so as well. For a detailed discussion of certain tenurial requirements, see C. McNeill (ed.), 'Lord Chancellor Gerrard's Notes of his Report on Ireland', *Anal. Hib.*, No. 2 (1931), pp. 93–291. See also S.G. Ellis, 'The Tudors and the Origins of the Modern Irish States: a Standing Army', in T. Bartlett and K. Jeffery (eds), *A Military History of Ireland* (Cambridge, 1996), p. 120.

[27] D. Edwards, 'The Escalation of Violence in Sixteenth-Century Ireland', in Edwards, Lenihan, and Tait (eds), *Age of Atrocity*, pp. 34–78.

In the 1590s, when Hugh O'Neill and his Confederates challenged the English crown's right to the island of Ireland, the nature and consequences of border defence changed dramatically. This revolt was no short-term disruption of life like Gaelic raiding of years past; it was a long drawn out war in which soldiers had to be constantly ready for battle and the country prepared to supply their needs. Within a very short time the Ulster rebellion had engulfed the other provinces, but it was the threat posed to the Pale which made this rebellion so worrying because it was only through the Pale, and specifically Dublin, that one could hope to control Ireland.[28] As early as 1594 Sir George Carew had warned that O'Neill was fully aware of Dublin's strategic importance, it 'beinge the onlie place wheare the Deputee, and the Counsaile make their aboade, where the munycion is kepte, wheare the Recordes of the Realme are remayninge, And is neighboured to Englande.' He felt compelled to remind his readers that the Confederates were formidable adversaries, and 'lett vs not thinke that theie are soe ffoolysh, sithence all theyse comodities by theire comynge to Dublin will attend them'.[29] Carew's anxieties about Pale security were held by all, and the extreme importance of that place for English government and authority is best illustrated through contemporary allegory. Secretary Fenton frequently likened Ireland to a human body, its metaphorical heart being the Pale and the provinces its limbs.[30] Like a body, the English administration could survive the loss of a gangrenous limb or two, but could not survive without its heart, palpitating though it may have been. In times of crisis, when the army was weak, when rebellion raged throughout the provinces, and when rebel forces threatened the Pale, the administration's primary concern was like that of a field surgeon: keep the heart beating and cut circulation to the limbs because without the first there was no hope of treating the rest.

The Pale had become a serious strategic problem, especially if we consider the difficulties posed by the retention of fortified outposts like Monaghan, Enniskillen, the Blackwater, and Carrickfergus, all of which the crown was determined to keep. As Hayes-McCoy has noted, the queen's holdings in Ulster demanded constant reinforcements and supply convoys which usually required the deployment of the army's entire strength.[31] While these relief convoys helped solidify distant garrisons, they had to be dispatched from the Pale, leaving the heart unguarded. The fact that campaigning outside Leinster left the Pale vulnerable to rebel attack meant the administration had to either resign itself to a defensive war, abandoning isolated holdings and efforts to pursue the enemy in his own territory, or take a perilous offensive course

---

[28] TNA, SP 63/178/68 (Fenton to Burghley, 3 Mar. 1595).
[29] TNA, SP 63/174/13(1) (Carew's treatise on Ireland, Apr. 1594).
[30] TNA, SP 63/186/90 (Fenton to Burghley, 29 Feb. 1596).
[31] Hayes-McCoy, *Irish Battles*, p. 92.

in the hope of hunting down and eliminating the enemy before he could launch an assault on the undefended Pale. Striving to solve this technical problem, numerous military treatises were penned during this period, and notwithstanding a sincere desire to preserve remote forts, the authors' recommendations concerning Pale defences were always of the utmost importance.[32] Most reform proposals advocated the erection of garrisons along the Pale frontier, to be manned by English companies. In theory, the idea was solid; however, the crown army, for the most part, was either too weak to provide adequate defence or too preoccupied with pursuing insurgents in other regions to bother guarding the frontier.

This dilemma was clearly articulated by Lord Deputy Russell in August 1595. Although willing to march his English companies, then stationed along the borders of the Pale, into Connacht to assist Sir Richard Bingham, Russell was acutely conscious that the rebels would take his absence as an opportunity to harass the Pale. If, on the other hand, Russell did not go to Bingham's assistance, the president would be left with far too small a force to successfully subdue Connacht before proceeding into Tyrconnell to confront Hugh O'Donnell.[33] As Russell had discovered, the English forces at the government's disposal were insufficient for the task at hand; they were unable to protect the Pale and simultaneously confront the enemy. Faced with this reality, it became apparent that if viceroys hoped to campaign against rebels further afield they would have no alternative but to rely on the Palesmen to defend the seat and heart of English authority in Ireland.

Although the weakness of crown forces meant the Old English Palesmen were principally responsible for Pale defences during the Nine Years' War, it was desperation which had driven the administration to rely on them, not trust in their allegiances or respect for their traditional military role. It was doubts about the Palesmen's loyalties which had heightened administrative fears about Pale security. As fearsome a threat as Hugh O'Neill may have posed, it was discord obtaining within the Pale which made this rebellion all the more alarming. Even though the majority had held out against O'Neill's initial call to arms, Fenton, like others, was confident that the moment O'Neill declared himself for the Catholic cause many Palesmen would be prepared to support him.[34] It was also believed that if the rebels succeeded in gaining territory within the Pale or its environs many of the crown's traditional supporters would

---

32 For example, TNA, SP 63/174/62(I) (Dawtrey's discourse on Ireland, 24 May 1594). See also TNA, SP 63/180/61 (discourse by J. Goringe, June 1595).

33 TNA, SP 63/182/10 (Russell to Burghley, 4 Aug. 1595). Mountjoy found himself in a similar predicament in October 1600, TNA, SP 63/207(5)/121 (Irish Council to Privy Council, 28 Oct. 1600).

34 TNA, SP 63/185/33 (Fenton to Burghley, 26 Dec. 1595).

quickly fall away.[35] The religious cause and the rebels' impressive progress was a dangerous combination, but add to this the much awaited arrival of Spanish aid, and the consequences could be fatal.[36] Should Dublin fall to the rebels and their Spanish allies, Carew was 'perswaded the papystes and malcontents of the english pale… will not be dyspleased', adding that 'I knowe not anye citie, or almoste villaige in all Irelande, but in affection is Spanysh'.[37] As early as January 1595 Russell was already convinced that O'Neill had won the sympathy of many within the Pale and that some of these were now conspiring with their exiled colleagues to assure themselves of a receptive audience for the anticipated Spanish invasion.[38] As the war unfolded, very few of these negative predictions actually materialised, yet it did little to temper official pessimism. Indeed, by spring 1601, Mountjoy was given to assert that 'the baseness and dishonesty of the English-Irish inhabitants hath been the chief cause of the hazard of this kingdom'.[39] Existing evidence would indicate otherwise.

Cynical denouncements, like that by Mountjoy, were relentless. Yet, the fact that the Old English were primarily responsible for Pale defences during this period suggests that their contribution and dedication to the crown's military enterprise was a decisive factor in the outcome of the war. At the very least, their defence of the administrative heart preserved the government during periods of weakness until such time as crown forces could successfully regain control of Ireland's limbs.

The Pale Host

By the 1590s English administrators were deeply sceptical of Old English allegiances, largely on account of their Irish birth and increasing attachment to the Catholic faith. Most prominent Palesmen, however, continued to hold some vain hope of finally proving that they were not polluted by these affiliations and that they had remained unshakeably loyal to their English sovereign throughout the many controversies of the century.[40] The Nine Years' War was to put their loyalty to the ultimate test and the most effective means of demonstrating

---

[35] For example, TNA, SP 63/209(2)/124 (Fenton to Cecil, 3 Oct. 1601); TNA, SP 63/209(2)/155 (Bishop of Meath to Cecil, 20 Oct. 1601).

[36] TNA, SP 63/209(2)/261 (Carew to Cecil, 28 Dec. 1601).

[37] TNA, SP 63/174/13(1) (Carew's treatise on Ireland, Apr. 1594). See also TNA, SP 63/191/45 (J. Norreys' instructions to H. Norreys, 27 July 1596); TNA, SP 63/194/21 (Russell and Council to Privy Council, 16 Oct. 1596).

[38] TNA, SP 63/178/3 (Russell to Burghley, 8 Jan. 1595); TNA, SP 63/178/24 (R. Brown to Russell, 28 Jan. 1595).

[39] *CSPI, 1600–1601*, p. 267.

[40] For example, see Clarke, 'Alternative Allegiances', p. 258.

their continuing fidelity 'was to actively support the military enterprise against O'Neill' through 'the traditional aristocratic duty of providing men and provisions for military expeditions'.[41]

Hostings remained commonplace throughout the Nine Years' War, but over the course of the war, fewer and fewer were officially documented. Instead, State Paper records focus on military campaigns as the means for judging the crown's progress against its enemies, particularly in terms of territorial and combative gains and losses and the numbers of leading rebels killed. By the closing years of this war, unless it was to criticise defensive proceedings, the State Papers do not afford much attention to this vital Old English contribution.[42] It is possible that English officials took the task for granted as the natural and expected duty of the Pale population, or maybe they were reluctant to give credit to a community they did not entirely trust. Alternatively, those English officials who were normally in charge of reporting on risings out may have been too preoccupied with other wartime activities to fully acknowledge this service. Whatever the case, the early stages of the conflict offer a sample illustration for the frequency and duration of Pale hostings during this war, and because rebel encounters along the borders became more frequent during the war's closing years, we may assume that this commitment increased correspondingly.

During the eight-month period between January and September 1595, the Dublin administration called upon the Palesmen for at least four separate risings out. The first occurred in January. It was hoped at this time that the Palesmen would take charge of border defences while Lord Deputy Russell, with the strength of the crown army, pursued Feagh McHugh O'Byrne in the neighbouring mountains. On this occasion, Lane stated that certain regions of the Pale readily volunteered their services without any need for compulsion by the administration.[43] According to other members of the Irish Council, assistance from the Palesmen as a whole was not forthcoming. Russell complained that 'onely the cittie of Dublin, the countie of Dublin, and the countie of Kildare, haue voluntarylie yielded to furnish vs with 300 footemen, viz. 100 for eich of them Armed, paied and vitled at their owne chardges for 2 monthes to aunswere this prosecucion'.[44] It is unclear what was demanded of other regions or how they responded to the call, but the city of Dublin and the counties of Dublin and Kildare should have been commended for their willingness to provide the men, supplies, and money for a project which clearly infringed upon their prescribed

---

41 McGowan-Doyle, "'Spent Blood'", p. 182.

42 There was some attention given to a series of hostings during 1599 and 1600, but the records do not afford enough consistent details to piece together a coherent representation of the Palesmen's contribution during this interval.

43 TNA, SP 63/178/31 (Lane to Burghley, 2 Feb. 1595).

44 TNA, SP 63/178/14 (Irish Council to Privy Council, 23 Jan. 1595).

forty-day term of service. And, if there had been any recalcitrance among sections of the Pale community, the circumstances under which this hosting had been called cannot be discounted. This action was to be conducted during the winter, a most depressing time for service and an unseasonable time for travelling troops to make their way to musters. What is more, only two months had passed since the last Pale host.[45] Such considerations did not temper Russell's objections, who protested to Sir Robert Cecil that '[t]he Lords of the pale had direction... to assemble the whole forces of the pale... but so slowly and coldly yt was handled, that within a fewe daies they, returning, pretended only want of vittles and horsemeate'. Russell then concluded that '[t]here is nothing nowe to lett the Rebelles from coming to the gates of this Cittie'.[46]

Poor though their turnout may have been, in accordance with the terms set out in January, the earl of Kildare had taken up the leadership of the Palesmen's defensive proceedings.[47] And, within weeks of commencing the January host, Kildare and the other Pale lords were again summoned to the Irish Council to discuss further security arrangements.[48] As anticipated, the northern Confederates seized Russell's campaign in Wicklow as an opportunity to harry the Pale and, by the end of February, several depredations along the Pale's northern borders prompted a call for another hosting which was to consist of 'the strength of the Pale'.[49] Unfortunately, the total number of men to be raised from every Pale shire is not explicit, but 400 men were directed to rise out from County Meath, thus indicating that this operation was a substantial undertaking.[50] The duration of the intended campaign is also not specified but, having issued orders to assemble on 12 March, the administration decided to adjourn the service on several occasions. This may have been a tactical decision due to the scale of the operation so as to make the most of local military support, but it also may have been necessary since the Palesmen had been given unusually short notice to prepare themselves.[51]

Then, in late June, following the proclamation of treason against Hugh O'Neill, the Dublin administration called upon the Palesmen to defend the borders for another thirty days. Having held consultations with 'Kildare, the

---

[45] For the hosting of 27 November 1594 see Lambeth, Carew MS, 612, No. 270, f. 10 (Russell's journal).

[46] TNA, SP 63/178/55 (Russell to Cecil, 26 Feb.1595).

[47] TNA, SP 63/178/54 (Irish Council to Privy Council, 26 Feb. 1595).

[48] TNA, SP 63/178/39 (Irish Council to Privy Council, 7 Feb. 1596).

[49] TNA, SP 63/178/54 (Irish Council to Privy Council, 26 Feb. 1595); TNA, SP 63/178/55 (Russell to Cecil, 26 Feb. 1595); TNA, SP 63/178/80 (Irish Council to Privy Council, 8 Mar. 1595).

[50] TNA, SP 63/178/88 (acts and orders in Her Majesty's exchequer, 12 Mar. 1595).

[51] TNA, SP 63/178/68 (Fenton to Burghley, 3 Mar. 1595); TNA, SP 63/178/80 (Irish Council to Privy Council, 8 Mar. 1595); TNA, SP 63/178/82 (Russell to Cecil, 11 Mar. 1595).

Lord of Delvyn, & other lords of the fyve englishe counties', it was agreed that the Pale would raise 500 footmen and that the 'sherifes & principall gentlemen' would 'muster all men 16 yeres to 60 yeres to be in a redines'.[52] In addition to the 500 foot levied from the Pale, this hosting included provisions for a further 200 foot to be stationed in both Dundalk and Ardee.[53] After making these detailed arrangements with the Pale nobility, Russell and the Irish Council were soon displeased and informed the Privy Council that the Palesmen had yet again failed to fulfil their promises. Although Kildare had likewise complained that some Palesmen 'do not attende the service in sorte as they should', his actual tally of Pale forces demonstrates that many did in fact respond, including 'The Lord of Gormanston with 40 horsmen and the carbines to the Nobber. The Lord of Delvine, with the horsmen and the hundredth foote of Westmeath to Firmanagh. And my self heare at kelles with some 400 foote and not past 30 horsse.'[54]

The final hosting recorded for 1595 was also the largest that year. In August the incessant problem of border defence arose again and there was little hope that the repeatedly requested 1,000 foot and 100 horse from England would be forthcoming. Even if English reinforcements did arrive, the Irish Council warned that the problem of border defence remained unresolved because these recruits were badly needed in 'Mounster, Leinster, Knockfergus, the Newry and other places in Ulster'.[55] Only a few months had passed since the last hosting, but the Dublin administration was again compelled to hold consultations with the Pale nobility in the hope of gaining their assistance. This time the Irish Council appealed to them in personal terms, 'vrging to them the present daungerous estate of the tyme and what belonged to them to do in honor for their owne saffetie and defence'. Fortunately for the administration, the Pale lords acceded to yet another rising out so that 'thenglish pale and the borders thereof is left to the defence of the Noblitie and contrey'.[56] The Palesmen were ordered to assemble 1,000 foot and 300 horse by 16 August and these were to serve for thirty days at the expense of the country.[57]

It is for this August–September hosting that the State Papers offer the most comprehensive assessment of the Palesmen's proceedings. These contemporary accounts, which represent the government's position, offer great detail on how the Palesmen responded to the administration's needs, or to be

---

52 TNA, SP 63/180/48 (Fenton to Burghley, 24 June 1595); TNA, SP 63/181/7(I) (state of Ireland, July 1595).
53 TNA, SP 63/180/48 (Fenton to Burghley, 24 June1595).
54 TNA, SP 63/181/26 (Kildare to Russell, 13 July 1595).
55 TNA, SP 63/182/13 (Irish Council to Privy Council, 6 Aug. 1595).
56 Ibid.
57 Ibid.; TNA, SP 63/183/48(I) (lord chancellor and others to Burghley, 18 Sep. 1595).

more accurate, the administration's perception of their response. While the intended contribution of the Pale in this action appears impressive, English official reports imply that the project of raising the 1,000 foot and 300 horse was not taken so seriously by the Palesmen. On his arrival at the borders on 12 September, Russell reported that there were 'skarse 300 foote and 100 horse vpon this border, besydes my Lord of Kildare whom I found in readi- ness'.[58] Two days later, Russell again wrote that the numbers were insufficient, claiming there were fewer than 400 foot and 100 horse.[59] This he blamed on the 'exceeding backwardness in this people which I cannot but greatly complain of, for that the service thereby hath received no small hinderance'.[60] According to these letters, 100 more footmen had arrived at the borders within two days but, within a week, they had diminished again by 100 foot and twenty horse.[61] It is remarkable that Russell's appraisals of the strength of Pale forces varied significantly from one report to the next; in fact, numbers are not even consistent in letters written on the same day. Such discrepancies were not unique to this hosting, and similar inconsistencies can be found in records detailing the forces attending Ormond in December 1599.[62] This begs the question as to whether the Palesmen's numbers actually did change so noticeably from one day to the next, or was this symptomatic of a general predilection to disparage the Palesmen's services and, by implication, their loyalties?

It is necessary to establish some gauge by which to judge the Palesmen's proceedings on this occasion, and for this purpose reference is made to the Irish Council's joint report on 21 September:

> At our cominge to these borders, wee found here therle of Kyldare with 4 weake companies of foote and 100 horse of the Countrey forces, beinge part of the 1,000 foote and 300 horse agreed vpon to be leavyed by thenglish Pale and other contribu- tarie Countyes, the residue beinge not ready nor as wee perceaue, to be hoped for at this tyme, and wee brought with vs onely 3 companies of foote and 100 horse sent last owt of England, with 70 horse more compounded vpon the retynues of me the Deputy and some other smale broken companies, besides 80 horse and 200 foote which therle of Ormonde brought hether yesterdaie well appointed and prouided of vittles at his owne chardges... so as the whole force wee haue here for defence of the Pale, is but 7 companies of foote, weake in nombers and furniture, and vnder 400 horse.[63]

58 TNA, SP 63/183/28 (Russell to Burghley, 12 Sep. 1595).
59 TNA, SP 63/183/32 (Russell to Burghley, 14 Sep. 1595).
60 CSPI, 1592–96, p. 393.
61 TNA, SP 63/183/42 (Russell to Privy Council, 21 Sep. 1595).
62 TNA, SP 63/206/63 (Irish Council to Privy Council, 3 Dec. 1599); TNA, SP 63/206/68 (Ormond to Privy Council, 4 Dec. 1599).
63 TNA, SP 63/183/43 (Russell and others to Burghley, 21 Sep. 1595).

It is conceivable that the Pale lords had not fulfilled their consensual obligation, yet Russell's first tallies were compiled twenty-six days into the agreed thirty-day hosting and the Council's report was composed a full week after the host was entitled to disband. There is no denying that the Palesmen had not raised the number of men required, for which consideration will soon be offered, but it is also possible that their forces had already begun dispersing. Regardless of admin- istrative censures, the fact remains that between the native forces commanded by the earls of Kildare and Ormond, the Old English contribution to this project was at least double that of the English themselves. There were only three English companies and 170 English horse whereas the Palesmen, under Kildare's leadership, had raised four foot companies and 100 horse, while Ormond had presented himself with a further 200 foot and eighty horse. What is more, all these native servitors, Ormond included, personally bore the expenses of their military contribution 'without any allowance from Her Majesty'.[64] Therefore, complaints about the Palesmen aside, on this occasion, and on many others, they were the mainstay of Pale defence both physically and fiscally.

Notwithstanding their habitual criticisms of the Palesmen's activities and enthusiasm, English administrators relied heavily on Pale hosts for border defence and other helps throughout this war. Although he frequently complained that the country answered 'the general hosting exceeding slowly and backwardly', Lord Deputy Mountjoy's communications betray the admin- istration's heavy dependence on the Palesmen's traditional services.[65] Upon rumours of the imminent Spanish invasion, Mountjoy specifically requested that Kildare be stayed from going into England because he was an indis- pensable agent for arranging border defences.[66] When the Spanish invasion did materialise, Mountjoy left 'thenglishe Pale… to the defence of God and the Contrey' while he and the crown army confronted del Aguila's forces in Kinsale.[67] In addition to these border responsibilities, special charges were given to Kildare, Delvin, Dunsany, and Sir Francis Shane 'to coste and followe the Rebells and empeach them in there Iournay as mutch as they may'.[68] And,

---

[64] *CSPI, 1592–96*, p. 410.

[65] TNA, SP 63/208(3)/83 (Mountjoy, Wingfield, and Bourchier to Privy Council, 19 July 1601).

[66] TNA, SP 63/209(1)/101A (Mountjoy to Fenton, 22 Sep. 1601). Other Old English, including the barons of Dunsany and Delvin, and Sir Theobald Dillon, were likewise charged with making arrangements for border defences. TNA, SP 63/209(2)/152 (T. Dillon to Cecil, 17 Oct. 1601); TNA, SP 63/209(2)/155 (Bishop of Meath to Cecil, 20 Oct. 1601); TNA, SP 63/209(1)/112 (Fenton to Cecil, 29 Sep. 1601). See also TNA, SP 63/209(2)/199 (Carey to Cecil, 23 Nov. 1601).

[67] TNA, SP 63/209(2)/179 (lord chancellor and Council to Privy Council, 7 Nov. 1601); TNA, SP 63/209(2)/118 (Irish Council to Privy Council, 1 Oct. 1601).

[68] TNA, SP 63/209(2)/199 (Carey to Cecil, 23 Nov. 1601); TNA, SP 63/209(2)/168A (Mountjoy and Councillors to Loftus and Dublin Council, 25 Oct. 1601); TNA, SP 63/210/8 (Loftus and Council to Privy Council, 12 Jan. 1602).

following the Spanish–Confederate defeat at Kinsale, the Pale lords were charged with intercepting retreating rebels as they passed through the Pale and its environs.[69] As usual, officials found much to be desired in the Palesmen's conduct and informed the Privy Council that 'notwithstandinge theis direccions, given tymely ynough to haue given him some stopp or interrupcion in his passage… wee vnderstand that he [O'Neill] with the Rabble he brought with him, passed all alonge without encounter'.[70] The speed at which the rebels fled Kinsale was dizzying and the Palesmen hardly had time to prepare; nevertheless, their failure to obstruct the rebels' passage north was used against some individuals, namely Christopher Nugent of Delvin, as evidence of rebel collusion.[71] While the less than impressive performance of crown forces at Kinsale and elsewhere was partially excused on account of their extreme weakness and the hardships of winter service, the Palesmen were not afforded the same consideration. For reasons like these, official complaints about the Palesmen's services and dedication must be judged within the context from which they arose.

The English Army's Irish Contingent

During the Nine Years' War, Old English martial pursuits far exceeded what was traditionally expected of them. Besides formal summons for risings out, the government made additional and frequent appeals to the Palesmen to prepare and arm themselves for self-defence. It is impossible to estimate the extent or scale of this contribution, but there is little doubt that it was substantial.[72] Like hostings, these services were expected and generally considered an extension of their natural duty to their sovereign and state. In addition to carrying out these customary military obligations, the native contribution included participation in fully functioning companies wholly composed of native troops.[73] There were full companies of Irish kerne – as Irish foot soldiers were known – which were often on the queen's payroll but led by their traditional territorial captains.[74] Other companies were composed of loyalist volunteers or the adherents of Irish

---

[69] TNA, SP 63/210/8 (Loftus and Council to Privy Council, 12 Jan. 1602).

[70] Ibid.; TNA, SP 63/209(2)/155 (Bishop of Meath to Cecil, 20 Oct. 1601).

[71] TNA, SP 63/212/2(c) (articles against Delvin, n.d.).

[72] For example, TNA, SP 63/186/51 (Irish Council to Privy Council, 9 Feb. 1596); TNA, SP 63/191/15(I) (J. Norreys and Fenton to Russell and Council, 27 June 1596); Lambeth, Carew MS, 612, No. 270, ff. 4–5v (Russell's journal); CUL, MS Kk. I. 15, ff. 387–89v ('Some errors to be reformed', Aug. 1598).

[73] For example, TNA, SP 63/178/31(Lane to Burghley, 2 Feb. 1595).

[74] Nicholls, *Gaelic and Gaelicised Ireland*, p. 98; Ó Báille, 'The Buannadha', pp. 49–94; F. Cannan, '"Hags of Hell": Late Medieval Irish Kern', *History Ireland*, Vol. 19, No. 1 (2011), pp. 14–17.

magnates and landowners like the baron of Dunsany and John Talbot.[75] The service tenure of these Irish companies varied; some were only temporary bands, erected when occasion warranted emergency measures, while others formed a more permanent part of the military establishment. Amongst these, some served at their own expense, some were commissioned and paid by their 'chief', and others were directly employed by the crown, though it is not unusual to find all three employment scenarios in a single company.[76] Undoubtedly, the native captains leading these companies were as money-grubbing as their English counterparts, but there is copious evidence to show that they accrued great personal debts in their efforts to maintain their forces while they vainly awaited salaries and rewards from England.[77] Moreover, as crown servitor Sir Edward Moore explained, although 'evell spirited persons' at court would argue otherwise, his lands were spoiled, his pay was long overdue, he cessed soldiers at his own expense, and yet he was still expected to pay his annual rent of nearly £600, for which he was utterly disabled.[78]

Assuredly, many Irish servitors had more worldly motivations than the patriotic defence of an English Ireland, but there is no avoiding the fact that they made a significant contribution to the crown's military machine. Captain John Goringe's June 1595 report on available forces demonstrates just how important Irish companies were to the numerical strength of the crown army:

> her Ma:ties Armie in Ireland consisteth in theis forces followinge; of the olde companies 7, of the Britanie Companies 13, of the new supplie 10 companies, and some 7 or 8 companies levied in the contrie, so that her Ma:ties whole foote forces cannot be aboue 4000 men, and in lykesorte to the number of 400 horsmen.[79]

---

[75] TNA, SP 63/175/5(XXVII) (note of new erected companies, 1594); TNA, SP 63/175/10(I) (disposition of forces in Leinster and Ulster, 10 June 1594); HMC *Salisbury MSS*, vi, 543–4; Moryson, *Itinerary*, ii, p. 43.

[76] For example, Theobald Dillon of Westmeath commanded twenty-five horsemen paid by the queen; he also commanded a group of kerne and, although it is unclear who paid these troops, it is very likely that he personally employed these men. TNA, SP 63/197/29 (J. Dillon to Cecil, 15 Jan. 1597).

[77] For example, TNA, SP 63/125/2 (Dunsany to Burghley, 1 July 1586); TNA, SP 63/128/86 (Dunsany's petition, 9 Mar. 1587); TNA, SP 63/133/65 (Dunsany to Burghley, 18 Feb. 1588); TNA, SP 63/142/55 (Dunsany to Burghley, 28 Mar. 1589); TNA, PC 2/17(2)/63 (Privy Council meeting, 13 May 1590); TNA, SP 63/173/31 (Dunsany to Burghley, 15 Feb. 1594); TNA, SP 63/173/63 (Dunsany to Burghley, 27 Feb. 1594.); TNA, SP 63/177/21 (Dunsany to Cecil, 18 Nov. 1594); TNA, SP 63/177/21(I) (petition of Dunsany, 18 Nov. 1594); TNA, SP 63/178/64 (docquet of Irish suitors, Feb. 1595); HMC *Salisbury MSS*, viii, 6; HMC *Salisbury MSS*, ix, 183; C. Brady, 'The Captain's Games: Army and Society in Elizabethan Ireland', in Bartlett and Jeffery (eds), *Military History of Ireland*, pp. 136–59.

[78] TNA, SP 63/207(2)/57 (E. Moore to Cecil, 27 Mar. 1600).

[79] TNA, SP 63/180/61 (discourse by Goringe, June 1595).

Here, companies raised in Ireland, composed wholly of the native population, amounted to approximately 20 per cent of the army, a figure which could be significantly higher if those 'olde companies' included any native companies, and if the native component within 'English' companies is taken into account.[80]

James Sedgrave, and many others like him, can be found amongst the ranks of what were purportedly exclusively English companies. This is not entirely surprising since any army which intends to campaign in a foreign country must enlist the help of at least a few natives. These provide valuable services: they act as translators; intelligence operators; provide expertise on local social and political norms; may have experience with native military practices; know where and how to find material necessities; and can serve as guides in an unfamiliar and hostile land.[81] But while native recruits are necessary, conquerors have always found it prudent to limit their numbers and this rule holds true in sixteenth-century Ireland.

In former times the Old English had been regarded as acceptable substitutes for English-born soldiers, but this attitude had been undergoing some change since the middle of the century, largely on account of the perceived degeneration of the Old English and their stubborn recusancy.[82] By the later part of the century it was felt that English companies should be composed of the crown's English-born subjects, and these were not to be confused with the loyal lieges of a dependent kingdom who were, for all intents and purposes, Irish. Sometime before the 1590s conflict, Francis Walsingham, the queen's principal secretary, made this abundantly clear, stipulating that 'very fewe, & but twoo or three of the yrish' should be permitted in English companies.[83] At the height of the war, the author of the *Dialogue of Silvynne and Peregrynne* referred to a statute dictating that 'there shoulde but six Ireland men in a band of a hundreth, and that of English race to'.[84] This may have been the ideal ratio, but the military reality of the 1590s necessitated some drastic modifications to policy. As early as July 1595 the Dublin administration had already authorised army captains 'to take a supplye of 20 soldiers of this contrey birth into every companie of 100'.[85] As the war

---

[80] This figure is an estimate based on the numbers given by Goringe; 18.9% if there were seven native companies out of thirty-seven or 21% if there were eight native companies out of a total of thirty-eight. And, assuming a conservative estimate that the English companies were composed of 20% Irish = 600 out of 3,000, this would mean that of Goringe's 4,000 estimate 1,300 to 1,400 were Irish, making the Irish component of the army between 32.5% and 35%.

[81] P. Palmer, 'Interpreters and the Politics of Translation and Traduction in Sixteenth-Century Ireland', *IHS*, Vol. 33, No. 131 (2003), pp. 257–77.

[82] Canny, *Making Ireland British*, p. 68.

[83] BL, Cotton Titus B XII, ff. 35–43, esp. 37b.

[84] H. Collier, *Dialogue of Silvynne and Peregrynne*, ed. Morgan (CELT), p. 135.

[85] TNA, SP 63/181/66 (Fenton to Buckhurst, 30 July 1595); BL, Add. MS 4819, f. 75 (collections made by Perrott for his *Chronicle of Ireland*).

progressed this figure was subject to unofficial inflation as government records reveal increasing numbers of Irishmen in English military ranks. By February 1598 it was estimated that Irishmen made up at least 'three partes of 4' in the crown army.[86] A month later Ralph Lane reported the army consisted of 9,904 men, of which the Council reckoned 'there are not one thowsand English bodyes to serue in the Army, but that the whole rest are compounded or subborned with Irish'.[87] Admittedly, the official record was prone to all sorts of exaggeration, yet there is a consistent theme: the English army's Irish component was in the ascendancy. With the benefit of hindsight, Barnaby Rich lamented that the employment of Irish soldiers had become so general that 'it might haue beene called a speciall and a choise company, that had not three Irish for one English'.[88] Consequently, maintaining an English majority was a bragging point for officers like Sir John Norreys who boasted that the horse companies commanded by him and his brother were the only bands in Ireland still filled with Englishmen.[89]

For all those concerned with the queen's service, the employment of native troops was regarded as a last resort to be used during times of dire need. However, dire need was the order of the day throughout this conflict because the weaknesses of English forces made relying on native military cooperation an absolute necessity. Advertisements from the Irish Council portray an army in a condition little short of abysmal. John Norreys asserted in 1596 that 'of the 3,500 [English] men sent ouer wythyn thys yeer ther are not 1,000 that doe nowe bear armes, but are either dead, run away, or conuerted into Irish'.[90] Throughout the war the Irish Council repeatedly requested greater numbers of soldiers, victuals, and money from the English Privy Council, but their requests were never met in full and, in many cases, not at all. Upon viewing the purportedly 600 soldiers recently sent from England in late 1600, Carew discovered that their numbers were only 350.[91] And, already insufficient in numbers, these English reinforcements were also giving cause for concern in respect of their calibre. It was often reported that a significant proportion of

---

86 TNA, SP 63/202(1)/56 (Loftus, Gardener, Ormond, and Council to Privy Council, 27 Feb. 1598).

87 This would make the Irish component 90% of the English army's strength, a very improbable calculation. TNA, SP 63/202(1)/66 (Lane to Burghley, 1 Mar. 1598); TNA, SP 63/202(2)/17 (Loftus, Gardener, and Wallop to Privy Council, 21 Apr. 1598). This problem was not restricted to foot companies; in December 1598 Captain Thomas Reade informed Cecil that there were 700 horse serving the queen in Ireland, but 'they are weake and vnserviceable, and besides they consiste moste of Irishe'. TNA, SP 63/202(4)/19 (Reade to Cecil, 10 Dec. 1598); TNA, SP 63/203/45 (Reade to Cecil, 14 Feb. 1599).

88 Riche, *New Description*, p. 109.

89 CUL, MS Kk. I. 15, f. 223 (instructions from J. Norreys, 27 July 1596); TNA, SP 63/191/45 (J. Norreys' instructions to H. Norreys, 27 July 1596).

90 TNA, SP 63/191/9 (J. Norreys to Burghley, 7 July 1596).

91 TNA, SP 63/207(5)/113 (Carew to Privy Council, 25 Oct. 1600).

English levies sent to Ireland were pressed men, many of whom were criminals and vagrants with neither the military training nor the money to equip themselves for war.[92] This was not an accident; the mayor of Chester reported that he '[h]ad search made "in the streets and other suspected houses for idle and vagrant persons. Divers were apprehended, fourteen of whom he impressed and put into pay."'[93]

It was not until the viceroyalty of Robert Devereux, the earl of Essex, that the queen finally committed to waging an all-out war for Ireland, reluctantly yielding to the tremendous associated costs. But even under Essex, Sir George Carey reckoned that the supposedly 17,000 or 18,000 strong army had no more than 10,000 serviceable troops.[94] Although Essex's failures in Ireland can be blamed on poor judgement and bad advice, he had come to appreciate that his impressive army was ill-prepared for the task confronting it. The main issues were the soldiers' lack of training and equipment, along with their melting away through sickness and desertion.[95] These were not problems for which the deployment of English reinforcements could wholly compensate. The conditions of Irish service were as loathsome as the war itself and the plight of the average soldier, be he Irish or English, was not an easy one. First, his pay was rarely issued in a timely fashion, if at all, with the result that he was forced to fend for himself in an extremely inhospitable environment.[96] Deprived of a disposable income, out of which he was expected to arm, clothe, and feed himself, the soldier was also faced with subsisting in an increasingly desolate landscape. In fact, it was commonly said that the soldiers' greatest Irish enemies were 'Captaine Travell, Captaine Sicknes, Captaine Hunger, Captaine Colde'.[97] These hardships made it extremely difficult to effect the kind of services the queen and Privy Council expected from men like Essex. Lacking the pomp and ceremony which surrounded Essex's lord lieutenancy, his predecessors had found themselves in even more difficult predicaments when any urgent occasion of service arose. Whether it was to meet an imminent threat or march to the relief of a teetering outpost, these viceroys invariably discovered that the forces at their disposal were inadequate for the task.[98] Crippled by weakened companies and the chronically slow dispatch of reinforcements from England, deputies and

---

[92] C. McNeill (ed.), 'Fitzwilliam Manuscripts at Milton, England', *Anal. Hib.*, No. 4 (1932), p. 313; McGurk, *Elizabethan Conquest*; Falls, *Elizabeth's Irish Wars*, ch. 3.
[93] *CSPI, 1600*, p. 412.
[94] TNA, SP 63/205/151 (Carey to Cecil, 26 Aug. 1599).
[95] TNA, SP 63/205/164 (journal of Essex's proceedings, 8 Sep. 1599); TNA, SP 63/206/25 (Irish Council to Privy Council, 17 Nov. 1599); TNA, SP 63/206/105 (Sentleger to Privy Council, 25 Dec. 1599).
[96] TNA, SP 63/202(2)/96 (Ormond to Cecil, 5 July 1598).
[97] TNA, SP 63/202(4)/75 ('A discourse', 1598).
[98] For example, TNA, SP 63/185/28 (Irish Council to Privy Council, 26 Dec. 1595).

lieutenants were left with little choice but to augment their army with the only manpower available to them: the Irish.

Lord Deputy Russell's experiences exemplify the dilemma faced by all Irish viceroys. Within a week of being sworn in he complained that the old garrison companies were predominantly Irish and that 'there was some 500 mere Irish men lately erected of which I still continwe my former opinion that they had bene better borne Englishe'.[99] But, in April 1595, when the recently arrived Brittany forces fell far short of the expected 2,000, Russell was insistent that he would have to levy up to 900 native troops to fill the incomplete bands.[100] His experience was not unique and other viceroys found themselves in similar predicaments.[101] In 1597, the Blackwater fort was in dire straits, but a relief convoy would require a great military escort; thus Lord Deputy Burgh was driven to recruit large numbers of Irishmen into his army.[102] This had become an unofficial, but universal, practice, and Essex, Mountjoy, and the lords justice all requested like permission to implement similar measures as official policy.[103] Notwithstanding such appeals for deviations and amendments to military protocol, the extraordinary enlistment of Irish troops by viceroys should not be interpreted as a lenient or favourable toleration of Irishmen in the crown army. For all of these men, necessity required the enrolment of Irish troops, but, like so many others, they were adamant that this was not a safe course of action.[104]

The Advantages of Employing Irishmen

In May 1598 Captain Stafford concluded that the queen's army 'standeth composed of twoe Nacions: Englishe & Irishe, both Subiects to the dignitie of her Crowne. The first naturall, obedient and faithfull, and the fewest in nomber. The seconde discontented, perfideouse & vngrategull, ever disposed to innovacion and apte to Rebellion. And they are by twoe partes in three

---

[99] TNA, SP 63/175/52 (Russell to Cecil, 16 Aug. 1594); Falls, *Irish Wars*, p. 185.

[100] TNA, SP 63/178/101 (Russell to Privy Council, 20 Mar. 1595); TNA, SP 63/179/5 (Russell to Burghley, 3 Apr. 1595).

[101] For examples of requests for reinforcements under Mountjoy, see TNA, SP 63/207(3)/81 (Irish Council to Privy Council, 7 June 1600); TNA, SP 63/207(3)/85 (F. Stafford to Cecil, 7 June 1600); TNA, SP 63/212/13 (Irish Council to Privy Council, 12 Aug. 1602).

[102] TNA, SP 63/202(3)/1 (Irish Council to Privy Council, 2 Aug. 1598); TNA, SP 63/202(3)/91 (Irish Council to Privy Council, 2 Oct. 1598).

[103] TNA, SP 63/205/30 (Privy Council to Essex, 17 Apr. 1599); TNA, SP 63/205/109 (Essex and Council to Privy Council, 15 July 1599); TNA, SP 63/205/131 (Elizabeth to Essex and Council, 9 Aug. 1599); TNA, SP 63/208(2)/35 (Mountjoy to Privy Council, 1 May 1601); TNA, SP 63/208(3)/83 (Mountjoy, Wingfield, and Bourchier to Privy Council, 19 July 1601).

[104] TNA, SP 63/202(2)/96 (Ormond to Cecil, 5 July 1598).

the stronger.'[105] But, for all the official moaning about the prevalence of Irish soldiers, crown administrators must be held partially accountable. The overwhelming admission of Irishmen into the crown's English army was largely the result of two factors: necessity and greed. These faults were recognised by many contemporaries and persistent complaints from officials in Ireland met frosty responses in England. For instance, when acknowledging certain difficulties with the Irish service in 1598, the Privy Council reprimanded its Irish counterpart because, 'by you giving passports daily for English to come away, and by your tolerating the Captains to take in Irish for gain, that will serve for half pays to fill up the bands... you are absolutely guilty of that inconvenience'.[106] For English observers, this was a war between English supremacy and Irish sovereignty and it is understandable that they expected the opposing forces to embody that struggle. Yet English rule could not be secured by England alone. Caught up in a series of international debacles, Elizabeth was unable, or unwilling, to yield to the escalating demands of the Irish conflict, so necessity dictated that the administration seek significant local endorsement. While it was essential that the administration strengthen English forces with additional manpower from the only available source, there were certain considerations which made such recourse less abhorrent: native soldiers were cheaper, more self-sufficient, often better skilled, and their employment deprived the enemy of their numbers.[107]

The Irish were cheap. They cost the crown half that of their English counterparts and many army captains eagerly embraced the financial benefits of employing them. Irishmen were specifically recruited for muster checks to fill places left vacant by sickness and desertion and, in order to make the most of their Irish recruits, captains made a habit dressing these men in English apparel and entering them into the rolls under English names so that they could draw the full pay of an English soldier but dispense with only a portion of it, and sometimes none at all, to their Irish charges.[108] It was not just the captains who abused the Irish soldiers in this respect; the crown may have made an allowance of half rate for Irish soldiers, but many government administrators expected them to live off the country without any remuneration whatsoever.[109] In August 1599 the Irish Council admitted this by noting that they had made provisions

[105] TNA, SP 63/202(2)/54 (memorandum by Captain Stafford, May 1598).
[106] CSPI, 1598–99, p. 201.
[107] McGurk has briefly acknowledged these benefits of Irish employment in his study of English mobilisation for the Irish war. McGurk, Elizabethan Conquest, p. 42.
[108] TNA, SP 63/178/31 (Lane to Burghley, 2 Feb. 1595); TNA, SP 63/202(2)/100 (Privy Council to Irish Council, 13 July 1598); Brady, 'Captain's Games', pp. 136–59; Canny, Making Ireland British, ch. 2.
[109] TNA, SP 63/202(2)/100 (Privy Council to Irish Council, 13 July 1598).

to pay Irish troops only one month out of every four.[110] And the lowly Irish foot soldier was not the only one who received less pay. When compared to their English peers, high-ranking Old English and Gaelic Irish military servitors received significantly reduced crown entertainments.[111] This is corroborated by Fynes Moryson's account of the pay allotted to companies of horse in 1600. Horse companies under Lord Deputy Mountjoy, Munster President George Carew, Henry Danvers, and Henry Docwra received 18 pence *per diem*, while companies under the earls of Ormond, Kildare, and Clanricard, the barons of Dunsany and Dunkellin, and Sir Christopher St Lawrence received only 12 pence.[112] And this was only a partial subsidy; most of the native servitors who put their personal retinues at the crown's disposal were expected to finance at least a portion of these forces themselves.[113] It might be fair to say that the crown was getting 'a good deal' when it utilised the services of Ireland's native inhabitants.

The financial benefits of native employment were attractive to a cash-strapped administration; more interesting though is that some English officials argued that the Irish were better soldiers. In his reform treatise, Captain Nicholas Dawtrey made what must have seemed an astounding statement: 'I will say this for the Irish souldier, I had rather haue him to serue under me, than any Countryman in the world, so he be well paide and punished for his faultes, according to ther natures, and then I think ther cannot be a better souldier under the sune.'[114] Irish soldiers were considered a hardier breed than their English counterparts, and capable of enduring unimaginable toil and dearth.[115] Thus, in August 1602, the usually cautious Mountjoy said he would prefer to fill army ranks with 2,000 Irish recruits rather than English ones because 'those that came over newly, when they were presently to enduer the hardnes of a winter warr... decayed so fast, and were of so little vse or helpe vnto vs, as wee ar verie much discouraged to move your L[ord]s for any more of them'.[116] It was also believed that Irish incivility was responsible for an astonishing quality of fearlessness; Ralph Lane went so far as to say that the cowardice of English

---

[110] TNA, SP 63/205/139 (Essex and Council to Privy Council, 14 Aug. 1599).

[111] TNA, SP 63/178/31 (Lane to Burghley, 2 Feb. 1595).

[112] Moryson, *Itinerary*, ii, p. 59.

[113] For example, see TNA, SP 63/177/21(I) (Dunsany to Privy Council, 18 Nov. 1594). See also TNA, SP 63/201/144 (suit of Dunsany, 1597); TNA, SP 63/207(3)/24 (Countess of Ormond, to Cecil, 8 May 1600) HMC *Salisbury* MSS, vii, 476; CUL, MS Kk. I. 15, f. 21v.

[114] H. Morgan (ed.), 'A Booke of Questions and Answars Concerning the Warrs of Rebellions of the Kingdome of Ireland', *Anal. Hib.*, No. 36 (1995), p. 93.

[115] The same argument was used when urging the employment of Scottish troops for the Irish wars. TNA, SP 63/207(5)/66 (Dockwra to Privy Council, 1 Oct. 1600).

[116] TNA, SP 63/212/13 (Mountjoy and Councilors to Privy Council, 12 Aug. 1602).

troops set a bad example for their otherwise courageous Irish colleagues.[117] In a similar manner of admiration, some English commentators deemed the Irish more accurate marksmen than their English counterparts and there were times when the crown's Irish soldiers provided the core strength of the army in battle.[118] In October 1595 Richard Bingham described a rebel encounter during which his Irish troops had unexpectedly proved their mettle. Because his English companies were 'unserviceable for the most parte', in the heat of battle Bingham's captains 'were driven to take the bullettes and powther from many of them [English soldiers] to giue it to the Irish shott which stood in best steed that daye'.[119]

This does not mean that Bingham endorsed the employment of Irishmen; it was merely proof that English soldiers were in short supply and that those who were there were of poor quality and training. Despite their valiant service at this particular skirmish, Bingham still insisted that the loyalty and dependability of Irish troops was always tenuous. In the very same letter describing their good performance, Bingham warned that 'Irish souldiers be so treasonable as we cannot with assurance adventure to much vppon their service seing by many examples how they will serve with us this daye and tomorow cut our throats'.[120] That Bingham could appreciate the merits of Irish soldiers and still refuse to trust them is not surprising considering the bloody end his cousin met at the hands of his most trusted Irish subordinate. George Bingham had been treacherously murdered by his Irish ensign, Ulick Burke, who then delivered Sligo Castle to the enemy.[121] But the provincial president's criticisms were specifically reserved for Gaelic Irish troops. When requesting 2,000 reinforcements for Connacht in August 1595, Bingham stipulated that half of these were to be English and that the other half should be levied from amongst the Old English population of the Pale.[122] Six months later, Bingham specifically requested the dispatch of the baron of Delvin and his forces to assist him in Connacht.[123] If his appeal for Pale recruits may be taken as evidence, Bingham made a clear distinction between the Gaelic Irish and Old English and this reflected his opinion on the reliability of these two groups when employed in crown service. Bingham's personal confidence in the Palesmen is corroborated

[117] TNA, SP 63/178/31 (Lane to Burghley, 2 Feb. 1595); TNA, SP 63/212/13 (Mountjoy and Councilors in Camp to Privy Council, 12 Aug. 1602); Cannan, "'Hags of Hell'", pp. 14–17.
[118] TNA, SP 63/194/42 (Lane to Essex, 23 Oct. 1596); TNA, SP 63/207(4)/83 (Carew to Mountjoy, 20 Aug. 1600); Stafford, *Pacata Hibernia*, p. 43.
[119] TNA, SP 63/183/82 (R. Bingham to Burghley, 10 Oct. 1595); Falls, *Irish Wars*, pp. 191–2.
[120] TNA, SP 63/183/82 (Bingham to Burghley, 10 Oct. 1595).
[121] AFM, p. 1973.
[122] TNA, SP 63/182/13 (Irish Council to Privy Council, 6 Aug. 1595).
[123] TNA, SP 63/186/86(XII) (R. Bingham to Russell, 22 Feb. 1596).

by his statement: 'I do not think any alteration will happen in the Pale so long as Her Majesty's sword stand up in strength.'[124]

Depriving the enemy of numbers was also a consideration when accepting submissions and offers of service from former rebels.[125] Though defection was a risk, many officials considered it a necessary evil and one which did not always end as badly as anticipated. In 1602 Mountjoy recommended topping up army ranks with 2,000 Irish submittees because they would 'otherwise goe to the Spaniards, but being enterteyned once with vs, wee found by experience that last yeare, that they both stucke vnto our partie as well and served as gallantly as our Englishe old soldiers'.[126] With respect to the traditionally loyal Irish lords and gentlemen, it was deemed a wise policy to keep them content because it was their example and authority which kept their retainers and followers from revolt.[127] The administration depended on this political reality, as was evident when Mountjoy instructed the Dublin Council to notify 'all the Lords and principall men therabout' of the Spaniards arrival so that 'their light and vnruly followers maie… be by them restreyned from Revolt or growing into anie other vndewtifull action'.[128] There was, therefore, an appreciation within government circles that native servitors could be very valuable assets in the fight against O'Neill's Irish Catholic Confederacy.

In addition to these practical considerations, the reality was that the labours of native soldiers and servitors did much to buoy up the English war effort. The importance of the Pale's leading gentlemen, especially those living along the region's endangered frontier, is highlighted through reference to the services performed by Christopher Nugent, baron of Delvin, and Patrick Plunkett, baron of Dunsany. From 1593 to 1597 Delvin displayed 'great activity' in defending the Pale borders, especially against incursions by the neighbouring O'Farrells and O'Reillys.[129] In 1593 he was appointed leader of the Westmeath forces, and in 1595 he was amongst the Pale nobility called to government conferences at which he received additional commissions to levy and lead the forces of his lordship.[130] In February 1596 Delvin was given even greater authority to pursue

---

124 *CSPI, 1592–96*, p. 362.

125 TNA, SP 63/207(6)/59 (J. Lye to Cecil, 5 Dec. 1600); TNA, SP 63/209(2)/123 (Irish Council to Privy Council, 3 Oct. 1601).

126 TNA, SP 63/212/13 (Mountjoy and Councilors to Privy Council, 12 Aug. 1602).

127 For example, TNA, SP 63/202(3)/171(IV) (speeches between T. Lee and R. Hoper, 24 Nov. 1598); TNA, SP 63/209(2)/123 (Irish Council to Privy Council, 3 Oct. 1601).

128 TNA, SP 63/209(1)/103A (Mountjoy and others to Irish Council, 24 Sep. 1601).

129 S. Lee (ed.), *Dictionary of National Biography* (London, 1909), p. 258; Lennon, 'Christopher Nugent', *ODNB*. See also BL, Add. MS 4819, f. 147.

130 TNA, SP 63/180/48 (Fenton to Burghley, 24 June 1595); TNA, SP 63/181/7(I) ('State of Ireland', July 1595); TNA, SP 63/182/13 (Irish Council to Privy Council, 6 Aug. 1595); BL, Add. MS 4,763, f. 429.

rebels in bordering counties and was charged with the maintenance of two crown fortifications in Cavan, without which 'her highness hath no footing in all that countrey'.[131] As a justice of the peace in Westmeath, he was responsible for signing Richard Tyrrell's arrest warrant and, following Tyrrell's escape from Mullingar gaol, Delvin again served against the notorious rebel commander.[132] By January 1600 Delvin was in command of 1,050 men, an immense command for a servitor of Irish birth, and a very significant contribution towards the numerical strength of the crown army.[133] According to his own account, between 1596 and February 1600 Delvin had either apprehended or killed a total of 246 rebels and sent many heads to Dublin.[134] Although there is no way of verifying this number through other accounts, Russell's campaign journal includes several entries noting Delvin's delivery of prisoners and rebel heads, as well as a number of his victories against the insurgents.[135]

The baron of Dunsany's services were no less distinguished. In 1594 and 1595 he commanded twenty horsemen assigned by the queen and another 'thirtie which he held allwaies as marshall'.[136] Also in 1595, he and his forces were listed among companies campaigning in the north under the command of Sir John Norreys. Norreys, however, expressed doubts about the value and dedication of the Palesmen's services so far from their homes with the result that Dunsany, along with twelve of his horsemen, were directed to Dundalk where they provided the equally vital service of guarding the borders against rebel stealths.[137] The following July, Dunsany and his company of horse were appointed to the borders to assist the lord deputy and provost marshal with the execution of martial law against any unpardoned rebels entering the Pale.[138] By September 1599, Dunsany was a colonel of foot, in command of fifty horse and 150 foot at Kells and Navan and was listed again in 1600 as commanding the same number of troops in Leinster.[139] Dunsany's charge of 200 soldiers was one of the largest amongst Old English servitors at this time, commensurate with the earls of Kildare and Clanricard, and only surpassed by Ormond,

---

[131] TNA, SP 63/186/51 (Irish Council to Privy Council, 9 Feb. 1596).

[132] Nicholls, 'Richard Tyrrell', pp. 163–4; TNA, SP 63/199/53 (J. Norreys to Cecil, 24 May 1597).

[133] TNA, SP 63/207/40(V) (Delvin to Ormond, 21 Jan. 1600).

[134] TNA, SP 63/207/88(I) (services done by Delvin, [n.d.] 1600).

[135] Lambeth, Carew MS, 612, No. 270 (Russell's journal). See also TNA, SP 63/202(2)/13 (note of principal traitors slain or executed, 19 Apr. 1598).

[136] TNA, SP 63/103/48 (Queen to Lords Justices, 30 July 1583); TNA, SP 63/177/21 (Dunsany to Cecil, 18 Nov. 1594); TNA, SP 63/177/21(I) (petition of Dunsany, 18 Nov. 1594); TNA, SP 63/178/64 (docquet of Irish suitors, Feb. 1595).

[137] TNA, SP 63/183/12 (J. Norreys to Burghley, 8 Sep. 1595); Lambeth, Carew MS, 612, No. 270 (Russell's journal, 21 Sep. 1595).

[138] TNA, SP 63/191/46(I) (notes by J. Norreys, [Enclosure], 27 July 1596); BL, Add. MS 4819, f. 147.

[139] Moryson, Itinerary, ii, pp. 43, 61.

Delvin, and Christopher St Lawrence.[140] Significantly, of the 350 horse and 3,200 foot registered by Moryson as available for taking the field in March 1600, Dunsany was listed with his full complement of fifty horse and 150 foot, thus making him a large contributor to Mountjoy's campaign against O'Neill.[141] As the examples of Delvin and Dunsany illustrate, the contributions of Old English servitors were instrumental in securing the crown's eventual victory over Hugh O'Neill and the Irish Confederacy. Presumably there were many more Palesmen who performed services equally proportional to their status; regrettably, the specific details of their services have escaped greater detail in official records.

The Problem with the Irish

'[B]eware of thine owne companies', warned the author of *The Supplication*, 'seeke for Englishe soldiers, whose quarell it is, is now in hand: who will not faile thee, because in failinge thee, they shall faile themselves.'[142] Although the crown enjoyed substantial support from the Old English Pale community, there was no escaping the fact that those who came to the aid of the government could also harbour certain sympathies for the plight of their rebellious compatriots. As Maurice Kyffin cautioned Burghley, 'how dangerous a matter it is to wage warre, and vse such forces against their own Countrymen, kinsmen, and allys… They runne away and revolt to the Rebels daily and howerly. They betray forts, castles, howses, and villages ordinarily.'[143] Kyffin's pessimism was warranted and the English had good reasons to doubt the valour and constancy of Irish soldiers who encountered kinsmen and neighbours on the opposite side of the battlefield. And confront each other they did, because the Nine Years' War was as much a civil war as it was a war of independence. Most families were divided; for example, Delvin's exertions in the vicinity of Meath/Westmeath bolstered the crown's military position, but many of his relatives, including his own nephew, Richard Nugent, took up the rebel standard.[144] Similarly, the loyalist Captain John Tyrrell often engaged his infamous rebel kinsman, Captain Richard Tyrrell.[145] In doing so, both Delvin and Tyrrell displayed a resolute commitment to the queen's cause, but many others did not show the same kind of fortitude.

---

[140] Ibid., pp. 59–61.

[141] Ibid., p. 61.

[142] Maley (ed.), 'The Supplication', p. 37.

[143] TNA, SP 63/201/ 33 (Kyffin to Burghley, 27 Oct. 1597).

[144] For more on Richard Nugent, see Anne Fogarty's introduction to R. Nugent, *Cynthia* (1604), ed. A. Lynch (Dublin, 2010), Introduction.

[145] TNA, SP 63/196/2 (observations, 3 Dec. 1596).

In addition to the suspected fickleness of Irish-born servitors was a fear that the crown was inadvertently equipping its enemies for war. Many believed that in its effort to promote Irish civility the English crown had unwittingly maintained the Old English in a position of competence and arrogance while raising the Gaelic Irish to a level that they could now confront the English government and military establishment on its own terms. Since they had been trained in English politics and styles of warfare, any sudden clash with the crown made these men formidable enemies, both inside the council chamber and on the battlefield.[146] Hugh O'Neill was a prime example. According to Dawtrey, the upstart earl could never have posed such a threat to the crown had he not previously enjoyed the queen's good favour. Hoping to use him as her pawn in Ulster, Elizabeth had spared no expense when nursing O'Neill up to great power, but she would have to expend much more to chastise the monster that generosity had created.[147] She had learned the hard way that 'we cannot expect pleasant fruit from thistles'.[148]

Having spent his youth in the Pale, O'Neill had been endowed with a typical English military education. While still nominally loyal in the years leading up to his revolt, he had also made the most of English 'butter captains' to train his Ulster forces.[149] In addition to the military expertise he had exploited prior to the war, it was deeply suspected that O'Neill continued to encourage Irishmen to enter English ranks to ensure they obtained adequate training, intelligence, and arms.[150] Thus, the most serious problem posed by Irish soldiers was that after receiving their military education in the English army they might defect to the rebels, taking with them a knowledge of English strengths, weaknesses, and intentions. It was to this factor that many English observers attributed the good training of O'Neill's forces.[151] There was, moreover, a general belief that the Irish character was predisposed to deceit and defection. This opinion was symptomatic of derogatory attitudes towards the native Irish, but was not without precedent as examples of Irish treachery abounded during the conflict. In 1598 the loyalist James Fitzpiers Fitzgerald turned traitor and delivered

---

[146] TNA, SP 63/203/96 (instructions for Essex, 25 Mar. 1599); Maley (ed.), 'The Supplication', pp. 37–8. See also Canny, *Making Ireland British*, p. 68.

[147] Morgan (ed.), 'Questions and Answers', pp. 70–134.

[148] *CSPI, 1599–1600*, p. 230.

[149] Hayes-McCoy, *Irish Battles*, p. 96; Hayes-McCoy, 'Strategy and Tactics in Irish Warfare, 1593–1601', *IHS*, Vol. 2, No. 7 (1941), p. 262; Morgan, *Tyrone's Rebellion*, ch. 5; O'Neill, *The Nine Years War*, p. 202; TNA, SP 63/174/62(I) (Dawtrey's discourse on Ireland, 24 May 1594).

[150] BL, Harl. MS 292, f. 172 ('A Direction to the Queenes Majestie how to conquer Ireland A.D. 1599').

[151] Morgan (ed.), 'Questions and Answers', pp. 92–3; TNA, SP 63/206/119(I) (caveat delivered to Her Majesty in November 1591, Dec. 1599); TNA, SP 63/207(6)/126 (paper on the causes of rebellion, Dec. 1600). For a complete study of the military revolution under O'Neill, see O'Neill, *The Nine Years War*, pp. 196–208.

several crown fortifications to the rebels; also in 1598, 'no lesse then 300 of the mere Irishe' defected to the enemy during the battle at Yellow Ford; and, in 1599, Dunsany's foot company at Kells fled to the rebels during their commander's absence.[152]

English observers had long been convinced that the Gaelic Irish were naturally inclined towards disobedience and rebellion, but by the closing decade of the sixteenth century it was felt that the Old English had come to share a similar penchant.[153] Although the crown had found unwavering support amongst sections of this population, it was all too aware that there were many within this community whose adherence was purely conditional. In their desire to overtop the rebels, governors had deliberately accepted offers of service from known traitors in return for pardons.[154] Although pardons were used as a means to draw adherents away from the Confederates, numerous commentators advised against this tactic, arguing that it only served as a respite for rebels to renew their strength under more peaceful conditions.[155] Very few of these former rebels had defected to the crown over a crisis of conscience; instead, hoping to preserve their lives and lands, they had only submitted when they found themselves momentarily overcome by the crown army.[156] So long as it served their turns, many individuals, regardless of what camp they had initially supported, were ready to forsake political and religious ideals for the prospect of survival and advancement. When opportunity arose to resume former behaviour, it was unlikely they would hesitate.

Interestingly, English administrators were not alone in their reservations about Irish recruits. Like those rebels who submitted to the crown, many crown servitors had abruptly joined the rebellion following devastating rebel assaults or convincing threats of imminent destruction.[157] This did not make for steadfast Confederate allies, and O'Neill used these men with caution. For similar reasons, O'Neill had qualms about some of the Irish mercenary forces, or *buannadha*, in his pay. He trusted those of Ulster since they were wholly dependent on him,

---

[152] AFM, 1973; Canning, 'James Fitzpiers Fitzgerald', pp. 573–94; Falls, *Irish Wars*, p. 219. Concerning desertions at the Blackwater, the examinant also noted that two English soldiers of recent arrival also defected: SP 63/202(III)/34(I) (declaration of Captains Ferdinando and George Kingsmill, 23 Aug. 1598). About Dunsany's forces: TNA, SP 63/206/31(I) (R. Heath to Irish Council, 17 Nov. 1599); TNA, SP 63/206/33 (R. Napper to Cecil, 18 Nov. 1599).

[153] TNA, SP 63/180/53 (Irish Council to Privy Council, 27 June 1595).

[154] TNA, SP 63/202(1)/66 (Lane to Burghley, 1 Mar. 1598); O'Sullivan Beare, *History of Ireland*, p. 56.

[155] For example, TNA, SP 63/205/154 (G. Comerford to Cecil, 27 Aug. 1599); TNA, SP 63/207(6)/126 (paper on the causes of rebellion, Dec. 1600); TNA, SP 63/209(2)/155 (Bishop of Meath to Cecil, 20 Oct. 1601).

[156] This occurred with increasing frequency during the closing years of the war. For example, TNA, SP 63/207(5)/38 (W. Yelverton to Cecil, 20 Sep. 1600).

[157] TNA, SP 63/207(3)/92 (H. Bird to Cecil, 8 June 1600).

but he was apprehensive about those from Connacht.[158] They were exactly what they were designed to be: hired killers who fought for personal gain rather than any high-minded ideal. Possibly more surprising though is that Viscount Mountgarrett did not trust his fellow Leinster Confederates and followers, and 'in his own distrust of the natives of the country, has wholly committed the ward of his castles to Ulster men, and has displaced his own'.[159] But Mountgarrett would know; his distrust was built upon personal experience, since he had switched sides on many occasions depending on which contender offered him the greatest prize – or more specifically, which side offered him the greatest chance to seize the earldom of Ormond. Official opinions on the duplicitous character of Irish troops were, therefore, justifiable; yet an entire population cannot be tarred with the same brush, nor are the reasons for betrayal always the fault of the betrayer.

The hardness of service was a contributing factor in defections from the crown. Irregular pay, poor equipment, and severe food shortages drove many to seek solace where they could. Shipments of treasure and victuals from England were appallingly inadequate, and the overburdened loyalist regions of Ireland were increasingly incapable of yielding to the demands of the expanding crown army. The scarcity of locally accessible provisions was certainly the case in Leinster, Munster, and Connacht; Ulster, however, had never seemed so productive.[160] Until the closing stages of the war, crown forces had been unable to penetrate O'Neill's stronghold, where he had made arrangements for an abundance of agricultural supplies to feed his growing army. For those in the queen's service who knew how well prepared O'Neill was, the prospect of survival with the enemy must have been somewhat more attractive than almost certain death with the crown. Furthermore, O'Neill's promises of monetary rewards must have been especially alluring to men who could never be sure of a payday in the queen's employ.[161] Considering that English troops were a

---

[158] Ó Báille, 'The Buannadha', pp. 62–3.

[159] CSPI, 1598–99, p. 410; Ó Báille, 'The Buannadha', p. 83.

[160] For example, TNA, SP 63/200/143 (Clifford to Burghley, 30 Sep. 1597); TNA, SP 63/207(4)/59 (Mountjoy to Cecil, 7 Aug. 1600). G.A. Hayes-McCoy, 'The Army of Ulster, 1593–1601', in Irishmen in War from the Crusades to 1798: Essays from the Irish Sword, Vol. 1 (Dublin, 2005), pp. 74–5.

[161] O'Neill's Spanish allies had delivered him several shipments of treasure which he could use to hire men and buy munitions. TNA, SP 63/198/32(I) (E. Moore to Russell, 22 Mar. 1597); TNA, SP 63/198/32(II) (T. Wingfield to W. Clarke, 22 Mar. 1597); TNA, SP 63/198/35 (Fenton to Cecil, 24 Mar. 1597); TNA, SP 63/198/41 (Irish Council to Privy Council, 25 Mar. 1597); TNA, SP 63/198/82 (Lane to Burghley, 11 Apr. 1597); TNA, SP 63/198/125 (Irish Council to Privy Council, 29 Apr. 1597); TNA, SP 63/202(3)/135 (Loftus, Gardener, Bingham, and Council to Privy Council, 31 Oct. 1598); Moryson, Itinerary, iii, p. 7; TNA, SP 63/208(1)/44 (Dunsany to R. Cecil, 10 Feb. 1601); TNA, SP 63/209(2)/159 (Irish Council to Privy Council, 24 Oct. 1601); TNA, SP 63/209(2)/199A (advertisements, 1 Nov. 1601); TNA, SP 63/210/22 (F. Stafford to

perpetual flight risk and known to defect, Irish troops must have been equally, if not more, inclined to break away.[162]

Extenuating Circumstances

The vast majority of documentation for this period comes from English official correspondence, and since there is little recourse to evidence representing the Old English or Gaelic Irish point of view, one must approach these records with a degree of scepticism. Complaints about the Palesmen's military performance, whether directed towards border defence or other martial services, are a recurring theme throughout contemporary records on the Nine Years' War. The queen and Privy Council were so inundated with an unrelenting torrent of complaints that it is small wonder Elizabeth expressed outrage:

> when we obserue howe litle they ether preuented the vyolence to our good subiectes, howe short tyme they made their aboade abroad, and howe slenderly they excused them selues by want of victuall, none of them being 20 myles from their owne house, surely wee cannot forbeare to let you knowe that it doth not a little offende vs to think that the world shall note men of their byrth and calling to be of so small abilitie to serue their contrie.[163]

There was, of course, some truth in official criticism of the Palesmen's enthusiasm and conduct, and this community did have its reluctant and conspiratorial members. The State Papers contain numerous examples of poor service and betrayal which serve to validate official indignation, but a thorough assessment of existing evidence also demonstrates that English commentators' most negative predictions rarely came to fruition. In spite of overwhelming fears of massive defections if a foreign invasion were to succeed, many administrators must have been shocked by how few inhabitants actually joined the Confederacy following the Spanish arrival at Kinsale.[164] It is, therefore, necessary to examine testimonies which represent the Palesmen's sincere efforts to provide the crown with military service and the struggles they endured by doing so.

War was a common affair in sixteenth-century Ireland. Contemporary sources sometimes recorded two or three unrelated wars within the space of a single year, but these were usually small in scale and the product of dynastic

---

Cecil, 14 Jan. 1602); Morgan (ed.), 'Questions and Answars', pp. 91–2; S. Ó Domhnaill, 'Warfare in Sixteenth-Century Ireland', *IHS*, Vol. 5, No. 17 (1946), p. 43.

[162] SP 63/206/100 (Warren to Cecil, 24 Dec. 1599).

[163] TNA, SP 63/178/99 (Elizabeth to Russell and Council, 20 Mar. 1595). See also CUL, MS Kk. I. 15, ff. 93–93v (Elizabeth to Russell and Council, 20 Mar. 1594/5).

[164] TNA, SP 63/209(2)/198 (Loftus and Council to Privy Council, 23 Nov. 1601).

or territorial disputes between a few semi-autonomous lordships.[165] As David Edwards has asserted, 'no lord, no matter how powerful, had the capacity to continue long-range warfare year after year'.[166] The Nine Years' War required just that and the military demands of 1595 alone were colossal compared to anything experienced by the Pale community previously. As hostilities escalated over the next eight years, so too did the government's demands on this population, yet the local military machinery from which the crown could draw had not evolved sufficiently to meet the needs of the struggle. Rather inconveniently, Ulster had undergone a military revolution of sorts under the leadership of Shane O'Neill and then Hugh, and this had enabled the northern leaders to assemble a host within three days' notice; Hayes-McCoy has asserted that 'it would take the English more than three weeks to mobilise against them'.[167] This would suggest that Old English society had failed to modernise, but certain considerations must be taken into account before accepting official irritation over delays in convening Pale hosts.

According to custom, the administration was required to give the Irish nobility forty days' notice to rise out before the expected host would actually assemble.[168] Excepting the armed retainers of great magnates, the vast majority of Ireland's inhabitants did not make their livings by military service and it took time for these men to settle their personal affairs, collect materials for war, and travel to the places appointed for mustering. They were already handicapped by delays in assembling the host, and an annual service obligation of forty days was constraining when a situation necessitated prolonged campaigning or full-scale war. The problem was difficult to circumvent, but administrators had devised a partial solution: prorogation. This tactic, used to suspend parliamentary sessions without actually disbanding parliament, had definite advantages when applied to military affairs, as was demonstrated in March 1595.[169] On this occasion Pale forces had been assembled in accordance with their service obligations, but by proroguing the intended session of service the soldiers were retained at the appointed place of assembly without infringing on their forty days' service. Proroguing prevented the disbandment of the host; it also ensured that the time during which these forces were assembled did not violate tenurial agreements since the men were not actually employed in action. This indicates that forces could be kept at the ready for an indeterminate length of time before becoming

---

[165] Ó Domhnaill, 'Warfare', p. 31. See esp., *AFM*.

[166] Edwards, 'Escalation of Violence', p. 66.

[167] Hayes-McCoy, *Irish Battles*, p. 110. For a more recent evaluation, see O'Neill, *The Nine Years War*, pp. 14, 33, 53, 99.

[168] TNA, SP 63/178/68 (Fenton to Burghley, 3 Mar. 1595); TNA, SP 63/199/41 (Irish Council to Privy Council, 20 May 1597); TNA, SP 63/199/66 (Irish Council to Privy Council, 31 May 1597).

[169] TNA, SP 63/178/68 (Fenton to Burghley, 3 Mar. 1595).

fully operational and that the time considered active service was subject to government opinion. While it suggests that such a policy could be employed, it is doubtful that it became the norm since the maintenance of idle soldiers – food, accommodation, and entertainment – would have placed serious financial strains on both the government and the local inhabitants.

Closely related to the issue of gathering men together from the various reaches of the Pale to serve along an endangered frontier was the question about the dedication such men showed when serving in regions far removed from their own.[170] For much of 1595 and 1596 Sir John Norreys commanded a large force of mixed backgrounds in the northern regions of Ireland. Norreys showed a definite preference for companies composed of English-born soldiers but, in spite of repeated appeals for companies sent directly from England, was obliged to accept many native foot and horse companies into his charge. These included forces under the earl of Thomond, baron of Dunsany, and Captain Christopher St Lawrence, but even many of his 'English' companies had been largely converted to Irish under their English captains.[171] Deeply frustrated, Norreys announced that these native servitors were of little use to him, specifically alleging that the Palesmen were unwilling to perform any meaningful service when appointed to locations like his because they were too far removed from their homes. Norreys appealed to the Irish Council to exchange his native and contaminated companies with some English companies then stationed around the Pale under Lord Deputy Russell's command. In doing so, he contended that his native forces would be of more use if relocated to posts in and around the Pale while Russell's English companies would be better deployed in the pursuit of rebels further abroad, specifically with Norreys in the north.[172] There was some merit to Norreys' concerns; human instinct dictates that one would defend one's own possessions more ferociously than those of others.[173] On the other hand, English soldiers, with a few exceptions, had no personal interest in any specific Irish region and it, therefore, made little difference to them where they served. Whether Norreys genuinely believed that the Palesmen were undependable and of little use is hard to say. The rivalry between the great military general and the queen's viceroy is well known and it could be argued that both men were as concerned about their personal reputations as they were

---

[170] TNA, SP 63/182/77(I) (J. Norreys to Russell, 25 Aug. 1595). See also TNA, SP 63/178/99 (Elizabeth to Russell and Council, 20 Mar. 1595); CUL, MS Kk. I. 15, ff. 93–93v (Elizabeth to Russell and Council, 20 Mar. 1594/5).

[171] TNA, SP 63/183/42(III) (companies to be sent to J. Norreys, 19 Sep. 1595).

[172] TNA, SP 63/182/77(I) (J. Norreys to Russell, 25 Aug. 1595); TNA, SP 63/183/12 (J. Norreys to Burghley, 8 Sep. 1595); TNA, SP 63/183/42(II) (J. Norreys to Russell, 16 Sep. 1595); TNA, SP 63/191/46(I) (notes by J. Norreys, 1596); CUL, MS Kk. I. 15, ff. 223 (instructions from J. Norreys, 27 July 1596).

[173] John Lye put forward a similar argument. TNA, SP 63/207(6)/59 (J. Lye to Cecil, 5 Dec. 1600).

with the service. It is conceivable that Norreys was trying to pass these doubtful companies to the lord deputy so that if some reverse were to befall the queen's service, particularly if it could be blamed on the expected slackness of Irish servitors, it would be Russell, not Norreys, who would suffer Elizabeth's sharp rebuke. That Norreys' ambition provided the stronger motive seems likely considering Bingham did not share the same hesitation when he requested the recruitment of 1,000 Palesmen to serve under him in distant Connacht.[174] Lord Deputy Mountjoy, likewise, had few reservations when requesting the dispatch of large numbers of Palesmen to help him against the Spanish in Kinsale.[175]

The question as to where native servitors were most effective was debated throughout the war and arguments were offered in support of both cases. By the time of Mountjoy's viceroyalty, the perception that Irish servitors were greedily absorbing the profits of crown employment, in terms of pay and land rewards, without performing any actual service provided the impetus for their employment further afield.[176] Yet, even at this late stage, Mountjoy was given to complain that he was receiving contradictory instructions:

For I have received direction from Her Majesty to employ them out of their own countries, and not to suffer them to enjoy the benefit of her pay for the keeping of their own cows. And now of late I am advised by their Lordships to consider whether the fittest men to be employed in Leinster be not the landed gentry of that province, who in likelyhood will endeavour themselves to recover and secure their own lands.[177]

As inconvenient as these conflicting advices were, Mountjoy was not actually in favour of either policy. He argued that Irish forces were as useless at home as they were abroad or in garrison.[178]

There were, of course, legitimate reasons to doubt the commitment of men serving in distant and unfamiliar locations and one might ascribe the Palesmen's lack of fervour on such occasions to any of three possible considerations. First, fighting a war in unfamiliar territory could be reason enough for a degree of cowardliness; second, these individuals did not have a vested interest in the areas to which they were assigned and were, therefore, less likely to sacrifice themselves for its defence; and third, many men, quite naturally, feared what might happen to their own lands, goods, and people during their absence abroad. Security of distant holdings was always a genuine concern and, in the absence of a detailed example from the Pale, the experiences of the inhabitants of County Tipperary may illustrate the negative repercussions of service abroad. In October

[174] TNA, SP 63/182/13 (Irish Council to Privy Council, 6 Aug. 1595).
[175] TNA, SP 63/209(2)/168B (companies appointed for Kinsale, 25 Oct. 1601).
[176] TNA, SP 63/207(5)/116 ('Heads of things', 27 Oct. 1600).
[177] CSPI, 1600, p. 507; Moryson, Itinerary, ii, p. 284.
[178] TNA, SP 63/208(1)/38 (Irish Council to Privy Council, 7 Feb. 1601).

1595 a company commanded by Ormond and composed of Tipperary gentlemen was assigned to the vulnerable, but distant, borders of Louth. In their absence, Ormond and his men risked the deterioration of their own properties.[179] Besides neglecting their own possessions, the Irish nobility and gentry had responsibilities to defend the interests of their dependants and tenants back home – and it was not just the rebels from whom they needed protection. While Ormond was faithfully executing his duty to his prince, government commissioners seized upon his absence as an opportunity to investigate the Munster composition and extend these obligations into Ormond's palatine. With no lord to defend them from the administration's onerous demands, Ormond's tenants were subjected to further financial exactions for the queen's Irish wars.[180] Florence Fitzpatrick, baron of Upper Ossory, had a similar experience in late 1599. He alleged that his properties in the Grange and St Mary's Abbey were exempt from country charges yet, when he was absent on campaign, crown 'cessors and collectors doth charge the same, and oftentimes the soldiers do rifle and take away all my poor tenants' goods'.[181] There must have been many other Palesmen who had experiences comparable to those of Fitzpatrick, Ormond, and the men of Tipperary. Bearing in mind the actual hardships of service abroad and the consequences for those left behind, the services of Ormond and the men of Tipperary in Louth was no small feat and should be taken as confirmation of their honest desire to protect crown authority in Ireland.

Contrary to English administrators' statements that the Palesmen had failed to fulfil their military obligations, by the end of 1595 they had far exceeded the annual requirement of forty days' service. Unfortunately, certain ambiguities in contemporary records render a perfect assessment of the Pale's contribution impossible. The exact numbers of men called upon is rarely explicit, nor is the kind of men (freeholder, tenant, labourer, etc.), their barony of origin, or the precise duration of service. It is unclear whether levies for each hosting were composed of the same men as before or fresh recruits. It is also unclear if or to what extent natives paid scutage in lieu of personal service or hired paid substitutes to stand in their place.[182] In all likelihood, the reality was a combination of these scenarios. Nevertheless, it can be assumed that by the August–September hosting of 1595, being the fourth that year, the population from which the Pale

---

179 For example, TNA, SP 63/206/43 (baron of Upper Ossory to Cecil, 27 Nov. 1599).

180 TNA, SP 63/183/96 (Wallop, Gardiner, Napper, Sentleger and Wilbraham to Burghley, 20 Oct. 1595).

181 CSPI, 1599–1600, p. 263.

182 S.G. Ellis, 'Taxation and Defence in Late Medieval Ireland: The Survival of Scutage', Journal of the Royal Society of Antiquaries of Ireland, Vol. 107 (1977), pp. 5–28; J. Otway-Ruthven, 'Royal Service in Ireland', The Journal of the Royal Society of Antiquaries of Ireland, Vol. 98, No. 1 (1968), pp. 37–46; Otway-Ruthven, 'Knight Service in Ireland', The Journal of the Royal Society of Antiquaries of Ireland, Vol. 89, No. 1 (1959), pp. 1–15.

lords could draw serviceable men had been greatly depleted as a consequence of the community's previous contributions as well as the hazards of war. Remarkably, even Russell was forced to concede that the nobility had appreciable difficulties raising men on this occasion because 'they are very hardly able to find them'.[183] Besides the number of fatalities and men incapable of serving again due to serious injury, many of those who had escaped bodily harm must have been exhausted and unable to provide further service with respect to both their enthusiasm and armaments. Moreover, having already fulfilled their annual military obligation, these individuals were not legally bound to serve again.[184] In order to meet enlistment quotas over the course of multiple risings out, the Pale nobility and gentry must have been driven to recruit poor and inexperienced men who had neither the means to arm themselves nor the training to engage a tricky enemy.

Although government officials frequently complained about the quality of local troops mustered for hostings, their feeble condition was hardly intentional. Undoubtedly, the gentlemen leading these Pale forces not only wanted a sufficient number of troops under their command, but also desired that those soldiers be reasonably equipped and trained for war. The ultimate ambition of sixteenth-century martial men was honour and glory on the battlefield and the lords of the Pale were no different from their peers elsewhere. They put their own honour and welfare at stake when they led the forces of their lordships and it was in their own best interest to avoid combat until they had assembled the strongest body of troops possible. As early as February 1595 the Pale lords had already complained of 'the vntowardness of their people who for the most parte weare vnserviceable, and therefore daungerus for persons of their sort to adventure their honour and lyves'.[185] The situation must have been considerably worse nearly five years later when the baron of Howth swore that the 200 foot and horse he had recruited from Dublin were 'so badly appointed... he would never venture his life with them'.[186] Also in connection with the December 1599 rising out, Lord Trimblestown announced the general response to his efforts to raise local forces was that 'they had rather be hanged at their doors at home, than be killed in the field'.[187] In a similar mood of frustration, Ormond reported 'my Lord of Slane, my Lord of Louth, and my Lord of Killeen, affirmed that the countries under their command denied either aid of horse or foot'.[188] Crown officials may have considered this a dishonour to the queen's

---

[183] TNA, SP 63/183/42 (Russell to Privy Council, 21 Sep. 1595).

[184] Sir Arthur Savage discussed conflicting demands on the Palesmen and how that hindered their service. TNA, SP 63/207/85 (A. Savage to Cecil, 3 Feb. 1600).

[185] TNA, SP 63/178/54 (Irish Council to Privy Council, 26 Feb. 1595).

[186] CSPI, 1599–1600, p. 292.

[187] Ibid., p. 298.

[188] Ibid.

service but, as the situation continued to deteriorate over nine years, the local population was probably far more concerned with basic survival.

Traditionally, the Pale community's primary obligation had been to answer risings out, but during the Nine Years' War they were pressed by multiple and conflicting demands which proved detrimental to that service. Although the Palesmen were constantly berated for careless attendance at hostings and accused of providing insufficient forces for border defence, by August 1598 even the English Privy Council was forced to acknowledge that the manpower available for these tasks had been critically diminished due to the large-scale enrolment of Palesmen into the regular army corps.[189] In addition to these incompatible forms of martial participation, the Palesmen were also obliged to subsidise the queen's military establishment by way of composition. Prior efforts to demilitarise the Irish lordship and do away with arbitrary forms of military taxation had led to the foundation of composition. This aimed to commute both the cessing of government troops and the need for personal military service into a single tax to be used towards financing a more permanent English garrison.[190] But in the 1590s, with the outbreak of war on an unprecedented scale, the English military presence was entirely incapable of meeting the challenge without local reinforcement. With far greater urgency and frequency than was custom, the Palesmen were called upon to physically serve their prince, yet they were still required to render a significant portion of the army's financial and material needs. Despite repeated pleas for arrangements to offset these overlapping contributions, the Palesmen were expected to provide active military service on top of paying the composition which had been established as an economic substitute for that obligation.[191]

Notwithstanding the general tenor of State Paper records, not all English officials were agreed that the Palesmen's efforts were unsatisfactory. Captain Thomas Lee corroborated the Palesmen's readiness to serve during this war. He contended that if reinforcements could not be sent from England, 'your majesty's subjects in the English pale would willingly yield to your highness 600 soldiers, horse and foot, at their own charge for six months, and longer if need require'.[192]

---

[189] TNA, SP 63/202(3)/1 (Irish Council to Privy Council, 2 Aug. 1598).

[190] The details of this development have been recounted by a number of other historians. For example, see Bradshaw, *Constitutional Revolution*; Brady, *Chief Governors*, pp. 141–54; B. Cunningham, 'The Composition of Connacht in the Lordships of Clanricard and Thomond, 1577–1641', *IHS*, Vol. 24, No. 93 (1984), pp. 1–14; TNA, SP 63/166/57(II) (note concerning the composition, 13 Sep. 1592).

[191] TNA, SP 63/180/61 (discourse by Goringe, June 1595); TNA, SP 63/196/13(I) (memorial, 7 Dec. 1596). For the collection of composition during this period, see A.J. Sheehan, 'Irish Revenues and English Subventions, 1559–1622', *PRIA*, Vol. 90C (1990), p. 45.

[192] Lee, 'Brief Declaration of the Government', p. 135.

Four years later a group of Palesmen reiterated this. They insisted that the Palesmen had a sincere desire to serve their prince but that they suffered certain disabilities, specifically a lack of war-like equipment and training. In an effort to rectify this, they had appealed to crown for basic assistance:

> to haue Armor and municion delivered to thinhabytaunts for some of the money due to them for contry chardges, and that certayne bands should be erected of the Englishe Pale to be trayned by some expert man at the chardge of the contry, to be reddie at their owne chardge to withstand any invacion or sudden brunt of Rebells. And if need required their service for any long tyme, then they to serve your Highenes for ordinary pay without burthen to the contry.[193]

Whether this suit was ever answered is uncertain, but disability, impoverishment, and conflicting commitments were common themes in the supplications submitted by Palesmen. As the war dragged on, supporting the queen's military enterprise became more and more arduous and the inhabitants found meeting the government's military demands for men, supplies, and money increasingly difficult. Besides presenting defensively detailed accounts of their own services, personal and corporate petitions were usually requests for men, money, and munitions, both as reward for services already done as well as essential prerequisites for their ability to continue in crown service.[194] According to the Palesmen, if fault could be found with their military conduct it was only because they lacked the means and opportunity to do better and, for this, they had looked to the crown and administration which had failed them.

The Blunders of State

Accusations of Irish treachery and deceit abound in the State Papers, and even though native defections were almost always attributed to the dishonest character of Irish servitors, there are occasional admissions that these men had been driven to such recourse through ill treatment by the crown, its representatives, and above all, its military officers. The corruption of army captains was endemic and by no means a new phenomenon, but during a crisis like this war it proved seriously prejudicial to the service.[195] Even the author of *Dialogue of Silvynne and Peregrynne*, who was vehemently opposed to the employment of

---

[193] TNA, SP 63/202(4)/60 ('greevances', 1598).

[194] TNA, SP 63/177/21 (Dunsany to Cecil, 18 Nov. 1594); TNA, SP 63/177/21(I) (petition of Dunsany, 18 Nov. 1594); TNA, SP 63/178/20 (W. Smythe to Burghley, 25 Jan. 1595); TNA, SP 63/178/64 (docquet of Irish suitors, Feb. 1595); TNA, SP 63/178/65 (Dunsany to Burghley, Feb. 1595); *CSPI, 1599–1600*, p. 431.

[195] TNA, SP 63/202(2)/100 (Privy Council to Irish Council, 13 July 1598). Brady, 'Captain's Games', pp. 136–59; Canny, *Making Ireland British*, pp. 74–5.

Irish soldiers under any circumstances, laid partial blame for Irish defections on their English captains. Peregrynne, recounting his experiences in Phillipstown, asked a group of Irish soldiers why they had 'forsaken theire alledgiances to her maiesty' and absconded to the rebels. Their response was that:

> theire officers misvsed them, theire Captens stole theire pay… we coulde neither get cloathes vppon credit to kepe our bodyes from weather, nor scarce victualles to houlde lyfe and soulde togither, so that we were compelled, by the negligence of such, that shoulde haue supplyed our wantes with the premisses, to rely vnto the rebelles, for vnder theire protection, we are lycensed to live as Libertynes without conptrolment.[196]

How to rectify the situation left administrators in a quandary. Notwithstanding legislative measures to regulate numbers, during periods of emergency governors had little choice but to augment weak English companies with Irish recruits. This was done as a necessary but temporary fix with the intention that Irish soldiers would be either disbanded as soon as peace was established or replaced by Englishmen when fresh recruits were sent from England. It was a tricky course to navigate. Whether men were cashiered during the multiple truces and ceasefires or replaced during the height of conflict, the problem remained the same. Once they were armed, trained, and idle, it was to be greatly feared what action these Irishmen would take since they now sought employment as martial men, not as civilians.[197] Although the arrival of English reinforcements would bolster the numerical strength of the army's English component, if these new men were exchanged with their Irish opposites it was universally assumed that the disbanded Irish would seek employment with the enemy.[198] The most common solution offered was that proposed by Sir Henry Wallop in November 1595. Rather than disbanding Irish troops, who 'will happelie afterwards depend on soch here as are not best affected to the state', Wallop suggested sending six foot companies and 160 horsemen of Irish birth to serve in the French wars.[199] This proposal was short-sighted; as had already transpired, Irish soldiers transferred to the Netherlands could, and did, defect to the forces of Catholic Spain at the siege of Deventer in 1587. Having gained useful military experience and

---

[196] Collier, *Dialogue of Silvynne and Peregrynne*, pp. 133–4.

[197] This applies to men all over Europe, who found both the honour and the pay of military service preferable to crafts and trade. See G. Parker, *The Military Revolution: Military Innovation and the Rise of the West, 1500–1800* (Cambridge, 1996), p. 47.

[198] TNA, SP 63/198/82 (Lane to Burghley, 11 Apr. 1597); TNA, SP 63/207(2)/1 (Irish Council to Privy Council, 1 Mar. 1600).

[199] TNA, SP 63/184/34 (Wallop to Burghley, 26 Nov. 1595). This proposal was repeated by many other officials over the course of the war. See TNA, SP 63/202(2)/26 (Loftus and Gardener, Ormond, and Council to Privy Council, 4 May 1598); TNA, SP 63/206/92 (declaration by C. Clifford, 20 Dec. 1599); TNA, SP 63/207(4)/116 (H. Cuff to Carew, Aug. 1600); Morgan (ed.), 'Questions and Answers', pp. 93–4.

expertise on the continent, some of these defectors later returned to Ireland where they helped O'Neill and others train Irish soldiers to fight the crown.[200] A more common and desirable solution was that no further Irishmen would be drawn into the queen's employment and that those who were already so employed would be allowed to diminish naturally through the hardships of war.[201] As Mountjoy and the Irish Council assured the Privy Council in August 1602, they would 'expose' the Irish 'to services of greatest danger, and have not so great care to preserve them as the Englishe'.[202] Mountjoy regarded the employment of Irishmen as a useful way to purge the country of its inhabitants and defended his decision to admit them because 'it hath been ever seen that more than three parts of four of these countrymen never return'.[203] Mountjoy's estimate of this wastage, however, was a direct reflection of how destructive this war really was for all those serving in the crown army.[204] And, as Mountjoy unhappily discovered at the war's conclusion, he had failed to waste enough Irishmen through battle and was instead consumed by a flood of Irish submittees seeking pardons and new employment.[205]

Many Irish servitors were aware of how they were regarded by the administration and it is no surprise that they felt disenchanted. Some observers asserted that so long as Irish troops felt unappreciated and fearful of imminent unemployment they would stand on fickle terms.[206] According to one muster clerk, Richard Wackely, the government had only itself to blame for Irish infidelity. He averred native soldiers lived in constant fear of disbandment which:

> put vs all, of Ierlande beirth, in a mistrust, that you will cashier vs all, and supplie the bands in our steed, with the supplies that are to come of Englishe, this is the beste construccion wee can make of it, but the myer irishe doe not sticke to saye, that they are vsed, but to serve our tornes, but that they will provide for them selves if theer be not better regarde had of them.[207]

The administration's cynical view of Irish soldiers and its indifferent treatment of them had given all Irishmen cause to distrust the very regime they were

---

[200] TNA, SP 63/207(4)/116 (H. Cuff to Carew, Aug. 1600).
[201] CSPI, 1598–99, p. 156; TNA, SP 63/202(2)/100 (Privy Council to Irish Council, 13 July 1598); TNA, SP 63/202(3)/1 (Irish Council to Privy Council, 2 Aug. 1598); TNA, SP 63/207(5)/116 ('Heads of things', 27 Oct. 1600).
[202] TNA, SP 63/212/13 (Mountjoy and Councillors to Privy Council, 12 Aug. 1602).
[203] CSPI, 1600–1601, p. 305.
[204] For a discussion of soldier mortality rates during the early modern period, see Parker, Military Revolution, pp. 53–4.
[205] TNA, SP 63/212/135 (Irish Council to Privy Council, 24 Feb. 1603).
[206] For example, TNA, SP 63/207(2)/1 (Irish Council to Privy Council, 1 Mar. 1600). Mountjoy was, however, ordered to disband a number of native companies. TNA, SP 63/207(5)/116 ('Heads of things', 27 Oct. 1600).
[207] TNA, SP 63/202(1)/54 (Wackely to Lane, 19 Feb. 1598).

expected to defend. As far as Wackely was concerned, the crown was right not to trust the Irish as of late, but it was the government which was responsible for this because, seeing themselves so ill-used, the Irish had no incentive to remain steadfast. In effect, the crown's Irish administration was pushing its Irish partners into the arms of the rebels. Ralph Lane appreciated the judgement of his subordinate and affirmed that Irish loyalties could, in fact, be maintained through respect and fair handling:

> the greatest number of the meere Irishe and protected traitors may bee made as faithefull, and muche more seruiceable to her Ma:ty then enye newe companies that can for the presente bee sente out of England, allowinge them but reasonable contentments of apparell and lendings according to her Ma:ties gracious ordinances, and strictelie enioyinge a seconde dutie which is the contynuall attendance of theire Captens with them in theire garrisones and theire personall daielie presence amongste them.[208]

Unfortunately, the opinions expressed by both Wackely and Lane were not widely endorsed by other administrators nor is there any evidence to indicate that the advices of these two men were heeded. As a result, the crown's relationship with its native soldiers remained strained throughout the war and, no doubt, the effect would be enduring.[209]

To return to the battle of Clontibret: according to O'Sullivan Beare's account, 'there were generally more Irish than English in the Royalist army'.[210] A modern commentator, Lorcan Ó Mearáin, argues that O'Sullivan Beare was wrong and that fourteen of the English companies were 'exclusively English'.[211] In theory, Ó Mearáin is correct; after all, the army amassed was supposed to reduce the rebellious Irish in the name of the English queen. However, the reality was that no 'English' company was wholly English because they had all been diluted with Irish-born conscripts. Even if O'Sullivan Beare's declaration can be dismissed as hearsay, the accumulated evidence from surviving witness reports indicates that the exiled Catholic pundit was much closer to the truth.[212] By no means does this imply that the majority of Ireland's inhabitants supported the crown during

---

[208] TNA, SP 63/202(1)/66 (Lane to Burghley, 1 Mar. 1598).

[209] For example, TNA, SP 63/206/92 (declaration by Clifford, 20 Dec. 1599); TNA, SP 63/209(1)/17(a) (things shipped to Donegal, 6 Aug. 1601).

[210] O'Sullivan Beare, *History of Ireland*, p. 87.

[211] Ó Mearáin, 'Battle of Clontibret', p. 9.

[212] It may be posited that O'Sullivan Beare was unwilling to admit that O'Neill's defeat was due to the superiority of English arms, preferring to give partial credit to his loyalist compatriots. However, his work also strove to present the war as a national one which transcended Ireland's traditional particularism and he was unlikely to concede that the Irish Catholic nation he glorified was so fractional unless he had good reason to do so.

this conflict; there is plenty of documentation to argue otherwise. However, the evidence presented here does suggest that a very significant proportion of those forces which pursued the English crown's agenda in Ireland were, in fact, native. Try as they might to keep English forces 'English', no crown administrator could deny that the crown army had taken on a distinctly Irish flavour.

Existing evidence also concurs with O'Sullivan Beare's assertion that the crown's native adherents were largely drawn from the Old English population. For all his faults, O'Sullivan Beare provided reasonable justifications for this trend, and personal ambition and cautious clergymen feature prominently in his reasoning.[213] In addition to these influences, the words and actions of Old English Palesmen exude a desire to prove their loyalty to the English crown and actively supporting the crown's military enterprise would have seemed like a measurable expression of that. By managing border defences, hostings, personal retinues, and enlisting in the crown army, the Palesmen did in fact make up a very considerable part of that military machine. Yet for all their efforts, the Old English could not escape suspicions that they were corruptible by virtue of their Irish birth and attachment to Catholicism. Perhaps as the war unfolded the crown was right not to trust them. True, there were ideological incentives for turning their backs on their Protestant queen, but if that did not inspire, their treatment by the government certainly could have. As one anonymous Old Englishman lamented: 'These prooffes being had of them with their dayly protestation of faith and loyaltie, yf their trueth may not acquire truste, they thinke violence to be offered to nature her self in depriving the child of his mothers milke, and in taking from them the rewarde of their faith and valour.'[214] Paid less, if at all, exposed to greater hazards, required to serve far above statutory regulations, overtaxed, and over-criticised, it is a wonder that so many more did not defect to the Confederate cause. In light of all these tokens of disrespect, it would be understandable if the majority had just cut their losses and joined the rebellion in the faint hope of establishing a new order in Ireland. Remarkably, most leading Old English Palesmen were not so inclined and persevered in their support of the crown till the war's bitter end. As to what this meant for their identity, their military participation says a great deal because whichever side members of this community chose reflected how they regarded themselves and their relationship with both Ireland and England. Notwithstanding the overwhelming criticisms lodged by New English administrators, the physical exertions made by the majority of Old English Palesmen during this conflict stand as proof of their continuing dedication to crown interests in Ireland and symbolic of an enduring attachment to an English identity.

---

[213] O'Sullivan Beare, *History of Ireland*, pp. 51–5.
[214] TNA, SP 63/202(4)/75 ('A discourse', 1598).

5

'Road to Perdition': The Socio-Economic Impact of War on the Pale

Neuer was there [a] poore[r] kingdome, bearing any shew, or shadow of gouernment, so miserable afflicted, and distressed, as this is. It were lamentable to consider, whether the owtcryes of the soldiors, euery where, for want of pay, or of the country people, extreemely robbed and pillaged by the soldiors, be the more greeveous. Whole countryes, even within the English Pale, be left waste, with owt habitation, or tillage. And now, as the inhabitants of the land go, generally, a begging, with their wiues and children; so, the soldiors hauing left neither for others, nor yet for themselues, any furder mean of relief, doo, by the iust iudgement of God, most miserably starue and famish in many places. Betwene the Rebells, on th'one side and our own soldiors (... living altogether on the spoyle,) all is devowred, and destroyed ... The Captains (for their parts) exclaime. Our soldiors dye wretchedly in the open streets, and high wayes. The Native subiects spoiled, and brought to extreme beggery. No seruice in warre performed. No militare discipline or ciuile Iustice exercised. Briefly the whole kingdome ruined, and forrayed. This is true, and it greeves me to write so muche.

Maurice Kyffin, 1597[1]

Military strategy and feats of valour tend to dominate histories which focus on periods of war; yet, the burden of supporting a war and the trauma these conflicts inflict is felt far beyond the battlefield. By consuming human life, money, property, and goods, wars precipitate social and economic dislocation which can have significant implications for state–community relations. This was true of sixteenth-century Ireland where each war and rebellion chipped away at centuries-old ties between the Old English inhabitants and their distant English sovereign, and none more so than the Nine Years' War.[2] This war cost Elizabethan England more money and men than any other conflict. Historians have addressed the drain on England's manpower and resources, along with the miserable condition of English soldiers serving in Ireland.[3] There is no denying

---

[1] TNA, SP 63/197/91 (M. Kyffin to R. Cecil, 14 Feb. 1597).

[2] Anthony McCormack's study of social and economic dislocation in Munster during the Desmond Rebellion of 1579–83 has provided the most concise example of the hardships endured by Ireland's inhabitants during times of conflict and there is no reason to believe that the Nine Years' War was any less traumatic. A.M. McCormack, 'The Social and Economic Consequences of the Desmond Rebellion of 1579–83', *IHS*, Vol. 34, No. 133 (2004), pp. 1–15.

[3] McGurk, *Elizabethan Conquest*; McGurk, 'The Dead, Sick & Wounded of the Nine Years War (1594–1603)', *History Ireland*, Vol. 3, No. 4 (1995), pp. 16–22; Falls, *Elizabeth's Irish Wars*, ch. 3; H. Morgan, *The Welsh and the Shaping of Early Modern Ireland, 1558–1641*; Brady, 'The Captains', pp.

that this war took a toll on neighbouring England, but the impact on Ireland and its inhabitants was nothing short of devastating. Besides providing the crown with active military service, the Old English Pale community supported the crown's military enterprise by lending money, providing labourers, materials, victuals, and billeting crown soldiers in their own homes. To these voluntary and mandatory contributions must be added the depredations of rebels and the illegal and extortionate appropriations of the crown's military personnel. Not only were civilians killed, but they died of famine and disease, their lands were spoiled and left waste, their goods stolen, their homes abandoned, and money borrowed from them never repaid. It affected the daily lives and functioning of individuals and communities throughout the country, yet little attention has been paid to the efforts of the queen's loyal Irish lieges in sustaining the crown's military machine or how it contributed to their socio-economic deterioration. By assessing the contributions and hardships endured by the Palesmen, this chapter examines the experiences of Old Englishmen during a crucial juncture in that community's identity formation. In doing so, it will explore the ways in which the Palesmen assisted the crown's military establishment with food, money, and lodgings, and how the Palesmen bore a disproportionate share of that burden. It will consider how normal charges were quickly exceeded and how this led to extraordinary demands on the Palesmen's resources and their exploitation by frustrated military men. The economic crisis occasioned by the war will also be surveyed through an examination of agricultural decline, the administration's rising debts, and the effect of a failed coinage debasement scheme. By investigating the Palesmen's material contribution towards the grand finale of the Tudor conquest along with the collapse of the economy, this chapter will consider the social, economic, and physical impact of the Nine Years' War on the Pale and its residents.

Sustaining the Military Establishment

Over the course of the Nine Years' War the English military presence in Ireland swelled from an estimated 1,500 men in 1594 to a monstrous 19,000 with the arrival of the earl of Essex as lord lieutenant in April 1599.[4] As formidable as this army appeared on paper, the reality was that it was an underpaid, underfed, ill-armed force of mostly raw recruits which had been increasingly diluted with

136–59; V.P. Carey, '"As lief to the gallows as go to the Irish wars": Human Rights and the Abuse of the Elizabethan Soldier in Ireland, 1600–1603', *History*, Vol. 99 (2014), pp. 468–86.

[4] For a discussion on the English army during this period, see the preceding chapter of this study. See also J.S. Nolan, 'The Militarization of the Elizabethan State', *Journal of Military History*, Vol. 58, No. 3 (1994), pp. 391–420.

Irish-born conscripts.[5] According to State Paper records, the needs of these forces were rarely met in a timely fashion, and shipments of money, food, apparel, and munitions from England fell far short of the service's requirements.[6] With respect to munitions, the common soldier was generally poorly armed, and there were constant reports of defective weapons and powder shortages throughout the war.[7] For example, a 1597 shipment of calivers, or light muskets, 'without the ordinarie marke of prooffe accustomed to be stamped vpon the pece', were discovered to have 'croked stockes which nowe be out of vse [and] will never be issued to Tharmie but are like to lie and consume with rust as many other did'.[8] Gunpowder was always in short supply, but there were also faults with its shipment and storage. The famous Dublin explosion of March 1597 was wholly attributed to the negligence of ordinance officers in the Tower of London who had sent 'the powder without duble casque to defend it from the like mishappes'.[9] Shipments of other supplies were little better. Deficits in the delivery of soldiers' apparel were so severe that army captains frequently claimed their naked soldiers were pitifully succumbing to the natural elements.[10] Most prejudicial of all was the ineffective supply of food and victualling money. Not only were shipments of foodstuffs late and of meagre quantities, but there were incidents when large proportions of victuals spoiled on the journey and

5   TNA, SP 63/196/39 ('Memorandum on the state of Ireland', Dec. 1596).

6   For a detailed discussion of the English supply systems for Ireland, see R.W. Stewart, 'The "Irish Road": Military Supply and Arms for the Elizabethan Army during the O'Neill Rebellion in Ireland', in M.C. Fissel (ed.), *War and Government in Britain, 1598–1650* (Manchester, 1991), pp. 16–37. See also G. Parker, *The Military Revolution: Military Innovation and the Rise of the West, 1500–1800* (Cambridge, 1996), ch. 2.

7   For example, see TNA, SP 63/209(2)/227 (A. Chichester to Privy Council, 9 Dec. 1601). For a more detailed discussion on the distribution, allotment, and improvements in the armament system, see McGurk, *Elizabethan Conquest*, pp. 227–36.

8   TNA, SP 63/198/22 (G. Bourchier to Burghley, 16 Mar. 1597).

9   Ibid. See also TNA, SP 63/198/21 (J. Norreys to Cecil, 13 Mar. 1597); TNA, SP 63/198/24 (G. Fenton to Cecil, 18 Mar. 1597); TNA, SP 63/198/26 (Russell to Privy Council, 20 Mar. 1597); TNA, SP 63/198/26(IV) (examinations concerning powder explosion, 16 Mar. 1597); TNA, SP 63/198/26(V) (examination of John Shelton and Alexander Palles, Dublin sheriffs, and others, 18 Mar. 1597); TNA, SP 63/198/26(VI) (certificate by Mayor and sheriffs of Dublin, 18 Mar. 1597); TNA, SP 63/198/42 (Irish Council to Privy Council, 25 Mar. 1597); TNA, SP 63/198/42(I) (certificate of the number of dead by Mayor of Dublin, n.d.); TNA, SP 63/199/11 (Mayor and sheriffs of Dublin to Burghley, 6 May 1597); TNA, SP 63/199/12 (Mayor and sheriffs of Dublin to Cecil, 6 May 1597); TNA, SP 63/199/13 (Russell and Council to Burghley, 7 May 1597); Lennon, 'The Great Explosion in Dublin, 1597', pp. 7–20; Lennon, 'Dublin's Great Explosion of 1597', pp. 29–34.

10 TNA, SP 63/188/22 (H. Wallop to Burghley, 10 Apr. 1596); TNA, SP 63/196/39 ('Memorandum on the state of Ireland', Dec. 1596); TNA, SP 63/201/99 (Ormond to Privy Council, 10 Dec. 1597); TNA, SP 63/202(1)/22 (Irish Council to Privy Council, 21 Jan. 1598); TNA, SP 63/202(3)/168 (Irish Council to Privy Council, 23 Nov. 1598); TNA, SP 63/203/101 (Ormond to Privy Council, 26 Mar. 1599); TNA, SP 63/207(5)/44 (A. Yorke to Privy Council, 25 Sep. 1600).

were inedible by the time they reached Ireland.[11] The inadequate victualling system was by far the most damaging element in an already flawed military organisation.

Although the parsimonious habits of Elizabeth and her privy councillors were partly to blame for this state of affairs, the logistics of distribution presented significant obstacles. Transporting men and supplies across the Irish Sea was a challenging and time-consuming ordeal in the sixteenth century.[12] Shipping to Dublin was relatively easy, depending on the winds, but conveying supplies to Galway or Limerick was far more tedious and required good navigation and favourable weather for an extended period.[13] For these reasons shipments from England were usually directed to ports along the eastern seaboard, primarily to Dublin, but Waterford, Drogheda, and Cork were also commonly used. Upon the arrival of cargo at these ports, supplies were transported over land by large escorts for distribution to other regions. Even then, the country presented considerable difficulties for this kind of conveyance. The ruggedness of the terrain made passage extremely challenging at the best of times, and unfavourable weather and lurking rebels during times of war made it virtually impossible. This was compounded by the fact that as the war unfolded the means of land transport, being horses and carriages, became increasingly difficult to obtain locally.[14]

Owing to the unsatisfactory quantity and quality of shipments from England, as well as difficulties of transportation, the government was compelled to press the inhabitants of Ireland to supply the infinite material needs of the English administration and army. This burden was not distributed evenly, and the administration's supply and accommodation demands, as well as the illegal extortions of crown troops, were more severely imposed upon the loyalist Pale

---

[11] TNA, SP 63/200/7 (Burgh and Council to Privy Council, 4 July 1597); TNA, SP 63/200/86 (Loftus and other Councilors to Burghley, 11 Aug. 1597); TNA, SP 63/205/102 (Irish Council to Privy Council, 2 July 1599); TNA, SP 63/207(4)/62 (P. Barnewall to Cecil, 10 Aug. 1600); TNA, SP 63/207(5)/113 (G. Carew to Privy Council, 25 Oct. 1600).

[12] For a more detailed discussion on shipments and transport from England to Ireland, see McGurk, *Elizabethan Conquest*, especially chs 2 and 8; Stewart, 'The "Irish Road"', pp. 16–37. Examples of difficulties: TNA, SP 63/212/49 (G. Thornton to Cecil, 14 Oct. 1602).

[13] CUL, MS Kk. I. 15, ff. 24–5 ('Notes to be considered vppon for Irelande', 1591); TNA, SP 63/202(2)/38 ('The humble requests of the Captains of Ireland', 18 May 1598); TNA, SP 63/205/148 (F. Kingsmill to Cecil, 22 Aug. 1599); TNA, SP 63/207(5)/102 (Chichester to Cecil, 21 Oct. 1600). As Colm Lennon has previously noted, 'many of the 28 provisioning ships which set sail from England to Ireland between 1 April 1595 and 30 April 1596 were beaten back to Chester and Liverpool by tempest'. Lennon, 'The Great Explosion in Dublin', p. 13.

[14] TNA, SP 63/185/28 (Irish Council to Privy Council, 26 Dec. 1595); TNA, SP 63/183/57 (Wallop to Burghley, 27 Sep. 1595); TNA, SP 63/186/44(I) (declaration by the Council of War, 5 Feb. 1596); TNA, SP 63/208(3)/83 (Mountjoy, R. Wingfield, and Bourchier to Privy Council, 19 July 1601); Stewart, 'The "Irish Road"', p. 25.

community than elsewhere.[15] Although the most intense fighting occurred beyond the confines of the Pale, the indigenous populations of other regions were more inclined to join the Confederates, especially if they felt that these alien intruders were squandering their resources. It was likewise doubted that any supplies could be procured in those areas without the threat of physical force. By the closing years of the war, the implementation of scorched earth tactics by crown forces in Munster and Ulster further limited the army's supply base through the systematic destruction of agricultural production in the other provinces.[16] Thus, because the Pale was the most fertile district of Ireland and the only region where English authority and government writs were generally obeyed, the administration was inclined to rely more heavily on the inhabitants of the Pale than any other part of the country.

In addition to their tractability, there are a number of other reasons why the Palesmen were particularly hard-pressed to provision and billet crown forces during the Nine Years' War. First, Dublin was the primary port of disembarkation for thousands of reinforcements, sent from England and, while soldiers awaited muster checks and service appointments, it fell to the inhabitants of Dublin and its environs to accommodate them with lodgings and rations.[17] Second, because perennial supply problems could trigger mutinous conditions within the army rank and file, captains and higher military personnel frequently resorted to transferring troops from remote and inhospitable locations to more prosperous ones, and these were almost invariably located within the Pale. Third, until its closing years, this war was not continuous. Before 1599, fighting was intermittent, broken up by truces and the administration's inconsistent political and military policies.[18] Numerous cessations entailed withdrawing a large part of the crown army into the Pale and, during these intervals, the Palesmen were obliged to meet the needs of these forces. Also contributing to the spasmodic nature of the conflict was the need to protect the Pale's agricultural lands. In the hope of preserving and harvesting crops within the Pale, a number of officials recommended negotiating temporary ceasefires.[19] There were good reasons: the crops of the Pale were the sustenance of the army; drying grain stacks made easy prey for the pillager; and truces must have been welcomed by the husbandman

[15] For example, see CUL, MS Kk. I. 15, ff. 44–7 ('Articles contayning sondrie things to be considered of by the Lo: Deputie and Councell in Ireland, & to be answered to her Ma.tie', 1592).
[16] O'Neill, *The Nine Years War*, pp. 159–94; V.P. Carey, '"What pen can paint or tears atone?": Mountjoy's Scorched Earth Campaign', in Morgan (ed.), *Kinsale*, pp. 205–16.
[17] For example, see TNA, SP 63/199/21(V) (commission from the Privy Council, 14 Apr. 1597); TNA, SP 63/202(2)/38 ('Humble requests of the Captains', 18 May 1598).
[18] Morgan, *Tyrone's Rebellion*, ch. 8; Brady, 'Captain's Games', pp. 136–59.
[19] TNA, SP 63/182/62 (Norreys to Cecil, 26 Aug. 1595); TNA, SP 63/206/57 (Fenton to Cecil, 1 Dec. 1599).

who was permitted some respite while he harvested his crops.[20] This strategy, however, was not without consequence because the Palesmen were now obliged to share their hard-earned labours with the queen's ravenous army.[21] Finally, the Pale was the heart of English dominion in Ireland and it was from here that the vast majority of military campaigns were initiated. On these occasions, soldiers stationed throughout the country were called to Dublin for musters and, during their time in the area, were quartered among the civilian population. An equally onerous imposition was the expectation that the Palesmen would provide months' worth of victuals and other supplies before these newly mustered armies embarked on campaign.[22]

The system for levying supplies within Ireland was much the same as in England. Warrants were directed to county sheriffs specifying what was needed, along with when and where those supplies were to be delivered. The sheriffs were then required to arrange for the collection of provisions within their districts and, upon delivering the materials, an army receiving officer would issue bills or tickets confirming what had been delivered and what monies were due to the inhabitants for that contribution. Necessities were initially requisitioned in accordance with the Palesmen's annual service and taxation obligations but, during the Nine Years' War, government levies quickly surpassed the Palesmen's regular obligations with the result that the administration and its agents were driven to circulate supplementary warrants.[23]

Until the viceroyalty of Sir John Perrott the Palesmen had been bound by their tenures to provide the administration with military services by way of risings out for hostings, and this obligation could be converted into payments of cash or kind in order to support active forces. These mandatory contributions rarely met the needs of the administration and successive viceroys resorted to arbitrary exactions like cess[24] and even the abhorred Irish practice of coyne and livery in order to provide food and shelter for their forces. Through the middle of the century efforts were made to amend the system and demilitarise the Irish lordship by dissolving the private retinues of great magnates in favour of English

---

[20] TNA, SP 63/206/68 (Ormond to Privy Council, 4 Dec. 1599); TNA, SP 63/208(1)/86 (J. Bolles to Cecil, 16 Mar. 1601).

[21] TNA, SP 63/198/86 (Irish Council to Privy Council, 12 Apr. 1597); TNA, SP 63/203/39 (S. Bagenall to Privy Council, 8 Feb. 1599); BL, Cotton Titus C, VII, ff. 156–61 ('Sir Henry Wallops Relation of the Progresse of Tiroens rebellion', 1600).

[22] TNA, SP 63/198/86 (Irish Council to Privy Council, 12 Apr. 1597); TNA, SP 63/202(1)/29 (H. Brouncker to Cecil, 22 Jan. 1598).

[23] For example, TNA, SP 63/191/15(V) (Norreys and Fenton to Irish Council, 3 July 1596).

[24] The term 'cess' could be applied to a range of government impositions. It was initially imposed by viceroys as a prerogative right to provision their households and private retinues, but was later extended for the provisioning of crown garrisons. It was not established by agreement and was not imposed according to fixed rates.

garrisoned forces answerable to the administration.[25] This new army was to be funded by converting the Palesmen's traditional military obligations into monetary and material payments under a new universal taxation system known as composition.[26] In Munster and Connacht, composition revenues were designed to finance the administrative and military machinery of provincial presidencies. In the Pale, however, the composition was unambiguously categorised as a 'military' revenue.[27] The composition had, in effect, replaced traditional military obligations and the two had become mutually exclusive. This was to pose a serious stumbling block during the Nine Years' War.

Although composition had supplanted older forms of contribution, throughout these war years the Dublin administration employed both measures and converted them into whatever form of contribution was most needed. In June 1596 Sir John Norreys asked Lord Deputy Russell to 'giue direction vnto the countrie for the taking vpp of 200 garrons with provision for them for thirtie daies, which may be done vnder the terme of part of the risings out for this yeare'.[28] This was problematic because risings out were being used to supplement the physical strength of the crown army, as was a renewed reliance on the private militias of Irish magnates.[29] Besides, this did not alter the fact that risings out and composition were incompatible forms of local commitment. As Captain John Goringe cautioned during one of the many military crises of 1595, if a Pale host was called upon to defend the borders while the crown army campaigned in the north, 'the agreement for the Composicion money would have bine broken and the Armie would have eaten vpp all the provisions that should have releaved' them.[30] As judicious as Goringe's warning was, it fell on the deaf ears of desperate administrators who had little choice but to ignore this discrepancy.

Taxation by composition was quickly exhausted. The queen and her privy councillors repeatedly asked what had become of composition revenues but, as early as November 1595, Treasurer Sir Henry Wallop answered that supplies taken up within the Pale had already exceeded the terms established by their

---

25 For a discussion on military practices in early modern Ireland, see S.G. Ellis, 'The Tudors and the Origins of the Modern Irish States: A Standing Army', in Bartlett and Jeffery (eds), *A Military History of Ireland*, pp. 116–36.

26 Brady, *Chief Governors*, pp. 218–22.

27 In 1599 the composition of the Pale came to be included with the civil account, but by then no composition revenues were being collected. Sheehan, 'Irish Revenues and English Subventions, 1559–1622', p. 44.

28 TNA, SP 63/190/11(VII) (Norreys to Russell, 4 June 1596).

29 TNA, SP 63/180/61 (discourse by J. Goringe, June 1595); TNA, SP 63/196/13(I) (memorial on the state of Ireland, 7 Dec. 1596).

30 TNA, SP 63/180/61 (discourse by Goringe, June 1595). See also TNA, SP 63/199/66 (Burgh and Council to Privy Council, 31 May 1597).

composition agreements.[31] The decline in crown revenues by way of Pale composition is corroborated by Anthony Sheehan's tabulations. In the years preceding the war, Sheehan traced collections of £1,760 1s. 11d. sterling in 1589–90; £2,018 10s. 5d. in 1590–1; £1,765 2s. 5d. in 1591–2; and £2,144 17s. 1d. in 1592–3. With the outbreak of hostilities in 1593–4, the Pale composition amounted to an impressive £2,444 7s. 4d., and this figure was slighter greater the following year, £2,663 17s. 4d. In 1595–6 the Pale composition was worth only £880 0s. 8d., and the following year it dropped to the meagre sum of £354 7s. 4d. Between 1597 and 1603 there are no records to indicate that any composition payments had been collected within the Pale.[32] Although it is possible that such mundane record-keeping had escaped the registers of distracted crown officials, it is equally possible that this tax had been wholly converted to the war effort and that there was nothing left to line the queen's coffers. Responding to enquiries in January 1597, Wallop stated that 'there hath none thereof bene receaued this yeare and half, but the same is wholly left in the hands of the country people towards theire satisfaction for such beoves as they haue and do daily delyver... *surmounting farre the composicion they are to paye*'.[33] The following year, the Irish Council confirmed this, noting that 'wee cannot denie but yt is aunswered in beoues, and other helps taken vp for tharmy, to a far greater value then the composicion amounteth vnto'.[34]

The inhabitants of the Pale shouldered an indeterminately large proportion of the charges necessary for sustaining the crown's military enterprise during this period. Preserved in the Irish State Papers are scores of warrants directed to the mayors, sheriffs, and gentlemen of Pale towns and counties, some of which itemise the numbers of cows, sheep, hens, pigs, horses, and labourers to be levied within Pale shires. There are also numerous reports specifying to what extent certain warrants were answered by the Palesmen, but these almost always allege that government requirements were unsatisfactorily met by Irish subjects.[35] It is impossible to verify these complaints because they rarely accounted for what was in fact delivered. What is more, according to the sheriffs of Dublin, Meath, and Westmeath, government-appointed receivers refused to issue bills of receipt for supplies delivered by them, with the result that neither

---

[31] TNA, SP 63/184/11 (Wallop to Burghley, 8 Nov. 1595). See also TNA, SP 63/190/12 (Wallop to Burghley, 8 June 1596); TNA, SP 63/196/2 ('Observations', 3 Dec. 1596); TNA, SP 63/197/33 (Wallop to Burghley, 13 Jan. 1597); TNA, SP 63/202(1)/22 (Irish Council to Privy Council, 21 Jan. 1598).

[32] Sheehan, 'Irish Revenues', p. 45.

[33] Emphasis added. TNA, SP 63/197/33 (Wallop to Burghley, 13 Jan. 1597).

[34] TNA, SP 63/202(1)/22 (Irish Council to Privy Council, 21 Jan. 1598).

[35] Lambeth, Carew MS, 612, No. 270 (G. Harvey to Russell in Russell's journal, 10 Oct. 1595); TNA, SP 63/202(1)/29 (H. Brouncker to Cecil, 22 Jan. 1598); TNA, SP 63/207(5)/116 ('Heads of things', 27 Oct. 1600).

the council nor the country agents could prove, or disprove, whether deliveries were complete or deficient.[36] In most instances, warrants and recorded deliveries do not correspond, and there is no telling how many warrants, auditor reports, and complaints have not survived, nor is there any way of estimating how many escaped official recording.[37] In fact, the chronicler Sir James Perrott followed contemporary officials like Sir Geoffrey Fenton in asserting that even educated approximations of the charges imposed upon the Palesmen would greatly underestimate the actual burden they bore because '[t]he poore English pale did beare many secret and heauie burdens aboue the charges imposed by publicke authoritie'.[38]

Unfortunately, existing documentation reflects only a portion of what actually transpired. Nevertheless, the Irish State Papers do provide particulars from which we may infer certain trends, and probably the best extant example is offered by a list of warrants directed to the sheriff of Kildare. Between 1594 and 1596 the inhabitants of Kildare were required to answer twenty-three warrants issued by the Irish Council and army officials. Over the two years in question the county was expected to raise 450 footmen for military service, fifty pioneers to perform various forms of labour, 275 garrons[39] with 132 leaders[40] for transport, as well as 436 beeves and twenty-five barrels of oats to feed campaigning forces. In addition to these levies, the sheriff was also instructed to make billeting arrangements for 126 horsemen and fifty-six footmen along with their non-combatant followers. By the government's calculation, these impositions amounted to a charge of £2,690 2s.,[41] a sum which was approximately two-thirds of the composition due by the entire Pale for the same period.[42] According to Patrick Typper, agent for the inhabitants of Kildare, the actual charges borne by the county were considerably higher than those given by the Dublin administration and far in excess of the annual composition due by the combined five Pale shires,

---

[36] See the certificates submitted by the sheriffs of Dublin, Meath, and Westmeath: Lambeth, Carew MS, 612, No. 270 (Russell's journal). See also TNA, SP 63/207(6)/123 (answers to complaints, Dec. 1600); BL, Add MS 4757, Milles Collection, Vol. III, 27r–27v (Privy Council to Mountjoy, 20 Feb. 1599).

[37] For example, TNA, SP 63/182/35 (Fenton to Burghley, 14 Aug. 1595).

[38] BL, Add. MS 4819, f. 75v ('Collections made by Sir James Perrott'). See also TNA, SP 63/182/35 (Fenton to Burghley, 14 Aug. 1595).

[39] Small workhorses.

[40] Men in charge of handling and directing the horses and carts.

[41] TNA, SP 63/196/49 ('List of Warrants ranging from 1594 to 1596').

[42] This statement is based on the composition agreement established between the Palesmen and Perrot in 1585 along with amendments made to this agreement in 1592. See V. Treadwell, 'Sir John Perrot and the Irish Parliament of 1585–6', PRIA, Vol. 85 (1985), p. 302; TNA, SP 63/166/57(II) ('Note of the articles concerning the composition', 13 Sep. 1592). See also H. Morgan, 'Composition', in S.J. Connolly (ed.), The Oxford Companion to Irish History (Oxford, 2007), pp. 113–14; Sheehan, 'Irish Revenues', p. 46.

or even the whole of Leinster. Typper contended that over an eight-month period, from 19 September 1595 to 8 May 1596, the county's contribution had cost the inhabitants £2,118 2s.[43] On a monthly basis, this was nearly two and a half times greater than the government's estimate. Notwithstanding variations between the tabulations compiled by crown officials and Palesmen, even Ireland's English Treasurer-at-Wars was forced to concede on multiple occasions that what was both demanded of the Palesmen and delivered by them had far surpassed what they owed the crown and that it was the crown, in fact, which owed the Palesmen substantial compensation.[44]

Accommodating soldiers throughout the Pale was equally demanding on the Palesmen's resources. Essentially, the billeting of soldiers was a return to the formerly abolished practice of cess, which the Palesmen, along with many English bureaucrats, felt was unfair since recent legislation had been devised to establish a more equitable taxation system.[45] But in times of crisis, such as this, billeting had certain benefits. First, it served as a defensive procedure. Rebel raids on the Pale not only threatened lives by the sword, but also starvation through the destruction of crops. In addition to being the sustenance of its permanent residents, the Pale's agricultural output was the mainstay of the crown army and it therefore had to be protected. In an effort to preserve its farmland and husbandmen from spoliation, the Irish Council elected to billet soldiers throughout the Pale. In return for this protective barrier, inhabitants were expected to satisfy the needs of their defenders and thereby relieve the crown of that responsibility.[46] Unfortunately, this was not the symbiotic relationship envisioned by administrators and the system was routinely abused by disgruntled soldiers and frustrated officials.[47] These abuses are best exemplified by the proceedings of Sir John Norreys during his deployment to Connacht.

In May 1596 Norreys was commissioned to go into Connacht with a large crown force and treat with the province's rebels. As part of this commission he was instructed to investigate corruption charges lodged by the inhabitants against Sir Richard Bingham, the provincial president.[48] Reports of discord

---

[43] BL, Lansdowne MS, Vol. 81, f. 181 (petition of Co. Kildare, 8 May 1596).

[44] TNA, SP 63/184/11 (Wallop to Burghley, 8 Nov. 1595); TNA, SP 63/184/34 (Wallop to Burghley, 26 Nov. 1595); TNA, SP 63/184/38 (Wallop to Burghley, 30 Nov. 1595); TNA, SP 63/190/12 (Wallop to Burghley, 8 June 1596); TNA, SP 63/197/33 (Wallop to Burghley, 13 Jan. 1597); TNA, SP 63/202(1)/22 (Irish Council to Privy Council, 21 Jan. 1598).

[45] There were, however, some officials, most notably William Saxey, who advocated the reimplementation of the oppressive cess. BL, Cotton Titus B, XII, ff. 84–93b ('Mr. Saxeys Discourse', 1598).

[46] For example, TNA, SP 63/178/54 (Russell and Council to Privy Council, 26 Feb. 1595).

[47] Brady, *Chief Governors*, pp. 209–44; Canny, *Making Ireland British*, pp. 66–7.

[48] Composition agreements had been established between the State and provincials in the 1570s and 1580s. Yet, as late as the mid-1590s, the native population was still complaining of exploitation, accusing Bingham of overcharging them with the cessing of his forces and requisitioning

in Connacht had reached London the previous month, causing Burghley to write that 'the said Composition will houlde place, foreseeinge that in no wise any personn having his land answerable to the Composition should be chardged with any Cesse of the Souldior, or any other chardge whatsoeuer to be ymposed by the Lord Gouernor of the Cuntry'.[49] Following his own investigation into the matter, Norreys was convinced that Bingham's extortions had dishonoured the crown and abused the people, and he therefore recommended strict punishment for the president. Ironically, it was not long before Norreys began to implement the same abuses committed by the condemned Bingham.[50]

Owing to local scarcity, partially on account of Norreys's tenuous hold on the region as well as inadequate means for transporting victuals from other areas, Norreys's Connacht expedition soon encountered critical supply problems. John Nolan has explained that Norreys first attempted to relieve his forces by transferring them from temporary camps to surrounding garrisons; this proved insufficient for the very same reasons. Frustrated, Norreys and his troops resorted to wresting supplies from the already beleaguered inhabitants, which prompted a royal reprimand along with new orders restricting 'food gathering almost entirely to the loyal counties of the Pale'.[51] This was hardly the solution for feeding Norreys's army since their designated food supply remained a great distance from their place of service. As the situation continued to worsen, the only option available to Norreys was to divide his army because, by sending some away, it might be feasible to stretch existing resources for a smaller force.

In the end, Norreys's efforts to relieve his unpaid and ill-fed forces rested on passing the buck, so to speak, to the inhabitants of Dublin and Meath.[52] Between June 1595 and February 1596, Norreys issued at least four warrants to the sheriff of Dublin, three of which have survived.[53] The first existing warrant, dated 14 January 1596, referred to another, issued the previous June, in which Norreys had directed the sheriff to make preparations 'for the placing certen of my owne horsses, and some vnder my companie there. And to furnishe the saide horses sufficiently with horsmeate and likewise the boyes and groomes

their goods under colour of supporting his administration and its policing arm. On earlier composition agreements in Connacht, see Cunningham, 'The Composition of Connacht', pp. 1–14. See also R. Rapple, 'Taking Up Office in Elizabethan Connacht: The Case of Sir Richard Bingham', *English Historical Review*, Vol. 123 (2008), pp. 277–99.

[49] TNA, SP 63/189/48(I) ('Answers written by Lord Burghley', 13 Apr. 1596).

[50] J.S. Nolan, *Sir John Norreys and the Elizabethan Military World* (Exeter, 1997), p. 231.

[51] Ibid., p. 226.

[52] Ibid., p. 231.

[53] Lambeth, Carew MS, 612, No. 270 (Norreys's warrants to sheriff of Dublin in Russell's journal 14 and 25 Jan. 1596); TNA, SP 63/186/20 (warrant by Norreys to sheriff of Dublin, 25 Jan. 1596); TNA, SP 63/186/40 (warrant from Norreys to sheriff of Dublin, 5 Feb. 1596).

appointed to looke vnto them with their dyetts and lodgings.'[54] According to this warrant, prior efforts to transfer his companies' upkeep to the inhabitants of Dublin had met with objections and even forceful resistance.[55] Norreys therefore ordered the sheriff to be more diligent in his arrangements, investigate malefactors, and apprehend any persons who resisted further billeting arrangements.[56] This was evidently of no avail since eleven days later, in response to further reports of local defiance, Norreys wrote again to inform the sheriff that he had resolved to send one of his officers with fifty soldiers to assist the undersheriff in the execution of his decree.[57] A third warrant followed two weeks later. However, this time Norreys acquiesced to local agitation and transferred certain companies then lodged at Swords to Castleknock, for which he again directed the sheriff to make arrangements.[58] The tenor of Norreys's warrants clearly indicate that the inhabitants of County Dublin were not only irritated by the imposition of his companies but that some actually refused to receive his horsemen and 'moste maliciously turne them loose abroad'.[59] The number of soldiers quartered in Dublin and the costs incurred by the inhabitants are unclear, but similar complaints lodged against Norreys's forces by the inhabitants of County Meath offer some insight into this matter.

Although there are no extant warrants to the sheriff of Meath, two petitions submitted by the inhabitants of that county reveal that some of Norreys's companies had been distributed through Meath baronies. It is unclear whether these companies were transferred to Meath following Norreys's difficulties in Dublin, but because the Meathmen complained that 'they haue bene of longe tyme and yet are chardged with theis Companyes of horsse and foot', it is plausible that their presence there coincided with their abode in Dublin.[60] According to the inhabitants' first petition, they were at pains to support thirty-five horsemen along with their horses and boys.[61] The second petition revealed a similar story, this time listing whole companies, three of foot and three of horse, all of which the inhabitants were required to lodge and feed, usually at double and triple rates.[62] Although there is no documentation to suggest that Norreys's troops met with any aggression or confrontation in Meath, the

[54] Lambeth, Carew MS, 612, No. 270 (Russell's journal).
[55] Ibid.; TNA, SP 63/186/20 (warrant by Norreys to sheriff of Dublin, 25 Jan. 1596).
[56] Lambeth, Carew MS, 612, No. 270 (Russell's journal).
[57] TNA, SP 63/186/20 (warrant by Norreys to sheriff of Dublin, 25 Jan. 1596).
[58] TNA, SP 63/186/40 (warrant from Norreys to sheriff of Dublin, 5 Feb. 1596); Nolan, *John Norreys*, p. 226.
[59] TNA, SP 63/186/20 (warrant from Norreys to sheriff of Dublin, 5 Feb. 1596).
[60] TNA, SP 63/201/146 (petition of the inhabitants of Meath, 1597). See also TNA, SP 63/189/46(X) ('Note of the abuses committed … in the county of Meath', 22 May 1596).
[61] TNA, SP 63/189/46(X) ('Note of the abuses', 22 May 1596).
[62] TNA, SP 63/201/146 (petition of the inhabitants of Meath, 1597).

Meathmen's petitions made it abundantly clear that they were deeply perturbed by these impositions and that the 'burthen [was] at all tymes most heauy, and at this present most intolerable'.[63]

If the queen's councillors in England were in any doubt about the legitimacy of these particular complaints, they were seconded by a number of New English officials who had a vested interest in the prosperity of the country. It was noted that Thomas Jones, bishop of Meath, 'with manie of the rest, take great exceptions to Sir Iohn Norreys, for placing his troope of horse at Trymme'.[64] These, combined with the country complaints, put Norreys on the defensive. Although he had personal motives for encouraging Bingham's removal – having recommended his brother for the provincial presidency – Norreys's earlier verdict in favour of the inhabitants had shown a convincing degree of empathy for the plight of the poor countrymen. Yet, when defending himself from the Palesmen's criticisms, Norreys protested that 'practises are vsed in the country to haue the people exclaym and complayn of my horsemen… therefore I humbly pray… no creditt be geuen vnto them tyll I be herd'.[65] Assuredly, there were occasions when English officials had legitimate grounds to complain that the inhabitants were providing weak assistance; however, even under the extraordinary circumstances of this war, Norreys's exploitation of the Palesmen had overstepped anything which could be considered reasonable or fair. In fact, English officials took exception to the legality of Norreys's proceedings. In February 1596 Russell informed Burghley that despite his own presence in Dublin during this interval he had no knowledge of Norreys's billeting arrangements until complaints had reached him from the country. As far as Russell was concerned, Norreys had shown a flagrant disregard for administrative protocol by placing his forces in the Pale without prior approval from the lord deputy and council. This, Russell asserted, was deeply disturbing and potentially damaging for crown–community relations and he felt obliged to intervene so as to ensure that 'the service be not hindered by dissention'.[66] The Irish Council accordingly ordered some of those forces illegally lodged in Meath to disperse towards Kells and the Pale borders; Norreys's forces, however, contravened these orders and continued to reside around Trim.[67] It is perhaps unsurprising then that when Sir James Perrott reflected on Norreys's time in Ireland, he concluded that Norreys 'always preferred the soldiers benifitt [before] the poor contries satisfaction'.[68]

---

63 Ibid. See also TNA, SP 63/189/46(X) ('Note of the abuses', 22 May 1596).
64 TNA, SP 63/195/26 (Russell to Cecil, 22 Nov. 1596). See also, TNA, SP 63/195/25 (Russell to Privy Council, 22 Nov. 1596); TNA, SP 63/195/27 (Loftus and Jones to Burghley, 22 Nov. 1596).
65 TNA, SP 63/189/51 (Norreys to Cecil, 28 May 1596).
66 CSPI, 1592–6, p. 471.
67 TNA, SP 63/195/26 (Russell to Cecil, 22 Nov. 1596).
68 BL, Add. MS 4819, ff. 96–96v ('Collections made by Sir James Perrott').

Burdened by government-directed appropriations of food, materials, and housing, the Palesmen were growing ever-more irritated by the unfair demands imposed upon them by men like Norreys. But even more distressing than these quasi-legal impositions were the many abuses inflicted upon both their persons and possessions by large numbers of military men who felt their needs unsatisfactorily met by both the crown and civilian population. Tudor armies were plagued by 'chronic disciplinary problems', but the soldier's life in sixteenth-century Ireland was not an easy one.[69] Neglected by the crown for which he fought, the English soldier suffered from an intolerable shortage of pay, food, clothing, shelter, training, and arms, and was thrown into a war against an enemy who possessed a distinct local advantage with respect to terrain and tactics.[70] In the words of English army captains, 'the warre of Ireland is well knowne to be the most miserable warre for trauayle toyle and famyne in the worlde'.[71] Those soldiers who could afford to, paid huge fees to escape back to England, but for those who remained, Ireland was little better than a death sentence. Weakened in both body and mind, crown soldiers released their frustrations on the vulnerable civilian population who provided convenient soft targets.[72] As Lord Deputy Burgh lamented, the soldiers 'lived in manner by onely ayre, first having made spoyle of all they covld come by in towne as covntrey'.[73]

The most obvious culprits were those who had the greatest access. Technically, billeted soldiers were required to pay their hosts according to prescribed rates and, in 1596, the soldier's diet allowance, whether residing in garrison or among the inhabitants, was established at 6d. per day.[74] Rarely did this sum meet the dietary demands of the soldiery, nor did they have disposable cash to pay for their needs. As a result, the cost fell to the country and, according to the Kildare plaintiffs, the common soldier lodged there consumed 6d., and often more, for a single meal, and 'eche Corporall or other Officer taking 12d. 2s. or 3s. ster. a meale'.[75] The Meathmen claimed to have incurred far greater dieting

---

[69] Phillips, '"Home! Home!"', p. 316. McGurk, *Elizabethan Conquest*, ch. 9; McGurk, 'The Dead, Sick & Wounded', pp. 16–22; Falls, *Elizabeth's Irish Wars*, p. 61; J.E. Neal, 'Elizabeth and the Netherlands, 1586–7', *English Historical Review*, Vol. 45 (1930), p. 388.

[70] For a detailed discussion of Irish military tactics, see O'Neill, *The Nine Years War*.

[71] TNA, SP 63/202(2)/38 ('humble requests of the Captains', 18 May 1598).

[72] TNA, SP 63/195/6 (Kyffin to Cecil, 8 Nov. 1596); TNA, SP 63/196/39 ('Memorandum on the state of Ireland', Dec. 1596); TNA, SP 63/202(1)/56 (Irish Council to Privy Council, 27 Feb. 1598); TNA, SP 63/202(2)/16 (Fenton to Cecil or Burghley, 20 Apr. 1598); TNA, SP 63/202(2)/107 (R. Wilbraham to Cecil, 22 July 1598); TNA, SP 63/202(4)/62 (divers abuses done and suffered by the Council of Ireland, 1598); TNA, SP 63/203/101 (Ormond to Privy Council, 26 Mar. 1599). Canny, *Making Ireland British*, pp. 72–3; Carey, '"As lief to the gallows"', pp. 468–86.

[73] TNA, SP 63/199/58 (Burgh to Burghley, 25 May 1597).

[74] Lambeth, Carew MS, 612, No. 270 (Russell's journal).

[75] BL, Lansdowne MS, Vol. 81, f. 181 (petition of Co. Kildare, 8 May 1596).

costs, asserting that officers demanded at least double their allowed diet, with one particular officer consuming up to 18s. 6d. worth of food a day.[76] Although price inflation played a part in this cost, the reality was that soldiers forcibly demanded this maintenance at the expense of the subject, often denying their hosts the provisions they had carefully reserved for their families.

This sort of exploitation was not confined to soldiers who found semi-permanent accommodation among the Palesmen. Those troops who regularly passed through the Pale were equally guilty of abuses, and whether due to recent arrival at the Dublin port, times of cessation, or calls to musters, army discipline was appalling. It was hoped the eventual removal of these forces to distant garrisons or on campaign would provide some relief for the harassed locals and otherwise preoccupied administrators who were forced to investigate complaints of misconduct.[77] In the event, when these forces did receive marching orders they were in the habit of leaving 'a path of destruction in their wake'.[78] Regulations had been put in place to avoid these inconveniences, but they were to little avail. Military codes stipulated that travelling forces were to cover a minimum of ten miles each day and, if their posts happened to be further, soldiers were permitted only one night in any one place, 'taking of his host… competent meat & drinck such as the tyme and habillety of the partie can afforde… paying for the same ready mony or giveinge their Capten or officers ticquett'.[79] Crown soldiers rarely obeyed these orders and the Palesmen complained that horse companies travelled no more than four miles per day, repeatedly detouring from their course in search of habitations which might yield profitable gains to the would-be looter. Foot companies journeyed 'not aboue two or three myles in the day, and thoughe their appointed garrizons be not past ten myles of, yet do they often tymes goe thirty myles aboute'.[80] Worse still was that this traversing of the Pale occurred far more frequently than the service required, prompting the Palesmen to protest that 'since theis broyles, yt was ordinarie that every two monethes or there aboutes there should be drawn through the Pale two or three thowsand men from the partes of Mounster, Leynster, and Connoght'.[81] The problem had become so pervasive that by late 1600 the English Privy Council demanded to know why 'it is a common matter

[76] TNA, SP 63/189/46(X) ('Note of the abuses', 22 May 1596).

[77] For example, Lambeth, Carew MS, 612, No. 270 ('warrant for executing a soldier by marshall Lawe' in Russell's journal); TNA, SP 63/207(5)/116 ('Heads of things', 27 Oct. 1600).

[78] Canny, *Making Ireland British*, p. 67. TNA, SP 63/202(2)/38 ('humble requests of the Captains', 18 May 1598).

[79] TNA, SP 63/189/46(IX) ('Orders to be obserued', 18 Apr. 1596).

[80] TNA, SP 63/202(4)/60 ('greevances', 1598). See also TNA, SP 63/200/53 (petition of the inhabitants of Kildare, 24 July 1597); TNA, SP 63/207(3)/148 (petition of the inhabitants of the Pale, June 1600).

[81] TNA, SP 63/202(4)/60 ('greevances', 1598); TNA, SP 63/202(4)/75 ('A discourse', 1598).

to overrun the country with horse and foot for the convoy of one barrel of powder'.[82]

Although lying in garrison might sound more appealing than time on the march, crown soldiers found a peripatetic existence preferable to life in Irish garrisons where conditions were miserable and the risks of disease interminable.[83] However, the most immediate concern for garrisoned soldiers was acute food shortages. In 1598, army captains protested that 'it is well knowne and of truth to be auouched that there haue bene diuers garrisons in many places of Ireland which haue liued without the taste of bread or Drinke but with releif onelie of Beefe water. Some the space of 6 monthes, some 8, some more.'[84] Garrison life was indeed difficult, and there were periods of near famine for the warders, but the country did provide some direct relief. Delays and shortfalls in victual shipments from England compelled the administration to press the local population to raise and deliver provisions for these garrisons. According to the Palesmen, weekly levies were imposed for 'lardge proporciones of beoffes, muttons, and grayne', along with horses and men to deliver them. Little regard was had for whether the country could afford to surrender these provisions, and if the Palesmen failed to meet supply demands in full, 'the soildiors straight runneth into the contry'.[85] To the inhabitants, deficits in supplies were merely a pretext for overrunning the country because even when they had fully complied with government orders the soldiers still proceeded to 'vex and opresse thenhabytaunts next adioynyng to their garrizons moste extreamelie, consumyng wastfullie and needles suche provision as the people do make for the relief of them selves and their famylies'.[86]

By mid-1599, the English military presence in Ireland stood at 19,000 men, and one can well imagine the devastation wrought by these extra bodies in a region suffering from considerable political and economic instability. This figure, however, only accounts for men-at-arms; it does not include the army's sizable entourage, composed of soldiers' attendants, or 'boys' as they were known, wives, and mistresses.[87] The government had set restrictions on the army's non-combatant 'tail': six women were permitted to follow each company, and these, being the wives of select soldiers, were expected to serve as laundresses. Each horseman was entitled to employ one horseboy, and

---

[82] *CSPI, 1600*, p. 507.
[83] For example, O'Sullivan Beare noted: 'A great swarm of lice afflicted the garrison of Armagh and many perished of this plague. Famine soon followed.' O'Sullivan Beare, *History of Ireland*, p. 93. See also Canny, *Making Ireland British*, pp. 70–1; Phillips, '"Home! Home!"', p. 322.
[84] TNA, SP 63/202(2)/38 ('humble requests of the Captains', 18 May 1598).
[85] TNA, SP 63/202(4)/60 ('greevances', 1598).
[86] Ibid.
[87] Evidence for the 1590s concurs with Brady's assessment of official figures during the 1570s. Brady, *Chief Governors*, p. 221. See also Brady, 'Conservative Subversives', pp. 68–9.

foot soldiers were restricted to one boy for every two men.[88] Official decrees also stipulated that these non-combatants 'shalbe no waie chargeable to the Countrie or townes'.[89] However, like every other directive concerning army discipline, these regulations were routinely violated. It was commonly alleged that 'everie man' within a travelling horse company 'moste comonlie hath dobble horses, some officers treble, each of them one boy, and some two', and there were occasional reports of a single officer maintaining three boys to serve only himself.[90] Foot companies were little better, 'eache soildior with his boy at leaste, and for a greate parte with their woman, and many horses aswell of their owne, as of the contrie violentlie taken'.[91] Like the soldiers, these followers took their maintenance from the inhabitants 'farre more then competent, and... muche exceeding the peoples habylitie'.[92] For instance, the inhabitants of County Kildare complained that each woman demanded '4d. or 6d.' and each boy consumed 3d. per meal.[93]

Whether they were billeted, garrisoned, or just passing through, soldiers and officers illegally seized food, drink, lodging, money, and goods from the already frustrated locals, declaring 'their drom and collors a suffician[t] warrant'.[94] But, worse than the uncompensated pillage of livestock, goods, and money, was the manner in which these things were confiscated. According to one group of outraged Palesmen:

> if they be not satisfied with meate and money according their outradgious demaundes, then doe they beate their poore hostes, and their people, ransackinge their howses, taking away chattell and goodes of all sortes, not leaving soe muche as the tooles or instruments that craftes men doe excercise their occupacions withall, nor the garments to their backes, or clothes on their beddes.[95]

Some officials, most notably Mountjoy, dismissed these complaints, arguing that 'the manner of this country is to cry out in general that they are spoiled, and not to lay down in particular by whom, whereby... no course can be taken for redress'.[96] According to the Palesmen, they dared not name offenders because

[88] TNA, SP 63/189/46(IX) ('Orders to be obserued', 18 Apr. 1596). McGurk, *Elizabethan Conquest*, p. 199; Falls, *Elizabeth's Irish Wars*, p. 37.
[89] TNA, SP 63/189/46(IX) ('Orders to be obserued', 18 Apr. 1596).
[90] TNA, SP 63/202(4)/60 ('greevances', 1598); TNA, SP 63/189/46(X) ('Note of the abuses', 22 May 1596).
[91] TNA, SP 63/202(4)/60 ('greevances', 1598).
[92] Ibid.
[93] BL, Lansdowne MS, Vol. 81, f. 181 (petition of Co. Kildare, 8 May 1596). The inhabitants of Meath claimed to have incurred even greater charges. TNA, SP 63/189/46(X) ('Note of the abuses', 22 May 1596).
[94] TNA, SP 63/202(4)/60 ('greevances', 1598).
[95] Ibid.
[96] CSPI, 1600, p. 508.

'they do not onelie excersies all the crueltie they can against them, but doe also procure other companies to set a fresh vpon the poore Inhabytaunts and spoyle them in farre worse sorte then before in nature of a Revendge'.[97] The Palesmen's sense of despair on this point is prevalent throughout their wartime complaints, and not least of all because they were unsure whom to trust for justice or redress. This, no doubt, contributed to the Palesmen's growing irritation with crown forces and sense of alienation from the administration.

The advantages of exploiting the civilian population were appreciated by some rebels and non-combatants who attempted to emulate crown soldiers. Perhaps surprising though is Ó Báille's contention that the Confederates did not commit such abuses to the same extent.[98] Rebel depredations were generally opportunistic and tactical, with the intention of forcing certain individuals to submit or become neutral with the added goal of depriving the English army of its food source.[99] Excepting targeted raids, those Confederate forces which penetrated and occupied areas of Leinster did not perpetrate the same abuses as their opponents or comrades in Munster.[100] This was corroborated by the Palesmen, who averred that 'the soildiors entertayned and appointed by youre Maiesty for the contries savegarde and defence have... no lesse consumed, empoverished and anoyed moste parte of the Pale, then the traytors'.[101] Even officials like Lord Chancellor Loftus conceded that the Pale was 'miserably wasted and impoverished by those who are sent to defend it'.[102] This was good propaganda for the Confederates and Hugh O'Neill was quick to assert that he and his allies had refrained from fully assaulting the Pale in the vain hope that the Palesmen would re-evaluate their position and join the Irish Catholic Confederacy.[103]

The Confederates may have been less burdensome, but raiding did occur and the crown soldiers living off – or, to be more accurate, pilfering from – their Pale hosts did little to prevent it. In November 1596, while some of Norreys's forces continued to reside in Meath, northern Confederates launched a series of raids against Meath towns but the occupying soldiers

[97] TNA, SP 63/202(4)/60 ('greevances', 1598).
[98] Ó Báille, 'The Buannadha', pp. 49–94.
[99] For discussions on Gaelic Irish warfare, see Nicholls, *Gaelic and Gaelicised Ireland*; K. Simms, *From Kings to Warlords* (Rochester, NY, 1987); Simms, 'Warfare in the Medieval Gaelic Lordships', *Irish Sword*, Vol. 12 (1975), pp. 98–108; Hayes-McCoy, 'Strategy and Tactics in Irish Warfare', pp. 255–79; Ó Domhnaill, 'Warfare in Sixteenth-Century Ireland', pp. 29–54.
[100] Ó Báille, 'The Buannadha', pp. 49–94; TNA, SP 63/207(5)/110(I) (letters sent by O'Neill to lords in Munster, 20–21 Sep, 1600).
[101] TNA, SP 63/202(4)/60 ('greevances', 1598). See also Lee, 'The Discovery', ff. 79–81.
[102] *CSPI*, 1599–1600, p. 411.
[103] TNA, SP 63/202(3)/168(II) (O'Neill to Fitzpiers, 11 Mar. 1598); TNA, SP 63/206/63(II) (proceedings of Delvin's agents with Tyrone, 26 Nov. 1599).

did little to defend the territory from which they now took sustenance. Recounting the event, crown servitor Sir Edward Moore reported that '40 horsmen with some 3 or foure hundred foete did burne and spoyle within some thre or foure miles of Tarra, and not a man in her Maiesties cause to make head against them'.[104] This was not an isolated incident. In January 1599, the Irish Council noted that 800 rebels had passed through supposedly well-defended Westmeath 'even at noon time of the day... without stop or encounter of any of Her Majesty's forces'.[105]

Although it may be argued that the supplications of Old English Palesmen were designed to further their own agendas, financially or otherwise, similar testimonies were lodged by New English officials and settlers which serve to corroborate the Palesmen's accusations. Contrary to any assumption that New English servitors may have been exempt from the molestations of crown soldiers, petitions from men like Edward Moore suggest that no group of people was immune to the transgressions of crown troops.[106] The fact that Moore, a New English military servitor himself, had been spoiled by his own comrades-in-arms is indicative of how common and widespread these disorders were. The excessive and ubiquitous nature of army abuses is also demonstrated by the fact that the Irish Council was compelled to reissue military codes of conduct on multiple occasions and make severe, albeit episodic, examples of offenders.[107] The brutality of army offences is made manifest by the specific itemisation of prohibited crimes; for example, one of the many which incurred the death penalty was 'the raveshinge & Carnall knowledge of any women against her will'.[108] These regulations and punitive measures failed to correct what had become a systemic and endemic problem. Moreover, given the already weak condition of the crown army, most English officials were disinclined to enforce rigid disciplinary codes.[109]

---

[104] TNA, SP 63/195/39 (Moore to Loftus, 25 Nov. 1596). See also TNA, SP 63/195/40 (T. Wackes to Loftus and Council, 26 Nov. 1596); TNA, SP 63/202(1)/56 (Irish Council to Privy Council, 27 Feb. 1598); Lee, 'The Discovery', ff. 79–81; TNA, SP 63/197/16 (Norreys to Cecil, 13 Jan. 1597).
[105] *CSPI, 1598–99*, p. 463.
[106] TNA, SP 63/189/39 (E. Moore to Burghley, 22 May 1596).
[107] TNA, SP 63/189/46(IX) ('Orders to be obserued', 18 Apr. 1596); TNA, SP 63/197/86 ('Decree by the Lord Deputy and Council to restrain extortions by Captains and soldiers', 12 Feb. 1597); TNA, SP 63/207(5)/15 (Irish Council to Privy Council, 12 Sep. 1600); TNA, SP 63/207(6)/123 (answers to complaints, Dec. 1600); Lambeth, Carew MS, 612, No. 270 ('warrant for executing a soldier by marshall Lawe').
[108] TNA, SP 63/189/46(IX) ('Orders to be obserued', 18 Apr. 1596).
[109] TNA, SP 63/208(2)/91(I) (Chichester to Mountjoy, 14 May 1601); Moryson, *Itinerary*, iii, p. 137. TNA, SP 63/210/67 (Mountjoy and Carew to Privy Council, 18 Mar. 1602); TNA, SP 63/211/8 (draft of Queen's letter, 16 Apr. 1602).

Agricultural Decline in the Irish Hub

Advertisements from Ireland, like that by Maurice Kyffin at the beginning of this chapter, appear redundant; every month of every year came prophecies of Ireland's impending doom. Countless dispatches from the Dublin Council declared Ireland's resources exhausted and emphasised the desperation of soldier and countryman alike. Because the Pale was the mainstay of English authority in Ireland, particular emphasis was put on the dangerous depletion of all commodities within it.[110] Notwithstanding inevitable inaccuracies in tabulating the Palesmen's contribution to the crown's war effort, it is possible to make at least a partial assessment of how the demands of this conflict impacted the local population and landscape. With respect to ordinary charges, several county petitions, plus a handful of official communications, offer insight into the trials and tribulations of the Palesmen, and a synopsis of what occurred in County Meath between October 1595 and November 1596 may serve as an appropriate example.

In October 1595 a single warrant directed George Harvey, sheriff of Meath, to raise 450 beoves,[111] eighty garrons, and 100 pioneers[112] to serve the needs of Sir John Norreys in Dundalk.[113] A month later, Harvey received another order to prepare a joint levy with the sheriffs of Dublin and Louth for twenty garrons and ten leaders to serve the army for sixty days.[114] The following July, Harvey was instructed to levy a further 300 cows and deliver these into Connacht for Norreys's forces.[115] Considering the Irish Council reported the execution of twenty-three warrants in Kildare over a coinciding two-year period, it is assumed that the surviving warrants directed to Meath account for only a portion of what was actually levied within that county. What is more, these warrants were issued during the same period that a number of Norreys's soldiers and attendants were accommodated in Meath, all of whom exacted more than was their due or bearable for the inhabitants.[116] By November 1596, the situation in Meath had become so worrying that Bishop Jones and Lord Chancellor Loftus warned Burghley that 'if some speedy direction from Her Majesty... be not taken to

---

[110] For example, TNA, SP 63/207(I)/34 (Loftus to Cecil, 20 Jan. 1600); E. Hogan (ed.), *The Description of Ireland and the State Thereof as it is at This Present in Anno 1598* (Dublin, 1878), pp. 43–4.

[111] Beef cows or oxen.

[112] A person employed to dig trenches, and build or repair military fortifications.

[113] Lambeth, Carew MS, 612, No. 270 (Harvey to Russell, 10 Oct. 1595); *Cal. Carew*, iii, 125.

[114] TNA, SP 63/185/28(IV) ('Warrant directed severally to the sheriffs of Dublin, Meath, and Louth', 28 Nov. 1595).

[115] TNA, SP 63/191/15(V) (Norreys and Fenton to Irish Council, 3 July 1596).

[116] TNA, SP 63/189/46(X) ('Note of the abuses', 22 May 1596); TNA, SP 63/201/146 (petition of the inhabitants of Meath, 1597).

bridle the disorders of the soldiers, that "manurance" of the land will quite be given over in these parts'.[117]

It was widely accepted that crown soldiers placed the greatest strain upon the Palesmen's resources, but the devastation wrought by rebel assaults cannot be discounted. In mid-October 1596, the Irish Council announced 'manie burninges and spoylinges haue been and still wilbe committed... vpon the subiectes of the Pale, specially in the counties of Meath and Lowyth, who are so much impoverished by their incursions, as a great part of those contries are readie to be laid wast'.[118] Although many of these incursions escaped official recording, a few surviving advertisements describe significant destruction in County Meath. In August 1596, 200 Breifne rebels spoiled a great tract of land within a few miles of the bishop's house at Ardbraccan.[119] On 14 November 1596, Thomas Wackes, sheriff of Meath, reported a series of devastating rebel attacks whereby the towns of 'Donamore', 'Ballymulghan', 'Harreston', 'Kingeston', 'Heyeston', 'Dollardston', and 'the remain of the granges' were burned, and great preys were taken from the towns of 'Alestoneread', 'Brannanston', 'Ladirath', and 'Knough'.[120] Ten days later, Edward Moore reported further destruction of lands within a few miles of Tara.[121]

Combined, the toll on the shire was too much to bear. According to the Meathmen, the normal hardships of war had reduced the county to '240 plowelandes wasted and in a moytie'.[122] Even the ever-cynical Burgh admitted that 'the waste of the covntrey is svch, as many villages be dispeopled, and the grovnd is left vntilled: wherby it is apparent, no harvest is here to be expected'.[123] Already crippled by the destruction of their lands, the inhabitants' desperate situation was further exacerbated by several years of unseasonable weather during which time grim reports of crop failure abound.[124] Although poor weather was a contributing factor for many years during this conflict, the situation proved little better in years when the weather was conducive to good harvests.[125] Regardless of what climatic conditions meant for agricultural productivity, there were more mouths to feed than was practicable at the best of

---

[117] CSPI, 1596–97, p. 169.
[118] TNA, SP 63/194/19 (Irish Council to Privy Council, 15 Oct. 1596); TNA, SP 63/194/41 (Fenton to Burghley, 22 Oct. 1596).
[119] TNA, SP 63/192/7 (Irish Council to Privy Council, 13 Aug. 1596).
[120] TNA, SP 63/195/40 (Wackes to lord chancellor Loftus and Council, 26 Nov. 1596).
[121] TNA, SP 63/192/7 (Irish Council to Privy Council, 13 Aug. 1596); TNA, SP 63/195/39 (Moore to Loftus, 25 Nov. 1596); TNA, SP 63/195/40 (Wackes to Loftus and Council, 26 Nov. 1596). See also TNA, SP 63/196/5 (Fenton to Cecil, 4 Dec. 1596).
[122] TNA, SP 63/201/146 (petition of the inhabitants of Meath, 1597).
[123] TNA, SP 63/199/58 (Burgh to Burghley, 25 May 1597).
[124] McGurk, Elizabethan Conquest, p. 209; Lennon, 'The Great Explosion in Dublin, 1597', pp. 12–14.
[125] TNA, SP 63/203/14 (Ormond to Queen Elizabeth, 18 Jan. 1599).

times and government demands upon the country's currently strained resources proved dangerously detrimental to both short-term productivity and long-term recovery.

Besides the destruction of arable land, there was a significant reduction in the manpower available for farming. An unknown number of people had abandoned their lands, taking to the woods and bogs with the Confederates; another significant number had left off their regular occupations in favour of military employment with the crown or their local lord; others still were distracted from their tillage by being conscripted into the army to serve as labourers. Add to this the decline of local equine stocks – whether pilfered during rebel raiding, government requisitioning, or by purloining soldiers – and the means of local cultivation was severely reduced. As Fenton cautioned, 'yt is the waie to ruine them more, to take from them both their men and garrons, which they shold vse in the harvest'.[126] It was a vicious circle: by requisitioning the country's horses and labourers for the use of the army, the inhabitants were left with too few plough animals and other equipment to efficiently cultivate any lands which escaped destruction. As a result, crop yields continued to decrease, compromising the inhabitants' ability to provide for themselves, never mind the needs of an ever-growing, mismanaged, rapacious army.

What applied to the deterioration of agrarian production also applied to pastoral farming. In November 1596, Kyffin informed Cecil that '[t]he ground is laid waste, and in a maner desolate, yelding neither foode for man, nor forage for beast'.[127] He reiterated this a few months later, declaring that '[i]n travailing vp and down the country ther is no kynde of foode for man, or beast, to be had, but what one buyeth at vnreasonable rates'.[128] Like the people themselves, Ireland's livestock supplies were becoming increasingly fragile due to dwindling fodder stores.[129] Not only were herds dangerously depleted in numbers through government requisitioning and rebel raids, but what was available was generally unsuitable for service, having been 'made vnprofitable throvgh weaknes'.[130] As the war progressed and prices escalated, officials in Ireland sent urgent reports that they could not afford to feed the few horses they still had.[131] And, weakened by the lack of grain and grazing, diminishing numbers of horses and cattle were

---

[126] TNA, SP 63/182/63 (Fenton to Burghley, 26 Aug. 1595). See also Morgan (ed.), 'Questions and Answars', p. 99.

[127] TNA, SP 63/195/6 (Kyffin to Cecil, 8 Nov. 1596).

[128] TNA, SP 63/198/48 (Kyffin to Cecil, 26 Mar. 1597).

[129] McCormack, 'Social and Economic Consequences', p. 4.

[130] TNA, SP 63/199/58 (Burgh to Burghley, 25 May 1597).

[131] TNA, SP 63/208(1)/42 (N. Dawtrey to Cecil, 9 Feb. 1601); Moryson, *Itinerary*, iii, pp. 66–7. TNA, SP 63/209(2)/232 (Mountjoy and Councillors to Privy Council, 12 Dec. 1601).

increasingly susceptible to outbreaks of disease which, in turn, rendered them an unreliable food source.[132]

Between cattle raids, crop destruction, and increased consumption, the availability of local agricultural products diminished rapidly throughout the Pale and the rest of Ireland. Increased demand and decreasing local availability led to unsustainable inflation. A very conservative estimate would allow for a minimum twofold increase in market prices, but correspondence from Ireland usually reported prices to be much higher. In early 1597 Russell asserted that prices were five times the normal while other accounts suggested treble and quadruple rates.[133] Describing what he witnessed when arriving in Ireland, Burgh reported 'an exceding great famine in the land where wheat was sould at 18s. or 20s. the bushel'.[134] For those inhabitants and soldiers who were deprived of pay at even the usual rates, escalating prices on all commodities could, and did, prove fatal.

In an effort to avoid this eventuality and protect government purchasing interests over the long term, fixed prices had been established on victualling staples. With respect to beef, prescribed rates set in September 1595 stipulated that the crown paid 15s. sterling per cow; this proved grossly inadequate and by mid-1597 the fixed price on beef was raised to 20s.[135] The revised rate still fell far short of actual prices, but government officials were adamant that 20s. was the absolute most crown soldiers could afford to pay.[136] Establishing fixed costs like this was necessary for sustaining the average soldier and for estimating the crown's expected expenditure during wartime. However, the enforcement of these rates played a significant role in generating resentment among the local population. Considering the Palesmen paid anywhere between 40s. and 50s. for a cow in mid-1597 but were forced to surrender the same cow to the army for 20s. – that is, if they even received payment – it is hardly surprising that the inhabitants were reluctant to part with their goods.[137] More appalling was that while the inhabitants were compelled to deliver their livestock at below-market prices, rumour had it that profiteering English officials were secretly exporting the hides at higher prices than had been paid for the actual animal.[138] It was

---

[132] TNA, SP 63/207(2)/97 (Mountjoy to Cecil, 9 Apr. 1600); R. Gillespie, 'Harvest Crisis in Early Seventeenth-Century Ireland', *Irish Economic and Social History*, Vol. 11 (1984), pp. 5–18.

[133] TNA, SP 63/198/33 (Russell to Burghley, 24 Mar. 1597); TNA, SP 63/202(4)/60 ('greevances', 1598); BL, Add. MS 4819, f. 157v; TNA, SP 63/208(1)/42 (Dawtrey to Cecil, 9 Feb. 1601).

[134] BL, Add. MS 4819, f. 157v.

[135] TNA, SP 63/183/49 (Wallop to Burghley, 24 Sept. 1595).

[136] TNA, SP 63/207(6)/123 (answers to complaints, Dec. 1600); Lambeth, Carew MS, 632, No. 271 ('A declaration of the present state of the Englishe Pale', June 1597).

[137] TNA, SP 63/202(4)/60 ('greevances', 1598); Lambeth, Carew MS, 632, No. 271 ('A declaration of the present state of the Englishe Pale', June 1597).

[138] Canny, 'The Formation of the Old English Elite', p. 21.

an unsustainable practice, and yet this was only one of many symptoms of economic decay. In addition to agricultural decline, the economic consequences of this conflict were most detrimentally shaped by the Dublin administration's mounting debts and the soaring sums owed to the loyalist inhabitants of Ireland. When the government finally resorted to the desperate and ill-conceived measure of coinage debasement to alleviate these problems, the entire system teetered on the precipice of disaster.

The Irish Debt Crisis

As much as supply difficulties impeded military progress and burdened civilians, the root of administrative and military troubles was the government's chronic fiscal instability. In late 1602 Treasurer Carey noted that 'these Irish wars do exhaust the treasure of England… we expend faster here than you can gather it in in England'.[139] This was no exaggeration. While the estimated annual revenue of the English crown during this interval was approximately £300,000, the Nine Years' War had consumed an impressive £1,924,000 by the time it concluded.[140] Throughout the war Elizabeth had repeatedly implored her Irish deputies 'to ease our Kingdom of those great or rather infinite charges, which We have thus long sustained… [and] which our Crowne of England cannot indure'.[141] How to reduce Irish expenditure left many in a quandary. The most obvious solution, and the one most popular with privy councillors in England, was to reduce the number of men in crown pay. The diminution of forces, however, would be disastrous for the lord deputies charged with subduing Ireland; thus, the solution most favoured by those operating within Ireland was the employment of cheaper manpower in the form of native soldiers who, on paper, served at half rates, but in practice often received no pay at all.[142] Other measures were introduced, including selective supply contracts with London merchants, modifications in soldiers' pay, cashiering of weak companies, and enforcing fixed prices.[143] None of these measures succeeded in reducing costs, curbing inflation, or improving the standard of provisioning for soldiers. As the war drew into its final years and the supply situation continued to worsen, the administration resorted to debasing Irish coin in the hope of controlling the market, paying servitors, and satisfying its colossal debts.

---

[139] *CSPI, 1600*, p. 26.

[140] C.E. Challis, *The Tudor Coinage* (Manchester, 1978), p. 268; HMC *Salisbury MSS*, xv, 2.

[141] Elizabeth to Mountjoy, 9 Oct. 1602, in Moryson, *Itinerary*, iii, p. 225.

[142] For example, Moryson, *Itinerary*, iii, pp. 137–8; TNA, SP 63/210/67 (Mountjoy and Carew to Privy Council, 18 Mar. 1602).

[143] BL, Add MS 49609 A, ff. 29–65b; BL, Add MS 4757, ff. 19–21; 44–6.

The Nine Years' War precipitated a serious debt crisis which was further exacerbated by a failed coinage debasement scheme, yet the economic ramifications of this conflict have not received adequate attention. Much like English shipments of materials and victuals, consignments of treasure were always late, less than what was needed, and already accounted for by the administration's rising debts.[144] To no avail, Irish councillors begged their English counterparts for the speedy dispatch of money 'to pay the detts of the countrey and townes in some measure, aswell for the soldiers diet… and also to satysfie extraordinaries, which in this chardgable tyme, cannot but rise higher'.[145] On those rare occasions when money was available to answer the administration's titanic outlay, Irish councillors, especially Treasurers Wallop and Carey, were put in the awkward position of deciding between the welfare of the queen's deprived soldiers and her exasperated subjects.[146] Naturally, during wartime, the administration's most immediate concern was the army, yet soldiers' salaries were rarely paid in full and even partial payments were commonly delayed for months.[147] This, more than anything else, dictated the behaviour of military men and the afflictions of the civilian population.

Much as it did for material supplies, the administration regularly borrowed money from Palesmen, especially merchants and aldermen. Wallop and Carey issued countless certificates for the numerous loans secured, many of which list the names of Irish creditors, amounts borrowed, and to what purposes those sums were allocated. Although creditors were repeatedly promised repayment from the next expected treasure shipment, their certificates, as well as the petitions submitted by Palesmen, clearly show that these debts were rarely satisfied and that the sums owed to Palesmen escalated dramatically over the course of the war.[148] A great number of these certificates are preserved in the

---

[144] TNA, SP 63/184/11 (Wallop to Burghley, 8 Nov. 1595); TNA, SP 63/184/38 (Wallop to Burghley, 30 Nov. 1595); TNA, SP 63/198/42 (Irish Council to Privy Council, 25 Mar. 1597); TNA, SP 63/202(1)/56 (Irish Council to Privy Council, 27 Feb. 1598); TNA, SP 63/202(2)/16 (Fenton to Cecil or Burghley, 20 Apr. 1598).

[145] TNA, SP 63/202(1)/56 (Irish Council to Privy Council, 27 Feb. 1598).

[146] TNA, SP 63/184/38 (Wallop to Burghley, 30 Nov. 1595); TNA, SP 63/198/42 (Irish Council to Privy Council, 25 Mar. 1597); TNA, SP 63/207(6)/43 (memoranda on treasure, victuals, and arms, Nov. 1600).

[147] TNA, SP 63/195/6 (Kyffin to Cecil, 8 Nov. 1596); TNA, SP 63/196/39 ('Memorandum on the state of Ireland', Dec. 1596); TNA, SP 63/202(1)/56 (Irish Council to Privy Council, 27 Feb. 1598); TNA, SP 63/202(2)/16 (Fenton to Cecil or Burghley, 20 Apr. 1598); TNA, SP 63/202(2)/38 ('humble requests of the Captains', 18 May 1598); TNA, SP 63/202(2)/107 (Wilbraham to Cecil, 22 July 1598); TNA, SP 63/202(4)/62 ('divers abuses done and suffered by the Council of Ireland', 1598); TNA, SP 63/202(4)/81 ('Observations' endorsed by Cecil, 1598); TNA, SP 63/203/101 (Ormond to Privy Council, 26 Mar. 1599). Canny, *Making Ireland British*, pp. 72–3.

[148] TNA, SP 63/184/11 (Wallop to Burghley, 8 Nov. 1595); TNA, SP 63/185/25(II) ('Note of 2,401*li*. 10s. 0d. borrowed towards victualling the garrisons for November and December', 23 Dec.

State Papers and a few examples may serve to illustrate the scale of the ever-growing Irish debt crisis.

At the end of 1595 the Dublin administration borrowed a whopping £2,401 10s. in order to victual crown garrisons for two months. This sum, more than two and a half times the composition collected that year, had been raised from a number of individuals in both Ireland and England and, among the many Irish financiers, £600 was owed to four Dublin merchants.[149] Within five months the Irish Council gave out that it had exhausted all potential for raising further loans within Ireland 'by any Courss of Credytt' because, having experienced very slow returns on their monies, creditors were disinclined to advance any more.[150] This had serious consequences for the day-to-day functioning of the administration and army since financial subsidies from England continued to fall short of the government's escalating needs. In January 1597 Wallop succeeded in borrowing an additional £575 from several Dublin merchants in order to purchase beeves in Munster, promising the same merchants full reimbursement 'out of the next treasure'. Knowing such promises had proven empty in the past, Wallop prepared Burghley for the expected repayment of this and other debts, noting 'what a lardge share of the next Treasure wilbe deducted for this onely occasion'.[151] By March 1597, despite the arrival of an English treasure consignment only three months earlier, desperation drove the Council to seek out creditors yet again. This time the Irish Council secured £4,000 in loans; but, to do so, it had to pawn most of its plate as collateral. The Irish Council warned its English counterpart that unless some of these debts were presently answered in England it would be impossible to obtain any future financial assistance within Ireland.[152] This did not spur the dispatch of more funds, and the following December Wallop was driven to borrow a further £1,578 13s. 4d. from 'the Cittizens heare in Dublin & others... to pay lendings to suche of the companyes as are furthest from reliefe'.[153]

There is no evidence to indicate if or when these specific loans were satisfied, but the scale of the administration's debts is made apparent by the fact that the Irish Council was making arrangements in August 1598 for the repayment of £8,000 'borrowed here of the Citty of Dublin, and other marchaunts'.[154] The sudden expansion of the army under Essex in spring 1599 and the escalation of

1595); TNA, SP 63/187/26 (Wallop to Burghley, 10 Mar. 1596); TNA, SP 63/190/12 (Wallop to Burghley, 8 June 1596); TNA, SP 63/197/57 (Wallop to Burghley, 29 Jan. 1597); TNA, SP 63/199/112 (docket of Irish Suitors, 20 June 1597).
[149] TNA, SP 63/185/25(II) ('2,401*li*. 10s. 0d. borrowed', 23 Dec. 1595).
[150] TNA, SP 63/190/2(I) (draft of a letter by Fenton, 22 May 1596).
[151] TNA, SP 63/197/57 (Wallop to Burghley, 29 Jan. 1597).
[152] TNA, SP 63/198/41 (Irish Council to Privy Council, 24 Mar. 1597).
[153] TNA, SP 63/201/90 (Ormond to Burghley, 3 Dec. 1597).
[154] TNA, SP 63/202(3)/1 (Irish Council to Privy Council, 2 Aug. 1598).

hostilities during the war's later years saw these debts increase exponentially. 'A reckoning' of moneys borrowed in the city of Dublin between December and March 1600 concluded that the city was owed £51,916 16s. 7d., and noted that a further £10,000 had been borrowed for the payment of lendings.[155] This was an enormous sum, and one which less obedient subjects would surely have refused.

At the same time as the administration was amassing these monetary debts, it was also becoming ever more indebted to the Palesmen for their incalculable contributions towards the army's material and accommodation needs.[156] Although promised reimbursement for these services, particularly the unwonted billeting of soldiers, the reality was that these charges were becoming ever more oppressive and 'much slower in being recompensed'.[157] By no means did English officials deny this. As early as January 1597 Wallop estimated that 'there can be no less due to the inhabitaunts of the Tounes for Diett of Soldiers then 3 or 4000l. to whom more doth daylie growe due'.[158] It was inevitable that this debt would rise over the following five years, but even at this early stage Wallop's estimate was probably conservative and petitions submitted by the citizens of Dublin and Drogheda that same year indicate they were due significantly more.[159]

Discounting hefty outstanding loans and independently supplied materials advanced by members of the Corporation,[160] by June 1597 the citizens of Dublin claimed the government owed them £890 for billeting soldiers and a further £3,000 for their assistance 'in maintaining armed companies in the field and otherwise'.[161] If that was not enough to trouble the inhabitants, the Corporation's suit was made desperately urgent on account of the recent gunpowder explosion, the estimated damages coming to £14,076.[162] Add to this the cost of providing watchmen to be on duty round the clock and men for general hostings, and there can be little doubt that the inhabitants were struggling to meet all their obligations.[163] In fact, the burden of supporting

---

[155] TNA, SP 63/207(6)/114 (reckoning of moneys borrowed from city of Dublin, Dec. 1600).

[156] For example, TNA, SP 63/184/38 (Wallop to Burghley, 30 Nov. 1595); TNA, SP 63/200/7 (Irish Council to Privy Council, 4 July 1597); SP 12/262/5(I) ('Warrant to pay 5,520li. to the merchants', 9 Jan. 1597).

[157] Lennon, *Lords of Dublin*, pp. 123–4.

[158] TNA, SP 63/197/57 (Wallop to Burghley, 29 Jan. 1597).

[159] TNA, SP 63/195/6 (Kyffin to Cecil, 8 Nov. 1596).

[160] For example, Dublin Alderman James Bellew was owed '660 and odd poundes' for supplying 'dyvers of hir Maiesties Army with apparrell and other necessaries'. TNA, SP 63/198/78 (Loftus to Cecil, 7 Apr. 1597).

[161] HMC *Salisbury MSS*, xiv, 35; TNA, SP 63/199/127 (petition of Mayor and Citizens of Dublin, June 1597). See also, TNA, SP 63/199/11 (Mayor and sheriffs of Dublin, 6 May 1597); TNA, SP 63/199/12 (Mayor and sheriffs of Dublin to Cecil, 6 May 1597).

[162] In addition to extensive damages done to the physical geography of the city, the explosion killed 126 people, seventy-six of whom were confirmed citizens of the Dublin Corporation.

[163] HMC *Salisbury MSS*, xiv, 35; TNA, SP 63/199/127 (petition of Mayor and Citizens of Dublin,

crown soldiers had become so onerous that in May 1597 the twenty-four Dublin aldermen, who were statutorily exempt from billeting charges, resolved to waive their exemption and pay 12*d.* a day towards the victualling of soldiers so as to 'help the other citizens... considering the present scarcity and the poverty of the poor neighbours'.[164] At the very same time as the Dubliners were seeking compensation, the inhabitants of Drogheda petitioned Sir Robert Cecil for '338*l*. 8s. 7d. for the diet of souldiers lately assessed vppon this towne' as well as a further £254 owed to them since 1588 for maintaining 'certeine Spanishe and Italien prisoners'.[165] In spite of recommendations from the Irish Council, by the end of October 1597 the town of Drogheda had received 'onely 138*l*. 8s. as parte of the said diet money'.[166]

The Palesmen sought reimbursement for the ordinary and extraordinary demands placed upon their resources, and although many English officials were cognisant of the disaffection bred by these growing arrears, they protested that 'for lack of victuells in the stoar, they cannott be eased, nor yet paied the allowaunces sett downe for them thorough the want of Treasur'.[167] The Palesmen's difficulty in acquiring payment of debts within Ireland was a common affair and, much to the annoyance of the queen and Privy Council, Irish suitors and country agents flocked to her English court seeking restitution.[168] These individuals met with varying success; Dublin Alderman Nicholas Weston managed to obtain several bills for repayment but Patrick Typper, who had long battled for the welfare of the inhabitants of County Kildare, was confined to prison for a period.[169]

Nicholas Weston's name figures prominently in Wallop's lists of Irish creditors and his efforts to obtain satisfaction are typical of the situation for many Palesmen. In late 1595 Weston loaned the administration £200 towards the cost

June 1597); TNA, SP 63/207(I)/7 ('Considerations touching Ireland causes' by Lord Buckhurst, 6 Jan. 1600); TNA, SP 63/207(5)/130 (Fenton to Cecil, 31 Oct. 1600); Lennon, 'The Great Explosion in Dublin, 1597', esp. pp. 14–15.

[164] H.F. Berry, 'Minute Book of the Corporation of Dublin, Known as the "Friday Book." 1567–1611', *PRIA*, Vol. 30 (1912/13), p. 491.

[165] TNA, SP 63/201/30 (T. Hamling to Cecil, 25 Oct. 1597).

[166] TNA, SP 63/199/99 (Irish Council to Privy Council, 12 June 1597); TNA, SP 63/201/30 (Hamling to Cecil, 25 Oct. 1597).

[167] TNA, SP 63/184/37 (Wallop, Gardener, Sentleger, and Bourchier to Burghley, 30 Nov. 1595). Wallop wrote a separate letter to Burghley the same day about the great debts owed to the country for the supply of beeves and victuals. See TNA, SP 63/184/38 (Wallop to Burghley, 30 Nov. 1595).

[168] CUL, MS Kk. I. 15, ff. 207–9 ('A copie of my M[aste]rs letter to the Lo. Deputy of Ireland', 10 July 1596); Lambeth, Carew MS, 612, No. 270 (Cecil to Russell in Russell's journal, 10 July 1596); TNA, SP 63/202(3)/1 (Irish Council to Privy Council, 2 Aug. 1598).

[169] TNA, SP 63/200/40 (Irish Council to Privy Council, 20 July 1597); SP 2/22/217 (Privy Council meeting, 17 Aug. 1597); BL, Lansdowne MS, Vol. 81, f. 181 (petition of the county of Kildare, 8 May 1596); HMC *Salisbury MSS*, viii, 420–21; TNA, SP 63/207(5)/130 (Fenton to Cecil, 31 Oct. 1600); TNA, SP 63/208(2)/64 (memorial to Privy Council, 14 May 1601).

of victualling English garrisons, followed by another £300 shortly thereafter.[170] Although promised full reimbursement in 1595, even at this early date Weston doubted his £500 debt would be satisfied, so he travelled to the English court bearing letters recommending that his bills be honoured there.[171] It is unclear whether the debt was answered in England at that time, but Weston continued to supply the administration with rather liberal loans over the following war years so it is possible that his debts were satisfied, either partially or in full. Over the course of the war several certificates were issued ordering the repayment of certain sums to Weston. When Wallop solicited '250 barrells of danishe Rye' upon credit from Weston in July 1597, a number of Irish Councillors pleaded with the English Privy Council to pay him £400 for this victualling service and, within a month, the Privy Council had ordered the repayment of that same sum.[172] In this respect, Weston was unusually successful. Weston's Protestantism endeared him to administrators, and he also had the advantage of being wealthy enough to make regular trips to the English court. Very few of his compatriots experienced the same compensation or return on their loans, and this was at least partly due to their Catholicism and lesser means, whereby their access to favour and court solicitation was made more difficult.[173]

Without a doubt, the Palesmen desired satisfaction of debts, but it is unlikely that they wholeheartedly believed the crown would acquiesce to demands for repayment. Past experience had taught them that remuneration was rarely forthcoming and required persistent solicitation by patrons and representatives at home and at the English court.[174] Many of these Old English suitors were probably also aware of the massive outstanding bills due to New English servitors, and it was unlikely that the Old English natives of Ireland would be recompensed before New English men.[175] This might explain why, in June

---

170 TNA, SP 63/185/25(II) ('2,401*li*. 10*s*. 0*d*. borrowed', 23 Dec. 1595); TNA, SP 63/185/34 (Irish Council to Burghley, 28 Dec. 1595).

171 TNA, SP 63/185/34 (Irish Council to Burghley, 28 Dec. 1595).

172 TNA, SP 63/200/55 (Wallop to Cecil, 27 July 1597); TNA, SP 63/200/40 (Loftus and other Councillors to Privy Council, 20 July 1597); PC 2/22/217 (meeting of the Privy Council, 17 Aug. 1597).

173 For more on Weston's services and the activities of Old English merchants, see Canning, 'Profits and Patriotism', pp. 1–28.

174 Stephen Barron, acting on behalf of the citizens of Dublin city, submitted multiple suits to the State for compensation in 1594. TNA, SP 63/173/49; 58; 58(I); 59; 71 (suits presented by S. Barran, Feb. –Mar. 1594); TNA, SP 63/207(3)/24 (Countess of Ormond to Cecil, 8 May 1600).

175 For example, TNA, SP 63/186/89 (Norreys to Cecil, 29 Feb. 1596); TNA, SP 63/196/57 (Dr. Doyley's remembrances for Norreys, 1596). See also TNA, SP 63/195/28 (C. Eggerton to Burghley, 22 Nov. 1596); CUL, MS Kk. I. 15, ff. 299–330 ('A Booke of suche interteignments as are due to the Lord Deputy, Cheife Officers, and others of her Majestie's Armye and Garrisons in paye within [this] Realme', Sep. 1597); TNA, SP 63/207(5)/6 (Dawtrey to J. Fortescue, Chancellor of the Exchequer, 7 Sep. 1600); TNA, SP 63/207(5)/47 (Mountjoy to Cecil, 27 Sep. 1600); TNA, SP

1597, the citizens of Dublin did not demand direct satisfaction of debts and damages, but hoped 'her Maiestie may be pleased to grant vnto them and their Successors their humble requestes conteyned in the annexed articles'.[176] The annexed articles included the confirmation of certain judicial and commercial privileges, exemptions from English customs, and the restoration of fee farms which had since fallen into abeyance or the hands of corrupt government officials.[177] The request implies they were mindful that financial restitution would not be readily offered from England; however, the suggestion that their debts could be satisfied within Ireland might entice the queen to see them appeased. Equally noteworthy is that the supplicants asserted the bestowal – or restoration – of these rights would serve 'for their better encouragement & inhablinge to contynue their accustomed forwardnes in the furtherance of her Maiesties seruice wherein they wilbe readie to bestowe their accustomed lyves lands and goodes if occasion be offered'.[178] According to this petition, the resurrection of these civic privileges would remove the inhabitants' dependency on England by enabling them to compensate losses through their own initiatives.[179] It is possible that the symbolic importance of such a gesture was even more significant because the conferral of these rights would amount to the crown's acknowledgement of their sacrifices and, thereby, validate their suffering.[180]

As the war drew into its final years, the administration's debts continued to mount, but the costs incurred by Essex's 1599 expedition and defeating the Spaniards in Kinsale at the end of 1601 further exacerbated the situation.[181] Having tried everything else, by late 1600 recommendations for debasing Irish moneys gained traction as the last remaining device to control the Irish market and generate enough coin to pay crown soldiers, administrators, and creditors.[182] The Tudors had turned to coinage debasement on other occasions, but their experiments in manipulating currency had only succeeded in Ireland during periods of relative peace.[183] The Irish situation of 1600 was anything

---

63/207(6)/50 (Carew to Cecil, Nov. 1600); TNA, SP 63/212/135 (Irish Council to Privy Council, 24 Feb. 1603).

[176] TNA, SP 63/199/127 (petition of Mayor and Citizens of Dublin, June 1597).

[177] Ibid.; HMC Salisbury MSS, xv, 95.

[178] TNA, SP 63/199/127 (petition of Mayor and Citizens of Dublin, June 1597).

[179] Ibid.; HMC Salisbury MSS, xiv, 35.

[180] TNA, SP 63/199/127 (petition of Mayor and Citizens of Dublin, June 1597).

[181] Essex's grand tour of Leinster and Munster in summer 1599 cost £280,000, while confronting the Spanish at Kinsale during Mountjoy's viceroyalty amounted to £415,401. H.S. Pawlisch, Sir John Davies and the Conquest of Ireland: A Study in Legal Imperialism (Cambridge, 1985), pp. 143–4.

[182] TNA, SP 63/207(2)/25 (Carey to Cecil, 9 Mar. 1600); TNA, SP 63/207(6)/131 (reasons against sterling and making base money, Dec. 1600); TNA, SP 63/207(6)/132 (paper on abasing of money in Ireland, Dec. 1600); HMC Salisbury MSS, ix, 23. See also CSPI, 1600–1601, pp. 126–7.

[183] TNA, SP 63/212/109 (note on Irish coinage debasement in times past, 1602); Challis, Tudor Coinage, pp. 268–73.

but conducive to such an ambitious scheme, and the implementation of this new currency had immense consequences for the war, its participants, and the socio-economic situation of post-war Ireland.[184] In fact, according to Sir Oliver St John in 1602, 'The greatest evill that presently greeues this country is the newe money.'[185]

In May 1601, the intrinsic value of Irish coin was reduced from 9 oz. to 3 oz. fine of silver and all other monies were decried.[186] The new currency was to be put into circulation through the payment of soldiers' lendings and the repayment of debts owed to merchants and other creditors. In order to keep sterling in England and the new Irish currency in Ireland, 'banks', or exchanges, were established at Irish and English ports where merchants and discharged soldiers could exchange their moneys at favourable rates.[187] The success of the new monetary policy hinged on two conditions: that the debased coin was accepted at face rather than intrinsic value, and that all other currencies were withdrawn from the Irish market.[188] From the very outset problems became apparent, not least of all because arrears in debts and salaries far exceeded what the banks could supply. There was no mint in Ireland to produce the much needed currency, and the smiths contracted to mint coins in England lacked the knowledge and technology to strike coins of the same metallic consistency.[189] Counterfeit operations cropped up almost immediately in Ireland, England, Scotland, and the Continent, further undermining confidence in the new coin.[190] The unreliability of the coin and limited access to exchanges caused a near stoppage in foreign trade, thus reducing the importation of much

---

[184] With the exception of Hans Pawlisch, C.E. Challis, and Joseph McLaughlin, the enactment and impact of this policy has received very little attention from historians. J. McLaughlin, 'What Base Coin Wrought: the Effects of the Elizabethan Debasement in Ireland', in H. Morgan (ed.), *The Battle of Kinsale*, pp. 193–204; Pawlisch, *John Davies*, pp. 142–57; Challis, *Tudor Coinage*, pp. 268–74.

[185] SP 63/210/78 (O. St. John to Cecil, 27 Mar. 1602).

[186] Pawlisch, *John Davies*, p. 142; TNA, SP 63/208(2)/82 (proclamation concerning the new moneys, 20 May 1601); Lambeth, Carew MS, 617, No. 67 (proclamation of the new coinage, 20 May 1601).

[187] Irish monies could be exchanged at '6d. ster. proffitt in every pound', while those exchanging sterling for the Irish monies stood to gain '12d. proffitt in every pound in the new mony'. TNA, SP 63/208(2)/82 (proclamation concerning the new moneys, 20 May 1601); Lambeth, Carew MS, 617, No. 67 (proclamation of the new coinage, 20 May 1601); TNA, SP 63/208(2)/83 (abstract of proclamation concerning the new moneys, 20 May 1601). Challis, *Tudor Coinage*, p. 269.

[188] Challis, *Tudor Coinage*, p. 268. Copper pennies and halfpennies were also sent into Ireland to pay army wages and serve as a smaller denomination for daily business transactions.

[189] TNA, SP 63/209(1)/74 (Carey to Cecil, 13 Sep. 1601); TNA, SP 63/208(1)/28 ('The humble desire of Sir Richard Martin', Jan. 1601); TNA, SP 63/209(1)/68 (Fenton to Cecil, 11 Sep. 1601). McLaughlin, 'What Base Coin Wrought', p. 196.

[190] TNA, SP 63/209(1)/70 (Carew to Privy Council, 12 Sep. 1601); TNA, SP 63/209(1)/70A (examination of J. Nott, 6 Sep. 1601); TNA, SP 63/209(1)/74 (Carey to Cecil, 13 Sep. 1601);

needed foodstuffs.[191] But the root of the administration's troubles was that the withdrawing of sterling and other currencies 'cometh not on so fast a[s] weare meete', and the existence of two standards meant the new coin was refused at face value.[192] Far from solving the problem of ready cash for supplies, the new money was either flatly refused or, to compensate for its lower quality, prices were elevated beyond already unaffordable rates. As a 1602 report on the coinage averred, 'the excess of all prices in that kingdom is far beyond the memory of any age'.[193] This was corroborated by Irish councillors who lamented that 'the prizes of corne, victualls, cloath, Iron, and all other thinges... are growne to such a height as the multitude are not hable to reach therunto, no, nor many of the better sort of the servitors'.[194] Even Mountjoy gave out that he could no longer sustain himself in any decent fashion on his salary, with the result that he had fallen into an estimated debt of £4,000 or £5,000 within a very short space of time. [195] Surely, if the lord deputy was struggling to make ends meet, the situation must have been significantly worse for the average civilian. Having fretted about food shortages and price inflation throughout the war, by January 1603 the mayor and sheriffs of Dublin complained that famine threatened due to 'the greate and extreame scarsitie of all kind of victuals, in this Realme and especiallie the want of graine'.[196]

It has mystified historians that the government's inability to meet soldiers' basic needs did not incite mutiny, and thus far, no satisfactory explanation has been offered. As for the civilian population, Hans Pawlisch and Anthony Sheehan have laid a fair share of the blame for the 1603 urban 'recusancy revolts' on the townsmen's discontentment over the botched debasement scheme.[197] Within a month of O'Neill's submission, Mountjoy complained that '[t]he discontentment of the coin is infinite and more insupportable to us all for it is generally refused. I know of no way to make it current where I go but by the cannon'.[198] Many other administrators insisted that the new coin added yet another grievance to existing crown–community tensions, and that

---

TNA, SP 63/211/74 (Hadsor to Cecil, 4 July 1602); TNA, SP 63/212/146 (N. Walsh, R. Walsh, T. Colcloughe and R. Ailwarde to Mountjoy, 12 Mar. 1603).

[191] TNA, SP 63/210/51 (Irish Council to Privy Council, 5 Mar. 1602). See also TNA, SP 63/210/24 (Chichester to Cecil, 15 Jan. 1602).

[192] TNA, SP 63/209(1)/68 (Fenton to Cecil, 11 Sep. 1601).

[193] CSPI, 1601–1603, p. 550.

[194] TNA, SP 63/212/122 (Mountjoy and Council to Privy Council, 26 Jan. 1603).

[195] TNA, SP 63/209(2)/178 (Mountjoy to Cecil, 7 Nov. 1601); TNA, SP 63/212/124A (Mountjoy to Carey, 25 Jan. 1603); TNA, SP 63/212/136 (Mountjoy to Cecil, 28 Feb. 1603).

[196] TNA, SP 63/212/111 (Mayor and sheriffs of Dublin to Cecil, 7 Jan. 1603).

[197] Pawlisch, John Davies, pp. 142–57; A.J. Sheehan, 'The Recusancy Revolt of 1603: A Reinterpretation', Archivium Hibernicum, Vol. 38 (1983), pp. 3–13; Challis, Tudor Coinage, pp. 272–3.

[198] CSPI, 1603–1606, p. 26.

the situation was '[a] lamentable preparacion to a famyn, and other daungerous Inconveniences, which may break out in the State, yf they be not speedely prevented'.[199] The whole debasement debacle was nothing short of a disaster. In no way did it alleviate the situation in Ireland, nor did it secure for the crown any profit or savings; instead, the scheme initiated even greater price inflation and market instability which, in turn, led to local hostility towards the currency, the administration and, even the queen herself.[200]

Unrequited Loyalty

Charging the inhabitants of Ireland with the expenses of the English queen's Irish war was not something all administrators took lightly. A number of officials, prominent among whom were Fenton and Loftus, were cognisant that the authorised and unauthorised expropriations of crown and army had surpassed the means of the country and they feared that the continuation of these practices could expedite an irreconcilable disaffection among the loyalist Pale population. As early as September 1595 Fenton cautioned Burghley about the situation, stating that the Palesmen were already 'weary of their heavy burdens' and 'mens myndes are stirred'.[201] But the war continued, as did the pressures on the Pale, causing Fenton to reiterate the same warning two years later: 'the long bearing of the burden of the warr, hath not a litle altered the harts of the people'.[202]

The empathy expressed by officials like Fenton stemmed from personal anxieties, since over the course of his career he had accumulated extensive landed interests in Ireland. While this may have influenced his judgement, it does not negate the significance of his observations. Through long service and personal attachments in Ireland, Fenton was better attuned to the hardships besetting the country than new arrivals like Lord Deputy Burgh. Many of Burgh's comments seem callous and symptomatic of a subscription to the notion that the Irish, be they Gaelic or Old English, were uncivil, untrustworthy, and deserving of the suffering currently afflicting them.[203] Yet the observations of those English officials long acquainted with Ireland are sometimes surprisingly insightful. They could hardly be labelled optimists but,

199 TNA, SP 63/212/122 (Irish Council to Privy Council, 26 Jan. 1603).
200 TNA, SP 63/212/64 (Irish Council to Privy Council, 10 Nov. 1602); Moryson, *Itinerary*, iii, p. 266. TNA, SP 63/212/89 (Elizabeth's draft touching the exchange, 24 Dec. 1602); TNA, SP 63/212/107 (project concerning Irish Coinage, 1602). McLaughlin, 'What Base Coin Wrought', p. 194.
201 TNA, SP 63/183/9 (Fenton to Burghley, 7 Sep. 1595).
202 TNA, SP 63/200/137 (Fenton to Cecil, 23 Sep. 1597).
203 TNA, SP 63/201/25(I) (Burgh to Loftus and Irish Council, 26 Sep. 1597).

for these men, Irish defiance had not spontaneously erupted in a vacuum. As Fenton explained, 'the people are discontented, & from discontentment they begin to grow to contempt, which will soone sort to disobedience'.[204] This, he asserted, was not because Ireland's inhabitants were naturally inclined towards rebellion; instead, having been reduced to such desperate circumstances, the inhabitants were being forced to choose between what they might be led to believe was the lesser of two evils. Fenton and a few other English officials perceived that government pressures, army abuses, and vulnerability could be more persuasive sources of disaffection and conflicting loyalties than religion, birth place, or rebel overtures.[205] While rebel attacks, or the threat thereof, induced some nominally loyal subjects to join the Confederacy, the lack of defence provided them against these incursions was also an important contributing factor.[206] Equally concerning was the soldiers' unlawful seizures of livestock and goods: this 'cannot but imprinte in the harts of the people, a daungerus discontentment… which they know is contrary to the freedome of subiects'.[207]

Fenton's opinions regarding the Palesmen's material assistance mirrored those expressed by Richard Wackely and Sir Ralph Lane about the native martial man. As far as these men were concerned there was no such thing as unconditional obedience. The people resembled the land on which they lived; no matter how fertile the soil, without adequate nurturing the husbandman could expect ever-diminishing yields until the field finally succumbed to invading, but resilient, weeds.[208] For this reason, these more compassionate officials advised the queen and her government to be more attentive to her Irish subjects before they turned against her.[209] In order to avoid such an eventuality, they were adamant that the Palesmen's good services should be rewarded or, at the very least, acknowledged. Such consideration, it was contended, would not only encourage individuals to persist in their loyal behaviour, but it would also teach them and, by association, others, to aspire to great displays of loyalty and thus strengthen the bonds between subject and monarch.[210] The problem of

---

[204] TNA, SP 63/186/25 (Fenton to Burghley, 27 Jan. 1596).

[205] For example, see BL, Cotton Titus C, VII, ff. 156–61 ('Sir Henry Wallops Relation', 1600).

[206] TNA, SP 63/185/26 (Fenton to Burghley, 24 Dec. 1595); TNA, SP 63/195/39 (Moore to Loftus, 25 Nov. 1596); TNA, SP 63/186/25 (Fenton to Burghley, 27 Jan. 1596); TNA, SP 63/197/91 (Kyffin to Cecil, 14 Feb. 1597); TNA, SP 63/202(2)/28 (Fenton to Cecil, 7 May 1598); TNA, SP 63/202(3)/135 (Irish Council to Privy Council, 31 Oct. 1598); TNA, SP 63/203/25 ('Proclamation for Ireland' by Queen Elizabeth, 25 Jan. 1599).

[207] TNA, SP 63/200/88 (Fenton to Cecil, 11 Aug. 1597).

[208] TNA, SP 63/202(1)/54 (R. Wackely to R. Lane, 19 Feb. 1598); TNA, SP 63/202(1)/66 (Lane to Burghley, 1 Mar. 1598).

[209] TNA, SP 63/202(1)/53 (Fenton to Burghley, 19 Feb. 1598).

[210] BL, Lansdowne MS, Vol. 83, ff. 51–3 (Loftus to Cecil, 8 Feb. 1596).

rewarding loyal behaviour was not a new one; as early as 1574 Auditor Jenyson felt it necessary to remind Burghley that '[i]f the country were well paid... they would willingly pay all they do, yea even more'.[211] However, in the 1590s, existing evidence clearly demonstrates that the Palesmen were rarely compensated for their contributions and they were, therefore, given little incentive to remain on a dutiful course.

While official correspondence sheds certain light on the sufferings and consequences of this war, equally, if not more, important is how the Palesmen perceived the impact of war on their own community and their relationship with the English crown.[212] Objections to military charges was not a new phenomenon. Financing and supplying an English standing army was a long-established grievance and the cess controversy of the 1570s and 1580s had revealed just how vociferous the Palesmen could be when they felt unfairly encumbered by the crown's military establishment.[213] As onerous as the demands of the previous two decades had been, the Nine Years' War initiated an unprecedented drain on the Palesmen's resources. In 1598 one group of Palesmen asserted:

> Howbeit, the former misseries had never lighted vpon the Pale, yet is it chardged, and burdened by the State, with suche and so manyfold ymposicions of beoffes, muttons, Porckes, graine, carriages, pioners, and other provicions to be yealded to youre Maiesties fforces in campe, and garrizons, besides their great burdens in finding soildiors of their owne, for defence of the borders, with the charge of the ordinarie and yeerely Rising out to generall hostings, as if the Pale bare no other burden but the same, yt weare sufficient to bringe it to vtter Ruyn and desolacion.[214]

Unlike previous Irish wars, the Nine Years' War impinged on every aspect of life throughout the country, and especially within the administrative centre of the Pale. The rapidly declining prosperity of the Pale's urban and rural communities provoked great bitterness towards the administration, manifesting itself in a flurry of complaints which increased in both frequency and urgency as the war dragged on. Undoubtedly, there were incidents of forceful resistance to the impositions of government and army, yet the State Papers contain no formal description of any major clash between civilians

[211] As quoted in Brady, *Chief Governors*, p. 234.
[212] TNA, SP 63/202(4)/60 ('greevances', 1598). Two other copies of this treatise exist: Lambeth, Carew MS, 632, No. 271 ('A declaration of the present state of the Englishe Pale', June 1597); BL, Cotton Titus B XII, ff. 97–105b ('A declaration of the present state of the Englishe Pale', 1598). See also TNA, SP 63/202(4)/75 ('A discourse', 1598); a second version of this treatise exists: BL, Cotton Titus B XII, ff. 112–17.
[213] Brady, 'Conservative Subversives', pp. 11–32; Canny, 'Identity Formation in Ireland', pp. 163–5; McGowan-Doyle, *Book of Howth*, ch. 4.
[214] TNA, SP 63/202(4)/60 ('greevances', 1598).

and military personnel within the Pale.[215] Instead, it seems the Palesmen's preferred mode of protest was to exercise their constitutional rights by submitting grievances directly to the queen and Privy Council in the hope of arbitration and remedy. These petitions, being the Palesmen's favoured course for redress, provide valuable insight into the socio-political workings of the Old English Pale community.

The fact that the Palesmen continued to solicit the queen for the easing of their suffering indicates that they regarded themselves as crown subjects and that, as subjects, they felt it was their inalienable right to have those complaints heard and answered by their monarch. They made this clear in a 1600 group petition: 'We humblie expect from your Royall Ma:tie that comfforte and redresse in these our calamities, which our Loyalties at all tymes and… our vttermost endevoures to the Advancement of your highnes service… doth deserve.'[216] That the Palesmen regarded the queen as a protector concerned for their welfare is evident by the fact that they laid the blame for their unaddressed condition on Irish administrators, not the queen, and expressed hope that those officials would be held accountable. Some petitions were presented under the assumption that Elizabeth did not fully comprehend just how distressed her Irish subjects were because her delegates had neglected to inform her. As subjects, the Palesmen believed it was their duty to apprise their prince of the many abuses committed in her name because 'the vyolacion wherof must be most offencyve vnto her highnes'.[217] The Palesmen's petitions also mimicked a feature commonly found in the those of English officials in that they reported exactly how both they and the queen had been defrauded by her representatives, '[s]oe as her Maiestis bounty… is dishonored & dispised, the souldier beggered and defrauded, thinhabitants of the country robbed spoyled and abused, and all this wrought thorough the auarietie and abuse of the same'.[218] Supplicants may have believed that if Elizabeth was brought to understand their misery, she would be outraged and immediately seek to repair their present condition, or at least punish those responsible. Informing the queen of these abuses was more than just complaining; it was proof of their allegiance and an exercise in their rights as subjects.[219] As one Palesman explained in 1577, 'to

---

[215] The most detailed incident of local aggression towards the establishment occurred in Limerick in 1600; no similar incidents were recorded within the Pale. See TNA, SP 63/207(2)/7 ('Articles against the town of Limerick', 3 Mar. 1600).

[216] TNA, SP 63/207(4)/5(I) (petition of noblemen and gentlemen of the English Pale, 13 June 1600).

[217] TNA, SP 63/200/53 (petition of the inhabitants of Kildare, 24 July 1597); TNA, SP 63/200/53(I) (charges and impositions on inhabitants of Kildare, 24 July 1597); TNA, SP 63/207(4)/62 (Barnewall to Cecil, 10 Aug. 1600).

[218] Ibid.; TNA, SP 63/200/53(I) (charges and impositions on inhabitants of Kildare, 24 July 1597).

[219] TNA, SP 63/207(5)/23 (Howth to Cecil, 14 Sep. 1600). V. McGowan-Doyle, 'Elizabeth I, the

complaine was the gate of obedience by which they might enter with humble petition'.[220]

The queen did respond to the cries of her Irish subjects by intervening in specific disputes and directing general reprimands to officials in Ireland.[221] The explanations offered by these officers were almost always the same: the people of Ireland were backward, disloyal, and 'clamorous... above all nations in the world'.[222] Lord Deputy Mountjoy went so far as to assert that the Palesmen were 'the worst sort of people in all the kingdom' and that the soldiers had to use excessive force because nothing could be achieved by 'fair means'.[223] Queen Elizabeth was not so easily persuaded. She did not attribute the rebellion wholly to the evils of the Irishry and frequent complaints of administrative corruption convinced her that the behaviour of her representatives in Ireland had provoked dangerous resentment towards crown government.[224] Elizabeth was equally concerned that the administration's weak efforts in addressing and reforming government corruption and soldier misconduct provided 'so lytle shewe to the People of any purpose to right them, as ether they must needes thincke our hart allyenated from doeing them Iustice, or you our Governor ill chosen that haue not better dealt in it'.[225] In spite of these sporadic admonitions, the Irish Council failed to rectify the situation and complaints from the Palesmen continued unabated. By the latter years of the war, efforts were made to restrain suitors from coming to England, partially because their services were needed in Ireland, but largely because the queen and Privy Council were overwhelmed by the number of Irish suitors coming to court to plead cases for arrears, awards, and restitutions.[226]

In their petitions the Palesmen addressed a number of issues affecting their welfare, almost all of which related to the unremitting demands of the

---

Old English, and the Rhetoric of Counsel', in B. Kane and V. McGowan-Doyle (eds), *Elizabeth I and Ireland* (Cambridge, 2014), pp. 177–8.

[220] Cecil MS 60/130 (N. White to Burghley, 13 June 1577).

[221] For examples of specific disputes, see CUL, MS Kk. I. 15, ff. 91–91v, 196v–99v, 233–34v (various letters from Queen and Privy Council to Irish Council, Mar. 1594–Sep. 1596). See also TNA, SP 63/187/24 (Cecil to Norreys, 10 Mar. 1596); TNA, SP 63/187/44 (Norreys to Cecil, 20 Mar. 1596); TNA, SP 63/189/51 (Norreys to Cecil, 28 May 1596); TNA, SP 63/190/25 (Norreys to Burghley, 15 June 1596); TNA, SP 63/197/16 (Norreys to Cecil, 13 Jan. 1597).

[222] *CSPI*, 1600, p. 508.

[223] TNA, SP 63/209(2)/178 (Mountjoy to Cecil, 7 Nov. 1601); TNA, SP 63/207(5)/116 ('Heads of things', 27 Oct. 1600).

[224] TNA, SP 63/189/43 (Elizabeth to lord deputy and Council, 25 May 1596).

[225] Ibid.

[226] For example, TNA, SP 63/207(3)/139 ('Certain instructions conceived' by the Queen, June 1600). See also TNA, SP 63/207(6)/75 (Carew to Privy Council, 16 Dec. 1600); TNA, SP 63/208(2)/93 (Fenton to Cecil, 25 May 1601); TNA, SP 63/212/8 (Mountjoy to Cecil, 10 Aug. 1602).

administration and the vicious treatment meted out upon them by the queen's army. They also purposefully objected to official allegations that they had used various evasions to avoid meeting the administration's supply requirements. County petitions, usually forwarded by local officials like George Harvey of Meath, were emphatic that they had exerted themselves to their utmost at all times to satisfy the crown's needs.[227] Aiming to discredit official allegations of non-compliance, many petitions provided assessments of livestock, grains, monies, and materials levied, along with other help, including military services and manual labour. As the war progressed the inhabitants admitted that some deliveries had fallen short of what had been demanded but these deficits, they insisted, were due to the impoverished condition of the country rather than any underlying recalcitrance. The inhabitants of Kildare asserted in 1597 that '[i]t is nowe come to passe that your Supplicats are dishabled to liue and to performe such dueties & seruices of Loyaltie and allegiance vnto her Maiestie as they doe owe. Which causes of intollerable greif & Calamytie beinge contrary and repugnant to her Maiesties most royall and princely pleasure, and most tender regarde of her Subiectes.'[228]

As the costs associated with their cooperation mounted the Palesmen saw little sign of compensation for all their pains; instead, the administration and army continued to take up supplies and billet forces among them without any show of compunction. Thus, another common feature exhibited in these petitions was the insistence that their grievances rested largely on the excessive abuses of the army, not the cause itself, and that the Palesmen would willingly bear any legal and reasonable charges laid upon them. Characteristic of this were two petitions from the inhabitants of Meath. Having sought remedy for the illegal exactions of crown soldiers unlawfully billeted in the county by Norreys, their hopes for some restitution and the observing of the Council's resolution that soldiers live off their own pay were not realised.[229] Since their previous appeals for succour remained unresolved, in 1597 the distressed Meathmen requested the removal of those companies billeted in the county. Should this be misconstrued to mean that they refused to shoulder any further war costs, the Meathmen proposed that they simply pay composition 'equally with thother Ciuill partes of the Realme'.[230] Despite the repetitiveness and urgency of their appeals, there is no evidence to indicate that the Meathmen's request was granted or that they were alleviated in any way.

[227] *Cal. Carew*, iii, 125 (Harvey to Russell, 10 Oct. 1595). See also Clarke, 'Alternative Allegiances', p. 258.
[228] TNA, SP 63/200/53 (petition of the inhabitants of Kildare, 24 July 1597).
[229] TNA, SP 63/189/46(X) ('Note of the abuses', 22 May 1596); TNA, SP 63/201/146 (petition of the inhabitants of Meath, 1597).
[230] TNA, SP 63/201/146 (petition of the inhabitants of Meath, 1597).

The Palesmen were annoyed by the government's failure to rectify army violations, but they were also incensed by the lack of return on their investment, or, to be more precise, exploitation. While many Palesmen had rushed to the queen's side to assist her army in the fight against her Irish enemies, her army had not returned the favour. Even New English servitors could attest to this; a bewildered Edward Moore exclaimed that although the queen had employed 'some tenn thousand men, I holde yt a hard course, two hundred of them may not be imployed in defence of the princypall members of this kingedome'.[231] However, if the crown did not fully appreciate the worth of its loyalist border barons, Hugh O'Neill surely did. Steadfast borderers presented serious obstacles to the progress of his rebellion and their loyalty made them strategic targets. O'Neill's Confederates missed few opportunities to strike devastating blows against these men, either in order to persuade them to join the Confederacy or to disable them as serious threats.[232] After a series of rebel attacks on his lands and tenants in 1596, the baron of Delvin remarked, 'how much my distruction is required as a thing thought verie necesarie by them for the easier accomplishing of their traitorous designments'.[233] In late 1599, due to the virulence of perennial rebel assaults, Delvin admitted that many of his tenants and neighbours would probably revolt; some because they were that way inclined but, for others, it was simply because they had 'no defence'.[234] For Delvin, and many like him, O'Neill symbolised that Gaelic tyranny against which their Anglo-Norman ancestors had long fought and the idea of capitulating to this enemy was repugnant. But, without defensive help from the crown, there was little Delvin could do to deter his bitterly harassed followers from doing so.[235] In spite of warnings like this, crown soldiers did little to prevent the spoliation of the queen's Irish allies. Instead, the subjects' supposed protectors preferred to commit the same atrocities, but to a greater degree than their foes, and it became common parlance that crown soldiers were a greater menace than the rebels.[236] According to the Palesmen, they were 'assaulted and as Rigouroslie vsed as if they were disobedient, and disloyall Subiects' and they were lucky to escape with their lives.[237] This was hardly the way to win hearts and minds.

---

[231] TNA, SP 63/195/39 (Moore to Loftus, 25 Nov. 1596). See also TNA, SP 63/202(3)/135 (Irish Council to Privy Council, 31 Oct. 1598).

[232] TNA, SP 63/203/33 (Fenton to Cecil, 3 Feb. 1599).

[233] TNA, SP 63/192/7(VII) (Delvin to lord deputy and Council, 7 Aug. 1596). See also TNA, SP 63/202(1)/61(II) (O'Neill to Ormond, 25 Feb. 1598).

[234] TNA, SP 63/206/44(I) (Delvin to Loftus and Carey and Irish Council, 22 Nov. 1599).

[235] TNA, SP 63/192/7(VII) (Delvin to lord deputy and Council, 7 Aug. 1596); TNA, SP 63/203/48 (Fenton to Cecil, 15 Feb. 1599).

[236] TNA, SP 63/202(4)/60 ('greevances', 1598); Lee, 'The Discovery', ff. 79–81.

[237] Ibid.; Lambeth, Carew MS, 632, No. 271 ('A declaracion of the presente state of the Englishe Pale', June 1597). See also Lee, 'The Discovery', ff. 71–2.

Notwithstanding expressions of outrage, the Palesmen's petitions maintained that the majority of this community remained obedient and loyal. They went so far as to announce that no amount of anguish endured for the advancement of crown interests could remove them from their natural affection for the English crown. As one group of Palesmen declared in 1598: 'although the alurements of this vnhappie tyme did offer provocacions to carry vnstaied myndes astray, yet we as vnremoveable from our loyalties, doe remayne stedfast and constant, contynuallie accepting, and making choise of all callamities, misseries, and mischiefes what soever, rather then to be disloyall'.[238] Although official correspondence contains more criticism than praise, the fact that administrators like Fenton, Loftus, and Wallop frequently wrote to England recommending the suits of Old English individuals and municipalities is indicative of the confidence these officials had in the sincerity of many Palesmen's allegiances, or, at the very least, their recognition of the crown's dependence on the Palesmen's assistance.[239] They frequently praised the services of certain Old Englishmen and testified that these individuals always exerted themselves to support the crown. They also affirmed that in spite of the unimaginable torments endured at the hands of the crown's Irish administration and army these individuals had remained incontrovertibly loyal to their English sovereign. However, even for these moderate men, nothing lasted forever and there was a limit to what Elizabeth's loyal Irish subjects would tolerate; to discover what that limit was would mean it was already too late.

It is impossible to recreate the immense suffering endured by individuals in the past, but it is possible to represent descriptions of it. By the time Ireland's Nine Years' War concluded, these descriptions convey an image of desolation and desperation. Recounting the stories of survivors who fled Ireland in the aftermath of this conflict, Philip O'Sullivan Beare wrote:

> Thus the war was finished. Ireland was almost entirely laid waste and destroyed, and terrible want and famine oppressed all, so that many were forced to eat dogs and whelps: many not having even these, died. And not only men but even beasts were hungry. The wolves, coming out of the woods and mountains, attacked and tore to pieces, men weak from want. The dogs rooted from the graves rotten carcases partly decomposed. And so there was nought but abundance of misery and a faithful picture of ruined Troy.[240]

---

[238] TNA, SP 63/202(4)/60 ('greevances', 1598).
[239] BL, Lansdowne MS, Vol. 83, ff. 51–3 (Loftus to Cecil, 8 Feb. 1596); TNA, SP 63/198/78 (Loftus to Cecil, 7 Apr. 1597); TNA, SP 63/199/23 (Loftus to Cecil, 9 May 1597); TNA, SP 63/199/24 (Wallop to Burghley, 10 May 1597); TNA, SP 63/199/78 (Loftus to Cecil, 4 June 1597); TNA, SP 63/199/124 (Fenton to Cecil, 30 June 1597); TNA, SP 63/202(4)/18 (Fenton to Cecil, 10 Dec. 1598); TNA, SP 63/203/34 (Loftus to Cecil, 5 Feb. 1599).
[240] O'Sullivan Beare, *History of Ireland*, p. 181.

The Nine Years' War strained England's human, financial, and agricultural resources to breaking point.[241] But, in addition to the resources expended on the war itself, redundant reports of burning, pillaging, and destruction illustrate that it had done much worse to Ireland. By 1600, Irish Councillors fretted that the Palesmen were 'impoverished even to the bones by the long enduring rage of this rebellion', and worse was still to come with the arrival of the Spanish, the coinage debasement scheme, and Mountjoy's scorched earth tactics.[242] Given the state of crown finances and the military supply system, it is hard to imagine that the Tudor conquest could have been completed without the impressive support tendered by the Palesmen throughout this conflict. In a country at war one would assume that conscientious governors would be wise of the need to protect and appease their strongest native allies. Some obviously were, but they were too few to effect any major shift in policy. Instead, the Pale and its inhabitants were inexcusably exploited in the name of a queen and government which were ostensibly presented as their guardians. Thus, it would seem that the queen's Irish administration muddled through this war on luck; luck because, inexplicably, the increasing poverty, maltreatment, and alienation of its loyalist Pale partners had not sufficiently deterred them from their ancestral obedience to the English crown. The Palesmen did not go quietly into the night, however; there were grumbles, omens, and some defections. They were seriously aggrieved that crown government had not only failed to manage its obnoxious army or recompense their many losses, but they were also incensed that their personal sacrifices had received little acknowledgement, monetarily or otherwise, from the Dublin and London authorities. There can be little doubt that the Palesmen felt unappreciated and abused throughout this war and there is something very poignant and telling about viscount Gormanston's 1596 outburst: 'I pray your L. remember wee are Christians, and therfore good L. vse vs as xpians [Christians].'[243]

---

[241] Other historians have acknowledged the burden of Irish wars on the English populace, but John McGurk has provided the most detailed and itemised assessment on how the Nine Years' War impacted England. McGurk, *Elizabethan Conquest*, especially chs 2 and 3.

[242] *CSPI, 1600*, p. 472. TNA, SP 63/207(5)/92 (Loftus and Council to Privy Council, 12 Oct. 1600).

[243] TNA, SP 63/196/13(I) ('Memorial', 7 Dec. 1596).

Office and Influence: Defending
a Tradition of Privilege

Sixteenth- and seventeenth-century England witnessed what Lawrence Stone called 'the crisis of the aristocracy'.[1] According to Stone, between 1558 and 1640 the Tudor and Stuart aristocracy underwent a social, economic, and political transformation brought about by the rise of the 'middle classes' and a decline in the wealth and respect commanded by the old élite. The Tudor nobility, and their shifting role in society, has been scrutinised intensively since Stone's seminal work but, like Stone's book, these later studies have been geographically limited to the island of Britain and have failed to take account of the nobility and gentry living in Ireland.[2] Although they experienced the centralisation of the Tudor state in remarkably different ways, Ireland's Old English élite were very much a part of Tudor noble society and its factional political networks. They constitute an inconvenient anomaly for the study of Tudor politics due to their location, ancestry, and complex cultural affiliations, yet their experiences were no less significant to the course of English political history. These distinctive traits make them all the more worthy of inclusion since they offer an alternative narrative for the history of Tudor noble culture as it has thus far been understood. Far from being cut off from political trends obtaining in England, it is possible that the crisis of the aristocracy was even more traumatic for Ireland's Old English nobility.[3] Unlike their counterparts

---

[1] L. Stone, *The Crisis of the Aristocracy, 1558–1641* (Oxford, 1967).

[2] All of these studies have shed valuable light on the Tudor nobility, but the exclusion of Ireland's Gaelic and Old English nobility ignores another dimension in aristocratic relations during this period. For example, see F. Heal and C. Holmes, *The Gentry in England and Wales, 1500–1700* (Basingstoke, 1994); D. Hoak (ed.), *Tudor Political Culture* (Cambridge, 2002); J.F. McDiarmid (ed.), *The Monarchical Republic of Early Modern England: Essays in Response to Patrick Collinson* (Basingstoke, 2007); N. Mears, 'Courts, Courtiers, and Culture in Tudor England', *HJ*, Vol. 46, No. 3 (2003), pp. 703–22; J. Rose, 'Kingship and Counsel in Early Modern England', *HJ*, Vol. 54, No. 1 (2011), pp. 47–71; Stone, *Crisis of the Aristocracy*. Fortunately, Steven Ellis has conducted several comparative studies of frontier nobility in Ireland and England: S.G. Ellis, *Tudor Frontiers and Noble Power: The Making of the British State* (Oxford, 1995); Ellis, 'Civilizing Northumberland: Representations of Englishness in the Tudor State', *Journal of Historical Sociology*, Vol. 12, No. 2 (1999), pp. 103–25; Ellis, 'The Pale and the Far North: Government and Society in Two Early Tudor Borderlands', O'Donnell Lecture (Galway, 1986).

[3] The term 'aristocracy' is anachronistic in the Irish context, but the role the played in England was performed by the Old English nobility and gentry of Ireland. G. Power, *A European Frontier*

in England, the Old English existed on an isolated island periphery unencumbered by the personal presence of their prince; so isolated in fact that only three reigning English monarchs had visited Ireland since the twelfth-century Anglo-Norman invasion.[4] When urgent need arose, sporadic interventions had been made, yet the intrusion of deputies and commissioners from England was rarely lasting. As a result, upholding the English crown's right to the lordship of Ireland had fallen to the descendants of the original Anglo-Norman colony. Charged with preserving the administrative, judicial, and martial legitimacy of English overlordship, the Old English nobility were permitted an enormous amount of independence and authority, and certainly far more than their counterparts living in southern England.[5] Yet, in spite of being so far removed from the epicentre of English government, the curbing of noble power under the Tudors extended to those living in Ireland and, considering the liberty and unrivalled power this group had once enjoyed, the crisis of the aristocracy must have been felt particularly severely by the Old English élite. This is because the nature of the crisis in Ireland was driven by more than just economic and social factors; it was propelled by a sincere desire to root out Catholicism and a heightened concern for preserving the 'Englishness' of Ireland's English administration. For those in Ireland it was not the 'middle classes' which threatened to dilute their status; it was the systematic substitution of Old English Catholic officials for New English Protestants.

English critics presented what must have seemed legitimate reasons for removing native participation in a reformist English government. In spite of the crown's best, albeit inconsistent, efforts to establish a little England beyond the sea, the Old English community's failure to comply with Tudor religious and social reforms seemed ominous. Regardless of their professed political loyalties, the majority of Old English men were religious delinquents and their continuing attachment to Catholicism made them susceptible to competing church and state allegiances. Captain Thomas Lee alleged that the Catholic convictions of the supposedly loyal Palesmen were more poisonous than those of Hugh O'Neill and his Confederates.[6] While charges of Old English Gaelicisation, or degeneration, were certainly exaggerated, the fact remained

---

Elite: The Nobility of the English Pale in Tudor Ireland, 1496–1566 (Hannover, 2012); Power, 'Hidden in Plain Sight: The Nobility of Tudor Ireland', History Ireland, Vol. 20, No. 1 (2012), pp. 16–19; McGowan-Doyle, 'Elizabeth I, the Old English, and the Rhetoric of Counsel', p. 183.

[4]   The last of which was Richard II in 1399.

[5]   For example, see Ellis, Tudor Frontiers and Noble Power; D.B. Quinn, 'Anglo-Irish Local Government, 1485–1534', IHS, Vol. 1, No. 4 (1939), pp. 354–81.

[6]   Lee stated that O'Neill attended Protestant services when in the company of the lord deputy but that the Old English blocked their ears to avoid hearing a word of the service. Lee, 'Brief Declaration of the Government', p. 111. See also R. Rapple, Martial Power and Elizabethan Political Culture: Military Men in England and Ireland, 1558–1594 (Cambridge, 2009), pp. 157–9.

that the Palesmen were Irish by birth and there was no way of determining how that would sway their allegiances when they felt in any way maligned. By the later part of the century, these concerns, along with their fluency in English political culture and access to government, had convinced many New English officials that the Old English Palesmen were more of a menace to the realm's security than any potential Gaelic Irish traitor. As Edmund Spenser contended, the Old English were 'more stubborn and disobedient to law and government than the Irish be, and more malicious against the English that daily are sent over'.[7] For many English observers, these negative attributes had already been demonstrated in dangerously defiant behaviour and, since the Old English had shown their ability to rise and challenge the crown during the late 1570s and early 1580s, the queen and her representatives thought it prudent to limit Old English access to positions of power.[8]

However, herein lies something of a conundrum, because cause and effect were very much the same. Although they were not as yet entirely ostracised, many of the Old English had come to believe that they were not only losing their ability to influence and direct government policy in Ireland, but were also losing their right to consent to major administrative decisions. After constitutional methods had been tried, by means of petitions and delegations to court, a few more radical constituents thought action might succeed where diplomacy had failed. Although multiple motives can be attributed to earlier Old English uprisings, these were at least partially reactionary in nature and conducted in the vain hope that the status of the Old English would be recognised and maintained. The riotous actions of this minority did not persuade crown officials into concessions; instead, many English contemporaries regarded such bellicosity as added justification for curbing the power and influence of the original colony.[9] As argued in *The Supplication of the blood of the English*, experience taught the crown that no man of Irish birth could be trusted:

> If wee should preasume to perswade yore ma:tie to trust none Irishe, wee should perswad you to the safest course for yore kingedome, the safest course for yore subiects, the safest course for yore selfe Althoughe assuredly there are some, whose faith if it were thoroughly knowne doth well deserve trust. Yet that some are soe fewe as that it is better for you to trust none, then to hazard the lightinge on them that are disloyall.[10]

---

[7] Spenser, *A View*, p. 175.

[8] For example, see Maley (ed.), 'The Supplication', p. 53.

[9] See H. Coburn Walshe, 'The Rebellion of William Nugent 1581', in R.V. Comerford *et al.* (eds), *Religion, Conflict and Coexistence in Ireland* (Dublin, 1990), pp. 26–52; C. Maginn, *'Civilizing' Gaelic Leinster: The Extension of Tudor Rule in the O'Byrne and O'Toole Lordships* (Dublin, 2005); Maginn, 'Baltinglass Rebellion', pp. 205–32.

[10] Maley (ed.), 'The Supplication', pp. 36–7.

Old English alienation in the decades preceding the Nine Years' War has been much discussed.[11] Having for centuries possessed the highest administrative offices and directed all major decisions on Irish affairs, the Old English found themselves after the Kildare rebellion of 1534 undergoing gradual displacement in favour of English-born Protestant officials. Valerie McGowan-Doyle has noted that this decline was felt most markedly in relation to administrative, judicial, and military offices.[12] The positions of viceroy, lord justice, lord chancellor, and lord treasurer had been quickly transferred to men of English birth.[13] Displacement at other levels had been more gradual but, as the higher places in the administration and judiciary fell vacant, they too were filled with appointees from England. Also contributing to Old English alienation during the latter half of the century was the expansion of the crown bureaucracy. New offices were created, including provincial presidencies and deputy ministerial positions, and the vast majority of these were awarded to the friends and family of English viceroys or court favourites eager to reinforce their own factional networks. The military establishment was likewise enlarged during this period, but the Old English found little space for themselves among the army's officer ranks.

Modern historians have debated the degree and pace at which the Old English were supplanted by New English appointees, but the fact remains that the Old English themselves believed that their traditional role and status was under threat. Elizabeth's instructions to Lord Deputy Russell in 1594 demonstrate that she purposely appointed men out of England to replace Irish-born officials in the offices of master of the rolls, chief baron of the exchequer, and the two chief justices of the benches.[14] She had been doing this for some time, having officially entertained replacing the justices of common pleas and queen's bench in 1567 and again in 1577 upon accusations of the incumbents' supposed partiality and Gaelicisation.[15] According to the Palesmen, such accusations of degeneration and prejudice were made by 'evil affected' English officials who aimed to instil

---

[11] Ciaran Brady has argued that although the Old English were experiencing political displacement within the English administration, this was a slow process and there remained certain individuals who continued to enjoy a large degree of political influence. Brady has noted that the Old English held 75% of administrative offices in 1541, but their share in government posts had dropped to 50% by 1580. Brady, *Chief Governors*, esp. pp. 213–24; Brady, 'Conservative Subversives', pp. 26–8; Canny, 'Formation of the Old English Elite'; J.G. Crawford, *Anglicizing the Government of Ireland: The Irish Privy Council and the Expansion of Tudor Rule, 1556–1578* (Blackrock, 1993); McGowan-Doyle, *The Book of Howth*; McGowan-Doyle, 'Rhetoric of Counsel', pp. 163–83; Power, *A European Frontier Elite*.

[12] McGowan-Doyle, 'Rhetoric of Counsel', p. 167.

[13] As McGowan-Doyle notes, the viceroyalty was monopolised by New English appointees as of 1534, and by 1556 the offices of lord justice, lord chancellor and vice treasurer were also controlled by the New English. McGowan-Doyle, 'Rhetoric of Counsel', p. 169.

[14] *Cal. Carew*, iii, 90–1.

[15] McGowan-Doyle, 'Rhetoric of Counsel', p. 174.

'needless iealousies, & a pestilent opinion, that the place of any mans birth should breed him hurt being free from all imputation else and not to be taxed with any other crime'.[16] Even worse, according to the Palesmen, was that these malicious reports had nurtured a misperception amongst those in England that 'the descente of the Englishe (to their great greefe) are here [in England] called and counted Irishe'.[17] Given the personal experiences of some of their countrymen, this was a fair conclusion. When the baron of Howth visited the English court in 1562 Elizabeth enquired as to whether he could speak English.[18] Of course he could, and for him the implication of the question was deeply insulting.

Offence over the erroneous construction of an Irish identity for this group was a recurring theme in Old English complaints, and many supplicants made it abundantly clear that they understood allegations of their supposed degeneration were largely responsible for their increasing political alienation. Denying the assimilation which had inevitably occurred over many generations, Old English men commonly argued that they and their ancestors had successfully preserved both their Englishness and the authority of the English crown from the contamination and tyranny of the Gaelic Irish. They likewise drew on a long established tradition of disdain for Gaelic Irish culture within the towns and cities which made any notion of a united Irish Catholic confederacy inconceivable, since to combine with them would be an insult to all that they and their ancestors had achieved against the native barbarians.[19] For the majority of Old English men, this sense of cultural superiority negated any possibility of a pan-Irish alliance, even if it was to counter the onslaught of English heresy. As one Pale discourse argued:

we are iustlie moved to thinke, vpon suspicion of lacke of due affection in vs towards your Ma:ties service, of which Imaginacion we see no cause or collor, except it be for the generall opinion of difference in matters of conscience and Religion conceaved of this contry people, which seemeth a very falible argument of disloyaltie, and a frevolous suggestion, as the manner of your Highnes subiects carriadge here doth sufficientlie declare, the quarrell betwixt vs and the Irish proceeding not of matters of

---

[16] TNA, SP 63/207(3)/149 (petition of the inhabitants of the Pale, June 1600).

[17] TNA, SP 63/202(4)/75 ('A discourse to show 'that planting of colonies, and that to be begun only by the Dutch, will give best entrance to the reformation of Ulster', 1598). Another version is available in BL, Cotton Titus B XII, ff. 112–17.

[18] *Cal. Carew*, v, 201. Kane and McGowan-Doyle, 'Elizabeth I and Ireland: An Introduction', in Kane and McGowan-Doyle (eds), *Elizabeth I and Ireland*, p. 1.

[19] TNA, SP 63/202(4)/75 ('A discourse', 1598). For earlier examples of this argument, see N.P. Canny, 'Select Documents: XXXIV Rowland White's "Discors Touching Ireland", c. 1569', *IHS*, Vol. 20, No. 80 (1977), pp. 439–63; Canny, 'Rowland White's "The Dysorders of the Irisshery", 1571', *Studia Hibernica*, No. 19 (1979), pp. 147–60; D.B. Quinn, 'Edward Walshe's "Conjectures" Concerning the State of Ireland [1552]', *IHS*, Vol. 5, No. 20 (1947), pp. 303–22; Walshe, *The office and duety in fighting for our countrey*; Lennon, *Richard Stanihurst the Dubliner*; Canny, 'Identity Formation in Ireland: The Emergence of the Anglo-Irish', pp. 160–1.

Religion, but for land which we sithence the conquest have possessed and gotten by our auncestors bloodd.[20]

Interestingly, some members of the legal profession tackled the problem of political exclusion by focusing on how ethnic discrimination violated statutory laws. Both Richard Hadsor, Solicitor for Irish Causes in London, and the anonymous author of a 1598 discourse on plantation argued that the fabrication of a Gaelicised Old English identity had led to the misapplication of laws surrounding office-holding in Ireland, specifically with respect to regulations designed to bar Gaelic Irishmen from official positions in the crown's Irish administration.[21] The 1598 discourse explained:

> in some lawes there be exceptions taken against the Irishe as that none of them shalbe Gouuernors of certain named fortes and holdes, nor be elected Lords Iustices... those cautions were made against the meere Irishe, As appeares by the subsequent wordes, in euery such Act, naming Matcs and Oes, yet is the meaning thereof now erroneously enlarged to the excluding those of Englishe race from any such truste, contrarie to former Presedents.[22]

According to Hadsor and the author of the 1598 discourse, herein lay the root of Ireland's current troubles, because:

> so longe as they & theire posteritie were imployed as principall officers & Councellors of estate in tyme of warr and peace in the Realme, being such men who were thoroughly informed of all matters therein, and acquainted with the disposicion of the people, The Realme was well governed & daily increased in civilitie, & yelded some proffitt to the Crowne of England without chardge.[23]

This opinion was unanimous among the Old English and, as the Palesmen stipulated in their 1600 group petition, 'your Counsell for the greater part alwaies till now of late [was] consisting of your Subiects, born there'.[24]

Staunchly defending their Englishness, petitions submitted by representatives of the Old English nobility also defended their right to office and counsel

---

[20] TNA, SP 63/202(4)/60 ('greevances', 1598).

[21] TNA, SP 63/206/110 (Hadsor to Cecil, 30 Dec. 1599); TNA, SP 63/202(4)/75 ('A discourse', 1598); J. McLaughlin, 'New Light on Richard Hadsor, II. Select Documents XLVII: Richard Hadsor's "Discourse" on the Irish State, 1604', *Irish Historical Studies*, Vol. 30, No. 119 (1997), p. 346. Though Hadsor focused on the legal implications of this misrepresentation of the Old English, other members of his community had come to very similar conclusions, including the 7th baron of Howth. McGowan-Doyle, *Book of Howth*, pp. 94–7.

[22] TNA, SP 63/202(4)/75 ('A discourse', 1598). For Hadsor's comments on these laws, see McLaughlin, 'Richard Hadsor', p. 347.

[23] McLaughlin, 'Richard Hadsor', p. 346.

[24] TNA, SP 63/207(3)/149 (petition of the inhabitants of the Pale, June 1600); TNA, SP 63/207(6)/69 (Mountjoy to Cecil, 12 Dec. 1600).

by concentrating on tradition and the loss of privileges attached to high social status. Chief among the grievances was the administration's failure to consult them on matters of national importance. A fervent defender of Old English privilege, the baron of Delvin composed a treatise in 1584 which aimed to defend and define the role of Ireland's nobility, specifically in relation to administrative decisions on Irish affairs. In doing so, Delvin made his own position and that of many of his compatriots clear: the crown's Irish administration had absolutely no right 'to make warre or Peace with the Irishe without consent of the nobilitie & counsell'.[25] In theory, he was correct; in addition to personal and corporate business, matters of Irish war and taxation should have been discussed in a parliamentary forum. But the Irish parliament met only three times during Elizabeth's reign – 1560, 1569–70, and 1585–6 – and thus opportunities for consultation were limited.[26] The infrequency of parliaments did not prevent crown administrators from making weighty decisions, and this was particularly evident during the crisis of the Nine Years' War. Consequently, the problems of noble consent and consultation were broached on many occasions during this conflict, with particular objections raised over the legality of the proclamation against Hugh O'Neill and the government's billeting arrangements for soldiers.

Delvin's opinions on consent were echoed in a 1596 memorial submitted by Jenico Preston, viscount Gormanston, and endorsed by the earl of Kildare and the barons of Howth and Trimbleston. '[I]n the name of all the LLs. of the Pale', Gormanston expressed indignation that the administration had neglected to hold any consultation with the Pale nobility before publicly declaring O'Neill a traitor.[27] This should not be construed as sympathy for the rebel earl or his cause; rather, it was an expression of the Palesmen's interpretation of their own constitutional position. As Richard Hadsor specified in his 1604 discourse: 'The manner of tryall of Noblemen in Ireland for treason, ys by the Act of parliament in that Realme.' Based on Hadsor's understanding of former statutes, this meant that juries should be composed of the defendants' peers, which in this case would have been the nobility of Ireland.[28] Gormanston and his associates were of the same opinion. This was, after all, an Irish rebellion which affected the inhabitants of Ireland, not those of England. Unlike the queen's Privy Council in London or her English representatives in Dublin, the Pale nobility had a

---

[25] TNA, SP 63/108/58 (Delvin's plot for the reformation of Ireland, 26 Mar. 1584). See also V. Treadwell, 'Sir John Perrot and the Irish Parliament of 1585–6', *Proceedings of the Royal Irish Academy, Section C*, Vol. 85 (1985), p. 266.

[26] D.B. Quinn, 'Parliaments and Great Councils in Ireland, 1461–1586', *IHS*, Vol. 3, No. 9 (1943), pp. 60–77.

[27] TNA, SP 63/196/13(I) (memorial to be delivered by R. Gardener, 7 Dec. 1596).

[28] McLaughlin, 'Richard Hadsor', p. 347. See also Bodleian Library, MS Talbot B 11/25 (Hadsor to Salisbury, 9 Jan. 1607).

vested interest in all matters Irish, including the activities of Hugh O'Neill. And, unlike those councillors of English birth, the Palesmen were uniquely capable of understanding the circumstances of the revolt as well as the means towards achieving a more peaceful settlement. It therefore behoved English officials to take local expertise into account before embarking on any policy affecting Ireland or its leading lords.

In addition to their natural desire to exert influence over government decisions, the proclamation against O'Neill gave Gormanston and his colleagues good reason to doubt the security of their own status and privilege. Although Gaelic Irish, O'Neill was an established member of Ireland's nobility; if O'Neill, once the queen's favourite, could be handled in this way by English adminis-trators, what kind of treatment could the rest of his caste expect if they too came into conflict with the crown? At the heart of the Palesmen's unease was the fact that it was not the crown which had officially proclaimed O'Neill, but the queen's representatives on the Dublin council; not one of these men was an earl and, considering O'Neill should have been judged by his peers, the baser-born members of the Irish council were in no position to pass a verdict.[29] The administration's resolution on O'Neill's treasons must have made many an Irish noble wonder if they were already a spent force to be set up and pulled down according to the whims of lesser-born outsiders.[30]

The complete disregard shown for the traditional role of the nobility and gentry in implementing the necessary measures for managing wartime affairs was also offensive. Complaining about the *ad hoc* placement of Norreys's forces, Gormanston asserted that the lord deputy and his subordinates 'ought not to cesse vs without our owne consents'.[31] The Palesmen lodged another complaint in 1598, expressing outrage that levies and billeting arrangements were imposed 'without consent of the Nobylitie and gentlemen cheefelie entrested therein'.[32] Though these protests exude a concern for the greater good, they were primarily defending the privileges of the élite, specifically requesting that 'such Noblemen & Gentlemen, as haue ancient immunities and freedomes may still enioy the same without impeachment'.[33] The coalescing issues of consent and privilege were reminiscent of the 1570s cess dispute, yet, just as two decades earlier, the Palesmen's interests were largely ignored. In fact, having long been at the discretion of local sheriffs, during the Nine Years' War the Palesmen's control over accommodation arrangements had been transferred to quartermasters,

---

29 TNA, SP 63/196/13(I) (memorial, 7 Dec. 1596). See also Bodleian Library, MS Talbot B 11/25 (Hadsor to Salisbury, 9 Jan. 1607).

30 TNA, SP 63/196/13(I) (memorial, 7 Dec. 1596).

31 Ibid.

32 TNA, SP 63/202(4)/60 ('greevances', 1598).

33 TNA, SP 63/207(3)/149 (petition of the inhabitants of the Pale, June 1600).

another newly created office occupied by New English appointees. This, predictably, provoked strong objections from the Pale's representatives.

In spite of opposition from members of the Irish Council, the English Privy Council was partially amenable to Gormanston's 1596 remonstration. Although it upheld the proclamation against O'Neill, the Privy Council ruled in favour of the Pale nobility, concluding that in future, '[i]t was thought convenient to referre this opinion for calling the Nobelletie to Counsell in publecque cowses of the Realme, to the deputie and Counsell theare, to renewe the same, as hath been in former times accustomed in perill and danger'.[34] This was an exceptional verdict but, as too many Old English men would discover, the ruling was restricted to the matter at hand and not the role of the Old English as a whole. As it transpired, the Dublin Council only deferred to the Palesmen when they were sure of a favourable response or when there was no other alternative but to include them; these occasions of consultation were almost always in relation to hostings and border defence rather than issues of government policy.

Notwithstanding the Privy Council's rather encouraging 1596 judgment, other requests for similar opportunities to offer counsel were rebuked. In 1595 John Talbot of Louth urged the Irish Council to consider the advices of certain local gentlemen, carefully noting that these were to be of good reputation and experience. He probably had himself in mind, but the gentleman whom Talbot modestly recommended was Sir Patrick Barnewall. His endorsement was disregarded.[35] Earlier that year, in spite of Barnewall having served the government with financial assistance and intelligence on rebel and clerical activities, the Dublin administration had launched an investigation into his personal affairs, specifically in relation to rumours that he had been harbouring Catholic priests in his home.[36] It was not the first or last time Barnewall had been commended for his expertise, nor was it the first or last time he had come under scrutiny.[37] But, for Talbot, who believed he too had an advisory role to play, it must have been somewhat insulting that the administration had ignored his own counsels as well as his recommendation of Barnewall.[38]

Much debated throughout the war, the issue of consultation and the appointment of Old English councillors came to a head again in 1600. On

---

[34] TNA, SP 63/196/27 (opinions of the Privy Council, 26 Dec. 1596).

[35] TNA, SP 63/181/35 (J. Talbot to Cecil, 17 July 1595).

[36] TNA, SP 63/182/12(I) (docquet of 1,350*li.* Borrowed, Aug. 1595); TNA, SP 63/178/4 (P. Barnewall to Burghley, 9 Jan. 1595); McNeill (ed.), 'Harris: Collectanea De Rebus Hibernicis', p. 377.

[37] Barnewall was listed amongst the Pale's doubtful men in 1589 and again in 1598. TNA, SP 63/149/32 (Doubtful men in Ireland, 1589); TNA, SP 63/202(4)/26 (list of suspected gentlemen, 14 Dec. 1598).

[38] TNA, SP 63/181/35 (J. Talbot to Cecil, 17 July 1595); TNA, SP 63/180/45 (J. Talbot to Cecil, 21 June 1595)

behalf of the Palesmen, a delegation led by Sir Patrick Barnewall, the baron of Howth, and a Mr Rocheford travelled to the English court to present a series of complaints and proposals from the Pale. The list was long, and largely related to the transgressions of crown soldiers and other abuses. Among their many recommendations for remedy was a request to have one of their own elevated to the Irish Council, a thing which they insisted was 'no Innovation'.[39] Central to their proposal was the contention that the leading figures in the Pale were more attuned to the problems besetting Ireland and therefore better suited to offer counsel than men newly appointed out of England. The Palesmen's petition rationalised: 'it is impossible, that any should so well right the Causes of the Poore, as those that are best acquainted with their condition, the nature of theire griefes, and causes of their complaints, or that any should so much tender their good & Estate of any Kingdome, as he, whom nature doth oblige thereto, having no other place of refuge, & retruit'.[40]

Lord Deputy Mountjoy had previously denounced the inhabitants of Ireland as 'the worst subjects that any Prince hath in Christendom', yet he was surprisingly receptive to this particular proposal.[41] Irritated by 'their manner of complaint', he nonetheless informed Cecil that he was determined 'to do them right', and that 'it [were] fit that this table were strengthened both with respect and sufficiency, and not amiss that some of this country were members thereof'.[42] Mountjoy seemed to appreciate that the Palesmen were uniquely invested in the fate and fortunes of Ireland and were, by experience, supremely suited to offer guidance. Unfortunately, his personal authority did not permit him to promote anyone to the Council so he deferred to Cecil, cautioning him that 'here is matter for the strongest wits, and... we have not so many wise men amongst us as you think... wherein I could be well content with better assistance than I have, especially with such as, for a time at least, would forget their own private ends'.[43]

Unable to appoint candidates of his own choosing, Mountjoy recommended Howth and Barnewall as the best men for the task. Both men were popular and well connected within their community, so much so that the baron of Dunsany hailed Barnewall as 'a man endowed with parts that may challendge the trust of the best'.[44] Secretary Fenton much preferred Howth, whom he credited with assuaging the tempers of Palesmen angered by the spoils of crown soldiers.

39 TNA, SP 63/207(3)/149 (petition of the inhabitants of the Pale, June 1600); TNA, SP 63/207(6)/69 (Mountjoy to Cecil, 12 Dec. 1600).
40 TNA, SP 63/207(3)/149 (petition of the inhabitants of the Pale, June 1600).
41 CSPI, 1600, p. 301.
42 TNA, SP 63/207(6)/69 (Mountjoy to Cecil, 12 Dec. 1600).
43 CSPI, 1600–1601, pp. 57–8.
44 TNA, SP 63/207(3)/108 (Dunsany to Cecil, 15 June 1600).

Fenton rarely sanctioned the advancement of Irish-born individuals, yet he assured Cecil that the baron was 'a nobleman of great worthe and sincerely affected to her Ma:tie and her gouernment, Such a one as of his ranke, there are few his lyke in this kingdome'. Fenton went so far as to declare that 'yt will greatly stead her Ma:ties seruice, considering what good vse may be made of him'.[45] Howth was an ideal candidate; in addition to championing the political interests of his community, he was renowned for his martial skills and record.[46] During a period of such turmoil, the Council certainly could have made 'good vse' of an esteemed and practised native servitor like Howth, and members of his own community would have been glad of it. His appointment would have served as a move towards appeasing the Old English nobility while reassuring the loyalty of the Palesmen more broadly through this token recognition of their worth. As their group petition asserted, the elevation of one of their own 'will breed a generall great contentment to your People', and even the ever wary Fenton agreed that 'yt will satisfie the countrey to see one of themselues called to the trust of her Ma:ts weightie affaires'.[47]

This was at the height of the war, and if there was ever a time for Elizabeth to openly acknowledge the value of her Irish subjects and thereby soothe their sense of grief and estrangement, surely this would have been it. The queen, however, was in no mood to be dictated to by her subordinates. She empathised with the cruelties inflicted upon her subjects in Ireland, and she demanded that administrators investigate and reform the abuses described by the Palesmen's ambassadors.[48] That was as far as she was willing to allow Old English counsel to extend, and she duly reprimanded her Irish Council for entertaining the elevation of one of them to their membership. To ensure there would be no further deliberation on the matter, Elizabeth purposefully stipulated that 'it is not meet Her Majesty be prescribed in so royal a point by her subjects... let them surcease all further proceeding therein, and leave to Her Majesty's princely mind to call to that junction whom she will, and when she will'.[49] As McGowan-Doyle has so succinctly concluded, this was the 'pivotal moment during the Nine Years' War, when it was in her hands to reverse the declining status of the Old English, [yet] against the advice of virtually all her advisors and administrators, Elizabeth invoked royal prerogative to reject out of hand

---

[45] TNA, SP 63/207(5)/26 (Fenton to Cecil, 15 Sep. 1600).

[46] For example, TNA, SP 63/206/63 (Lords Justices, Ormond, and Council to Privy Council, 3 Dec. 1599).

[47] TNA, SP 63/207(3)/149 (petition of the inhabitants of the Pale, June 1600); TNA, SP 63/207(5)/26 (Fenton to Cecil, 15 Sep. 1600). McGowan-Doyle has explored the significance of this event in relation the rhetoric of counsel as exercised by the Old English community. McGowan-Doyle, 'Rhetoric of Counsel', pp. 163–83.

[48] TNA, SP 63/207(4)/34 (Queen to Mountjoy, 20 July 1600).

[49] CSPI, 1600–1601, p. 117.

the request for an Old English appointment to the Irish council'.[50] No doubt, her ruling in this instance was a devastating blow to the Palesmen's already flagging morale.

The 'Best Acquainted'

Presumably, there were some Old English men who saw the writing on the wall, yet continued to put up a robust defence for their ongoing role in Irish government and society. Alongside arguments defending their constitutional right to sit on the Irish Council, many within the Old English community maintained that the impact of their ostracism reached beyond their own concerns and actually ran counter to the crown's best interests. Generations of Irish residency, along with their vested interest in the country, meant that the Palesmen were better qualified than the New English to advise on matters of Irish policy. This argument had been put forward many times before, including by the baron of Delvin in the 1560s, 1580s, and 1590s. For men like him, their participation in the peculiarities of Ireland's mixed cultural and social life was strong grounds for their continuing presence in the Irish administration. As his 1564 primer on the Irish language intimated, it was only through the special cultural talents of Old Englishmen that some understanding could be achieved between the English crown and the Gaelic Irish. The primer was designed to instruct the queen on how to better understand and communicate with her Irish subjects, but it also served to demonstrate that Delvin and his compatriots were the medium though which such harmony could be fostered.[51] Notwithstanding their hunger for power, men like Delvin genuinely believed that their long experience in Ireland and acquaintance with its inhabitants made them better placed and better practised to govern Ireland than English-born *arrivistes*.[52] This was a widely held view and, put in more graphic terms by the baron of Howth; the Old English were the best qualified because they were 'the old experienced learned with bloody hands'.[53]

While the crown may have considered those of English birth more deserving of favour and office, it was the quality of these Englishmen which made the practice all the more galling.[54] For the Old English nobility, these newly

---

[50] McGowan-Doyle, 'Rhetoric of Counsel', p. 182.

[51] Nugent, 'Queen Elizabeth's Primer'; Palmer, 'Interpreters and the Politics of Translation', pp. 257–77.

[52] TNA, SP 63/108/58 (Delvin's plot for the reformation of Ireland, 26 Mar. 1584).

[53] McGowan-Doyle, *Book of Howth*, pp. 101–02.

[54] There were continual complaints about the calibre of English officers throughout this period. John Talbot's criticisms of the character of army captains is only one example of many. TNA, SP 63/181/35 (J. Talbot to Cecil, 17 July 1595).

appointed English officers were their social inferiors and it was a grievous affront to their honour that such men should now be in a position to judge and command their social betters.[55] Reflecting the opinions of many of his peers, Delvin made his feelings on the matter explicit in 1584 by insisting that Ireland's chief governor should 'be no man of base discent for in all adges men doo reverence such as discend from worthie famelies'.[56] Leaving aside Delvin's personal motive in making the statement, even Hugh O'Neill was adamant that the highest post in the Irish administration should be held by a man of no meaner standing than earl.[57] The appointment of men from England, whatever their rank, had serious consequences for the longevity of the native nobility and Lord Gormanston's 1596 complaint certainly indicated that he interpreted recent developments as such.[58]

The impression that untitled Englishmen had the ability to exert unqualified authority over the nobility and gentry of Ireland had become a genuine concern. The Palesmen had raised this point in connection with all levels of the administration and military organisation, and during the 1590s their complaints extended to control over the structures of local government. While they had long experienced exclusion from offices in the crown administration and army, the Old English had nonetheless maintained their control of local and municipal positions; but by the time of the Nine Years' War, Old English displacement had begun to trickle down to shire level, which naturally generated a great deal of bitterness. Much of the resentment was directed towards sheriffs and the newly instituted quartermasters. The corruption of one and the creation of the other not only infringed on the Palesmen's management of wartime affairs, but was also responsible for distressing the people through widespread incidents of oppression and injustice.

Technically, the shrievalty was supposed to be held by men who owned lands within the territories to which they were assigned. As had happened with so many other offices, vending and exploiting shrievalties had become a lucrative business for greedy governors who cared little about purchasers' credentials. The lawyer Richard Hadsor reserved his greatest venom for these sheriffs, asserting that the appointment of amoral outsiders had perverted the entire system of justice in Ireland and consequently alienated the hearts of the queen's rightful

---

[55] For instance, it is well known that the earl of Ormond resented the appointment of low-born Englishmen to administrative and military offices. Canny, *Making Ireland British*, p. 94.

[56] TNA, SP 63/108/58 (Delvin's plot, 26 May 1584). Treadwell, 'Perrot and the Irish Parliament', p. 266.

[57] TNA, SP 63/206/55 (Tyrone's articles, Nov. 1599).

[58] TNA, SP 63/196/13(I) (memorial, 7 Dec. 1596). For a thorough assessment of 'British' honour and the Nine Years' War, see B. Kane, *The Politics and Culture of Honour in Britain and Ireland, 1541–1641* (Cambridge, 2010), ch. 3.

subjects.[59] Having neither ties to the country or the people, these illegitimate sheriffs operated with impunity, having great liberty to 'sell & abuse ther power in executing justice, &... carry away there misdemeanors w[i]thout yeelding recompence to the people for ther oppression & wronges'.[60] Hadsor did not have a uniquely native take on the situation. William Saxey, Chief Justice in Munster, also mourned the fact that this jurisdiction was 'greedily sought... and too easily granted' to English military men of questionable principles 'whose insolency and ignorance' 'exercised oppression in place of justice'.[61] Guilty of unscrupulous behaviour themselves, even the crown's officer corps condemned the corruptions of sheriffs. In a 1598 petition, army captains alleged that the sheriffs charged with collecting supplies commonly took up more than was allotted by their warrants, and certainly 'more then he is appoynted to his owne vse'.[62]

The invention of quartermasters caused similar turmoil at local level by trespassing on customary responsibilities for directing and implementing wartime procedures.[63] Traditionally, billeting arrangements had been within the remit of local sheriffs, and the inhabitants considered their continued employment in this task acceptable so long as the sheriffs were themselves local men. The Palesmen certainly felt that when it came time to organise accommodation for travelling troops their local officers were far more inclined to consider their abilities than the army's new quartermasters, who 'doe plot and quarter the Souldiors with noe indifference or care haveinge noe knowledge of the countrey but overburtheninge some with over greate nombers to theire vtter vndoeinge, [and] doe for reward free others'.[64] The Palesmen had been complaining about quartermasters since at least 1597, but in 1600 Lord Deputy Mountjoy denied that any had existed since his arrival. Acting as the Palesmen's agent at court, Howth wryly retorted that the office of quartermaster had suddenly become known by the title of furrier, 'as thoughe the varietie of the name should alter

---

59 For a more detailed discussion on Hadsor and the corruption of laws in Ireland, see R.A. Canning, '"May she be rewarded in heauen for righting her poore subiects in Irelande": Lawyer Richard Hadsor and the Authorship of an Elizabethan Treatise on Ireland', *Irish Jurist*, Vol. 55 (2016), pp. 1–24.

60 TNA, SP 63/206/110 (Hadsor to Cecil, 30 Dec. 1599).

61 *CSPI, 1599-1600*, p. 285. Although Saxey was a vocal opponent of military rule and the corruption of sheriffs, he was equally critical of native appointees whom he accused of using their offices to acquire arms and munitions, some of which was used to aid the rebels.

62 TNA, SP 63/202(2)/38 (requests of the captains, 18 May 1598).

63 It is unclear when this post was officially established, or when it fell into disuse. Lambeth, Carew MS, 632, No. 271 ('Declaracion of the presente state of the Englishe Pale', June 1597); TNA, SP 63/207(3)/149 (petition of the inhabitants of the Pale, June 1600); TNA, SP 63/207(5)/23 (baron of Howth to Cecil, 14 Sep. 1600).

64 Lambeth, Carew MS, 632, No. 271 ('Declaracion of the presente state of the Englishe Pale, June 1597).

the nature of the matter'. Of course, changing the name of the office formerly known as quartermaster did not fool the Palesmen, nor did it change the fact that they wanted officials who were intimately acquainted with the affairs of each locale to manage those activities. Howth therefore pursued their case against quartermasters, diplomatically noting that the Palesmen did not question what officers the queen 'should vse for hir Armye', they merely aimed 'to showe what hurt the subiects receaued by the quartermasters'. By doing so, they hoped appropriate measures would be implemented to preserve the rights, properties, and goods of the inhabitants, a task for which they believed their local officers were supremely capable.[65]

Having made his own case against the appointment of corrupt newcomers, Richard Hadsor urged Cecil to consider how home-grown gentlemen were better candidates for local offices.[66] He further implored Cecil to instruct Irish governors to cease the sale of shrievalties and bestow all future appointments on 'such discreet honest men as shall haue lands within the same countie according the lawes of this and that kingdom'.[67] Hadsor's advice, along with similar protests from officials and civilians in Ireland, may well have been considered because in June 1600 Queen Elizabeth ordered Mountjoy to be 'more carefull to make good choice of Sheriffs... according the manner and custome of England, and not... to suffer those offices to be sold, and bought for money by which course they fall into the hands of vnworthie men'.[68] Her ruling did not necessarily imply that she thought these offices would be better executed by men of Irish birth; rather, she just hoped her deputy would be more diligent in his selection of future aspirants. Mountjoy assured the queen and her councillors that he would do his best to rectify the situation; however, it is unclear whether he actually installed native candidates in subsequent shrieval positions at the expense of decommissioned English martial men.[69]

Notwithstanding the general pessimism of English officials and commentators in Ireland, there were a number of experienced administrators who were more amenable to the idea that local appointees would have greater success than strangers when preforming the duties attached to local offices. In 1591, following the settlement of Monaghan and the murder of the first sheriff, a detested English captain named Willis,[70] Lord Chancellor Loftus recommended

[65] TNA, SP 63/207(5)/23 (Howth to Cecil, 14 Sep. 1600).
[66] TNA, SP 63/206/110 (Hadsor to Cecil, 30 Dec. 1599); McLaughlin, 'Richard Hadsor', p. 350.
[67] TNA, SP 63/206/110 (Hadsor to Cecil, 30 Dec. 1599).
[68] TNA, SP 63/207(3)/139 ('Certain instructions conceived' by the Queen, June 1600).
[69] TNA, SP 63/207(4)/5 (Mountjoy to Cecil, 4 July 1600); TNA, SP 63/207(4)/109 (Irish Council to Privy Council, Aug. 1600); TNA, SP 63/207(5)/15 (Irish Council to Privy Council, 12 Sep. 1600); TNA, SP 63/207(6)/69 (Mountjoy to Cecil, 12 Dec. 1600).
[70] This Captain Willis, murdered by the local MacMahon sept, is not to be confused with

John Talbot for the shrievalty.[71] Talbot's nomination was promptly blocked by Lord Deputy Fitzwilliam who claimed that Talbot was an unworthy candidate by virtue of his membership in the Old English community.[72] However, in light of the local reception afforded the former English appointee, Loftus had come around to the Palesmen's view that the Gaelic Irish would better tolerate the presence of Old English officials who consequently would be able to exert greater authority on behalf of the crown. It is regrettable that his senior colleagues did not agree. Indeed, had men like Talbot been preferred above unscrupulous English captains one might wonder if the subsequent course of events in Ulster have been different or, at the very least, if O'Neill's list of grievances have been somewhat altered. Richard Hadsor certainly thought they could have been; as he and the author of a 1600 discourse on the causes of the war opined, the appointment of corrupt non-native sheriffs was one of the chief contributing causes of rebellion in the 1590s.[73] This opinion applied to all levels of government and the Old English were sure that their displacement was the very reason why Ireland had descended into chaos.

Martial Matters

During the Nine Years' War the deteriorating position of the Old English was felt most noticeably within the military establishment. Over preceding decades, efforts had been made to demilitarise the existing political system and, where appropriate, replace the private retinues of local élites with forces loyal to the crown and government. As the professionalised English military presence increased in Ireland, these forces were granted to English newcomers who were appointed to captaincies at the expense of traditional commanders of Old English and Gaelic Irish extraction. The denial of martial authority was seen as a direct assault on the power and status of the Old English élite, which had always taken great pride in its military traditions. This shrinking military function was another issue raised by the baron of Delvin in 1584, and among his articles of contention was that border magnates should continue to 'haue the leadings of the people as they wear accustomed to haue vppon all occasions of service'.[74] This was obviously to little avail, for sixteen years later Lord Barry,

---

Humphrey Willis who served as a captain and sheriff in Connacht and was later nominated for the shievalty of Counties Fermanagh and Donegal. Canny, *Making Ireland British*, p. 102.

71 TNA, SP 63/158/11 (Loftus to Burghley, 20 May 1591).

72 TNA, SP 63/161/12 (Lord Deputy Fitzwilliam to Burghley, 5 Nov. 1591); Canny, *Making Ireland British*, pp. 102–03; Morgan, *Tyrone's Rebellion*, p. 68.

73 McLaughlin, 'Richard Hadsor', p. 349; TNA, SP 63/207(6)/126 (paper on the causes of the rebellion, Dec. 1600).

74 TNA, SP 63/108/58 (Delvin's plot, 26 May 1584).

viscount Buttevant, was still arguing the very same point.[75] In spite of objections from such powerful local lords, English commentators continued to recommend the exclusion of Irish-born individuals from the army's officer ranks, and even during the 1590s crisis administrators were reluctant to reverse the trend. At the very outset of this war Captain John Dowdall declared 'I wold not haue anie of the countrey Birthe to be a comaunder over the rest but every one that you please to hold protested as a subiect shall governe his owne familie and knowen folloers, and no further.'[76] This sentiment was shared by members of the Irish Council, who expressed great reservations about entrusting military commands to native servitors. When Mr Ashley, the English captain of Duncannon fort, absented himself for a prolonged stay in England, the Irish Council appealed to the English Privy Council for his immediate return because his charge had been left in the hands of a local man, 'Mr Itchingham, a gentleman of the county of Wexford, which in our opinion, is not so saffe for a place of that chardge in this daungerus tyme'.[77]

Although native exclusion had become general policy, the Old English élite had not been reduced to mere civilians and the heightened state of emergency during the Nine Years' War offered them plenty of scope to perform military services. Contrary to Delvin's implication that they could no longer command local forces, the border magnates continued to maintain private retinues and were routinely entrusted with arranging border defences and leading the risings out of their locales. This reflected necessity rather than confidence in the Palesmen's loyalties. The administration had effectively been forced to resort to these native supports because the crown army's English component was too weak to provide men for the Pale frontier while it pursued the enemy further afield. For similar reasons, a number of prominent Old English servitors did attain military offices, especially at the rank of captain. Even though access to higher military offices had contracted, there were some notable exceptions: Sir Christopher St Lawrence was awarded a captaincy and many local commands; Henry Fitzgerald, twelfth earl of Kildare, was granted a command over a large force sent directly out of England; the fourteenth earl of Kildare was entrusted with the government of Offaly; and the baron of Dunsany was granted like authority over Kells and the surrounding borders.[78] More surprising was that James Fitzpiers Fitzgerald was knighted and given a substantial command shortly after his ill-conceived

[75] TNA, SP 63/207(4)/115 (Lord Viscount Buttevant's humble requests, Aug. 1600).

[76] TNA, SP 63/174/37(IX) (J. Dowdall to lord deputy and Council, 2 May 1594). See also Maley (ed.), 'The Supplication', p. 36.

[77] TNA, SP 63/202(1)/56 (Loftus, Gardener, Ormond, and Council to Privy Council, 27 Feb. 1598).

[78] McGowan-Doyle, '"Spent Blood"', pp. 179–91; TNA, SP 63/194/29 (Kyffin to Cecil, 19 Oct. 1596); TNA, SP 63/194/30 (Kyffin to Burghley, 20 Oct. 1596); TNA, SP 63/194/30(I) (muster roll of Kildare's light horse, 19 Oct. 1596); TNA, SP 63/194/32 (draft by Burghley or Cecil to Kildare,

secret plot to act as a traitor.[79] Undoubtedly, the decision to promote him rested on the impressive control he held over his neighbours and the 'Bastard' Geraldines. Most remarkable of all was the appointment of Thomas Butler, tenth earl of Ormond, as lieutenant general of the queen's army in Ireland. This was the ultimate acknowledgement of an Old Englishman's valuable service to the crown; not only did it make him the head of all crown forces in Ireland, but it was proof that his military contribution was recognised as outstanding, even when compared to New English contenders. These examples point to an awareness within administrative circles that native support was necessary and that fostering that support required at least some positive reinforcement. Yet, these exceptions should be judged on their own merits; in Ormond's case, he was the queen's cousin and, much to the chagrin of her English officials, greatly favoured by her. Tempering official jealousies somewhat was Ormond's Protestantism, and in the eyes of many English reformers this rare act of conformity was worth rewarding as a means to encourage others to follow suit.[80]

Even though Ormond enjoyed unusual royal favour and esteem, his promotion to Ireland's highest military office was bittersweet. As he soon discovered, his executive authority had been undermined and he was unable to exercise certain prerogatives normally associated with his position. What proved most problematic in this respect was that he was deprived of the right to personally select and appoint deserving candidates, native or otherwise, to military captaincies.[81] The logic behind limiting his remit was to prevent the rapid expansion of the officer cadre and the inevitable cost to the crown in paying captains' salaries. It was, however, damaging for Ormond's reputation and authority since it was believed that it was he who possessed the power to promote men or, in this case, obstruct them. His inability to exercise this privilege also had wider implications and potentially catastrophic consequences for the crown's war effort because lack of reward bred dissent among servitors who felt they deserved better. Although his charge was subject to greater restraints, Ormond's experience was not unique and similar limitations endangered the powers of other officials, including English lords deputy. Mountjoy in particular complained that he bore the brunt of dissatisfied captains' malice since they held him responsible for all military affairs in Ireland, and especially

---

Oct. 1596); TNA, SP 63/194/38 (Kyffin to Burghley, 21 Oct. 1596); TNA, SP 63/194/57 (Irish Council to Privy Council, 31 Oct. 1596); TNA, SP 63/207(1)/2 (Dunsany to Cecil, 2 Jan. 1600).
[79] TNA, SP 63/207(3)/97 (Mountjoy to Cecil, 9 Apr. 1600); TNA, SP 63/207(3)/93 (Mountjoy to Privy Council, 9 June 1600). See Canning, 'James Fitzpiers Fitzgerald', pp. 573–94.
[80] Indeed, as Hugh Cuff, secretary to the earl of Essex, explained, the exclusion of Irish-born applicants should be upheld except in cases where the individual was 'known to be well affected in religion' because this 'would be a principal means to draw others to conformity'. No doubt Ormond met Cuff's criteria for one of these 'good teachers'. CSPI, 1600, p. 403.
[81] TNA, SP 63/202(3)/144 (Ormond to Privy Council, 5 Nov. 1598).

the welfare of all martial men who served in what had become known as 'the most miserable warre… in the worlde'.[82] Dissent in the army was a danger of which most commanders were all too well aware, and the curbing of their right to promote men and thereby reinforce military bonds was a very genuine concern. Paul Hammer has stated that 'Essex's dubbing of so many new knights in Ireland was not simply a sign of his rashness… but a calculated, rational gamble intended to preserve the fighting power of his army at a time of acute crisis'.[83] Other lords deputy had likewise found their situation troubling; but, already compromised by his place of birth, the restrictions placed upon Ormond's authority served to weaken further his control over the army and diminish the respect he commanded from his men.

Governors had been warned to be sparing in the conferral of knighthoods and commands, but permission to bestow these rewards on servitors of Irish birth was deliberately more restrictive than it was for men born in England.[84] As a result, the promotion of native servitors typically elicited detailed explanations to justify their deserts.[85] What is more, the scope of authority these natives enjoyed was subject to stricter limitations than their English counterparts and their rewards in entertainment were significantly reduced. Possibly even more disheartening was that appointments to higher commands could be challenged or reinterpreted by cautious English administrators, as had happened to the baron of Dunsany. In late 1599 Essex had appointed Dunsany to the government of Kells, but three months later the Irish Council refused to recognise his position, arguing that they were not sure how far Dunsany's authority was actually meant to extend. Despite Dunsany's appeals, the Council ruled that they would only reconsider the matter when the lord lieutenant returned, which, of course, he never did.[86] Therefore, as the experiences of Ormond and Dunsany demonstrate, even if esteemed and advanced, Old English servitors remained marginalised.

[82] TNA, SP 63/202(2)/38 (requests of the captains, 18 May 1598); TNA, SP 63/205/241 (proclamation by Elizabeth, Oct. 1599); TNA, SP 63/207(3)/82 (Mountjoy to Cecil, 7 June 1600); TNA, SP 63/207(4)/68 (Mountjoy to Privy Council, 13 Aug. 1600); TNA, SP 63/207(6)/35 (Mountjoy to Cecil, 27 Nov. 1600). Paul Hammer talks about this dilemma of in his discussion of Essex's bestowal of knighthoods and objections from England. P.E.J. Hammer, '"Base Rogues" and "Gentlemen of Quality": The Earl of Essex's Irish Knights and Royal Displeasure in 1599', in Kane and McGowan-Doyle (eds), *Elizabeth I and Ireland*, pp. 184–208.

[83] Hammer, '"Base Rogues"', p. 203.

[84] Mountjoy expressed reservations about being disallowed to bestow companies upon worthy Irish servitors. TNA, SP 63/207(2)/97 (Mountjoy to Cecil, 9 Apr. 1600); TNA, SP 63/207(5)/116 ('Heads of things', 27 Oct. 1600).

[85] TNA, SP 63/207(2)/97 (Mountjoy to Cecil, 9 Apr. 1600); TNA, SP 63/207(3)/105 (J. Harrington to Cecil, 12 June 1600); TNA, SP 63/207(6)/35 (Mountjoy to Cecil, 27 Nov. 1600).

[86] TNA, SP 63/207(I)/2 (Dunsany to Cecil, 2 Jan. 1600); TNA, SP 63/209(2)/155 (Bishop of Meath to Cecil, 20 Oct. 1601).

Such unequal treatment was hardly the way to encourage native co-operation but, in spite of the administration's poor usage of them, the Old English remained undeterred in their quest for military office and authority. This was made manifest by their many petitions, suits for commands, and their avowals of an ancestral obligation to serve their prince. Striving to prove their worth and ability, Old English supplicants went to great lengths to detail their many loyal services, even so far as counting the number of rebel heads they had delivered.[87] These petitions further functioned as declarations of personal and familial sacrifice by drawing attention to the financial and human costs of war in terms of military support proffered and the destruction of livings by rebels and marauding crown soldiers. All this they had endured for the sake of the crown and what they sought in return were the means to better serve their queen while protecting themselves from further harm. This became the typical formula when suing for favour. However, the Palesmen went beyond mere requests for reward and appealed for more apparent political parity, stipulating that all the services and suffering they had sustained merited the same appreciation and recompense as enjoyed by their English-born equivalents. Following a typically lengthy recital of his own services, the baron of Dunsany explained that '[i]f the causes of givinge entertaynemennt to any be either Trust, Desert, Power and skill to serue, or for fitness of State to restrayne the Enemye, I doe thinck my self in this respecte... not last of others to be regarded'.[88] Dunsany objected to the unjust tendency to discriminate against individuals born in Ireland and insisted that he deserved the same consideration as any subject born in England because the services performed by him and his family were comparable to the very best England had to offer.[89]

Having expressed his irritation at the promotion of less deserving men in 1595 and again in 1597, and having had his government of Kells questioned in early 1600, Dunsany remained determined to pursue military office. In late 1600 he urged Cecil to consider him for one of three vacant military commands: Knockfergus; Cavan; and the forts in Leix and Offaly.[90] On this occasion, Dunsany outlined his particular expertise and qualifications for each post, intentionally focusing on credentials which no English contender could legitimately possess. He insisted that whomever was entrusted with Knockfergus would need 'to be well vnderstode' of the Ulstermen's 'factions and fewdes ther

---

[87] For example, see the suits submitted by the baron of Delvin: TNA, SP 63/198/61 (brief of Delvin's suit, Mar. 1597); TNA, SP 63/207/88(I) (services done by Delvin, 1600); TNA, SP 63/207(6)/45 (statement by H. Dillon on services by Dunsany, Nov. 1600).

[88] TNA, SP 63/178/65 (Dunsany to Burghley, Feb. 1595).

[89] Ibid. Also see his 1597 petition: HMC Salisbury MSS, vii, 323; TNA, SP 63/201/144 (suit of Dunsany, 1597). Dunany reportedly delivered a speech to this effect in 1599. SP 63/206/33 (R. Napper, Chief Baron of the Exchequer, to Cecil, 18 Nov. 1599).

[90] TNA, SP 63/207(6)/46 (Dunsany to Cecil, Nov. 1600).

allyances and aptness to be emploied'. Dunsany bragged, 'I haue all the helpes & meanes that eny other man hathe, and I haue the language very well for advantage.' With respect to the position in Cavan, Dunsany noted his personal relations with the ruling O'Reillys, both through marriage and neighbourhood, 'wherby I haue good meanes to drawe in Oreylie and all that county from the Traytor'. His similar knowledge of the O'Moores, O'Connors, and O'Dempseys in Leix and Offaly likewise endowed him with advantageous connections for more successful negotiations.[91] This was, by all appearances, an application for office, and one which was unsuccessful. But the qualifications Dunsany touted were nonetheless vital in determining the outcome of this war. Old Englishmen proved extremely useful agents for conducting negotiations and securing pledges from Gaelic Irish rebels because ties of friendship, neighbourhood, and even kinship, permitted a degree of trust between the two parties which could never be achieved by some upstart New English outsider. These same connections were also indispensible for the acquisition of intelligence, while their fluency in the Irish language enabled them to translate intercepted rebel communications.[92] Dunsany made clear that he was not only as dignified as any New English servitor, but he possessed skills, experience, and relationships which they could not rival and it would therefore be a mistake to overlook him for these offices.

Like so many Old English supplicants, Dunsany had advised Burghley that tokens of favour and gratitude would do much to keep the Palesmen satisfied and loyal, by reassuring them that their queen appreciated their efforts.[93] He further insisted that his advancement would be embraced by his peers as a promising sign for their own possible preferment in the future; Dunsany even went so far as to insist that the rest of the Irish nobility would be offended if he did not receive favour in his suits.[94] This is not to pretend the Old English were anything like the three musketeers; the Irish political system was fraught with endemic factionalism and there was fierce competition for advancement. Nevertheless, Dunsany's claim of communal solidarity still has some merits. In

[91] Ibid.

[92] Delvin was particularly active in this regard. TNA, SP 63/186/86(XVII) (Delvin to Russell, 24 Feb. 1596); TNA, SP 63/186/86(XVIII) (P. O'Reilly to Delvin, 20 Feb. 1596); TNA, SP 63/190/11(V) (Bishop of Meath to Russell, 4 June 1596); TNA, SP 63/190/44(IX) (Bishop of Meath, Delvin, and Killeen to Russell, June 1596); TNA, SP 63/190/30(I) (Bishop of Meath to Russell, 18 June 1596).

[93] For another example of this opinion, see TNA, SP 63/178/20 (W. Smythe to Burghley, 25 Jan. 1595).

[94] 'Obieccion if there be any as that other noble men wold stomack that I shuld be preferred and not them selves maie be answered very truely thus, that wayinge my longe and chargeable abode here, they will with more reason dispise my goinge without it, then despite my havinge of it'. TNA, SP 63/178/65 (Dunsany to Burghley, Feb. 1595).

1594 Thomas Fleming, baron of Slane, strongly endorsed Ormond's elevation to the military leadership; Slane would almost certainly accrue some benefit from the promotion of his friend Ormond, but this does not negate the fact that Slane wished to see a man of his own background preferred and rewarded before English-born newcomers.[95] In 1595 John Talbot had likewise recommended the expertise and promotion of Sir Patrick Barnewall and, in 1600, Dunsany endorsed both Barnewall and the baron of Howth as men who were 'wise', 'honest', and 'well affected to his contry'.[96] While factional politics played a role in determining who advanced whom, each of these men believed that the individuals they recommended would represent their own interests as well as those of their community. In spite of many strong arguments for their promotion and preservation, in the end the Old English were to be disappointed.

Notwithstanding policies of exclusion and restrictions on the number of native soldiers allowed in English companies, native servitors made up a very substantial share of the crown's military establishment during the Nine Years' War. This fact was often acknowledged, yet did not translate into fair or equitable treatment. Indicative of the poor regard and handling of Old English servitors was the lower pay they were allowed, even at the level of captain. Another particularly conspicuous display of disrespect was that when lords deputy were instructed to reduce the number of military men in pay, the companies led by Old English captains were disbanded before those of the New English. Worse still, on some occasions these Old English-led companies were simply reassigned to Englishmen who had successfully petitioned for commands.[97] Many of the cashiered native leaders justly believed that this was a product of ethnic discrimination, and they sued crown administrators for the restoration of their forces. This was another cause taken up by Hadsor in London. In October 1601 he advocated on behalf of a Mr Plunkett whose foot company, formerly in the pay of the queen, had been recently cashiered. Hadsor implored Cecil to advance Plunkett's suit for the restoration of that company because 'he is an honest gentlman and able to do the Queene service being one of the best of his name and hath received great losse by the wasting of his lands by the rebels'.[98] In furthering Plunkett's suit, Hadsor also took the opportunity to argue that 'it were fitter in my opinion to imploy him and a number of other sufficient gentlmen of English race in the Pale who received great losse in these

---

95 TNA, SP 63/174/48(VII) (Slane to R. Gardener, W. Weston, A. Sentleger and G. Fenton, 12 May 1594).
96 TNA, SP 63/181/35 (J. Talbot to Cecil, 17 July 1595); TNA, SP 63/207(3)/108 (Dunsany to Cecil, 15 June 1600).
97 For example, see opinions expressed by muster officers Richard Wackely and Sir Ralph Lane: TNA, SP 63/202(1)/54 (R. Wackely to Lane, 19 Feb. 1598); TNA, SP 63/202(1)/66 (Lane to Burghley, 1 Mar. 1598).
98 TNA, SP 63/209(2)/153 (Hadsor to Cecil, 17 Oct. 1601).

warres and are knowen to the State there to be good subiects and faithfull to her Ma:tie'.[99]

John Lye, a native of County Kildare, was inclined to agree, and advised Cecil that 'the sevice here will be muche the better performed' if 'some of the contrie gent. dwellinge on the bordors maye be imployed therin'.[100] This, Lye asserted, could be done with little cost to the crown because, having been subjected to spoliation and ruin, the prospective rehabilitation of border lands and tenants was a far greater incentive than crown pay. According to him, all the border lords required was some guarantee for their preservation. Lye's second and equally rational argument was that these borderers were uniquely acquainted with Irish warfare, 'haveing good experience howe to prosecutte the rebles & are able to travell & byde both hunger and could'. Above all, Lye was adamant that these Old English Palesmen 'will adventure much where as others haveinge noe liueinge… & not able to byde the like sorowe, will not care to prolonge the same hereowte'.[101]

As emphasised by Lye, this conflict presented a direct threat to the welfare of those living along the Pale's frontier. But, in addition to their displacement within the military establishment, the tactical dilemmas of border defence were further accentuated by the Palesmen's increasing poverty through suffering so many physical and economic hardships. Warning Cecil that 'the gentlmen and inhabitants of the English Pale are vnarmed and vnfurnished to defend them selves or to do the Queene service', Richard Hadsor implored Cecil to grant them the succour they so needed to perform the duties expected of loyal subjects.[102] The Palesmen had been making similar appeals since the early stages of the war, complaining that they had neither the money nor the men to protect themselves and their holdings, never mind perform any meaningful service against the rebels.[103] As is evident from James Fitzpiers's 1594 petition, many within the community assumed they were entitled to some assistance in this respect. Collaborating with his uncle Edward Fitzgerald, Fitzpiers petitioned the crown for a company of men to help secure his position in County Kildare and exact revenge on the murderers of his parents. Explaining how 'we are in dayly danger of our lives threatned by those myschivous rebells', they begged for means and reinforcements to fend off future rebel assaults.[104] As loyal subjects

---

99   Ibid.; TNA, SP 63/202(4)/75 ('A discourse', 1598).
100 TNA, SP 63/207(6)/59 (J. Lye to Cecil, 5 Dec. 1600).
101 Ibid.
102 HMC *Salisbury MSS*, xi, 8–9; TNA, SP 63/209(2)/153 (Hadsor to Cecil, 17 Oct. 1601).
103 For example, TNA, SP 63/173/91(VI) (complaint of J. Fitzgerald, 18 Mar. 1594); TNA, SP 63/176/4 (petition of E. Fitzgerald, 2 Sep. 1594). See also TNA, SP 63/207(4)/1 (T. Dillon to Cecil, 1 July 1600).
104 TNA, SP 63/173/91(VI) (complaint of J. Fitzgerald, 18 Mar. 1594); TNA, SP 63/176/4 (petition of E. Fitzgerald, 2 Sep. 1594).

and servitors, Fitzpiers and his uncle believed they had a right to expect crown protection, or at the very least some assistance for their defence since they were among the primary targets of the same Gaelic Irish brutes who had revolted against the crown. By virtue of the shared enemy, Fitzpiers and his uncle imagined themselves irrevocably tied to the crown in this cause and, in return for the crown's assistance, they would fully commit to the queen's military enterprise. In their minds at least, this was supposed to be a mutually beneficial bond.[105] Fitzpiers and his uncle were successful in this particular suit and the English Privy Council directed its Irish counterpart to grant them command over twenty-five horse and fifty foot.[106] The two men later explained to the Cecils that the grant had not materialised and they required further letters from England before the Irish Council actually fulfilled the conditions of their reward.[107]

The duration and scale of the Nine Years' War compelled the crown to rely heavily on the Old English community, particularly in terms of augmenting the crown's military strength through hostings and border defence. Maintaining a native support base was imperative for the survival of crown government and, even though Old English representation had declined within the army's officer ranks, this ensured they continued to have some say in military affairs. Though still excluded from momentous decisions, like the proclamation against O'Neill, there were occasions when the Council opted to defer certain announcements until the Pale nobility had been consulted. This particular show of respect was most commonly allowed when events necessitated the assembly of a great army because administrators appreciated that Old English co-operation would be more effective if attained through consent rather than coercion. To this end, numerous consultations and 'councils' were held between Dublin officials and the Pale nobility. In March 1595 Fenton described the assembly of what he termed a 'grand Councell' for which 'manie matter weare to be prepared to be handled in that consultacion, which cold not suffer delaie the rather for that the resolucions for the North, and the defence of those borders depended vppon that conference'.[108] Because the particular matter at hand was border defence, English administrators were cognisant that this would be better handled by willing men than by those who felt their value taken for granted. Discussions took place again in June and, with the consent of those concerned, it was agreed that the earl of Kildare, 'assisted with the residue of their lordships', would hold executive command over the Palesmen.[109] Similar consultations were held again

---

105 TNA, SP 63/176/4 (petition of E. Fitzgerald, 2 Sep. 1594).
106 TNA, SP 63/176/3 (J. Fitzgerald to Cecil, 2 Sep. 1594).
107 Ibid.; TNA, SP 63/176/4 (E. Fitzgerald to Burghley, 2 Sep. 1594).
108 TNA, SP 63/178/68 (Fenton to Burghley, 3 Mar. 1595).
109 TNA, SP 63/180/48 (Fenton to Burghley, 24 June 1595).

in July and November 1595, to the same effect.[110] Such councils were convened regularly throughout the war and, in spite of the weakening condition of their people and estates, the Pale nobility remained pliable on these occasions largely because they felt their opinions and concerns were being recognised by higher authorities.[111]

For the crown administrators, consultation was not so much desirable as expedient. Rather than simply issuing orders for the assembly of Pale forces, the government consulted the nobility on border defences and risings out in an effort to avoid potential reluctance at such critical times. English officials were acutely conscious that Old English complicity in these matters required that they continue to play a role in government policy and decision-making, particularly when it concerned defending their own turf. Since hostings were usually – though not always – called in order to procure a defensive force along the Pale's borders, the administration was obliged to acknowledge local interests as a means to encourage local participation. On such occasions the lords of the Pale were consulted on the general progress of the war and could likewise expect their opinions to be heard. This had two benefits for the administration. First, the Palesmen, momentarily placated by the government's recognition of their value, were all the more willing to take on the responsibility of border defence and, released from this service, the crown's 'English' army had greater liberty and strength to campaign abroad. Second, keeping the Pale magnates on side was the best means to keeping the general Pale population obedient since the continuing loyalty of their lords served to deter tenants and weaker neighbours from going out against them. Ireland was a highly dynastic society, held together by familial and personal bonds and, as Captain Lee had said of Fitzpiers, his rebelliously inclined neighbours 'dare not whilest he stands in, ffor… they feare him muche, for he is a tall man, & a good executioner'.[112] Even though the Pale nobility had been increasingly excluded from official positions, that the administration felt a need to consult them on such matters suggests that they still had considerable influence in military affairs, especially those affecting their community. Furthermore, the participation of the Pale lords at these conferences and their co-operation in taking charge of border defence not only indicates their readiness to serve the crown, but also demonstrates that they were an indispensable part of the government's military machine.

---

[110] BL, Add. MS 4763, f. 429 (report of meeting between Council and nobility, 21 July 1595); Perrot, *Chronicle*, p. 103.

[111] For example, see TNA, SP 63/207(1)/59 (Mountgarrett, Dunboyne, W. Butler, and H. Folliott to Ormond, 29 Jan. 1600); TNA, SP 63/207(3)/63 (Irish Council to Privy Council, 27 May 1600); TNA, SP 63/207(5)/15 (Irish Council to Privy Council, 12 Sep. 1600).

[112] TNA, SP 63/202(3)/171(IV) (speeches between T. Lee and R. Hoper, 24 Nov. 1598).

This is not a definitive study of the crisis of the Old English élite; it does, however, provide a glimpse into a community undergoing a crisis of identity during an exceptionally traumatic time. Their weakened grasp on office-holding, counselling, and influence were all features of Old English demotion, and the Palesmen's petitions and treatises made it clear that they had become acutely sensitive to outside interference.[113] Concerns about their displacement and diminished political role had been articulated long before the outbreak of the Nine Years' War, and thus reveal a downward but consistent trend for Old English influence. The rapid expansion of the army during this conflict, and their deliberate exclusion from major administrative decisions, amplified the declining status of the Old English nobility. Equally offensive was that they were being systematically replaced by their social inferiors whose English birth and Protestant faith were their only superior credentials. Whatever advancement and promotion a few of them did attain was subject to restrictions which impeded their effective wielding of authority. As expected, there was a native reaction to policies of exclusion, but, for the most part, objection took the form of complaints, petitions, suits, and treatises rather than physical displays of discontent. This may come as a surprise, largely because Old English concerns about their declining political influence would probably have justified revolt in many eyes, especially at a time when matters of politics and religion were coalescing into one grand national cause. Rather than hitch themselves to O'Neill's invented Irish Catholic nation, the Old English remained adamant that they not only supported the English crown's Irish administration, but were still the best possible candidates for its civil and military offices. They referred to precedent, statute, and law; they listed credentials and qualifications, ancestral and personal records of service, and familiarity with the people and land to be subdued. Their profiles were impressive, as were the arguments they presented at court, yet there was no mistaking their deposition by green and largely unscrupulous men sent directly from England. Despite so many setbacks and obvious signs of disrespect, the Old English remained undeterred in their quest to prove their case throughout this war. However, the most decisive blow against this community came in December 1600 when Queen Elizabeth ruled once and for all that she was not obliged to listen to Old English counsel, and she most certainly had no intention of raising one of them to her Irish Council.[114] This may be looked on as an inevitable termination of Old English privilege and authority. On the other hand, it is arguable that, had it not been for this war, the Pale élite might have had more time to build their case, or at the very least, more time to enjoy the final days of their ascendancy.

[113] For example, TNA, SP 63/202(4)/60 ('greevances', 1598); TNA, SP 63/207(3)/149 (petition of the inhabitants of the Pale, June 1600); TNA, SP 63/207(4)/3 (intelligences for Her Majesty's services, 3 July 1600).
[114] *CSPI, 1600–1601*, p. 117.

Epilogue

An Inconclusive Aftermath

The war ended on 30 March 1603. Hugh O'Neill submitted to Lord Deputy Mountjoy at Mellifont Abbey only to discover that Queen Elizabeth had died six days earlier. Five days after his submission came news that James VI of Scotland was to be proclaimed King James I of England and Ireland. According to Fynes Moryson, the publication of this proclamation was met with 'joyfull acclamations... through the chiefe streets of Dublyn'.[1] Reaction in other urban centres was considerably less enthusiastic and certainly less obedient.

One might have expected a collective sigh of relief from the Palesmen and their colleagues in other parts of the country. The constant threat of violence had eased, the need to support large numbers of unruly soldiers had diminished and, although the debased coin was still circulating, there must have been hope that regular trading would soon resume. What is more, like the defeated Confederates, many loyalist Old English Catholics erroneously assumed that the new King James had Catholic sympathies and that it would be safe to publicly practise Catholicism again. But no one was actually this optimistic. Even before the war had concluded Mountjoy anticipated serious problems. He opined: 'The Nobility, Townes, and English-Irish, are for the most part as weary of the warre as any, but unwilling to have it ended, generally, for feare that uppon a peace, will ensue a severe reformation of Religion.'[2] He also fretted that 'generally over all the Kingdome, [is] the feare of a persecution for Religion, the debasing of the Coyne... and a dearth and famine, which is already begunne, and must of necessity grow shortly to extremity; the least of which alone, have been many times sufficient motives to drive the best and most quiet estates into sudden confusion'.[3] Mountjoy was correct: many Old English townsmen were frustrated by their hardships; they were anxious about their futures; and, having long done their bit for the crown, were now prepared to stand upon their rights.

The interregnum between the death of Elizabeth and the confirmation of James I brought with it a great deal of uncertainty because Elizabethan officials were left without a mandate until the new king confirmed or replaced them. Taking advantage of this power vacuum, between 11 April and 10 May 1603, fourteen towns in Leinster and Munster went into 'revolt'. These

[1] Moryson, *Itinerary*, iii, p. 303.
[2] Ibid., p. 274.
[3] Ibid., p. 275.

revolts were nothing like the war which had preceded them. There was no nationalist manifesto and there was no formal call to arms. The townsmen in many places merely delayed proclaiming King James and denied the authority of crown officials until letters patent from the king confirmed them in their positions. They did, however, become emboldened in other ways. The obstinate townsmen restored the mass and re-adorned the churches with the treasured ornaments and relics they had hidden decades earlier from crown commissioners. Catholic processions were boldly staged, and '[n]ow came abroad in open shewe the Jesuites, seminarie priests, and friars owt of euerie corner, and walked up and downe in euerie cittie and corporation'.[4] Books of Common Prayer were burned and, in many places, the Protestant minority was taunted, threatened, and even run out of town.[5] Such defiant religious displays are the reason why these protests were misleadingly dubbed 'recusancy revolts'. But they were about much more than just religion. As Hans Pawlisch and Anthony Sheehan have argued, outrage over the economic ramifications of the currency debasement scheme played a significant role.[6] The townsmen also took control of munitions caches and crown forts, declaring that these fell under their jurisdiction according to the ancient charters of freedom granted to the corporations. They likewise denied crown companies entry into the cities because their charters exempted them from such obligations.[7] This was not entirely unfair; these rights had been enshrined in their charters and, having forsaken these privileges for the duration of the war, the townsmen had borne more than their fair share in supporting crown soldiers. Now the war was over, and so too should the demands on their very limited resources.

These displays of disobedience could not be tolerated at such a precarious time. The country was devastated and now was the time to seize control of the whole island. Furious letters were exchanged between Lord Deputy Mountjoy, the Irish Council, and the mutinous corporations. The threat of force soon followed, and after making examples of Kilkenny and Waterford, along with the ringleaders in those towns, the remaining riotous corporations threw in the towel and professed obedience. Had the chief corporations within the Pale risen too, things might have been considerably more difficult for the administration. The Pale was the lynchpin of English rule in Ireland and, given the administration's and army's heavy reliance on this region throughout the Nine Years' War, the crown may well have had to make some major concessions. Curiously,

---

4 Falkiner (ed.), 'William Farmer's Chronicles of Ireland (Continued)', p. 530.
5 Moryson, *Itinerary*, iii, pp. 312–21.
6 Pawlisch, *John Davies*, pp. 142–57; Sheehan, 'The Recusancy Revolt', pp. 3–13.
7 In addition to Sheehan, for more detailed assessments of the recusancy revolts, see S. Carroll, 'Government Policy, Strategies of Negotiation and the Politics of Protest in Early Seventeenth-Century Ireland' (unpublished PhD thesis, Trinity College Dublin, 2013), ch. 1.

none of the major urban centres within the traditionally defined Pale took part in the recusancy revolts. So why were the Palesmen so submissive? Was it the continued presence of military forces in and around the Pale? Was it because the crown administration continued to function in Dublin? Were they so weakened by the war that they were unable to take a stand? Did they fail to see this as an opportunity to air their grievances in unison with their colleagues elsewhere? Or did they actually think that their special position as loyalist Catholics would be suddenly recognised, tolerated, or even cherished?

The presence of the army and administration may have served as a deterrent, but this is not a satisfactory explanation since there was a functioning presidency in Munster along with adequate forces to prop it up. The activities of President Carew and his army did not discourage the inhabitants of Cork city from seizing both crown forts and munitions stores, resuming Catholic practices, and harassing local Protestants. Similarly, it would be rather naïve to assume that the Palesmen wholeheartedly believed the crown would let them be half-subjects: politically loyal and religiously delinquent. Members of the Dublin Corporation were probably still smarting from a brief but punitive campaign against leading recusants in January 1603.[8] It is, however, conceivable that they had more worldly concerns at this time since the corporation seems to have been in the early stages of preparing a crown petition, like that of 1597, which was presented in London sometime between 1603 and 1604.[9] If this was the case, the Dublin patriciate would have been disinclined to act in any way which might hinder the furthering of those interests. This may explain the behaviour of Dublin's citizens, but Dublin did not represent the Pale as a whole, and so the question remains: why did the Palesmen not rise in April 1603? And this question could be easily reframed: why did they not rise sooner? Why didn't they join a nationwide revolt against the centralising forces of the English state when they had the chance?

There were, of course, many Old Englishmen who did rise up during the Nine Years' War. Examples like Captain Richard Tyrell, Richard Weston, and Walter Reagh Fitzgerald demonstrate that there was an alternative to being ignored by the queen and her government. But were the actions of these individuals actually inspired by emotive ideologies? Although it is possible to discern its pre-modern origins, many historians and sociologists have persuasively argued that nationalistic patriotism is the invention of the modern era.[10] Like most

---

[8] Lennon, *The Lords of Dublin*, p. 172.

[9] The petition itself has not survived, but it did receive answer in an undated 1604 document. *CSPI, 1603–1606*, p. 228.

[10] For example, see B. Anderson, *Imagined Communities: Reflections on the Origin and Spread of Nationalism* (London, 1991); D.G. Boyce, *Nationalism in Ireland* (London, 1995); R.V. Comerford, *Inventing the Nation: Ireland* (London, 2003); O.D. Edwards, 'Ireland', in O.D. Edwards, G. Evans,

of his contemporaries, many scholars doubt that O'Neill was guided by a selfless desire for national and religious liberation. People do, and always did, invent high-minded ideals to justify their actions, but these are often self-serving. The same is true for those who join one side or the other. Besides the patriotic tug of faith and fatherland ideology, there were numerous other incentives which prompted Old English Palesmen to join Hugh O'Neill's extraordinary revolt, or to disavow it. Faith and fatherland may have an attractive ring to it, but for many Palesmen philosophical principles were not enough to convince them to bear arms against their English sovereign – especially since O'Neill had not secured the requisite papal and Spanish backing which might have convinced them that English suzerainty was in its final days. Presumably, there were a few emotionally charged members of the Old English community for whom patriotic sentiment held some appeal. However, for the majority of those who joined the rebellion, or even just momentarily contemplated revolt, their concerns were far more practical and immediate. Prominent among their grievances were political exclusion, social displacement, factional rivalries, personal security, economic resentment, and, especially during this conflict, blatant exploitation by the English administration and army they were expected to serve regardless of the many slanders levelled at their community. Even Queen Elizabeth recognised this and, in a 1599 proclamation, she noted:

> we doe conceiue that all our people which are at this presente Actors in this rebellion, are not of one sorte, nor carried into it with one minde, but some out of feeling thie haue of hard measures heretofore perhaps offered them by some of our ministers, some for feare of the power and might that their aduerse sectes and fellowes haue by aduantage of this loose time growne into, and some for wante of due protection and defence against the wilde and barbarous Rebells, inveagled with superstitious impressions, wrought in them by the conning of seditious Preistes and seminaries, crept into them from forraine partes, suborned by those that are our open ennemyes, and a great parte out of a stronge but misconceaued opinion infused into them, by the heads of this Rebellion, that we intended an vtter extirpation and rootinge out of that nation and conquest of the countrie.[11]

Considering how genuine and pressing these social, political, and economic concerns were to the Old English Pale community – and these matters distressed everyone – it is surprising how many Palesmen actually resisted the lure of resistance. Many Palesmen readily admitted that these considerations

---

I. Rhys, and H. MacDiarmid (eds), *Celtic Nationalism* (London, 1968); E. Gellner, 'Nationalism', *Theory and Society*, Vol. 10, No. 6 (1981), pp. 753–76; M. Hechter, *Containing Nationalism* (Oxford, 2000); J. Leerssen, *Mere Irish and Fíor-Ghael: Studies in the Idea of Irish Nationality, its Development and Literary Expression Prior to the Nineteenth Century* (Cork, 1996); H. Seton-Watson, 'Unsatisfied Nationalism', *Journal of Contemporary History*, Vol. 6, No. 1 (1971), pp. 3–14.
11 TNA, SP 63/203/25 ('Proclamation for Ireland', 25 Jan. 1599).

could 'carry vnstaied myndes astray'; yet, those who petitioned the queen and her government were adamant that they remained 'as vnremoveable from our loyalties' as their loyal ancestors had been before them.[12] Of course, these were only words; the true test would be whether the Palesmen would put their money where their mouths were.

By necessity, the vast majority of source material utilised for this study comes directly from the pens of Englishmen. This, of course, lends itself to a biased assessment of the events and participants of this war. One would therefore expect a very pessimistic conclusion based on the incessant declarations of doubtful loyalties and allegations of Old English treachery made by crown officials. That was the unanimous official line and, as Secretary Fenton expounded to Cecil in 1601, 'to Reapose the saffety of the pale vpon the valor and trust of this contreybirthe onely, weare more to increase the daunger, then to prevent yt'.[13] Yet, between the lines, these English records reveal something of a different picture. English administrators never failed to express their belief that the entire country would revolt, but these very same letters provide testimonies indicating the very opposite. For every letter praising Delvin, Dunsany, James Fitzpiers, or Nicholas Weston as the only man of his nation worthy of trust, there is another commending the earls of Ormond and Kildare, the barons of Louth and Howth, Christopher St Lawrence, Christopher Finglas, Richard Bellings, and merchants like John Frith and James Bellew.[14] And surely, Cornett James Sedgrave was not the only battlefield hero of the war or, indeed, of his community. Similar accolades were attributed to Fitzpiers, Dunsany, Delvin, and Christopher St Lawrence, to name but a few. We also have the names of many other crown servitors who voluntarily put themselves and their retinues at the disposal of the English administration.[15] These are only a few of the so-called 'only man of his sort' praised in the Irish State Papers. Thus, it is clear there was

---

[12] TNA, SP 63/202(4)/60 ('greevances', 1598).

[13] TNA, SP 63/209(2)/124 (Fenton to Cecil, 3 Oct. 1601).

[14] For example, earl of Kildare: TNA, SP 63/203/34 (Loftus to Cecil, 5 Feb. 1599); baron of Louth: TNA, SP 63/196/31 (Russell to Burghley, 27 Dec. 1596); baron of Howth: TNA, SP 63/179/82 (Irish Council to Privy Council, 18 May 1595); Christopher Finglas: BL, Lansdowne MS, Vol. 83, ff. 51–3 (Loftus to Cecil, 8 Feb. 1596); Richard Bellings: TNA, SP 63/199/40 (Irish Council to Privy Council, 19 May 1597); TNA, SP 63/199/78 (Loftus to Cecil, 4 June 1597); John Frith: TNA, SP 63/199/13 (Irish Council to Burghley, 7 May 1597); James Bellew: TNA, SP 63/198/78 (Loftus to Cecil, 7 Apr. 1597); TNA, SP 63/199/52 (J. Norreys to Burghley, 24 May 1597); TNA, SP 63/207(5)/26 (Fenton to Cecil, 15 Sep. 1600).

[15] For example, Lord Gormanston: TNA, SP 63/181/26 (Kildare to Russell, 13 July 1595); John Talbot: TNA, SP 63/173/64(XI) (H. Bagenal to lord deputy, 25 Feb. 1594); TNA, SP 63/176/60(XI) (baron of Slane to lord deputy, 12 Oct. 1594); TNA, SP 63/175/5(XXVII) (note of the new erected companies and the places where they lie, 1595); TNA, SP 63/175/10(I) (disposition of forces in Leinster and Ulster, 10 June 1594); Moryson, An Itinerary, ii, p. 43; HMC Salisbury MSS, vi, 543; TNA, SP 63/208(1)/14 (Ormond to Cecil, 19 Jan. 1601).

more than *one* crown loyalist in the Pale, and it is probably safe to assume that many other loyal Palesmen went unrecognised in the official record.

It is not possible to treat the Old English Pale community as a single unit, nor can it be divided into those who supported the crown and those who did not. The peculiar experiences and interests of each individual dictated their actions and behaviour. Some were steadfast to one side or the other, some wavered or switched camps depending on the prize offered or the fortune to be lost, and there were still others who remained neutral or indeterminate in their attitudes and inclinations. Equally significant is that neither party acted in unison; both sides lacked the necessary leadership and organisation which might have directed the activities and purposes of those involved. Undoubtedly, religion, geography, and factional politics played a role in isolating one group of loyalists or dissenters from another. With respect to those who supported the crown, the inability of the Pale's principal members to participate fully and formally in the administration's policymaking process must have been a contributing factor to the somewhat chaotic native command structure and their reluctance to take matters into their own hands. Since determining how that structure should function was left to New English outsiders, Old English magnates were essentially debarred from making any weighty tactical decisions and effectively discouraged from assuming a proactive military position. When the earl of Kildare was nominated as superior commander over all Pale forces during the 1595 hostings, it was not a permanent posting as his authority had been established at informal consultations between the Irish Council and Pale nobility and only lasted for the duration of these enterprises. Furthermore, his command was titular in nature since men like the baron of Delvin held independent commands over their own retinues and dependants. In 1599 there was a glimmer of hope that the Old English might gain greater control in military matters as the next earl of Kildare, along with eighteen 'of the chiefs of Meath and Fingall', were set to play their part in Essex's campaign.[16] Those hopes were soon dashed when the ship carrying them from England to Ireland was lost at sea.[17] As for the earl of Ormond, who acted as lord general for a period, he was a Protestant and wholly dependent upon the favour his cousin Queen Elizabeth extended towards him; he, therefore, shared little affinity with the majority of his Old English compatriots. In effect, the queen's Old English allies were a disorganised coalition of sometimes disparate interests, thrown together when needed, but often left to their own devices.

One might wonder whether the Old English would have behaved differently if any sense of unity or concord had existed during the 1590s. It is clear that

---

[16] AFM, p. 2093.
[17] Ibid.; HMC *Salisbury MSS*, ix, 134–5, 144, 162, 192, 207, 276.

the vast majority of Palesmen were perilously disenchanted with the existing English establishment; therefore, if one or more of their heads, such as the earls of Kildare or Ormond, had endorsed the rebellion and gathered together large numbers of their dependants and the lesser nobility, would the Old English have been willing to rise up against Ireland's English administration at this time? Conversely, it is also apparent that the Old English community distrusted the Gaelic Irish and regarded Gaelic society and institutions with disdain; thus, had this community been capable of overcoming its factional and particularist divisions and accept the leadership of one or more of their own, would they have acted in unison? And, would they still have supported the English crown? The course of Irish history might have been quite different had the Old English acted as a group; this, however, they did not.

In spite of the many grievances held by this community, the fractious nature of Old English Pale politics, and the various ambitions of the individuals involved, the majority of the Pale's leading representatives remained loyal to their distant English Protestant queen. This was not a foregone conclusion, largely because Old English concerns about their declining political influence would probably have justified revolt in many eyes. Sections of the community had resorted to armed insurrection in the past, but their efforts had failed and become convenient excuses for the continuing demotion of Old English influence within the central administration and council chamber. It is possible that these experiences served as precedents when war broke out in the 1590s, but it also seems that the Old English believed that they still might be redeemed in the eyes of English officials if they continued to contribute to the impressive military enterprise then under way. As one Old English man yearned:

> I could wishe therefore, that the English were looked vpon w[i]th some good gracious aspect, at her highnes handes, that is the well of remorce, the Shryne of Iustice, and the true patterne of a good Prince, w[hi]ch by the square of Christianity leuelles all her proceedings, whoe I pray God may long prosper and abound in those blessings that haue gained her, the title of a Goddesse on earth, And highly may she be rewarded in heauen for righting her poore subiects in Irelande.[18]

Unfortunately for the Old English, they did not see the writing on the wall. Following the conclusion of hostilities and the accession of James I to the English throne, their expectations that their efforts would be appreciated and their status as Catholic loyalists be accepted were not realised. Believing that James I would be more tolerant or lenient in religious matters, the Old English clearly misunderstood the religious and political character of the new Scottish monarch of England. Following the suppression of the recusancy revolts, the

---

[18] TNA, SP 63/202(4)/75 ('A discourse', 1598).

Oath of Supremacy was more forcibly enforced against all would-be office-holders, and by 1605 a proclamation was issued ordering the banishment of all Jesuits and priests from Ireland. Thus, the apolitical stance of many Catholic clerics and the laymen who protected them went unrewarded. In 1607 the Flight of the Earls permitted the government to initiate extensive land confiscations for the establishment of new English and Scottish plantations, for which the Old English were not considered suitable settlers. Then, following the implementation of the Ulster Plantation, preparations were made for assembling the 1613 parliament, and English officials made concerted efforts to include as many Protestant members as possible through the creation of new boroughs, many of which did not warrant the status, so as to limit Catholic participation and opposition. The Old English, convinced that they had proven their worth to English officialdom through their military support and political concessions over proceeding decades, discovered that their efforts had been in vain. Rather than being participants in the formation of the new Irish establishment, they were required to conform to the established church more stringently than in the past and likewise found themselves increasingly excluded and demoted within the political establishment. The consequences of these developments would reverberate through the seventeenth century.

Bibliography

Guides and Bibliographies

Abbot, T. K., *Catalogue of the manuscripts in the library of Trinity College, Dublin.* (Dublin, 1900).

Donovan, B.C. and Edwards, D. (eds), *British Sources for Irish History 1485–1641: A Guide to Manuscripts in Local, Regional and Specialised Repositories in England, Scotland and Wales* (Dublin, 1997).

Edwards, R.W.D. and O'Dowd, M., *Sources for Early Modern Irish History, 1534–1641* (Cambridge, 1985).

Hayes, R.J. (ed.), *Manuscript Sources for the History of Irish Civilisation* (11 vols, Boston, MA, 1965).

Matthew, H.C.G. and Harrison, B. (eds), *Oxford Dictionary of National Biography* (60 vols, Oxford, 2004).

McGuire, J. and Quinn, J. (eds), *Dictionary of Irish Biography* (9 vols, Cambridge, 2009).

Manuscript Collections

Archivo General de Simancas:
    Estado, lejagos 612–106: 'Breuis rerum declaration', by Patrick Sedgrave, Brussels, c. 1595.
British Library:
    Additional MSS
        4757: Milles Collection
        4763: 'Letters and papers relating to the history of Ireland, c. 400–1680'
        4793: Papers of Sir James Ware
        4819: 'Collectanea de rebus hibernici'
        11,402
        49,609A
    Cottonian MSS
        Titus B X: 'Miscellaneous Irish Papers'
        Titus B XII: 'Miscellaneous Irish Papers'
        Titus B XIII: 'Miscellaneous Irish Papers'
        Titus C VII: 'Miscellaneous state papers'

Harleian MSS
   292
Lansdowne MSS
   81
   83
Bodleian Library, Oxford:
   Laud MSS
      612
   Talbot MSS:
      B 11
Exeter College, Oxford:
   MS 154: 'Discourse on the mere Irish of Ireland'
Hatfield House:
   Cecil Papers
Jesuits in Britain Archives, London:
   MS 46/4/18
   MS 46/17/8/4: L. Hicks, 'Notes on Ireland'
Lambeth Palace
   Carew Papers:
      MS 600: 'Miscellaneous Irish papers'
      MS 612: 'Journal of Sir William Russell, Lord Deputy', June 24, 1594 to
         May 27, 1597.
      MS 617: 'Official Papers, 1594–1602'
      MS 618: 'Letters and warrants of Sir George Carew'
      MS 623: 'The Book of Howth'
      MS 632: 'Miscellaneous State Papers'
The National Archives [of the UK], Kew:
   APC 2: 'Acts of Privy Council'
   SP 12: 'State Papers, Domestic'
   SP 52: 'State Papers, Scotland, series I, Elizabeth I'
   SP 59: 'State Papers, Scotland, border papers'
   SP 63: 'State Papers, Ireland'
National Library of Ireland:
   MS G 992: Duanaire Na Núinseannach (Poem Book of the Nugent Family)
Trinity College, Dublin
   MS 578/12
University Library, Cambridge:
   Additional MSS
      Ee III 56: 'Burghley's letters to his son, Robert'
      Kk 1 15: Papers on the Nine Years War

Printed Primary Sources

Acts of the Privy Council of England, 1542–1631, ed. J.R. Dasent (46 vols, London, 1890–1964).

Annála Ríoghachta Éireann: Annals of the Kingdom of Ireland by the Four Masters, from the Earliest Period to the Year 1616, ed. and trans. J. O'Donovan (7 vols, Dublin, 1848–51).

Bergin, O. (ed.), 'Unpublished Irish Poems. II: In Memoriam Ricardi Nugent', *Studies: An Irish Quarterly Review*, Vol. 7, No. 26 (1918), pp. 279–82.

Berry, Henry F. (ed.), 'Minute Book of the Corporation of Dublin, Known as the "Friday Book." 1567–1611', *Proceedings of the Royal Irish Academy*, Vol. 30 (1912/13), pp. 477–514.

Calendar of the Carew Manuscripts Preserved in the Archiepiscopal Library at Lambeth, 1515–1624, ed. J.S. Brewer and W. Bullen (6 vols, London, 1867–73).

Calendar of the Manuscripts of the Marquis of Salisbury, Preserved at Hatfield House, Hertfordshire, ed. R.A. Roberts, E. Salisbury, M.S. Giuseppi, and G.D. Owen (20 vols, London, 1872–1968).

Calendar of State Papers, Domestic, ed. R. Lemon and M.A.E. Green (12 vols, London, 1856–75).

Calendar of State Papers, Ireland, ed. H.C. Hamilton, E.G. Atkinson, and R.P. Mahaffy (24 vols, London, 1860–1912).

Calendar of State Papers, Spain (Simancas), 1558–1603, ed. M.A.S. Hume (4 vols, London, 1892–9).

Canny, N.P. (ed.), 'Rowland White's "The Dysorders of the Irisshery", 1571', *Studia Hibernica*, No. 19 (1979), pp. 147–60.

Canny, N.P. (ed.), 'Select Documents: XXXIV Rowland White's "Discors Touching Ireland", c. 1569', *Irish Historical Studies*, Vol. 20, No. 80 (1977), pp. 439–63.

Collier, H., *Dialogue of Silvynne and Peregrynne*, ed. H. Morgan (CELT, 2005).

Copinger, J., *Mnemosynim or Memoriall to the afflicted Catholickes in Irelande* (Bordeaux, 1606).

Falkiner, C.L. (ed.), 'William Farmer's Chronicles of Ireland from 1594–1613', *The English Historical Review*, Vol. 22, No. 85 (1907), pp. 104–30.

Falkiner, C.L. (ed.), 'William Farmer's Chronicles of Ireland (Continued)', *The English Historical Review*, Vol. 22, No. 87 (1907), pp. 527–52.

Fitzsimon, H., *Words of Comfort to Persecuted Catholics, Written in exile, anno 1607*, ed. E. Hogan (Dublin, 1881).

Gainsford, T., *The true exemplary, and remarkable history of the Earle of Tirone* (London, 1619).

Gilbert, J.T. (ed.), *Facsimiles of national manuscripts of Ireland* (4 vols, Dublin, 1874–84).

Harris, W. (ed.), *Hibernica: Or, some Antient Pieces relating to Ireland* (Dublin, 1757), pp. 39–52.

Hogan, E. (ed.), *The Description of Ireland and the State Thereof as it is at This Present in Anno 1598* (Dublin and London, 1878).

Hughes, C. (ed.), *Shakespeare's Europe: unpublished chapters of Fynes Moryson's Itinerary, being a survey of the condition of Europe at the end of the 16th century* (London, 1903).

Lee, T., 'A brief declaration of the government of Ireland' (1594), in J. Lodge (ed.), *Desiderata Curiosa Hibernica*, Vol. 1 (Dublin, 1772).

Lee, T., 'The Discovery and Recovery of Ireland with the Author's Apology, c. 1599–1600, (BL MS Add. 33743)', ed. J. McGurk (CELT, 2009).

Lodge, J. (ed.), *Desiderata curiosa Hibernica: or, A select collection of State papers* (2 vols, Dublin, 1772).

Lombard, P., *The Irish War of Defence, 1598–1600: Extracts from the De Hibernia Insula Commentarius*, ed. and trans. M.J. Byrne (Cork, 1930).

Maley, W. (ed.), 'The Supplication of the Blood of the English Most Lamentably Murdered in Ireland, Cryeng Out of the Yearth for Revenge (1598)', *Analecta Hibernica*, No. 36 (1995), pp. 3–77.

McLaughlin, J. (ed.), 'New Light on Richard Hadsor, II. Select Documents XLVII: Richard Hadsor's "Discourse" on the Irish State, 1604', *Irish Historical Studies*, Vol. 30, No. 119 (1997), pp. 337–53.

McNeill, C. (ed.), 'Fitzwilliam Manuscripts at Milton, England', *Analecta Hibernica*, No. 4 (1932), pp. 287–326.

McNeill, C. (ed.), 'Harris: Collectanea De Rebus Hibernicis', *Analecta Hibernica*, No. 6 (1934), pp. 248–450.

McNeill, C. (ed.), 'Lord Chancellor Gerrard's Notes of his Report on Ireland', *Analecta Hibernica*, No. 2 (1931), pp. 93–291.

Morgan, H. (ed.), 'A Booke of Questions and Answars Concerning the Warrs of Rebellions of the Kingdome of Ireland, (c. 1597?)', *Analecta Hibernica*, No. 36 (1995), pp. 70–134.

Moryson, F., *An itinerary containing his ten yeeres travell through the twelve dominions of Germany, Bohmerland, Scotland and Ireland* (4 vols, Glasgow, 1907).

Murphy, G. (ed.), 'Poems of exile by Uillim Nuinseann Mac Barúin Dealbhna', *Éigse*, Vol. 6 (1948–52), pp. 9–15.

Nugent, R., *Cynthia* (1604), ed. A. Lynch (Dublin, 2010).

O'Sullivan Beare, P. *Chapters Towards A History of Ireland in the Reign of Elizabeth, being a portion of the History of Catholic Ireland by Philip O'Sullivan Beare*, trans. M.J. Byrne (CELT, 1970).

Ó Tuathail, É. (ed.), 'Nugentiana', *Éigse*, Vol. 2 (1940), pp. 4–14.

Perrot, J., *The Chronicle of Ireland, 1584–1608*, H. Wood (Dublin, 1933).

Quinn, D.B. (ed.), 'Edward Walshe's "Conjectures" Concerning the State of Ireland [1552]', *Irish Historical Studies*, Vol. 5, No. 20 (1947), pp. 303–22.

Rich, B., *A New Description of Ireland: Wherein is described the disposition of the Irish Whereunto they are inclined* (London, 1610).

Sawyer, E. (ed.), *Memorials of Affairs of State in the Reigns of Queen Elizabeth and King James I*, Vol. 1 (London, 1725).

Spenser, E., *A View of the State of Ireland*, eds. A. Hadfield and W. Maley (Oxford, 1997).

Stafford, T., *Pacata Hibernia* (London, 1810).

Walshe, E., *The office and duety in fighting for our countrey* (London, 1545).

Secondary Sources

Anderson, B., *Imagined Communities: Reflections on the Origin and Spread of Nationalism* (London, 1991).

Anstruther, A., *The Seminary Priests: A Dictionary of the Secular Clergy of England and Wales 1558–1850, I Elizabethan 1558–1603* (Durham, 1968).

Bagwell, R., *Ireland under the Tudors* (London, 1885–90).

Bradshaw, B., *The Irish Constitutional Revolution of the Sixteenth Century* (Cambridge, 1979).

Bradshaw, B., *The Dissolution of the Religious Orders in Ireland Under Henry VIII* (Cambridge, 1974).

Brady, C., *The Chief Governors: The Rise and Fall of Reform Government in Tudor Ireland, 1536–1588* (Cambridge, 1994).

Brady, C., 'The Captain's Games: Army and Society in Elizabethan Ireland', in T. Bartlett and K. Jeffrey (eds), *A Military History of Ireland* (Cambridge, 1996), pp. 136–59.

Brady, C., 'Spenser's Irish Crisis: Humanism and Experience in the 1590s', *Past & Present*, No. 111 (1986), pp. 17–49.

Brady, C., 'Conservative Subversives: The Community of the Pale and the Dublin Administration, 1556–86', in P. Corish (ed.), *Radicals, Rebels and Establishments* (Belfast, 1985), pp. 11–32.

Boyce, D.G., *Nationalism in Ireland* (London, 1995).

Cannan, F., '"Hags of Hell": Late Medieval Irish Kern', *History Ireland*, Vol. 19, No. 1 (2011), pp. 14–17.

Canning, R.A., 'Profits and Patriotism: Nicholas Weston, Old English Merchants, and Ireland's Nine Years War, 1594–1603', *Irish Economic and Social History*, Vol. 43, No. 1 (2016), pp. 1–28.

Canning, R.A., '"May she be rewarded in heauen for righting her poore subiects in Irelande": Lawyer Richard Hadsor and the Authorship of an Elizabethan Treatise on Ireland', *The Irish Jurist*, Vol. 55 (2016), pp. 1–24.

Canning, R.A., 'James Fitzpiers Fitzgerald, Captain Thomas Lee, and the Problem of "Secret Traitors": Conflicted Loyalties During the Nine Years' War, 1594–1603', *Irish Historical Studies*, Vol. 39, No. 156 (2016), pp. 573–94.

Canny, N.P., *Making Ireland British, 1580–1650* (Oxford, 2001).

Canny, N.P., *Kingdom and Colony: Ireland in the Atlantic World, 1560–1800* (London, 1988).

Canny, N.P., 'Identity Formation in Ireland: The Emergence of the Anglo-Irish', in N.P. Canny and A. Pagden (eds), *Colonial Identity in the Atlantic World, 1500–1800* (Princeton, NJ, 1987), pp 159–212.

Canny, N.P., 'The Formation of the Old English Elite in Ireland', O'Donnell Lecture (Dublin, 1975).

Canny, N.P., 'Spenser's Irish Crisis: Humanism and Experience in the 1590s', *Past & Present*, No. 120 (1988), pp. 201–09.

Canny, N.P., 'Edmund Spenser and the Development of an Anglo-Irish Identity', *The Yearbook of English Studies*, Vol. 13 (1983), pp. 1–19.

Canny, N.P., 'The Formation of the Irish Mind: Religion, Politics and Gaelic Irish Literature 1580–1750', *Past & Present*, No. 95 (1982), pp. 91–116.

Canny, N.P., 'Hugh O'Neill, Earl of Tyrone, and the Changing Face of Gaelic Ulster', *Studia Hibernica*, No. 10 (1970), pp. 7–35.

Carey, V.P., *Surviving the Tudors: The 'Wizard' Earl of Kildare and English Rule in Ireland, 1537–1586* (Dublin, 2002).

Carey, V.P. and U. Lotz-Heumann (eds), *Taking Sides? Colonial and Confessional Mentalités in Early Modern Ireland: Essays in Honour of Karl S. Bottigheimer* (Dublin, 2003).

Carey, V.P., '"As lief to the gallows as go to the Irish wars": Human Rights and the Abuse of the Elizabethan Soldier in Ireland, 1600–1603', *History*, Vol. 99, No. 336 (2014), pp. 468–86.

Carey, V.P., '"What pen can paint or tears atone?": Mountjoy's Scorched Earth Campaign', in H. Morgan (ed.), *The Battle of Kinsale* (Bray, 2004), pp. 205–16.

Carey, V.P., '"Neither good English nor good Irish": Bi-lingualism and Identity Formation in Sixteenth-Century Ireland', in H. Morgan (ed.), *Political Ideology in Ireland, 1541–1641* (Dublin, 1999), pp. 45–61.

Carey, V.P., 'John Derricke's Image of Irelande, Sir Henry Sidney, and the Massacre at Mullaghmast, 1578', *Irish Historical Studies*, Vol. 31, No. 123 (1999), pp. 305–27.

Casey, D., *The Nugents of Westmeath and Queen Elizabeth's Irish Primer* (Dublin, 2016).

Challis, C.E., *The Tudor Coinage* (Manchester, 1978).

Clarke, A., *The Old English in Ireland, 1625–42* (Dublin, 2000).

Clarke, A., 'Alternative Allegiances in Early Modern Ireland', *Journal of Historical Sociology*, Vol. 5, No. 3 (1992), pp. 253–66.

Clarke, A., 'Colonial Identity in Early Seventeenth-Century Ireland', in Donnchadh Ó Corráin and T.D. Moody (eds), *Nationality and the Pursuit of National Independence, Historical Studies*, Vol. XI (Belfast, 1978), pp. 57–71.

Coburn-Walshe, H., 'The Rebellion of William Nugent 1581', in R.V. Comerford, M. Cullen, J.R. Hill, and C. Lennon (eds), *Religion, Conflict and Coexistence in Ireland: Essays Presented to Monsignor Patrick J. Corish* (Dublin, 1990), pp. 26–52.

Comerford, R.V., *Inventing the Nation: Ireland* (London, 2003).

Connolly, S.J. (ed.), *The Oxford Companion to Irish History* (Oxford, 2007).

Corboy, J., 'Father Henry Fitzsimon, S.J., 1566–1643', *Studies: An Irish Quarterly Review*, Vol. 32 (1943), pp. 260–6.

Corboy, J., 'Father Christopher Holywood, S.J., 1559–1626', *Studies: An Irish Quarterly Review*, Vol. 33 (1944), pp. 543–9.

Corboy, J., 'Father James Archer, S.J., 1550–1625(?)', *Studies: An Irish Quarterly Review*, Vol. 33 (1944), pp. 99–107.

Corish, P.J. and B. Millett (eds), *The Irish Martyrs* (Dublin, 2005).

Corish, P.J., 'The Origins of Catholic Nationalism', in P.J. Corish (ed.), *A History of Irish Catholicism* (Dublin, 1968).

Crawford, J.G., *Anglicizing the Government of Ireland: The Irish Privy Council and the Expansion of Tudor Rule, 1556–1578* (Blackrock, 1993).

Cruickshank, C.G., 'Dead-Pays in the Elizabethan Army', *The English Historical Review*, Vol. 53, No. 209 (1938), pp. 93–7.

Cunningham, B., 'The Anglicisation of East Breifne: The O'Reillys and the Emergence of County Cavan', in R. Gillespie (ed.), *Cavan: Essays on the History of an Irish County* (Dublin, 1995), pp. 51–72.

Cunningham, B., 'The Composition of Connacht in the Lordships of Clanricard and Thomond, 1577–1641', *Irish Historical Studies*, Vol. 24, No. 93 (1984), pp. 1–14.

Duffy, P.J., 'The Nature of the Medieval Frontier in Ireland', *Studia Hibernica*, No. 22/23 (1982/3), pp. 21–38.

Edwards, D., *The Ormond Lordship in County Kilkenny, 1515–1642: The Rise and Fall of Butler Feudal Power* (Dublin, 2003).

Edwards, D., 'The Escalation of Violence in Sixteenth-Century Ireland', in D. Edwards, P. Lenihan, and C. Tait (eds), *Age of Atrocity: Violence and Political Conflict in Early Modern Ireland* (Dublin, 2007), pp 34–78.

Edwards, D., 'A Haven of Popery: English Catholic Migration to Ireland in the Age of Plantations', in A. Ford and J. McCafferty (eds), *The Origins of Sectarianism in Early Modern Ireland* (Cambridge, 2005), pp. 95–126.

Edwards, R.D., *Church and State in Tudor Ireland: A History of Penal Laws Against Irish Catholics, 1534–1603* (Dublin, 1935).

Edwards, O.D., 'Ireland', in O.D. Edwards, G. Evans, I. Rhys, and H. MacDiarmid (eds), *Celtic Nationalism* (London, 1968).

Ellis, S.G., *Defending English Ground: War and Peace in Meath and Northumberland, 1460–1542* (Oxford, 2015).

Ellis, S.G. and C. Maginn, *The Making of the British Isles: The State of Britain and Ireland, 1450–1660* (London, 2007).

Ellis, S. G., *Ireland in the Age of the Tudors 1447–1603: English Expansion and the End of Gaelic Rule* (Harlow, 1998).

Ellis, S.G., *Tudor Frontiers and Noble Power: The Making of the British State* (Oxford, 1995).

Ellis, S.G., *Tudor Ireland: Crown, Community and the Conflict of Cultures, 1470–1603* (Harlow, 1985).

Ellis, S.G., 'Civilizing Northumberland: Representations of Englishness in the Tudor State', *Journal of Historical Sociology*, Vol. 12, No. 2 (1999), pp. 103–25.

Ellis, S.G., 'The Tudors and the Origins of the Modern Irish States: A Standing Army', in T. Bartlett and K. Jeffery (eds), *A Military History of Ireland* (Cambridge, 1996), pp. 116–35.

Ellis, S.G., 'A Border Baron and the Tudor State: The Rise and Fall of Lord Dacre of the North', *The Historical Journal*, Vol. 35, No. 2 (1992), pp. 253–77.

Ellis, S.G., 'The Pale and the Far North: Government and Society in Two Early Tudor Borderlands', O'Donnell Lecture (Galway, 1986).

Ellis, S.G., 'Taxation and Defence in Late Medieval Ireland: The Survival of Scutage', *Journal of the Royal Society of Antiquaries of Ireland*, Vol. 107 (1977), pp. 5–28.

Falls, C., *Elizabeth's Irish Wars* (London, 1996).

Fennessy, I., 'Richard Brady OFM, Bishop of Kilmore, 1580–1607', *Breifne*, Vol. 9 (2000), pp. 225–42.

FitzGerald, W., 'Walter Reagh Fitz Gerald, a Noted Outlaw of the Sixteenth Century', *Journal of the Royal Society of Antiquaries of Ireland*, 5th Ser., Vol. 8, No. 4 (1898), pp. 299–305.

Ford, A., *James Ussher: Theology, History, and Politics in Early-Modern Ireland and England* (Oxford, 2007).

Ford, A., 'Goliath and the Boy David: Henry Fitzsimon, James Ussher and the Birth of Irish Religious Debate', in S. Ryan and C. Tait (eds), *Religion and Politics in Urban Ireland, c. 1500–c. 1750* (Dublin, 2016), pp. 108–33.

Gellner, E., 'Nationalism', *Theory and Society*, Vol. 10, No. 6 (1981), pp. 753–76.

Gillespie, R., 'Harvest Crisis in Early Seventeenth-Century Ireland', *Irish Economic and Social History*, Vol. 11 (1984), pp. 5–18.

Hadfield, A., 'English Colonialism and National Identity in Early Modern Ireland', *Éire-Ireland*, Vol. 28, No. 1 (1993), pp. 69–86.

Hammer, P.E.J., '"Base Rogues" and "Gentlemen of Quality": the Earl of Essex's Irish Knights and Royal Displeasure in 1599', in B. Kane and V. McGowan-Doyle (eds), *Elizabeth I and Ireland* (Cambridge, 2014), pp. 184–208.

Hammerstein, H., 'Aspects of the Continental Education of Irish Students in the Reign of Queen Elizabeth', in T.D. Williams (ed.), *Historical Studies*, Vol. 8 (Dublin, 1971), pp. 137–53.

Hayes-McCoy, G.A., *Irish Battles: A Military History of Ireland* (Belfast, 2009).

Hayes-McCoy, G.A., 'The Army of Ulster, 1593–1601', *Irish Sword*, Vol. 1, No. 2 (Dublin, 1949–53), pp. 105–17.

Hayes-McCoy, G.A., 'The Tide of Victory and Defeat: I. The Battle of Clontibret, 1595', *Studies: An Irish Quarterly Review*, Vol. 38, No. 150 (1949), pp. 158–68.

Hayes-McCoy, G.A., 'Strategy and Tactics in Irish Warfare, 1593–1601', *Irish Historical Studies*, Vol. 2, No. 7 (1941), pp. 255–79.

Hazard, B., *Faith and Patronage: The Political Career of Flaithrí Ó Maolchonaire* (Dublin, 2010).

Heal, F., and C. Holmes, *The Gentry in England and Wales, 1500–1700* (Basingstoke, 1994).

Hechter, M., *Containing Nationalism* (Oxford, 2000).

Hoak, D. (ed.), *Tudor Political Culture* (Cambridge, 2002).

Hogan, E., *Distinguished Irishmen of the Sixteenth Century* (London, 1894).

Iske, B., *The Green Cockatrice* (Dublin, 1978).

Jackson, B., 'The Construction of Argument: Henry Fitzsimon, John Rider and Religious Controversy in Dublin, 1599–1614', in C. Brady and J. Ohlmeyer (eds), *British Interventions in Early Modern Ireland* (Cambridge, 2005), pp. 97–115.

Jefferies, H.A., *The Irish Church and the Tudor Reformations* (Dublin, 2010).

Jefferies, H.A., *Priests and Prelates of Armagh in the Age of Reformations, 1518–1558* (Dublin, 1997).

Jefferies, H.A., 'Why the Reformation Failed in Ireland', *Irish Historical Studies*, Vol. 40, No. 158 (2016), pp. 151–70.

Jefferies, H.A., 'The Early Tudor Reformations in the Irish Pale', *Journal of Ecclesiastical History*, Vol. 52, No. 1 (2001), pp. 34–62.

Jefferies, H.A., 'The Church Among Two Nations: Armagh on the Eve of the Tudor Reformations', *History Ireland*, Vol. 6, No. 1 (1998), pp. 17–21.

Jefferies, H.A., 'The Role of the Laity in the Parishes of Armagh *Inter Anglicos*, 1518–1553', *Archivium Hibernicum*, Vol. 52 (1998), pp. 73–84.

Jefferies, H.A., 'The Irish Parliament of 1560: The Anglican Reforms Authorised', *Irish Historical Studies*, Vol. 26, No. 102 (1988), pp. 128–41.

Kane, B., *The Politics and Culture of Honour in Britain and Ireland, 1541–1641* (Cambridge, 2010).

Kane, B. and V. McGowan-Doyle, 'Elizabeth I and Ireland: An Introduction', in B. Kane and V. McGowan-Doyle (eds), *Elizabeth I and Ireland* (Cambridge, 2014), pp. 1–14.

Kerney Walsh, M., 'Archbishop Magauran and His Return to Ireland, October 1592', *Seanchas Ardmhacha: Journal of the Armagh Diocesan Historical Society*, Vol. 14, No. 1 (1990), pp. 68–79.

Knowles, E.B., 'Thomas Shelton, Translator of Don Quixote', *Studies in the Renaissance*, Vol. 5 (1958), pp. 160–75.

Leerssen, J., *Mere Irish and Fíor-Ghael: Studies in the Idea of Irish Nationality, its Development and Literary Expression Prior to the Nineteenth Century* (Cork, 1996).

Lennon, C., *Archbishop Richard Creagh of Armagh, 1523–1586: An Irish Prisoner of Conscience of the Tudor Era* (Dublin, 2000).

Lennon, C., *The Lords of Dublin in the Age of Reformation* (Blackrock, 1989).

Lennon, C., *Richard Stanihurst the Dubliner, 1547–1618: A Biography with a Standard Text on Ireland's Past* (Blackrock, 1981).

Lennon, C., 'The Dissolution to the Foundation of St Anthony's College, Louvain, 1534–1607', in E. Bhreathnach, J. MacMahon, and J. McCafferty (eds), *The Irish Franciscans, 1534–1990* (Dublin, 2009), pp. 3–26.

Lennon, C., 'The Parish Fraternities of County Meath', *Ríocht na Midhe*, Vol. 19 (2008), pp. 85–101.

Lennon, C., 'Fraternity and Community in Early Modern Dublin', in R. Armstrong and T. Ó hAnnracháin (eds), *Community in Early Modern Ireland* (Dublin, 2006).

Lennon, C., 'The Nugent Family and the Diocese of Kilmore in the Sixteenth andEarly Seventeenth Centuries', *Breifne*, Vol. 10 (2001), pp. 360–74.

Lennon, C., 'Mass in the Manor House: The Counter-Reformation in Dublin, 1560–1630', in J. Kelly and D. Keogh (eds), *History of the Diocese of Dublin* (Dublin, 2000), pp. 137–53.

Lennon, C., 'Dublin's Great Explosion of 1597', *History Ireland*, Vol. 3, No. 3 (1995), pp. 29–34.

Lennon, C., 'The Chantries in the Irish Reformation: The Case of St Anne's Guild, Dublin, 1550–1630', in R.V. Comerford, M. Cullen, J.R. Hill, and C. Lennon (eds), *Religion, Conflict and Coexistence in Ireland* (Dublin, 1990), pp. 6–25.

Lennon, C., 'The Great Explosion in Dublin, 1597', *Dublin Historical Record*, Vol. 42, No. 1 (1988), pp. 7–20.

Lennon, C., 'The Counter-Reformation in Ireland, 1542–1641', in C. Brady and R. Gillespie (eds), *Natives and Newcomers* (Blackrock, 1986), pp. 75–92.

Lennon, C., 'Richard Stanihurst (1547–1618) and Old English Identity', *Irish Historical Studies*, Vol. 21, No. 82 (1978), pp. 121–43.

Maginn, C., *'Civilizing' Gaelic Leinster: The Extension of Tudor Rule in the O'Byrne and O'Toole Lordships* (Dublin, 2005).

Maginn, C., 'Gaelic Ireland's English Frontiers in the Late Middle Ages', *Proceedings of the Royal Irish Academy*, Vol. 110C (2010), pp. 173–90.

Maginn, C., 'Whose Island? Sovereignty in Late Medieval and Early Modern Ireland', *Éire-Ireland*, Vol. 44, Nos 3 & 4 (2009), pp. 229–47.

Maginn, C., 'The Baltinglass Rebellion, 1580: English Dissent or a Gaelic Uprising?', *The Historical Journal*, Vol. 47, No. 2 (2004), pp. 205–32.

Maginn, C., 'English Marcher Lineages in South Dublin in the Late Middle Ages', *Irish Historical Studies*, Vol. 34, No. 134 (2004), pp. 113–36.

Mannion, J., '"As trew Englishe as any man borne in Myddlesex": Sir Francis Shane, 1540–1614', in C. Maginn and G. Power (eds), *Frontiers, States and Identity in Early Modern Ireland and Beyond* (Dublin, 2016), pp. 164–87.

McCormack, A.M., *The Earldom of Desmond, 1463–1583* (Dublin, 2005).

McCormack, A.M., 'The Social and Economic Consequences of the Desmond Rebellion of 1579–83', *Irish Historical Studies*, Vol. 34, No. 133 (2004), pp. 1–15.

McDiarmid, J.F. (ed.), *The Monarchical Republic of Early Modern England: Essays in Response to Patrick Collinson* (Basingstoke, 2007).

McGettigan, D., *Red Hugh O'Donnell and the Nine Years' War* (Dublin, 2005).

McGowan-Doyle, V., *The Book of Howth: Elizabethan Conquest and the Old English* (Cork, 2011).

McGowan-Doyle, V., 'Elizabeth I, the Old English, and the Rhetoric of Counsel', in B. Kane and V. McGowan-Doyle (eds), *Elizabeth I and Ireland* (Cambridge, 2014), pp. 163–83.

McGowan-Doyle, V., '"Spent Blood": Christopher St Lawrence and Pale Loyalism', in H. Morgan (ed.), *The Battle of Kinsale* (Bray, 2004), pp. 179–92.

McGurk, J., *The Elizabethan Conquest of Ireland: The 1590s Crisis* (Manchester, 1997).

McGurk, J., 'A Soldier's Prescription for the Governance of Ireland, 1599–1601: Captain Thomas Lee and his Tracts', in B. MacCuarta (ed.), *Reshaping Ireland 1550–1700: Colonization and its Consequences* (Dublin, 2011), pp. 43–60.

McGurk, J., 'The Dead, Sick & Wounded of the Nine Years War (1594–1603)', *History Ireland*, Vol. 3, No. 4 (1995), pp. 16–22.

McLaughlin, J., 'What Base Coin Wrought: The Effects of the Elizabethan Debasement in Ireland', in H. Morgan (ed.), *The Battle of Kinsale* (Bray, 2004), pp. 193–204.

Mears, N., 'Courts, Courtiers, and Culture in Tudor England', *The Historical Journal*, Vol. 46, No. 3 (2003), pp. 703–22.

Moore, P., 'The Mac Mahons of Monaghan (1593–1603)', *Clogher Record*, Vol. 1, No. 4 (1956), pp. 85–107.

Moore, P., 'The Mac Mahons of Monaghan (1500–1593)', *Clogher Record*, Vol. 1, No. 3 (1955), pp. 22–38.

Morgan, H., *Tyrone's Rebellion: The Outbreak of the Nine Years War in Tudor Ireland* (Woodbridge, 1993).

Morgan, H. (ed.), *The Battle of Kinsale* (Bray, 2004).

Morgan, H. (ed.), *Political Ideology in Ireland, 1541–1641* (Dublin, 1999).

Morgan, H., 'Policy and Propaganda in Hugh O'Neill's Connection with Europe', in M.A. Lyons and T. O'Connor (eds), *The Ulster Earls and Baroque Europe: Refashioning Irish Identities, 1600–1800* (Dublin, 2010), pp. 18–52.

Morgan, H., '"Slán Dé fút go hoíche": Hugh O'Neill's Murders', in D. Edwards, P. Lenihan, and C. Tait (eds), *Age of Atrocity: Violence and Political Conflict in Early Modern Ireland* (Dublin, 2007), pp. 95–118.

Morgan, H., '"Never Any Realm Worse Governed": Queen Elizabeth and Ireland', *Transactions of the Royal Historical Society*, Vol. 14 (2004), pp. 295–308.

Morgan, H., 'The 1597 Ceasefire Documents', *Dúiche Néill*, Vol. 11 (1997), pp. 1–21.

Morgan, H., 'Faith and Fatherland in Sixteenth-Century Ireland', *History Ireland*, Vol. 3, No. 2 (1995), pp. 13–20.

Morgan, H., 'Faith and Fatherland or Queen and Country? An Unpublished Exchange Between O'Neill and the State at the Height of the Nine Years War', *Dúiche Néill*, Vol. 9 (1994), pp. 1–49.

Morgan, H., 'Hugh O'Neill and the Nine Years War in Tudor Ireland', *Historical Journal*, Vol. 36, No. 1 (1993), pp. 21–37.

Morgan, R., *The Welsh and the Shaping of Early Modern Ireland, 1558–1641* (Woodbridge, 2014).

Morgan, R. and G. Power, 'Enduring Borderlands: The Marches of Ireland and Wales in the Early Modern Period', in S.G. Ellis, R. Esser, J. Berdah, and M. Rezník (eds), *Frontiers, Regions and Identities in Europe* (Pisa, 2009), pp. 101–28.

Morrissey, T.J., *James Archer of Kilkenny, an Elizabethan Jesuit* (Dublin, 1979).

Murray, J., *Enforcing the English Reformation in Ireland: Clerical Resistance and Political Conflict in the Diocese of Dublin, 1534–1590* (Cambridge, 2009).

Myers, J.P., '"Murdering Heart ... Murdering Hand": Captain Thomas Lee of Ireland, Elizabethan Assassin', *The Sixteenth Century Journal*, Vol. 22, No. 1 (1991), pp. 47–60.

Neale, J.E., 'Elizabeth and the Netherlands, 1586–7', *English Historical Review*, Vol. 45 (1930), pp. 373–96.

Nicholls, K.W., *Gaelic and Gaelicised Ireland in the Middle Ages* (2nd ed., Dublin, 2003).

Nicholls, K.W., 'Richard Tyrrell, Soldier Extraordinary', in H. Morgan (ed.), *The Battle of Kinsale* (Bray, 2004), pp. 161–78.

Nolan, J.S., *Sir John Norreys and the Elizabethan Military World* (Exeter, 1997).

Nolan, J.S., 'The Militarization of the Elizabethan State', *The Journal of Military History*, Vol. 58 (1994), pp. 391–420.

Ó Báille, M., 'The Buannadha: Irish Professional Soldiery of the Sixteenth Century', *Journal of the Galway Archaeological and Historical Society*, Vol. 22, No. 1/2 (1946), pp. 49–94.

Ó Domhnaill, S., 'Warfare in Sixteenth-Century Ireland', *Irish Historical Studies*, Vol. 5, No. 17 (1946), pp. 29–54.

Ó Faoláin, S., *The Great O'Neill: A Biography of Hugh O'Neill, Earl of Tyrone, 1550–1616* (New York, 1942).

Ó Mearáin, L., 'The Battle of Clontibret', *Clogher Record*, Vol. 1, No. 4 (1956), pp. 1–28.

Ó Néill, E., 'Towards a New Interpretation of the Nine Years' War', *Irish Sword*, Vol. 26, No. 105 (2009), pp. 241–62.

O'Neill, J., *The Nine Years War, 1593–1603: O'Neill, Mountjoy and the Military Revolution* (Dublin, 2017).

O'Reilly, M., *Memorials of Those Who Suffered for the Catholic Faith in Ireland in the 16th, 17th and 18th Centuries* (London, 1868).

Otway-Ruthven, J., 'Royal Service in Ireland', *The Journal of the Royal Society of Antiquaries of Ireland*, Vol. 98, No. 1 (1968), pp. 37–46.

Otway-Ruthven, J., 'Knight Service in Ireland', *The Journal of the Royal Society of Antiquaries of Ireland*, Vol. 89, No. 1 (1959), pp. 1–15.

Palmer, P., 'Interpreters and the Politics of Translation and Traduction in Sixteenth-Century Ireland', *Irish Historical Studies*, Vol. 33, No. 131 (2003), pp. 257–77.

Parker, C., 'Paterfamilias and Parentela: The Le Poer Lineage in Fourteenth-Century Waterford', *Proceedings of the Royal Irish Academy*, Vol. 95C, No. 2 (1995), pp. 93–117.

Parker, G., *The Military Revolution: Military Innovation and the Rise of the West, 1500–1800* (2nd ed., Cambridge, 1996).

Pawlisch, H.S., *Sir John Davies and the Conquest of Ireland: A Study in Legal Imperialism* (Cambridge, 1985).

Phillips, G., '"Home! Home!": Mutiny, Morale, and Indiscipline in Tudor Armies', *The Journal of Military History*, Vol. 65, No. 2 (2001), pp. 313–32.

Power, G., *A European Frontier Elite: The Nobility of the English Pale in Tudor Ireland, 1496–1566* (Hannover, 2012).

Power, G., 'Hidden in Plain Sight: The Nobility of Tudor Ireland', *History Ireland*, Vol. 20, No. 1 (2012), pp. 16–19.

Quinn, D.B., 'Anglo-Irish Local Government, 1485–1534', *Irish Historical Studies*, Vol. 1, No. 4 (1939), pp. 354–81.

Quinn, D.B., 'Parliaments and Great Councils in Ireland, 1461–1586', *IHS*, Vol. 3, No. 9 (1943), pp. 60–77.

Rapple, R., *Martial Power and Elizabethan Political Culture: Military Men in England and Ireland, 1558–1594* (Cambridge, 2009).

Rapple, R., 'Taking Up Office in Elizabethan Connacht: The Case of Sir Richard Bingham', *English Historical Review*, Vol. 123, No. 501 (2008), pp. 277–99.

Rose, J., 'Kingship and Counsel in Early Modern England', *Historical Journal*, Vol. 54, No. 1 (2011), pp. 47–71.

Seton-Watson, H., 'Unsatisfied Nationalism', *Journal of Contemporary History*, Vol. 6, No. 1 (1971), pp. 3–14.

Sheehan, A.J., 'Irish Revenues and English Subventions, 1559–1622', *Proceedings of the Royal Irish Academy*, Vol. 90C (1990), pp. 35–65.

Sheehan, A.J., 'The Recusancy Revolt of 1603: A Reinterpretation', *Archivium Hibernicum*, Vol. 38 (1983), pp. 3–13.

Silke, J.J., *Kinsale: The Spanish Intervention in Ireland at the End of the Elizabethan Wars* (Liverpool, 1970).

Silke, J.J., 'The Irish Peter Lombard', *Studies*, Vol. 64, No. 254 (1975), pp. 143–55.

Silke, J.J., 'The Irish Appeal of 1593 to Spain', *The Irish Ecclesiastical Record*, 5th Ser., Vol. 92 (1959), pp. 279–90, 361–71.

Simms, K., *From Kings to Warlords* (Rochester, NY, 1987).

Simms, K., 'Warfare in the Medieval Gaelic Lordships', *Irish Sword*, Vol. 12 (1975), pp. 98–108.

Stewart, R.W., 'The "Irish Road": Military Supply and Arms for Elizabeth's Army During the O'Neill Rebellion in Ireland, 1598–1601', in M.C. Fissel (ed.), *War and Government in Britain, 1598–1650* (Manchester, 1991).

Stone, L., *The Crisis of the Aristocracy, 1558–1641* (Oxford, 1967).

Tait, C., 'Adored for Saints: Catholic Martyrdom in Ireland, c. 1560–1655', *Journal of Early Modern History*, Vol. 5, No. 2 (2001), pp. 128–59.

Treadwell, V., 'Sir John Perrot and the Irish Parliament of 1585–6', *Proceedings of the Royal Irish Academy, Section C*, Vol. 85 (1985), pp. 259–308.

Walsh, M., 'The Military Order of Saint Patrick, 1593', *Seanchas Ardmhacha: Journal of the Armagh Diocesan Historical Society*, Vol. 9 (1979), pp. 274–85.

Unpublished Theses and Other Works

Carroll, S., 'Government Policy, Strategies of Negotiation and the Politics of Protest in Early Seventeenth-Century Ireland', Unpublished PhD Thesis, Trinity College Dublin, 2013.

McGowan-Doyle, V., 'The Book of Howth: The Old English and the Elizabethan Conquest of Ireland', Unpublished PhD Thesis, University College Cork, 2005.

Index

Pius V, pope, 32
plantations, 3, 6, 26n, 53, 74, 172
Plunkett, Patrick, baron of Dunsany, 11,
    46, 58, 61, 100, 176, 186–88, 197
  government of Kells, 183, 185, 186
  military services, 65, 98, 106, 108,
    109–10, 112, 116
Preston, Jenico, Viscount Gormanston,
    96, 166
  memorial (1596), 173–74, 175, 179
price inflation, 70–71, 140, 148–49, 157,
    158
priests. *see* Catholic clergy
private armies. *see* militias
Privy Council (London), 7, 89, 96, 99,
    102, 103, 105, 114, 120, 123, 140,
    153, 154, 161, 162, 173, 175, 183,
    190
prorogation, 115–16
Protestants, 6, 30, 35–36, 39, 42, 57, 58,
    63; *see also* Dublin administration;
    New English

Raleigh, Sir Walter, 75
rebellion of 1641, 8
recusants, 2, 7, 11–12, 14, 31, 70, 101
  anti-recusancy laws, 41
  indictments of, 21–22, 37, 39
  'recusancy revolts' (1603), 157,
    193–95, 199
Reformation, 6, 42
religious crusade. *see* Catholic crusade
religious persecution, 39, 40, 41, 82, 193
religious toleration, 41–43, 44
Rich, Barnaby, 102
Rider, Dean John, 36
Rocheford, Mr, 176
Rome, 15, 22, 66, 73
royal army. *see* crown forces
Russell, Sir William, lord deputy, 16, 21,
    24, 27, 29, 36, 71, 92, 94, 95, 96,
    97, 98, 104, 109, 116, 117, 119,
    132, 138, 148, 170

St John, Sir Oliver, 156
St Lawrence, Christopher, 77, 106, 110,
    116, 183, 197
St Malo (Brittany), 25
St Mary's Abbey, Dublin, 118
St Patrick's Purgatory, 42

Sanders, Dr Nicholas, 19
Saxey, William, 180
Scotland, 12, 19, 21, 23, 69, 156, 193
Scottish plantation, 200
Sedgrave, James, 84–86, 101, 197
Shane, Sir Francis, 44, 98
Sheehan, Anthony, 133, 157, 194
Shelton, John, 54, 75
Shelton, Thomas, 75n
sheriffs, 11, 56, 146, 157
  billeting of soldiers, arrangement of. *see*
    billeting of soldiers
  corruption of, 179–80, 181–82
  military provisions, collection of, 131,
    133–34, 136–37, 145, 180
  New English appointees, 179, 181–82
shipments, 5, 23, 113, 128–29, 141, 150
shipping, 23, 70, 129
Silke, John, 9
Slane, baron of. *see* Fleming, Thomas
Sligo Castle, 107
Society of Jesus. *see* Jesuits
Solicitor for Irish Causes in London. *see*
    Hadsor, Richard
Spain, 9, 15, 28, 37, 69, 72, 77, 93; *see*
    also Philip II
Spanish aid, soliciting of, 17, 20–26, 37,
    45
  bishops' plot (1593), 44
Spanish forces, 9, 24, 98; *see also* Kinsale,
    battle of (1601)
  Irish soldiers in, 108, 122–23
Spanish invasion, 73, 93, 98, 108, 114,
    166
Spenser, Edmund, 15, 169
Stafford, Captain, 104–5
Stafford, Thomas, 70
Stanihurst, Richard, 4, 7, 49
Stanley (priest), 38
State Papers, 14, 19n, 25n, 28, 36, 44, 46,
    48, 58, 88n, 94, 96, 114, 120, 121,
    128, 133, 134, 150–51, 160, 197
Stone, Lawrence, 167
Stuart aristrocracy, 167
Supplication of the Blood of the English,
    The, 110, 169
Swords, Co. Dublin, 33, 137

Talbot, John, 100, 175, 182, 188
Tara, Co. Meath, 144, 146

Irish Historical Monographs previous volumes